RESTORATION DRAMA AND
"THE CIRCLE OF COMMERCE"

Beginning with John Dryden's valuation of the importance of Beaumont and Fletcher for Restoration playwrights like himself, this book traces the genealogy of Restoration drama back to the beginning of the seventeenth century. It shows how tragicomedy was a means of deliberating on the political issues that define the seventeenth century, a means of increasingly understanding the effects of trade in the wake of the founding of the East India Company (1600), and a means of linking Harvey's discovery of the circulation of the blood, published in 1628, with both of these concerns. Tragicomedy is also shown to be a key to understanding William Davenant, Dryden's predecessor as Poet Laureate. The book concludes with a reading of six individual Restoration plays to show how the habits of the tragicomic tradition became the means of deliberating on the nature of late Stuart power, and its increasing implication in the world of seaborne commerce.

RICHARD KROLL is Professor of English at the University of California, Irvine. He is author of *The Material Word: Literate Culture in the Restoration and Early Eighteenth Century* (1991). He is the editor of *The English Novel: 1700–Fielding* and *Smollett to Austen* (both 1998). He is co-editor with Richard Ashcraft and Perez Zagorin of *Philosophy, Science, and Religion in England, 1640–1700* (Cambridge, 1992).

RESTORATION DRAMA AND "THE CIRCLE OF COMMERCE"

Tragicomedy, Politics, and Trade in the Seventeenth Century

RICHARD KROLL

University of California, Irvine

CAMBRIDGE
UNIVERSITY PRESS

CAMBRIDGE UNIVERSITY PRESS
Cambridge, New York, Melbourne, Madrid, Cape Town, Singapore, São Paulo

Cambridge University Press
The Edinburgh Building, Cambridge CB2 8RU, UK

Published in the United States of America by Cambridge University Press, New York

www.cambridge.org
Information on this title: www.cambridge.org/9780521828376

First published 2007

Printed in the United Kingdom at the University Press, Cambridge

A catalogue record for this publication is available from the British Library

ISBN 978-0-521-82837-6 hardback

For Alan Roper

Contents

PART III

SOME RESTORATION PLAYS FROM DRYDEN TO CONGREVE

Illustrations

Acknowledgments

Over the dozen years or so that I've been thinking about what has become *Restoration Drama and "The Circle of Commerce,"* I have accumulated many debts. The first and overwhelming debt I owe to the UCI English department, filled as it is with numerous colleagues who have almost all, in their different ways, lent me assistance. Less formally, and of greater importance, I have almost daily found myself intellectually challenged and deepened. For all these reasons, there are many I'd like to name – some have long departed (I mention especially Homer Brown and Al Wlecke), some are still here after a good number of years, and some have recently arrived. But my most consistent readers have been Elizabeth Allen, Mike Clark, Jayne Lewis, Vicky Silver, Jim Steintrager, Elisa Tamarkin, and Brook Thomas. I am also grateful for friends and colleagues in Art History, East Asian Studies, French and Italian, History, Philosophy, and Drama. And I am grateful too for our student-run Group for Early Modern Studies, which, more than any single other, has invariably provided a forum for a frank, impassioned, and unfettered exchange of ideas.

In the wider profession, I have again been fortunate in friends, supporters, and advisors. These include, in no particular order of importance, Doug Canfield, Brian Corman, Margaret Doody, Fraser Easton, Susan and Larry Green, Tom Habinek, Brean Hammond, Beth Hedrick, Derek Hughes, Paul Hunter, Claudia Johnson, Carol Kay, Mark Knights, Jonathan Lamb, John Marshall, Michael McKeon, Earl Miner, David Norbrook, Max Novak, Deborah Payne (Fisk), Mark Phillips, Steve Pincus, Alan Roper, Eric Rothstein, Howard Weinbrot, Mark Wilson-Jones, Rose Zimbardo, and Steve Zwicker.

I have received consistent funding for research and writing, involving full fellowships from the Folger Shakespeare Library, Washington DC, the National Endowment for the Humanities, and the UC President's Research Fellowship in the Humanities. I have received short-term fellowships from the Henry E. Huntington Library, San Marino, and the William Andrews

Clark Memorial Library, Los Angeles. And I have received grants closer to home, from the UCI Humanities Committee on Research and Travel, the UCI Humanities Center, and the UCI International Center for Writing and Translation. My department has also been exceedingly generous.

Direct support in research was also lavishly forthcoming from the following: apart from the staffs of the Clark, Folger, and Huntington Libraries, I received assistance from the staffs of the Bodleian Library, Oxford, and the British Library and British Museum. My foray into Inigo Jones revealed how generous people can be. Apart from invaluable help from Dr. Anthony Johnson, Dr. John Newman, and Dr. Joanna Parker, Librarian at Worcester College, Oxford, I am grateful to the staff of the Centre Canadienne d'Architecture, Montreal; Charles Noble and the staff of the Devonshire Collection, Chatsworth, Derbyshire; the staff of the library of the Royal Institute of British Architects; and Ken Tomio and the staff of the Tyler Museum of Art, Tyler, Texas, where I got to see Jones's personal copy of Vitruvius.

My chapters on *Marriage a la Mode*, *All for Love*, *Don Sebastian*, and *The Way of the World* are revised versions of essays that originally appeared in J. Douglas Canfield and Deborah C. Payne, eds. *Cultural Readings of Restoration and Eighteenth-Century Theater* (Athens, 1995), Jayne Lewis and Maximillian E. Novak, eds. *Enchanted Ground: Reimagining John Dryden* (Toronto, 2004), *The Huntington Library Quarterly*, and *REAL*.

My wife Allison has been a perfect companion in every way. This book is dedicated to one of the deans of Dryden studies, and the best teacher I ever had.

Introduction

As I imagine is true of many books, this book began with a hunch. In my career teaching neoclassical literature between the Restoration and the later eighteenth century, I became increasingly interested in the idea of circulation: some important texts, from Wycherley's *The Country Wife* (1675) and Behn's *The Rover* (1677) to Pope's *The Rape of the Lock* (1714), to Smollett's *Peregrine Pickle* (1751) and *Ferdinand Count Fathom* (1753), with its portrait of the benevolent Jew Joshua Manassch, appeared to link ideas of economic circulation or trade with ideas of the circulation of the blood or other bodily fluids. Both of these conceptions in turn seemed to inform, indeed determine, the behavior of the plot, since the resolutions of the plot were often brought about by money or objects either returning literally or symbolically to their point of origin; alternatively the shape of the plot echoed a wider system of circulation played out by objects and bodies in the course of the narrative. A further implication was that the economy of plot so conceived, whether in drama, poetry, or the novel, served as a material expression of the kinds of habits that, however contingently, sustain civil society, so that to admit the satisfactions of the *dénouement* was to welcome the corresponding satisfactions of human intercourse. Literature thus acted to secure as well as to express our need for the institutions that underwrite social life.

The crucial dynamics at play struck me as mainly twofold. First, the idea of circulation was systemic, describing and motivating the entire economy of the text, informing the behavior not only of objects and characters in it, but the machinery of the plot, considered purely as a verbal or literary device. Second, unlike the cruder or more primitive conceptions of barter – in which objects are traded on a one-time basis – circulation was mobile and self-proliferating, involving systems of exchange that assume a certain disequilibrium of the kind expressed, in post-Harveian physiology, in the difference between the diastolic and systolic motion of the blood, not a complete equivalence of value. This differential is endemic to the view, more fully articulated in the eighteenth century proper, that the competitive atmosphere of commerce partook in a general refinement – and in that sense feminization – of manners, which made the English, in Blackstone's estimation, a polite and commercial people. Thus it is typical that, in sentimental novels offering a late version of what I describe, individuals' intense consciousness of the movements of the pulse corresponds to the forward movement of the plot itself, as well as the fortuitous circulation of objects in it, whether money or atoms in Smollett or snuff-boxes in Sterne. Though incorporated in the action of a given plot, the health of the system presupposes a certain competition or *frisson* among its constitutive elements, so that coherence depends less on complete absorption of *différence* into some kind of literary singularity than on a willingness to sustain ambivalence to the end, an ambivalence bent on projecting the dialectical action of the plot into the world outside itself. For that reason alone, many neoclassical texts involve conclusions in which nothing is concluded.

When I applied those ideas to a field with which, since the 1970s, I have been consistently engaged, namely Restoration drama, it struck me that the dynamic I had defined for myself described, albeit slightly differently, the behavior of tragicomedy, a dramatic mode with a continuous history through the seventeenth century. Tragicomedy is distinguished by enormous internal tensions, in which a technically comic ending seems often violently threatened in the course of the action, in which many different genres and plots compete for attention, and in which the normal demands of probability frequently appear irrelevant. It also seems to relish or celebrate the extent to which all literary devices are purely artificial, and can easily incline to hyperbole, so drawing attention to itself, rather than inviting the illusion of some seamless relation to individual psychology or the external world. As an internally competitive mode, it acts easily as a form of anatomy, and so, according to my thesis, it assisted historically in the clarification of political debate in the course of the seventeenth century, in the gradual emergence of economics as an autonomous discipline, and, following the revolution effected by Harvey's *De Motu Cordis* (1628), in conceptions of the human body, and accordingly in conceptions of the body politic, as well as in conceptions of world trade that more or less demanded something like circulation to explain what might be involved. This confluence of forces forms the general topic of what is to follow.

My first chapter, "'This War of Opinions' in the 'Empire of Wit': tragicomedy, politics, and trade," lays out the major parameters of the argument. This belongs to the first of three main parts of which the book is composed. I argue, first, that John Dryden, the most important writer in the

Restoration period (1660–1700), had highly significant reasons for asserting that, for the later seventeenth century, the plays of Beaumont and Fletcher presented the most valuable models for playwrights, rather than Shakespeare or Jonson. This is of course a well-known story, but it is worth reemphasizing that what will strike many as Dryden's oddly inverted judgment actually stems from period practice: from 1660 and well into the early eighteenth century, plays by Beaumont and Fletcher were performed about twice as frequently as those by Shakespeare and Jonson combined. I then argue that these plays – often spoken of as "tragicomedies" – became, for Dryden and others, heuristic devices by which their age could deliberate on issues which were for it the profoundest sources of anxiety. Because tragicomedy by definition was generically indeterminate, often pitting incommensurable ways of seeing the world against each other, it permitted various kinds of thought experiment, as it were, in the single most obviously contested arena in the seventeenth century, namely political theory. It enabled dramatists and their audiences to ask a number of related questions: what were the sources of power in the state; what was the extent of the King's prerogative; how far was the King obliged to traditional sources of counsel in the political nation or parliament; and what was the relation between the common law and the dispensing power?

My argument may invite resistance because I believe, with Dryden, that the history of early Stuart drama and the history of Restoration drama are more closely related than is often thought. In short, Dryden's fondness for Fletcher has something to tell us both about the behavior of Restoration drama and about our deepest assumptions about what "literature" is or should be in the first place. Accordingly, it is important to recognize that although there are a good number of scholars who also wish to see seventeenth-century drama on a continuum, what one might call "the Shakespearean prejudice" has of course great popular appeal and is still visible in some scholarly or quasi-scholarly attitudes. The problem is both subtle and real, because it is largely through a mythic version of "Shakespeare" that, both in Germany and England, the Romantics developed criteria of literary judgment from which we still have difficulty freeing ourselves. For the Romantics, the specter of "Shakespeare" guaranteed the coherence of the author *vis-à-vis* his text, the coherence of the literary career, and the coherence of stage character and language. The idea of genius, the appeal to biography to explain literary effects, and the notion of the internal integrity of "literature" all militate against the humanist (or Ciceronian) conception that all constituents of culture are perennially in mutual competition in a kind of open-ended game.

Even if increasingly under challenge by sixteenth- and early seventeenth-century scholars, this reverential view of Shakespeare evidently persists. Thus a recent article in the *London Review of Books* in effect castigates Dryden for not being Shakespeare, the test case being *Hamlet* treated as a naturalistic masterpiece. This is an instance of the Eliotic dissociation of sensibility writ large, for here we see how the Romantic Shakespeare supports the demand that literature should express life itself, whereas, the objection goes, the Restoration – apart from Pepys's diary – is altogether a more mechanical, technical, artificial, specious, and hollow age. However, I do not think it is a case of special pleading in response to say that what is at stake is not a matter of literary quality. The point is much more cogently an opposition between two very different conceptions of language in general and literary language in particular. On the one hand, we have what we might call the lyric and expressive view of the literary, which inclines to a certain naturalism; on the other we have a more thoroughgoing commitment to the artificial nature of all linguistic expressions, with the result that utterances do less to describe a given state of things than draw attention to themselves and, in so doing, seek to alter their circumstances. That is, on this view, the effectiveness of an expression is rhetorical in a special sense: because it foregrounds its own argumentative devices, it seeks not to describe a given state of things, but by depending on the audience recognizing and relishing the mechanisms involved, attempts to draw the audience into its contestatory and even polemical atmosphere, so that naturalistic appeals are characteristically treated as a form of bad faith.

The opposition between the lyric and rhetorical modes that I have perhaps inadequately sketched is endemic to the history of modernism, for the modernists, in reacting against the Romantic naturalism of the Victorians, found themselves confronted with the problem of how they were to explain the exaggerated artifice of the baroque. Was this merely a hyperbolic, empty, and histrionic mode, or was there some way to intellectualize its ambitions? In a nutshell, this was the problem that, in the wake of Jacob Burckhardt's valuation of the high Renaissance in *Die Kultur der Renaissance in Italien* (*The Civilization of the Renaissance in Italy* [1860]), occupied figures like Heinrich Wölfflin (in *Renaissance und Barock* [1888]) and Walter Benjamin (in *Ursprung des deutschen Trauerspiels* [*The Origin of German Tragic Drama*, 1928]), and more indirectly, Johan Huizinga, whose book on the late middle ages (*Herfstij der Middeleeuwen* [*The Autumn of the Middle Ages*, 1919; 2nd edn. 1924]) confronts the problem of how we are to make sense of a culture that on the face of it appears merely decadent. Though he mapped his account against a scrupulous description of the level of violence and ambition that infused public life in the fourteenth century, Burckhardt, influenced by Hegelian idealism, saw in Renaissance Italy the vindication of the self-possessed, psychologically coherent individual, now capable of a rich private life, so that for him the Renaissance expressed "human nature in its deepest essence"; and he treated the sonnet as a literary genre capable of elegantly reconciling all the different realms of experience and an expressive vehicle of the "inward life." Indeed for him, in this moment in human history – also expressed in the genius of Shakespeare – "the human spirit had taken a mighty step towards the consciousness of its own secret life." Given the comprehensiveness of this conception, it was almost inevitable that, like Wölfflin, who saw the baroque as the style "into which the Renaissance degenerated," Benjamin turned his attention to the German baroque *Trauerspiel*, defending its excessive and artificial forms as a special case of the purely rhetorical condition of all human activities. As he writes, "The new theatre has artifice as its God."

Despite its oracular and hermetic aura, there is much in *The Origin of German Tragic Drama* which might apply to my argument. Centrally, I think I agree with Benjamin that the hyperbole and theatricality of the baroque is argumentatively and ideologically instrumental in the culture at large. And I think we share the notion that the lyric postulate encourages the view that literature is epiphenomenal, operating as a reflection on and at a remove from the messy business of the world, while the rhetorical view cleaves to the notion that literature competes for attention with the entire panoply of human activities, however mundane, which take place within language. This is one reason for its aesthetic urgencies and extremes.

I therefore argue in my first chapter that tragicomedy served as an heuristic device not only for the ambiguities built into different forms of political argumentation, but, less expectedly, for a series of related imponderables which accompanied the massive growth in trade during the century. The East India Company was founded in 1600, and England went to war with the Dutch thrice (in 1652, 1665, and 1672). This produced two conundra: how was economics to become a theoretical field in its own right; and how was the perception that national power increasingly depended on trade to inform political theory more largely? As the century wore on, it became increasingly clear that there were conceptual analogies between debate in the trade pamphlets and political debate. The one centered on the difference between the value of bullion – which seemed absolutely guaranteed by the nature of precious metals ("intrinsick" value) – and the value of trade, which depended on complex forms of agreement, habit, trust, and custom among the worldwide community of merchants ("extrinsick" value).

The other could be said to focus on a related distinction between the potentially absolute powers of the monarch by virtue of prerogative, and the customary and vernacular world best expressed in the common law; or alternatively between law as a potentially rigid and a priori code of behavior, and equity as a flexible means of securing proper ends, given the endless variations in human nature and the contingencies of historical experience. This analogy, I show below, is clarified fully for the first time in the context of the first Dutch War, when, in publishing *Gondibert*, Davenant begins to attach by now familiar elements of political debate to more recent debates in the discourse of trade, of the kind that prompted the 1651 Navigation Act, though one could imagine that his participation in *Britannia Triumphans*, performed during the ship money crisis, might have prepared him for that connection. (In *Mammon's Music* [2002], Blair Hoxby has recently argued that the same polemical climate made Milton sympathetic to trade as a basis of republican power under the Rump.) But I also argue that a number of other events allowed an increasing consciousness of the theoretical parameters at stake in both discourses: the coinage crisis of 1620; William Harvey's announcement of the circulation of the blood in 1628; the calling of the Long Parliament in 1640; and the King's *Answer to the Nineteen Propositions* (1642).

As I proceed with an account of the heuristic role that drama seems to have played in political and economic theory, however, I am engaged on a more covert methodological exercise in intellectual history. Because the oppositions within political theory were only dimly understood at first, and because at the beginning of the seventeenth century there was as yet no such discipline as "economics," I am also asking my reader to notice two related effects. First, as drama tests and retests various postulates to observe how they either match or collide in some way, it allows the outlines of what we now regard as a discipline to emerge with greater clarity than hitherto. This is very much the problem that occupies Joseph Schumpeter's epic *History of Economic Analysis* (1954), in which Schumpeter suggests that a discipline in embryo might emerge in the context of discourses which we no longer associate with that science or which even, to us, may be implicitly opposed to it. Thus echoing the conflictual nature of tragicomedy, it might be that greater disciplinary specificity is achieved by testing a half-formed conception against analogies that either reinforce that specificity or undercut it, in both cases helping to distill what is at stake.

In the case of the particular relationship between physiology and emerging economic models, the situation, it transpires, is yet more complex. Because early disputants in the discourse of trade knew they were debating matters of national importance, they naturally resorted to the metaphor of the body politic, even though they were writing in a climate as yet uninformed by Harveian circulation. When Malynes, Mun, and Misselden lock horns in the 1620s, we see that one of the theoretical difficulties for them is the role of bills of exchange, signifying systems of credit that bind, for example, traders in Europe, the Levant, India, and the Spice Islands. To accommodate what is in effect a cycle of obligation, it becomes clear that in the interests of disciplinary clarity, and well before *De Motu Cordis*, the physiological presumptions inhabiting the discourse of trade are clearly putting pressure on physiology proper to develop a full theory of circulation.

Second, this disciplinary clarity issues in large part from the fact that, because they are forced to occupy the same frame or stage space, incommensurable positions increasingly clearly emerge as the conceptual opposites or choices that we now understand them to be. I see this activity as assisted by several different circumstances or kinds of circumstance: the projection of incommensurables into the generically competitive atmosphere of tragicomedy; the effect of the Harveian model that now subordinates the variety of physiological elements into the workings of a single coherent system, namely circulation; the polemical machinery through which, after 1620 and 1640 respectively, the discourse of trade and political argument could increasingly descry the outlines of opponents, a process assisted by rapid publication in print, and (especially in the discourse of trade) the habit of republishing key pamphlets in response to new crises, so that a given point of view appeared increasingly less occasional and increasingly generalizable; the fact of print alone, which, as happened with architectural theory in the sixteenth century, allowed the development of a more disciplined second-order discourse; and the increasing formalization not only of stage space, as the indoor theater develops into the true proscenium stage, but, in the wake of Inigo Jones, the spatialization of English culture as a whole in the form of neo-Palladian architecture, which, I argue in Chapter Four, supplies the context for Davenant's reform of the stage in 1656.

As regards drama specifically, there is also a third consequence of these changes. The extremities of Fletcherian tragicomedy help account for the powerfully histrionic effect of a play like *Philaster*, where the dramatic effect issues from sudden and surprising twists which seem in many cases unmotivated by the usual expectations of plot and character. But the effect is both spectacular and somewhat ingrown, as if the play were preoccupied by the enormous irrational energies it unleashes. As the seventeenth century progresses, however, and as tragicomedy becomes more comfortable with itself, so to speak, the energy of the play – certainly by the Restoration – is now directed out from the stage and towards an implied audience: the history of tragicomedy in the period also becomes, I submit, a history of the creation of a specific kind of theatrical public. That audience becomes identified increasingly, I believe, with the King and the political nation, so that the purpose of drama in the Restoration is almost invariably advisory.

Hence by the time the Restoration occurred, drama was confident of its role as a vehicle of political economy, though this confidence seems most assured after the third Dutch War in the 1670s. My first chapter therefore concludes with readings of the Lord Mayor's shows mounted by Thomas Jordan after the Great Fire; *The Adventures of Five Hours* – one of the most successful plays in the 1660s; and *The Country Wife*, whose "china scene," the most famous moment in Restoration drama, simultaneously deliberates on language, politics, stage space, and the consumerism made possible by trade. Taken together, these plays and public performances show how metaphors of trade and politics serve as mutually enforcing analogies, and how the new proscenium stage allows theatrical space itself to serve as another symbolic expression of the conceptual issues involved. Though Evelyn meant his phrase in the singular to apply to the world of commerce, I am arguing that the constitutive role that literature played in this period truly made Davenant and the inheritors of the Fletcherian tradition "Authors of Traffick."

To lend contemporary weight to my argument that the drama of this period was understood to be hortatory in intent, I consider humanist rhetoric. My second chapter, "'This Mimic State': Cicero, Quintilian, and the theatrical scene of culture," has two sections. The first shows how, with the emergence of histories of drama at the end of the seventeenth century, and with the emergence of general aesthetic theories of the role drama plays in culture as a whole, especially in France, seventeenth-century drama became an "institution" in the way Homer Brown describes: not just a practice on the ground, but an entire cultural matrix readable through a theoretical lens afforded by its now having its own history and genealogy. One consequence of this shift is the emergence among late seventeenth- and early eighteenth-century writers of a consistent view that English drama, like that of the Greeks and Romans, was a prime vehicle of political debate in the state, and that the closest equivalents in that role were the orations of Demosthenes and Cicero. In the second section of the chapter I then turn to a close reading of the major texts of humanism, namely Cicero's *De Oratore*, *Brutus*, and *Orator*, and Quintilian's *Institutes*. This shows how, since *actio* (delivery) is for both thinkers the crown of oratory, the closest competitor to the fully finished orator is of course the actor. For Cicero this figure is commonly Roscius, his friend; but since both Cicero and Quintilian see the criteria of persuasive speech as being *copia* (ideally knowing everything that can be known) and *aptus* (speaking effectively to the occasion), the dramatic expression of the well-rounded speaker is the actor who excels both in comedy and tragedy, or two different actors representing both genres. Since for Cicero and Quintilian the orator serves to mediate between law and equity in the state, it follows that the competition between tragedy and comedy in the actor's training represents that symbolic function.

At this point I take issue with Benjamin's implication that baroque drama served the interests of political absolutism, because, in England, I believe the opposite to be true. Cicero had already linked the notion of *copia* – the contingent and composite grounds of effective speech – to Roman ideals of a mixed constitution, so Englishmen trained in humanist rhetoric were in effect expected to translate the multiple effects of tragi-comedy into a symbol of the "mixed" and vernacular modes of imagining the English polity, which were, if anything, anti-absolutist in implication. Thus while the regimen of a single genre could denominate the strictures of "law," the unstable combinations of genres in tragicomedy, echoing Ciceronian copiousness, could denote a world of contingency and the possibility of equity. Consequently, not only many Restoration plays, but also the masques that Davenant wrote in the 1630s were, I believe, forms of advice to the King and political nation, not instruments of Stuart absolutism.

The second part of my book is devoted to the career of William Davenant. Because Davenant is proof of powerful continuities between early and late Stuart drama, I originally planned Chapter Three to discuss his entire career. Davenant is critically important in the history of the theater because he got his start as a playwright in the 1620s; collaborated with Inigo Jones on the last few Stuart masques performed after Jones fell out with Ben Jonson in 1631, famously producing the last-ever Caroline masque, *Salmacida Spolia*, in 1640; introduced the modern proscenium stage, with actresses and moveable scenery, in *The Siege of Rhodes* in 1656, working now with Jones's collaborator since 1628, John Webb; and was one of the two figures granted theatrical patents at the Restoration in 1660. In the 1660s shortly before his death he "revised" *The Tempest* with John Dryden, who, when Davenant did die, assumed the post of Poet Laureate. Davenant poses something of a problem for the intellectual and cultural historian because he is a middling playwright and worse poet whose intellectual ambitions are nevertheless of the highest order: it is not for nothing that he was a personal friend of Hobbes, Milton, and Dryden. The consequence of his literary mediocrity is that scholars have tended not to read his work carefully and have almost universally failed to see how intelligent his various projects are.

The present Chapter Three restricts itself to a close account of Davenant's early career as a playwright, culminating in the plays of the 1630s. I demonstrate how the tradition of performances for "private" theaters increasingly exploits two possibilities afforded by the indoor stage, for all that we are still a long way from the staging conventions initiated by *The Siege of Rhodes*. First, the epistemological limitations symbolized by a more distinct and confined acting space, and a space moreover shared by members of the audience to which the players must therefore appeal, becomes a means of underscoring the public and entirely artificial nature of human endeavor: stage space alone serves as a device to rebuke the kind of naturalistic urges of the dogmatist or absolutist, who often remains blithely unconscious of the generic conventions, and so constraints, by which all dramatic characters must realize themselves. A consciousness of the artifice and necessity of genre is often further urged by a satyr–satirist figure in the plot, whose behavior places him at odds with those who are more deeply embedded within it: it is he who often reminds us that stagecraft and statecraft have much in common. In parallel with that development, and echoing the importance of the biometric metaphor in architectural theory (which, we discover, is central to ideas of stage design), as well as responding after 1628 to the Harveian conception of the body-as-space, characters also experience the spatial limits of their own bodies as a similar form of constraint, as if the theater as building were a kind of body (as Vitruvius would say), or the body a kind of theater.

Second, Davenant uses the position of characters on the stage as a symbolic device in its own right, one not truly available to Shakespeare, and one which partly explains the fact that the linguistic temperature of the plays cools relative to Shakespeare, where all the work – at least until the late plays – is done by the language alone. The contrasts between characters placed differently, I argue, serve to make the audience conscious of how the stage visually manufactures examples out of arrangements of characters on stage, yet serve to reveal the limiting force of perspective, and correspond to two other kinds of difference that Davenant seeks to harness. The differences between men and women in the audience and in the plots of these "Fletcherian" plays are, among other things, means to address the Caroline cult of platonic love, which Davenant shows to be functionally impossible in the physically and epistemologically limited world of the stage; and the claims women make in his plots correspond to the view that the King has obligations to the nation within the inherited conventions of rule he seeks to reform. The feminine principle, like the stage itself, serves as a kind of obstruction to the urgencies of masculine desire, and also corresponds to the hortatory effects of humanist education, which implicitly favors theories of the mixed constitution. Second, Davenant exploits the generic and symbolic tensions between tragedy and comedy in the tragicomic tradition out of which he writes, so that now we begin to experience a general spatializing of dramatic action in anticipation of *The Siege of Rhodes*, which claims a new "Art of Prospective in Scenes."

When I began to think of the masques, somewhat to my chagrin I realized that I would have to think about the entire masque tradition, and Inigo Jones's role in it. I did so already committed to the postulate that tragicomedy comprises a source of political advice to the King and political nation and does not simply wallow in adulation at the glories of Stuart rule, which from the start was plagued by obvious problems it would be irresponsible for loyalists to ignore. Here a difficulty was that the main arbiter of masque criticism, Stephen Orgel, has since the 1970s argued that masques were neoplatonic machines for aggrandizing the monarchy, and that though there is a strain of complexity in Jonson's masques, that tension disappears with Davenant, which Orgel takes to be proof that Charles I now assumed the role of orchestrating the action. I do not believe that royalists were ever, in the seventeenth century, uncritical promoters of the monarchy; and I believe that literary artists from the ancients on always distinguished what they were doing from outright flattery; so that it is unlikely that Davenant would have viewed Caroline rule with wide-eyed enthusiasm. A hint that the masques, like the plays, were rhetorically rather than propagandistically motivated appears in the polemics surrounding the famous artistic divorce between Jonson and Jones, in which Jonson in particular loudly mocks the idea that Jones, as architect, has any rhetorical expertise to compare with the poet. The historiography is largely given over to accepting that characterization: Jones's late career becomes a matter of increasingly sophisticated uses of stagecraft without any deepening of symbolic effect, so paradoxically revealing an antitheatrical prejudice in the criticism.

Feeling my way forward, I stumbled on a goldmine which has become the basis of my fourth chapter. This chapter reveals at length how Jones's stagecraft was – possibly after 1608, but at least after 1613 – indebted to his knowledge of architecture: from Vitruvius on, architectural theory always treated matters of stage design as a subset of public architecture; and from Vitruvius on, architecture was already the most vivid plastic expression of the rhetorical values espoused and propounded by Cicero and Quintilian, a consciousness further cultivated by the attitudes of the great Italian theorists of the sixteenth century. Jones owned copies of all the major architectural theorists (including two editions of Serlio) and obsessively annotated them at length, especially after the crucial Italian visit of 1613–14, so expressing his own architectural theory. Just as the power of Ciceronian speech depended on local uses of the enormous range of styles of which language is capable, and just as that variety symbolized for Cicero a healthy attachment to the mixed nature of the Roman constitution, so Renaissance architectural theorists gradually elaborated on the difference among the orders of architecture, with Serlio formalizing five such orders: the Tuscan, Doric, Ionic, Corinthian, and finally the Composite, the first and last of these orders being associated with vernacular Roman values, the middle three with Greece. I show that, in combining the different orders, in developing a clear interest in the Tuscan and in rustication, and in his curious work on Stonehenge, Jones was signaling his commitment to the mixed constitution, seeing his architectural designs as well as his work on the masques as a form of political counsel, as advice rather than adulation. By concluding with some of the masques Davenant wrote in the 1630s, I demonstrate not only how fully he had absorbed ideas derived from architectural theory, but also how he had put them to work in masques whose implicit criticisms of Caroline rule – and not only in *Salmacida Spolia* – make it highly unlikely that these were productions choreographed by the King himself.

Chapter Five brings Davenant's career to an end by considering *Gondibert*, the poem he wrote in the early 1650s when the theaters were closed; *The Siege of Rhodes*, first performed in a private production in 1656, then again in 1658, and in an expanded version in 1661; and his revision, in collaboration with Dryden, of *The Tempest*, performed five months before he died. Perhaps unsurprisingly, we discover that all three texts comprise Hobbesian deliberations on the construction of a viable polity, beginning with the famous exchange between Davenant and Hobbes over the forthcoming *Gondibert*. Even that poem belongs, it transpires, to Davenant's developing conception of the drama, because it was planned as a kind of theatrical poem in five cantos. The artificial quality of the drama is played out in the poem as a spatialized and explicitly architectural conception, showing how all human endeavor, including warfare, must be thought of as a ritualized and aesthetic affair, which Davenant treats dramatistically by making both his readers and audiences in the poem aware of how, in observing what they see as patternings and arrangements, they participate in making the world to which they belong. The degree of participation involved corresponds to a running argument about the mixed constitution, resisting on the one hand the empty effusions of popular opinion and on the other singular expressions of magisterial authority. Written on the brink of the first Dutch War, Davenant's poem now begins to fold the discourse of trade into the political theories on which he draws, treating the bullionist alternative as a metaphor for political authoritarianism, and the idea of trade as an expression of the communal and customary values it always behooves a ruler to consider. I believe that Davenant never finished his poem not because events intervened, but because, as in *The Platonick Lovers*, he held that the formal and public institution of marriage, both an Aristotelian and Erastian conception reconciling male and female, body and soul, perfectly expressed his commitment to the mixed constitution; so that once we reach Orna and Hurgonil's marriage, the conceptual problem the poem has set out to expound has been resolved, and so to continue would be to indulge in narrative for its own sake.

These arguments about the mixed constitution and trade also inform the curious dramatic preludes to the two performances of the original *Siege of Rhodes* (in 1656 and 1658), which also involve a consciousness of stage space. The "opera" itself becomes an exercise in political theory, in which Solyman the Magnificent embodies the perfection of civic *virtù*, while, apart from Ianthe (his Christian counterpart), others are distracted by private motives like desire and jealousy. But it is only in Part II of the "opera," first performed in 1661, that Davenant can exploit to its fullest extent the proscenium and perspective stage that marked the revolution in 1656. A key scene in Act IV reveals how the stage as a public space already ironizes the private instincts on which Roxalana is inclined to act, and in such a way as to guide her to a more politic outcome than unqualified jealousy or revenge might recommend. I conclude this chapter with a reading of the Davenant/Dryden *Tempest*, to show how the new staging conditions belong to a world that is entirely phenomenal in its aspect, and where politics, rather than having to account for metaphysical problems like the existence of evil, is purely a matter of statecraft and *Realpolitik*, of a kind Charles II would have done well to cultivate.

The final part of the book is devoted to a series of readings of six individual plays, from Dryden's *Marriage a la Mode* (1671) to Congreve's *The Way of the World* (1700). I have selected to write about a limited number, and for a number of different reasons. First, and most arbitrarily, I have chosen texts that I like because they are good plays too infrequently performed; or, as with *The Plain Dealer* and *Don Sebastian*, I have chosen texts I find intriguing on intellectual grounds, without being convinced that they would necessarily work well today on stage. Second, following a thread through the whole book, I have taken Dryden as a kind of touchstone, so that his three plays – *Marriage a la Mode*, *All for Love*, and *Don Sebastian* – provide some internal architecture for this part and can be seen as developing essays not only on the different political circumstances they address, but on the uses of stage space: Melantha watching what is going on offstage, then rushing out in a gesture both comic and pathetic; the startling arrival of Cleopatra and Octavia from different sides of the stage; and the dialectical uses of different stage spaces in *Don Sebastian* to correspond to the play's complex articulation of Dryden's loyalist crisis at the Revolution. Third, following the earlier portions of the book, the general drift in all the readings is that a presiding consciousness of the purely mediated nature of language, a recognition of the generic constraints on dramatic action, and the material conditions of the proscenium stage – which are conventions understood and enforced by the audiences – all cohere to produce a rhetorical effect. Together, they reveal the epistemological delusions of those characters who fail to read themselves in terms of shared institutional limitations, and implicitly the unwisdom, on the part of any member of the audience (which could include the King), of demanding more political authority than the native and mixed constitution in practice permits. Fourth, the field is in no need of books that aim at a comprehensive account of Restoration plays, since it is abundantly served by excellent studies covering the entire spectrum of possibilities, from Martin Butler's *Theatre and Crisis* (1984), for the early Stuart period; to Dale Randall's *Winter Fruit* (1995) and Susan Wiseman's *Drama and Politics in the English Civil War* (1998), for the Civil War and Interregnum; and, for the Restoration proper, Robert Hume's *The Development of English Drama in the Late Seventeenth Century* (1976), Susan Staves's *Players' Scepters* (1979), Eric Rothstein and Frances Kavenick's *The "Designs" of Carolean Comedy* (1988), and, most recently, Derek Hughes's *English Drama, 1660–1700* (1996). Finally, the reader may rightly object that these are all plays by loyalists, and that I do not discuss figures like Shadwell. This is partly owing to the fact that I cannot on symbolic grounds account for features of, say, *The Virtuoso*, like the play's inclination to farce, to which Dryden also objected. But it is much more motivated by my own formalist commitments, which are dispositional, are linked to my sense of how to teach my students how to read responsibly, and follow a principle announced by Roland Barthes, to the effect that "the more a system is specifically defined in its forms, the more amenable it is to historical criticism." A limited study of select plays has allowed me to show how their formal features – involving plot, language, and uses of stage space – were both conditioned by and sought to condition a series of very specific historical circumstances, and how, by the end of the century, the dialectical power of Fletcherian tragicomedy had run its course.

PART I

Conditions of Restoration drama

CHAPTER I

"This War of Opinions" in the "Empire of Wit":
tragicomedy, politics, and trade

Because John Dryden will be one of the intellectual heroes of this book, I begin with his *Of Dramatic Poesy: An Essay*. Dryden created the fiction that he had discovered the manuscript by accident among his "loose papers" to explain why, though he had written it in country retirement during the plague of 1665, he waited two more years to publish it. In many ways, this *topos* of accidental discovery, introduced in the poet's dedication to Buckhurst, distills the entire epistemological and ethical disposition of Dryden's dialogue.[1] Like Locke's *Essay concerning Human Understanding*, whose genesis is in the random conversation of a group of friends, Dryden remains committed throughout to exploring rather than settling matters, not least because for both authors, a demonstrative and conclusive method symbolizes, in the world of letters, a Cartesian dogmatism, and, in the world of politics, the aura of French absolutism. Just as Locke diffidently refers to his essay as proceeding by incoherent parcels, so Dryden sees his as similarly "incorrect" (17). And while Dryden's critical masterpiece begins with the Battle of Lowestoft, in which the English and Dutch fleets, in Dryden's resonant phrases, "disputed the command of the greater half of the globe, the commerce of nations, and the riches of the universe" (18), his tract ends slightly comically on two separate but related notes. Neander, rhapsodizing on rhyme in serious drama, is rudely interrupted and so deflated by the sudden arrival of the boat at Somerset stairs; and the friends go their several ways "through a crowd of French people, who were merrily dancing in the open air, and nothing concerned for the noise of the guns that had alarmed the town that afternoon" (92).

In Neander – a figure for Dryden himself – and the dancing French, Dryden gently satirizes the incipient self-regard of the author as well as a smugly autocratic state. The implication is that a sustained attention to the world, whether in literature or politics, urges on the individual as well as the national consciousness a respect for the contingencies of experience, whose rhetorical expression the prescriptivist may indeed deem fragmentary and incorrect, but whose actual behavior is, properly speaking, dialectical. It is accordingly one of the basic theses of what is to follow that Dryden's essay is a representative defense of the formal power and political significance of that uniquely English dramatic form or mode known as tragicomedy.[2] Echoing the structure of tragicomedy itself, Dryden's imagination in this regard has a kind of dual valency, because, like Virgil, he seeks in all seriousness to forge a viable literary mode from the ashes of the Civil War and Protectorate. And like the ancient genius, he also suffuses his endeavors with an ironic aura, supplying us with a precise sense of his place not only relative to the ancients and French to whom he is indebted, but also his place within the literary topography of English literature (and so not accidentally inventing English literary history). In the very act of creation, Dryden is almost unique in being able to watch and describe himself at work.

Because Shakespeare looms so large in our critical and cultural consciousness, it is easy to imagine that it is to Shakespeare above all that Dryden must appeal, with the qualification that Jonson will always be allowed to play a secondary role. It is true that in seeking to lay the groundwork for a renewed dramatic tradition in the first decade of the Restoration, Dryden pays homage to Shakespeare as providing a general foundation for the new edifice. But critical paraphrases of Dryden's position, especially when they cite Dryden's love of Shakespeare contrasted with his sterner admiration for Jonson, tend to forget that *Of Dramatic Poesy* and numerous pronouncements elsewhere and throughout his career almost invariably link Shakespeare, Jonson, *and Fletcher* as the reigning triumvirate of the former age. Indeed, it would also be true to say that whereas for Dryden Shakespeare represents a general idea about drama, it is specifically Jonson on the one hand and Beaumont and Fletcher on the other that provide concrete models for dramatic practice after 1660. (Vaughan's commendatory poem to *The Conquest of Granada* was to declare that "*Ben Johnson, Beaumont, Fletcher, Shakespear*, are /As well as you, to have a Poet's share.")[3] Dryden may allude to Shakespeare's history plays as a genre and perhaps at one point to *Henry V*, but he specifically names *Cataline* and *Sejanus* more than once, talks about *The Alchemist, Volpone*, and *Every Man in His Humor*, and famously engages in an extended examen of *The Silent Woman* (49; 65; 70–9). By "Fletcher" it is clear that Dryden primarily means Beaumont and Fletcher, though he expresses admiration for *The Faithful Shepherdess*, along with *The Humorous Lieutenant* and *The Island Princess*, one of the most successful Fletcher plays on the Restoration stage (66; 85). Dryden himself remarks that twice as many plays by Beaumont and Fletcher are performed in the 1660s than plays by Shakespeare and Jonson, and critical histories of the drama have consistently since then confirmed that preponderance, which only began to change at the end of the century (69).[4] Consequently, Dryden speaks of Fletcher more frequently than of either Shakespeare or Jonson, who get roughly the same billing, though it is also clear that his interest in the Fletcherian canon is absorbed primarily by *The Maid's Tragedy* and *A King and No King*.

Some critics may view Dryden's apparent preference for Beaumont and Fletcher as yet another sign that, as Wordsworth, Arnold, and Eliot agree, the neoclassical age had lost its moorings in literary history, if not its taste altogether. But Dryden's interest in these figures is not primarily populist or governed by their success in the 1660s: it is conceptual and principled, closely allied to the suspended, contingent, and dialectical ethic which informs Dryden's entire dialogue. There are a number of ways to see what is more largely at stake. First, Dryden wrote *Of Dramatic Poesy* in 1665, apparently celebrating the Duke of York's victory in the Battle of Lowestoft, fought on 3 June 1665, early in the second Dutch War, so that, like Conrad's interlocutors at the beginning of *Heart of Darkness*, the four friends float on the Thames while the battle rages off the coast of Suffolk, listening to "the noise of distant thunder, or of swallows in a chimney" (19). However, Dryden only entered the title in the Stationers' Register on 7 August 1667, by which time the jubilance of victory had been transformed into scenes of naval incompetence and political embarrassment for the Stuarts. In 1666, the war produced a punishing draw for the English fleet in the four-day Battle of the Downs, though the advantage went to the Dutch, which was offset by an English victory on 25 July off North Foreland. But by June 1667, this victory had been eclipsed first by the Fire of London and then by Cornelius de Witt sailing up the Medway, breaking into the English fleet at anchor, bombarding Chatham, burning three ships, and towing away the flagship, the *Royal Charles*. When *Of Dramatic Poesy* was entered in the Stationers' Register in August, the ink was dry on the Treaty of Breda signed on 21 July 1667, by which time negotiations for the peace revealed once again how Anglo-Dutch affairs were enmeshed in Louis XIV's expansionist designs, in the face of which Charles II so often appeared recumbent.

For two very obvious reasons, quite apart from the setting to which we will return, Dryden's language is highly sensitive to political conditions. And it also reveals how his conception of literature is pragmatic and rhetorical, embedded in the uncertainties of political pressures, attempting to define and qualify them, rather than merely responding to circumstance or glossing events *après la lettre*. For it would be a mistake to suppose that any one of the four friends scores an out-and-out victory for the position he espouses. Just as in 1667, it would be naïve to imagine that the Battle of Lowestoft was a conclusive victory, so it would be both naïve and offensive to revel in the view that, in the course of the verbal contest that accompanies the battle, the moderns defeat the ancients, the English defeat the French, or rhyme defeats blank verse. Though perhaps one effect of the dialogue is to register Dryden's preference for the moderns, the English, and rhyme, another effect is only to claim that he cannot escape being what he is, namely an English Modern (though he has more choice concerning rhyme), and yet another is of course to recognize the mutual dependence between the ancients and moderns, between the French and English, and between rhyme and other poetic modes of expression.

It is for exactly these reasons that *Of Dramatic Poesy* mounts a sustained defense of the dialectical and political power of vernacular English drama, which, for Dryden, the acknowledged peculiarities of Beaumont and Fletcher most vividly represent. Part of the difference between the French and English Dryden ascribes to differences in national character. The prescriptive severity of tragedy provides emotional ballast for the "airy and gay temper" of the French, while the more melancholy English need a dose of comedy intermingled with serious drama (60). But here Dryden is himself being playful in the midst of a more serious discourse, for one implicitly political principle is that no position should unequivocally prevail over any other, so that an important moment in the dialogue occurs when Crites – despite his name a man of moderation – interrupts Eugenius's praise of the moderns to remark, to everyone's satisfaction, that "Eugenius and I are never like to have this question decided between us" (42).

Crites's admission has all the force of what I will henceforth call an heuristic position. Like all the other speakers, he seems aware that though he may begin with a certain conviction about his ideas, hearing someone with a different point of view allows him, precisely, to moderate his own attachment to his argument, and his interrupting Eugenius – with benign motives to be sure – has also the effect of moderating that position too, just as Dryden gently mocks his own commitment to rhyme by showing how the boat arriving at its destination interrupts Neander in full flight. Dryden, that is, is exploring how the various positions look when they are squared off against each other, and is inviting his reader on the journey. The dialogue is sprinkled with approving references to the new natural philosophy, and Dryden's entire procedure is experimental much in the mode espoused by Boyle and Hooke. For him, the juxtaposition of points of view (which is skeptical in habit) can have no predetermined outcome (which would be altogether too dogmatic) and clearly rehearses what he says not only about English drama in general but Fletcherian drama in particular. Structurally, Dryden's own text is itself Fletcherian in this sense because it floats several technically incommensurable theses at once, theses which are incommensurable perhaps on epistemological grounds and on grounds of taste, but most importantly on political grounds. For the behavior of the mixed plots in English drama – in Shakespeare and Fletcher above all – have as their most exact corollary differences between different kinds of political institution. Above all – unlike the French claiming ancient precedent – the English abjure the unities. According to Dryden tragicomedy precisely differentiates English habits, customs, and institutions from the French, denoting what the friends enjoy on the boat, namely the mingled "freedom of discourse" (16), a more masculine fancy (65), a response to the variety and copiousness of the literary and natural world (65), and to the mixed nature of audiences (86). Though in criticizing the promiscuity of tragicomedy, Lisideus thinks he is scoring a point for the French, Dryden wants us, I think, to approve the ironic economy that tragicomedy delivers precisely because it is less ideologically tendentious than French statism:

[The French] do not burden [their plays], as the English do; which is the reason why so many scenes of our tragi-comedies carry on a design that is nothing of kin to the main plot; and that we see two distinct webs in a play, like those in ill wrought stuffs; and two actions, that is, two plays, carried on together, to the confounding of the audience; who, before they are warm in their concernments for one part, are diverted to another; and by that means espouse the interest of neither. (45)

The real irony is that the interest of the French state is so monolithic that Corneille's *Cinna* and *Pompey* "are not so properly to be called plays as long discourses of reason of state" (60), as if they were prosaic expositions of a Bodinian absolutism. Accordingly, when Richelieu died, French playwrights, feeling "too strictly tied up" by the unities (63), asserted their new-found freedom by experimenting with mixed plots (57).

Dryden's latitudinarian temperament is visible at this point, because he has a precise idea of how split-plot or "mixed" plays should work. Employing the cosmological metaphor that informs his Dedication to Danby in *All for Love*, as well as a number of seventeenth-century political tracts, Dryden sees the relation of the subplot to the main plot as reproducing the architecture of the solar system, which in turn pictures the proper relation between monarch and subject. Their orbits act eccentrically relative to each other, with the greater body indirectly determining the behavior of the lesser, so avoiding both tyranny – the complete dominance of the political cosmos by a single body – and what Dryden calls "coordination," which, like the Levellers to whom he also refers (21), "is as dangerous and unnatural [in a play] as in a State" (59). Though Dryden did not yet of course know that the cause was universal gravitation, for him the image of a lesser planet orbiting the sun in an ellipse exactly captures the dialectical possibilities of English tragicomedy, whose rhetorical aim was to contribute to the climate of good counsel in the state. When Dryden writes that the mixed or promiscuous quality of English drama comprises what he calls an "olio" (49), he means I think to allude to his implied ideal of mixed monarchy, but also to recall the relation between drama so conceived and the *satura*, a mixed body of discourse with its own internal metabolism, and whose effects on the body politic are themselves medicinal or therapeutic.

MIXED PLAYS AND POLITICAL THEORY

In *The Tragedies of the Last Age Consider'd* (1678), Thomas Rymer complains that *The Maid's Tragedy* fails to focus the audience on a chief character. Thus he writes,

> Whil'st . . . we are uncertain what ought to be the *title*, we may suspect that the *Action* of the Tragedy is *double*; where there seems two centers, neither can be right, and the lines leading towards them must all be false and confus'd; the *preparation*, I mean, and conduct must all be at random, since not directed to any one certain end.[5]

While Rymer's rigid application of the criterion of dramatic probability also misled him, infamously, into mocking Othello's motive for killing his wife, his irritation at Beaumont and Fletcher's play evidently blinded him to a profounder observation. That is, the mixed nature of the play is, as Dryden implies, deliberate. Craik believes that "political ideas are not important in this play";[6] but I would argue that this spectacularly theatrical drama – written in 1610 or 1611 and performed at the Blackfriars theater – feeds off the violent, indeed lurid collision between different conceptions of political and social order, all operating eccentrically relative to each other. The play itself is an heuristic device responding to the early Stuart world in which, above all, kingship has newly been redefined as divine, and yet in which no single analysis of human order predominates. Different and conflicting energies are released in an atmosphere where there seems no overarching logic to which characters or audience can appeal, perhaps one reason why the play is apparently set in a world with many obscure deities.

By exercising a grotesque version of *droit de seigneur*, the King forces Amintor into breach of contract with his betrothed, Aspatia, in order to marry Evadne, whose sexual favors as mistress the King wishes to prolong. Evadne reveals this secret to Amintor on their wedding night; out of friendship Amintor tells Evadne's brother, Melantius; Melantius then confronts Evadne, who confesses; Evadne agrees to an assignation with the King, ties him to the bed, and stabs him; Amintor fatally wounds Aspatia, who cross-dresses as her brother, but they are reconciled after Evadne kills herself and in time for Amintor then to join Aspatia in death. In the meantime, the King's brother Lysippus has smoothly assumed the throne, Melantius is prevented from killing himself as well, and Lysippus concludes with the moral:

> May this a fair example be to me
> To rule with temper, for on lustful kings
> Unlooked-for sudden deaths from God are sent:
> But curs'd is he that is their instrument.
>
> (V,ii,292–5)

Critics of Beaumont and Fletcher have often derided their plays as *merely* operatic or atmospheric, an impression that any summary of their plays tends to reinforce. But part of the problem is that the arguments of the plays, if that is what we can call them, occur as purely theatrical or melodramatic events without the extensive verbal glossing we expect from Shakespeare. The logic unfolds more situationally than verbally or metaphorically, such that the sudden immersion of developed possibilities into new and surprising configurations anticipates what Alan Roper sees as the casuistical rhetoric of plays like *The Conquest of Granada*.[7] Recognizing that political affairs are more mutable than "Naturall and Mathematicall causes," for example, Antony Ascham, writing in 1648, and directly alluding to casuistry several times, perfectly describes the mechanism: "as circumstance hath power to change the matter, so in the forme of the action, it leaves in the middle a latitude and extent, sometimes inclining to one extreme, sometimes to another."[8] Casuistry, one could say, proceeds more by raising questions than offering solutions, so that rather than focusing on the development of character – a psychologistic illusion – mixed plays in the English tradition (including many by Shakespeare) treat characters as conceptual postulates launched into a series of highly varied experiments, whose mutual relation cannot be parsed causally. That is, accounts as to why one scene follows from or is juxtaposed to the last often make the plot appear highly improbable, if not downright silly, not unlike the activity of romance in which characters also appear similarly as types. Drama is the best medium for the desired effect precisely because meaning on stage is made by such juxtaposition: we are asked to infer as much why one scene is symbolically unlike, as why it is like, what surrounds it, and the less we can rely on the illusion of character development to provide us with the comforts of continuity, the more the total effect (where it doesn't reproduce the experience of outright incommensurability) is, precisely, dialectical.

This mechanism militates against other modern critical presumptions that further explain Rymer's frustration with *The Maid's Tragedy*: its meaning cannot be identified with a single author any more than it can be identified with a single character. Not only is it a matter of historical record that between one-half and two-thirds of early Stuart plays were written by more than one author,[9] but Aubrey reports on the relationship between Beaumont and Fletcher in highly equivocal terms which disturb their mutual identities in numerous different ways, so that when in *Of Dramatic Poesy* Dryden refers to Fletcher in the singular, he assumes that the name encompasses two people at once. Aubrey writes,

They lived together on the Banke side, not far from the play-house, both batchelors; lay together; had one Wench in the house between them, which they did so admire; the same cloathes and cloake, &c; betweene them.[10]

The equivocations driving this account – as well as the title-page of the Beaumont and Fletcher folio of 1647 (see figure 1) – inform the behavior of *The Maid's Tragedy* because in 1610–11 the play exploits the mutual incomprehension of different accounts of the political order. On the one hand it exaggerates the language of Divine Right with which (though there are medieval precedents for the idea) James I had newly clothed himself. Declaring that the very name of "King" is itself sacred (II,i,308), the play proclaims at the start that "The breath of kings is like the breath of gods" (I,i,15), while in Act IV, Amintor's sword is "charmed" out of his hand by the royal aura (IV,ii,314); and though in Act III, Melantus and Calianax contemplate revenge, it rigidly reinforces the principle of nonresistance in the play's chief political officers ("We may not think revenge" [IV,ii,329]).

On the other hand it reveals a corruption at the heart of prerogative power. The chief problem that emerges raises the question that, prior to the early 1640s, early Stuart political theorists struggled in vain to answer. What, apart from expressions of Divine Right, exactly were the sources of law in the state? What are the relations between private, familial, and public conceptions of order? And what are the bonds of friendship, as opposed to those of family and alliance? Although we know that the King

Figure 1: Frontispiece to Beaumont and Fletcher, *Comedies and Tragedies*
(1647 Folio)

has done wrong, it is much less clear what moral scheme, precisely, he has disrupted, or on what grounds resistance might be justified. Amintor complains, for example, that "I only broke a promise / And 'twas the King that forc'd me" (II,i,135–6). But there are obviously different grounds for obligation – the play is filled with the language of promises, oaths, and vows. Breaking his "troth" to Aspatia, Amintor promises the King to marry Evadne instead; Evadne has "sworn" not to sleep with Amintor (II,ii,151); and Amintor (without knowing it is the King) swears he will kill the man that has wronged Evadne. And though Evadne kills the King for personal motives, they seem not entirely distinct from questions of family honor, since her action is spurred by confessing to her brother.

The play, in short, refuses to answer the question whether the King has breached natural law, a *consensus gentium* about the inviolability of exogamy, the patriarchal order more loosely, statutory law, customary common law, or divine positive law; and it evades the question of what legitimates his punishment, outside the arbitrary action of poetic justice. Yet while the play relishes the chaos that ensues, it is careful to protect the integrity of kingship and marriage as such: the King's brother, who plays no dramatic role, guarantees a seamless succession, and all who have violated marriage die. Since the characters have no second-order languages by which to navigate, the conflicts within the plot are motivated by mutual incomprehension, such that the activity of the play appears somewhat ingrown. In *The Maid's Tragedy*, theatrical spectacle seems unfocused by a clear sense of audience, since the characters are preoccupied by the puzzles of their local and shifting conditions, so that part of its *frisson* appeals to our position as voyeurs. In fact, like *The Tempest*, also performed at Blackfriars in the same season, the play is deliberating on what genres best serve the different implied arguments at issue, with a heightened sense (in both plays) that masques, most clearly tied to court entertainment, tend in particular to evade the contingencies of the plot, as well as of power itself. Masques, we hear within ten lines, "are tied to rules of flattery" (I,i,10) and so provide a stark contrast to Melantius's rough-hewn world of military glory. That flattery is not merely a personal disposition towards those in power, but connotes a principled defense of royal prerogative (or "Acts of Grace") is suggested by *The Subjects Libertie* (1643), a tract defending radical popular sovereignty to which we will shortly return.[11]

In sum, *The Maid's Tragedy*, while genuflecting to the language of Divine Right and the necessities of order, remains, like its characters, arbitrarily marooned in their circumstances, largely inchoate about the relative force of the various political languages it espouses. The pressures it unleashes are spectacularly successful as theater, but it seems that the play is not quite the conceptually self-conscious and politically ironic device that Dryden, speaking a half century later, imagines. That this is the situation in 1610 should not surprise us. At a global level, Skinner has taxonomized the huge range of political ideas that emerged both from the Renaissance at large and the Reformation more particularly, in which numerous different arguments about order were confronted by equally numerous arguments advocating resistance. For example, he shows how the constitutionalist ideas so influential in the English seventeenth century have their origins in large part in the Jesuit counter-Reformation, where conciliarists like Bellarmine and Suárez argued that papal authority should be mediated by church councils, representing the Catholic body more generally; and this view in turn, enriched by a scholastic ontology, serves as one source of theories of popular consent.[12]

Second, commentators roughly agree on the view that though the Tudors had succeeded in forging the lineaments of a modern state, and had regularly acted autocratically, the way that they governed owed a great deal to medieval conceptions of rule, in which the fiction was that the King, though sanctioned by God, took counsel from various different communities in the nation; and the relation between King and parliament, summoned irregularly, was similarly one of mutuality, not least because Privy Councillors served as political leaders and managers in the Commons.[13] Thus, though a theory of royal prerogative did exist, there were many practical, political, legal, and customary restrictions on the King's power to act, and yet none of these restrictions could be considered mutually coherent, so that royal power had to wend its way through a maze of different avenues and obstructions. Wootton remarks in this connection that "the early seventeenth-century state was highly decentralized and underfunded."[14] Claims and counterclaims within the political realm were first of all occasional and stimulated by local challenges, so that they did not invoke any universal language of rights, obligations, or sovereignty. This is a teleology foisted onto events by the great nineteenth-century Whig historians.

By contrast, Sir David Lindsay Keir's, F. W. Maitland's, Wallace Notestein's, and J. R. Tanner's accounts of the increasing conflicts between their parliaments and the early Stuarts make it clear that rather than insisting on their rights and privileges as a matter of principle and as a coherent and stable repository of arguments, members of the political nation were increasingly demanding to be included in the exercise of power by using entirely practical strategies on the ground (for example, by exploiting the potential of the Commons' committee system) and by using different kinds of appeal.[15] Commenting on the political scene in the period between the end of Elizabeth's reign and a fairly coherent sense of parliamentary opposition emerging between 1621 and 1626, Notestein could almost be describing the logic of Fletcherian tragicomedy when he writes that "It is easier to feel power in action than to explain it."[16] Like the mechanism of *The Maid's Tragedy*, the atmosphere of political contestation drew on what we might call numerous generically incommensurable arguments, of the kind superbly taxonomized by Margaret Judson. Citing McIlwain, Judson remarks that the reader of early seventeenth-century political tracts "is constantly impressed by the failure of either the royalists or their parliamentary opponents to meet squarely the arguments and precedents on the other side. In their arguments 'they slid past each other,' each side citing its own precedents and each side presenting an interpretation of opposing precedents which made them of little avail."[17] And Pocock's characterization of the Putney debates fits the entire situation between 1603 and 1649, as well as the action of *The Maid's Tragedy*, when he writes that this period "presents us with a case, not simply of minds seeking to regularize a delegitimized and chaotic situation, but of a new level of civic consciousness finding means of becoming articulate."[18]

Third, in practical terms, the notion that parliament as a corporate entity with a life of its own – quite apart from the summoning, prorogation, and dissolution of individual parliaments – was still, in the early seventeenth century, in its infancy. As Tanner has shown, for example, the entire constitutional history of the century could be written in terms of dealings between individual monarchs and individual parliaments, and the events of the period, endowed with Carlylean scope by S. R. Gardiner, could perhaps more properly be understood by looking at the individual monarch's abilities to handle people.[19] This was a rather basic but essential art that entirely eluded James I, who talked too much, Charles I and James II, who had little notion of political horsetrading, and Charles II, the least legible of all four, but perhaps because he was, owing to his experiences as a young man, entirely cynical about politics altogether. Notestein makes the penetrating remark that although the Tudors had no systematic way of mediating power in the state, Elizabeth deliberately remained rather reticent and mysterious in her dealings with parliament for rhetorical effect, whereas – like the language of *The Maid's Tragedy* – James liked to lecture the commons on the king's prerogatives.[20]

Finally, 1610 marked the end of James's first parliament. Called originally in 1604, this parliament had five sessions. By 1610, it was clear not only that the religious question was a potential source of considerable animus, but that James's problems, like those of his two successors, were financial. Compared with Elizabeth, who was famously tight-fisted, James's household alone was more expensive to run, quite apart from the fact that his wife was notoriously spendthrift; and the problems were exacerbated by the fact that James emerged from the relatively primitive and clannish world of Scotland into a more cosmopolitan and correspondingly less malleable political climate. In 1606, the royal debt stood at £700,000, and Salisbury was hard put to increase the King's revenues, which depended on aspects of his prerogatives, such as wardship, purveyance, and customs on imported goods. The latter was challenged by a Levant merchant in Bate's Case (1606), the first of many such judicial tests of the extent of the King's prerogative, most of which – including the ship money case, until the unequivocal defeat of James II in the trial of the Seven Bishops in June 1688 – went technically in the King's favor. But for two reasons, the vindication of prerogative was equivocal. In an atmosphere where the nature and limits of royal prerogative were poorly defined, Sir Thomas Fleming's much cited definition of sovereignty in Bate's Case suggests that it was internally fissured, to be distinguished between the prince's *absolute* and *ordinary* powers. He opined,

The king's power is double, ordinary and absolute, and they have several lawes and ends. That of the ordinary is for the profit of particular subjects, for the execution of civil justice, and the determining of *meum*; and this is exercised by equitie and justice in ordinary courts, and by civilians is nominated *jus privatum* and with us, common law; and these laws cannot be changed without parliament. . . The absolute power of the King is not that which is converted or executed to private use, to the benefit of any particular person, but is only that which is applied to the general benefit of the people, and is *salus populi*.[21]

The uncertain boundaries between parliamentary privilege and the King's absolute prerogative detectable here were revealed in the summer and autumn of 1610 in the failure of the Great Contract. Salisbury's idea was that parliament should provide a permanent royal grant-in-supply of £200,000 *per annum*, while the King would resign his rights to wardship and purveyance. During the summer, this practical plan for demarcating rights and powers in the state apparently met with some favor, but by the autumn, both parties involved had thought better of the idea, so that the balance between royal prerogative and parliamentary privilege remained unresolved as a theoretical question for the rest of the century, until the political events of 1688 placed legal sovereignty entirely in the hands of parliament. So when Dryden sees the Fletcherian mode as deliberating on affairs of state, he is aware that there is a genetic relationship between the climate to which *The Maid's Tragedy* responds and the related questions that it fell to his generation to mediate.[22]

BLOOD, SOVEREIGNTY, AND CIRCULATION

If the reader can concede that *The Maid's Tragedy* exploits the dramatic possibilities of early Stuart political languages vying for recognition, with the benefit of hindsight Dryden assumes that by the Restoration the Fletcherian mode also serves as an heuristic device for asking how they might become systemically or methodically contrasted. The King's action centrally exposes the divide between private passion and the public good, though the play also seeks to accommodate the familial metaphor through which kingship was imagined. (*The Subjects Libertie* almost provides a perfect gloss when it declares, "Kings are men, and have their passions, and must have time to digest them, and return where they should be, and happy shall they be when they understand their powers aright.")[23] If I am correct about the situation in 1610, it should not surprise us that the strains the plot places on its characters reveal themselves as an uncertainty about what languages are proper for their moral conundra. This in turn is expressed in three verbal habits, the first two of which Dryden was to use to great effect in *All for Love*, and all of which tend to arrest the forward movement of the action and contribute to the operatic effect of which critics have complained: the tendency to stop in mid action to objectify and examine a word as if it has temporally failed as a rhetorical instrument; the desire to convert the self into some legible emblem interpretable at least to the speaker imagining himself as a body in dramatic space; and a related obsession by which characters constantly measure their pulses both within and against the circumstances in which they find themselves.

The play refers to blood and the veins about twenty-five different times; and given the strongly physiological cast of many of those references, this is clearly an imagistic means of questioning the conceptual divide between private health – the workings of the individual body – and the commonwealth – the body politic.[24] Since the analogy rides on a Galenic view of the somatic economy, it can recognize that the blood is qualitatively essential to life without being able precisely to trace connections between individuals – whose dispositions or humors might themselves be incommensurable – and the state conceived of as a corporal or corporate entity. Thus Melantius imagines a kind of transfusion occurring between him and Calianax by which Calianax would gain in courage: "Would that blood / That sea of blood, that I have lost in fight, / Were running in thy veins" (I,ii,85–7). And since it presumes a qualitative distinction among different metabolisms, the Galenic hypothesis surely prevents direct analogies among and between different persons, though it does allow for sympathy. Observing Aspatia's grief at her abandonment, Amintor mutters, "Methinks I feel / Her grief shoot suddenly through all my veins; / Mine eyes run . . ." (II,i,127–9). So to secure the analogy between private and public bodies as far as possible, the key scene in which Evadne stabs the King is imagined very precisely as an anatomical experiment, best symbolized by the letting of blood:

Evadne: Stay, sir, stay;
        You are too hot, and I have brought you physic
        To temper your high veins.
King: Prithee to bed then; let me take it warm;
        Here thou shalt know the state of my body better.
Evadne: I know you have a surfeited foul body,
        And you must bleed. (V,i,52–8)[25]

The frequency and urgency with which such interests are espoused in the play indicate that Beaumont and Fletcher see the analogy of the body politic as more than merely decorative, as indeed constitutive of a certain kind of political analysis. At the same time, however, they seem to be asking the Galenic hypothesis to deliver more than it can. The imagery of blood, though persistent, provides less of a clear analysis of relations among individuals, or of relations between individuals and the state, than a series of suggestions that they might, somehow, be connected. Because the metaphor comprises an essential way of talking about something dimly perceived, and because it evidently cannot clarify the relations among elements in the system (either imagined as the individual body or the state as body politic), a premium lies on how the various ideas at issue might submit themselves to global description. That is, from our point of view, because political analysis clearly needs to move in the direction of theorizing about the state as such, in which different elements of the body politic can play mutually articulated roles, that heuristic puts pressure on physiology to develop a correspondingly more coherent and economic picture of the human metabolism.

It is obvious that, for Dryden, by 1665 the Fletcherian mode could provide precisely such an anatomy of the body politic. It is not that constitutional issues have definitively been settled, but that now they are evenly subject to dialectical analysis by the activity of the mixed plot. And the mixed plot serves a dual function, since, echoing the language of many of the tracts from the 1640s, the *topos* of the mixed monarchy represents one ideal of the polity that Dryden arguably espouses (so reflecting a wider political vocabulary); and the mixed plot also represents the best way of analyzing political questions (so helping to constitute them).

Dryden can fruitfully make these assumptions because by 1642 three shifts have occurred which allow polemicists to understand what is at stake. First, on the long view, Figgis brilliantly argues, the chief conceptual issue that the Stuart century spent eighty-five years deciding involves the nature of sovereignty as such. Figgis's account, which remains pertinent is that Divine Right theory, energetically adopted by the Stuarts, and most fully articulated after the Restoration,[26] served as the chief indigenous device by which seventeenth-century theorists realized that arguments about prerogative and parliamentary privilege were in fact arguments about what center of power defines the state as a single and coherent organism.[27] There are of course precedents in Marsilius of Padua, William of Ockham, and Jean Bodin, who is generally credited with endowing the problematic of sovereignty with its distinctively modern form; but English polemicists also defined the issue in their own terms, though as the century wore on, Bodin increasingly inflected the discussion (Richard Knolles's translation of *The Six Books of the Commonweale* appeared in 1606). The actuality of the Tudor state, with law-making as a distinctive feature, meant that "the facts of English history had for the first time rendered complete sovereignty a necessity in English national life."[28] And this was a necessity demanding a conceptual vocabulary. Before 1642, Weston and Greenberg believe, such a vocabulary was unlikely fully to emerge because no one had "either isolated the law-making power for an independent consideration or perceived in that power the key to sovereignty in the state."[29] Skinner argues that such global analysis, announced by Bodin, initiates the modern science of politics. In these conditions, we arrive at a "conceptualization of the state as a locus of power which can be institutionalized in a number of ways, and which remains distinct from and superior to both its citizens and their magistrates."[30] It is also important for my argument that Figgis depicts this view of the state in organic terms, writing that in using Divine Right as an heuristic, seventeenth-century royalists were embracing the view that "the State as such is an organism with a life of its own, and is subject to laws of development distinct from those of the Church," or, put more simply, for them the state is "a natural organism."[31]

Furthermore, political events after the calling of the Long Parliament in 1640, which involved among other things a lapse in censorship, encouraged a huge outburst of pamphleteering. The mere fact of the polemics, as well as their dependence on a newly energized printing market, has, first, important implications for Dryden's view of the Fletcherian mode, since they created a vivid sense of a political public, and a political public subject to suasion in print. So for Dryden the assumption is that, whereas *The Maid's Tragedy* may have been somewhat ingrown at its inception, drama after 1660, like the political pamphlets after 1640, is directed at a political audience, an audience comprised both of the King and the political nation, and perhaps this supplies the rhetorical motive for revising early Stuart plays. Moreover, unlike early Stuart dramatists, Restoration playwrights could depend on print as well as performance for much of their plays' immediate effect. Though the theaters were closed in 1642, the decision to issue the plays of Beaumont and Fletcher in folio in 1647 testifies to the power of print as a political medium with which drama is inevitably associated. In fact, in his Epistle "To the Reader" prefacing this production, Shirley writes that printing alone provides a fresh perspective on the dramatic and political events of the age:

And now Reader in this *Tragicall Age* where the *Theater* hath been so much out-acted, congratulate thy owne happinesse, that in this silence of the Stage, thou hast a liberty to reade these inimitable Playes, to dwell and converse in these immortal Groves, which were only shewed by our Fathers in a conjuring glasse, as suddenly removed as represented, the Landscrap is now brought home by this optick, and the Presse thought too pregnant before shall be now look'd upon as [the] greatest Benefactor to Englishmen, that must *acknowledge* all the felicity of *witt* and *words* to this Derivation.[32]

We will see in Chapters Three to Five how this notion of perspective becomes increasingly central in the history and theory of drama from mid century on. Clearly influenced by the Galilean advances in astronomy and here applied to reading plays as printed artifacts, in the 1650s Davenant exploits the idea to promote his use of the proscenium stage. Later it also serves as a metaphor for the capacity of Restoration drama – inheriting, partly through Davenant's reform of the stage, the critical power of the "mixed" Fletcherian mode – to deliberate on affairs of state.

The printed debates of the 1640s strike the modern reader not only with their range and intensity, but, as Shirley states, with a new clarity about how to frame the issues. Perhaps the key moment occurred, as Wallace, Pocock, and Weston and Greenberg argue, on 18 June 1642, with the King's *Answer to the Nineteen Propositions*.[33] This statement drafted by the moderate royalists Falkland and Colepeper supplies the classic account of mixed monarchy, and reveals, Kenyon believes, how the royalists always held the high ground in matters of constitutional theory. It reads,

There being three kinds of government among men, absolute monarchy, aristocracy and democracy, and all these having their particular conveniences and inconveniences, the experience and wisdom of your ancestors hath so moulded this out of a mixture of these as to give to this kingdom (as far as human prudence can provide) the conveniences of all three, without the inconveniences of any one, as long as the balance hangs even between the three estates, and they run jointly on in their proper channel (begetting verdure and fertility in the meadows on both sides) and the overflowing of either on either side raise no deluge or inundation.[34]

The combination of political realities on the ground and increasingly articulate proponents for the different positions meant that polemicists had an increasingly clearer view of what was at stake. Nevertheless, as *Of Dramatic Poesy* shows, it is not that a more comprehensive sense of the polity as a whole quells debate. If anything, it is rather that greater polemical precision provides a clearer idea of what alternatives are being espoused, throwing the contrasts into greater relief. All this was already true of the polemics in 1642–3 among Henry Ferne, who denied the subject's right to resist, Henry Parker and Charles Herle, who argued that sovereignty depended on popular consent (Herle providing a classic definition of co-ordination in *A Fuller Answer* [1642][35]), and Hunton's more moderate royalism as depicted in *A Treatise of Monarchy* (1642).

Evidently Hunton in particular had somehow crystallized the terms of debate; and this impression is confirmed by three features of the text. First, like Ferne, Hunton can see that the central issue concerns sovereignty in the state, for he writes that the magistrate's power "cannot be well divided into severall species; for it is one simple thing, an indivisible Beam of Divine Perfection."[36] Second, a kind of architectonic imagination allows him to taxonomize – or "frame" – issues very precisely. For instance, he qualifies the sentence above as follows: "yet for our more distinct conceiving thereof, men have framed several distinctions of it: so with respect of its measure it is absolute or limited, in respect of its manner, it is, as St. *Peter* divides it, Supreme or Subordinate; in respect of its mean[s] of acquiring, it is Elective or Successive."[37] Though the language of architecture – figuring the economy of the body politic as such – predominates, Hunton is also thinking along parallel lines through the somatic and physiological metaphor, so that his preference for a mixed constitution can be imagined either as "the frame and composure of our Monarchy" defining "the Architecture of this Government," or "Government of a mixt temperature" in which the temporary appearance of "Epidemical division" acts "as Physick [which] while it is working disturbs the natural body, if the peccant humors make strong opposition; but sure it tends to health, and so doth this resistance of disorder to Order."[38]

Third, the clarity – even disinterestedness – with which Hunton was able to approach his subject was confirmed by the subsequent popularity of his *Treatise*. Originally published in 1643, it was, like the tracts on trade to which we will shortly turn, reissued at critical moments of political crisis after 1660, in this case in 1680 – in response to the Exclusion Crisis – and in 1689 – in response to the Revolution. His *Vindication of the Treatise of Monarchy* (1644) was reissued in 1650 – after the execution of Charles I and perhaps during the Engagement Controversy to which *Leviathan* was also a response, and, bound with the *Treatise*, in 1689. (Antony Ascham's equally comprehensive *A Discourse wherein is Examined what is Particularly Lawful during the Confusions and Revolutions of Government*, published in 1648, was reissued under its subtitle in 1689.) We have seen that Hunton declares that, even within broadly uncontested conceptions of mixed monarchy, the questions of whether the monarch is absolute or limited, supreme or subordinate, or elective or successive remain unresolved; and the reissuing of such tracts at the Restoration, in the Exclusion Crisis, at the succession of James II, and at the Revolution obviously served to underscore and clarify the grounds of disagreement. This habit during the Restoration period confirms Weston and Greenberg's view that the chronic tension between the order theory of kingship and theories of co-ordination energized political debate until 1688–9; and it likewise confirms Howard Nenner's view that the same period still had to determine the distinctions between successive and elective monarchy.[39] It also suggests that whereas the Fletcherian mode originally served to expose the dizzying complexities of politics in 1611, for Dryden and his generation, it could serve, like Hunton's tract, as a dialectical device for anatomizing disagreements that emerged clearly in the 1640s (when drama could not actively participate in the polemical climate), remained objects of intense debate during the Restoration period (to which, I am arguing, drama contributed significantly), and were only settled by political events at the Revolution (which caused Dryden to return to drama as a vehicle of political critique).

The fact that political analysis proceeds in the 1640s altogether more comprehensively is not only, as I have argued, owing to an increasingly clearer conception that sovereignty is the key point at issue, or to the increasing sophistication of the pamphlet wars; it is also owing to a purely discursive shift that occurred in 1628. In that year, famously, William Harvey published *De Motu Cordis*, announcing his discovery of the circulation of the blood. (*De Circulatione Sanguinis* was published in 1649; *De Generatione* in 1651; and all three treatises appeared in translation as the *Anatomical Exercitations* in 1653.) Viewed from our perspective, *The Maid's Tragedy* is struggling with the intrinsic limits of the Galenic hypothesis; but since the circulation of the blood reveals a systemic and largely mechanical (rather than qualitative) description of bodily processes, in which the heart is as important as the head (if not more so), the Harveian revolution in physiology allows political thinkers, for whom the metaphor of the body politic is second nature, to think more uniformly about the implications of their arguments for the state as a whole.[40] (Harvey criticizes Galen by writing that "he could not find a vessel which from the heart should distribute the blood into the whole body.")[41]

The effects are subtle, but nonetheless real. Both Hunton and Ascham evidently see some correspondence between their desire to anatomize political conditions in general and the new physiology which, rather than differentiating elements that comprise bodily processes – as does, for example, *Galen's Art of Physick* (1652), translated by Nicholas Culpeper, a "Gent. Student in Physick and Astrology" – seeks to link the elements of the body in a single economy. Hunton writes that to understand the body politic we should look "where the *apex potestas* is, [for] there is the Government." A pure theory of co-ordination "is against all Common Reason: For the King, is he not King of the Kingdom? and what is the Kingdom but all united? All the particulars knit together in one body politick?"[42] And Ascham argues that earlier legislation still has force, "For we are still the same society or body politique, which dies not, no fundamental change intervening: Though the particular persons of past ages be no more, yet the society is the same; just as the *Rhine* is the same river it was at the beginning, though its waters still runne away, and are every moment buried in the sea." He declares within a few lines, "The Body Politique can be considered but as one particular person, and what it acts is usually for itself."[43] Many of the *topoi* are so conventional, such as the idea of the King as the fountain of justice, that it is hard to know, locally, whether they have now shifted ground. But surely an image like the fountain – which in Harvey alludes to the heart[44] – must have a different aspect to its users once *De Motu Cordis* has entered the political bloodstream. Now that Harvey has founded the bodily economy on fluid processes, they become key illustrations in the King's *Answer to the Nineteen Propositions* (the powers of each estate run in their own channel), in Ascham's conception of the historical coherence of the polity (over time the Rhine remains the same river), and in Hunton, when he writes:

Soveraign Power being so conferred on that person [of the sovereign], the person and power cannot be really sundered, but the force which is used to the one, must also violate the other: for power is not in the Soveraign as it is in inferior officers: as water is otherwise in the spring then in the channels, and pipes deriving it.[45]

But the clearest and most radical proof of the shift occurs in an anonymous pamphlet from 1643 whose title alone makes the point. It reads:

The Subjects Libertie. Set Forth in the Royall and Politique Power of England. The First Intent that Makes a King is the Peoples Consent, Fortesc. Cap. 13. And it is as the Effluxe of Blood from the Heart to the Head, and Lives before it. The Laws as Sinewes Unite all the Members, and the Head can no more Change them, then the Head of a Naturall Body can Alter the Ligaments of all the Members.

Drawing on the usual range of sources – the Bible, Aristotle, Augustine, Hooker, Fortescue, Bracton, the conciliarists, natural law, Roman history – and alluding to the Grand Remonstrance of 2 November 1642, the author lays out an aggressive argument in favor of popular consent, without which, in effect, the King is powerless. His culminating gambit is to draw on Harvey. Drawing directly on Harvey's discussion of life in the womb,[46] there must, he argues, be a head of state, but that head must draw its nourishment from the heart:

The Embrion begins the naturall body in all the lineaments, and the heart is the first that liveth, and by vitall blood quickens all the Members: so in the politique, the peoples Intent is the first living thing, and gives life to the head, the Lawes as sinews bind the bones and bodies of Men together, which of strong become weake, when they shrink or are stretched out of compass . . . The head is a fountaine as well as the heart, and should be the colder in well tempered Spirits. The blood begins at the liver, and is refined in the heart, tempered in the head, and by the sinews give sense and motion. So the king is *fons justitiae*, that the lusts of the people might not bee left to an Arbitrary, irascible, and concupiscible commotion.[47]

By 1660, then, the mixed-plot play serves at once as the symbol of the ideal mixed monarchy that Dryden recommends in *Of Dramatic Poesy*, and, for all the reasons we have considered, a sophisticated instrument for anatomizing the body politic, understood as the metabolic organism Harvey describes, and for debating alternative ways of imagining it.

MIXED PLAYS AND POLITICAL ECONOMY

The dramatic setting of *Of Dramatic Poesy* not only reflects but capitalizes on a further and revolutionary change in the conditions separating early from late Stuart conceptions of the state. Dryden's use of the Battle of Lowestoft during the second Dutch War is no more cosmetic for his purposes than his interest in Fletcherian tragicomedy, since, like the mixed plots whose corollary is the mixed constitution, the very nature of what was at stake in the war symbolizes for Dryden a political order willing to accommodate "traffick." Trade or commerce as a source of English national pride Dryden had already celebrated before the second Dutch War in 1662, in his epistle "To My Honour'd Friend, Dr. Charleton." Dryden depicts the displacement of scholastic dogmatism by English natural philosophy; and the genealogy of a newly skeptical science (embodied in Bacon, Gilbert, Boyle, Harvey, and Ent) simultaneously links the Harveian revolution with a new conception of world trade. On the one hand, English discoveries of magnetism (Gilbert) and circulation (Harvey) guarantee that world trade will become an English prerogative ("British fleets the boundless ocean awe" [l. 26]); on the other, the fraternal conjunction of Robert Boyle, the chemist, and Roger Boyle, Earl of Orrery, links the new science to political counsel and marries good counsel to the power of the revived theater, for which Orrery had written some successful heroic plays.

These *topoi*, one might remark, were not original. Already in 1653, the dedicatory poem to Harvey's *De Generationis* declared with similar celebratory tones,

> There didst thou trace the *Blood*, and first behold
> What *Dreams* mistaken Sages coin'd of *old*.
> For till thy *Pegasus* the *fountain brake*,
> The *crimson Blood*, was but a *crimson Lake*,
> Which first from Thee did *Tyde* and *Motion* gaine,
> And *Veins* became its *Channel*, not its *Chaine*.
> With *Drake* and *Candish* hence thy *Bays* is curl'd,
> Fam'd *Circulator* of the *Lesser World*.[48]

And, as Ronald Knowles and Blair Hoxby have shown, John Ogilby's *Relation of His Majestie's Entertainment Passing through the City of London to his Coronation* (1661) records how the King was confronted in his progress with a dense series of emblematic triumphal arches and *tableaux vivants*, governed in part, like Dryden's *Astrea Redux*, by Virgilian allusions to the return of a golden age.[49] As the King approached "the *East-India* House," a youth in Indian habit attended by "two *Black-Moors*" offered the tribute due an English monarch, and a second such youth, similarly accompanied, appeared on a camel "having two Panniers fill'd with Jewels, Spices and Silks" (9). He addressed the King as a phoenix risen from the ashes of civil discord, a national treasure more precious than the accumulated riches of the East, yet an eastern potentate of sorts like Solomon, capable of repelling the Dutch and eclipsing the Spanish by reviving the vigor of English trade:

> We'll blame that Fire no more, that scorch'd our Nest
> Of Spicy Trade, since we see You, the Best
> Of Kings, Rise from the Ashes of that Flame,
> That burnt our First Right *Phoenix* of Your Name.
> For you have out-done *Solomon*, and made
> Provision for a more than *Ophir* Trade;
> Among Your first of unexpected Cares
> Enlarg'd our Charter, and dispel'd our Fears
> Of the incroaching *Holland*'s Rival Force.
> Nor can we doubt, but by the bounteous Source
> Of Your Successful Right, not only We,
> But all the Merchants of Your Realm shall see
> This *Empory* the *Magazine* of All
> That's Rich, from *Phoebus* Rising to his Fall.
>
> (10; italics reversed)

Near the Exchange, the second arch was *"Naval,"* declaring Charles a British Neptune, with niches representing variously the arts of "ARITHMETICK, GEOMETRY, ASTRONOMY, and NAVIGATION" (13). As the nobility passed, it was serenaded by a group of seamen recounting their adventures on the high seas. Finally, in St. Paul's churchyard, the pupils of Christ's Hospital, beneficiaries of the City's charity, sang a hymn to the King. During the third Dutch War, in 1673, it was that very foundation, of which Pepys was a governor, which was to house the Royal Mathematical School. In 1681, William Hanway and John Potenger were to celebrate the King's munificence in creating the school "for the Improvement of *Naval Knowledge*, and the necessary advantages of *Maritime Dominion* and *Commerce*, depending thereon"; and they recall that, at the urging of Sir Jonas Moore, also a governor of Christ's Hospital, "His MAJESTY had of his own Bounty, and by the Mediation of His Royal Highnesse, then Lord High Admiral of *England*, been pleas'd to Order a liberal Allowance, for the maintainance of a Select number of the ablest and fittest Youths of the said *Hospital*, to be Annually chosen, as also for that of a Master, to instruct them, in such Parts of the *Mathematics* as are requisite in a Skilful *Sea-man*."[50] So in 1667, when Dryden concluded *Annus Mirabilis* with a prospect of a loyal London serving as a world emporium,[51] he was simply drawing on well-worn tropes, some of his own devising.

Almost exactly thirty years later, Dryden could justifiably revisit his prophecies about commerce in his Dedication to the *Aeneis*, though now applied to the fecundity of English, which imports words and then enriches them by a process of domestic circulation.[52] He could do this in confidence because, we now know, owing especially to conditions after the third Dutch War but really initiated by the Navigation Act of 1651, the period between 1660 and 1700 experienced revolutionary changes in the nature of public finance. Modern historians have labelled this transformation a "commerical revolution." In 1667, it is difficult to imagine Dryden being fully conscious of the disturbances beneath his feet, but by the end of the century Charles Davenant – the dramatist's son – could write that since 1660 England had experienced a four-fold increase in world trade, involving exotic products from America, the West Indies, and India, and involving a major reexport trade besides.[53] Although the conclusions are still spectacular, by focusing on the three most important exotic imports of the century, namely tobacco, sugar, and calicoes, Ralph Davis's estimates are slightly more cautious. In the period from 1663–9 to 1699–1701, calico imports rose from 240,000 to 861,000 pieces, and sugar imports rose from 148,000 cwt. to 371,000 cwt. But the figures for tobacco are remarkable: in 1619, imports stood at 20,000 lb., rising to 1,000,000 lb. in the 1630s, then to 7,000,000 lb. in 1662–3, and finally to 27,000,000 lb. in 1699–1701.[54] Davis also writes that over the century the tonnage of English merchant shipping increased between six- and seven-fold, though until 1640 half of the sailors worked for the domestic coal and fisheries industries.[55] These numbers accompanied major shifts in habits of domestic consumption, because what were formerly prohibitively expensive luxuries became affordable to members of the middling and lower classes. That Davenant exaggerated his estimate merely testifies to the enormous changes of which Englishmen became increasingly conscious and in response to which they sought to develop appropriate ways of thinking and speaking.

These changes, Steven Pincus has shown convincingly, had already taken place as a result of the first Dutch War – the effect of enforcing the Navigation Act against the Dutch carrying trade.[56] Partly because, of all three wars, this was militarily the most successful, numerous Commonwealthmen were touting the benefits of trade for the Rump parliament and the Protectorate. Pincus also argues that this conception of trade amounted to a theory of the political personality, one capable of incorporating conceptions of commerce into statecraft, one different from the classical republicanism described by Pocock and espoused at some points by Milton, and one equally distinct from MacPherson's possessive individualism.[57] In fact, these polemicists had happened upon what is properly understood as a form of political economy before William Petty, who is generally credited with founding the discipline: in what Petty also called "political anatomy," the health and disposition of the polity could be read through the lens of trade, its relation to the internal economy of the state, and the degree to which subjects participated in either. Thus it is obvious that figures like William Davenant, Evelyn, Ogilby, and Dryden were in fact inheriting a well-developed language about the benefits of trade from the very political figures the Restoration reviled.

All parties were appropriating and refashioning a language of trade whose origins lie in the establishment of the East India Company in 1600, and then the currency crisis which hit in 1620, a moment which not coincidentally helped further crystallize parliament's sense of its own privileges.[58] (Jan de Vries also sees this moment as comprising a turning-point in European economic history.)[59] Echoing the challenges facing political theorists before 1640, apparently disparate facts on the ground confronted merchants and men of affairs with a series of practical problems which they could not address easily through a developed vocabulary or a fully articulated theory about economic behavior. If anything, they were somewhat hampered in their endeavor by inherited prejudices against financial dealings, such as the fears of usury expressed in Thomas Wilson's *A Discourse upon Usury* (1572), even though the author was a hard-headed businessman acquainted with government affairs. It almost follows logically that the emergence of a discourse of trade as a distinct genre, in which writers mutually recognize each other even as they often vigorously disagree, involves a story of the emergence of increasingly defined tools for addressing specifically economic problems. But as Johnson, Letwin, and Schumpeter all remark, what Letwin calls "the origin of scientific economics" cannot be disentangled from languages that to us have neither to do with science nor narrowly with economics in its modern sense.[60] Several questions then arise: What concrete events push writers in the direction of thinking in economic terms? What heuristic devices do they draw on in seeking to articulate themselves? And how do these devices drive economic questions into wider, and perhaps to us different, moral and political ramifications? Or to put it another way, what local analogies invite connections between the economic concerns involved and other related issues, such as sovereignty, and how do those analogies also serve to render the analysis more systemic?

The first quarter of the century proved foundational for the discourse of trade for four reasons. First, the fact of India as an outpost of trade raised anxieties, repeated through the century, about the degree to which paying for exotic products with bullion at great distance sapped national wealth, since, for bullionists, wealth was measured by the amount of gold and silver within state borders. Second, the currency crisis in the 1620s intensified discussions about the distinctions among coinage (specie or hard cash), currency (money more generally), and instruments of credit, most often spoken of as bills of exchange, and it also began to stimulate interest in what economists now call money supply.[61] Third, the East Indies served as the dramatic setting for increasing conflicts between English and Dutch trading interests.[62] This reveals how one backdrop for the discourse of trade involved the collapse of Antwerp as the world *entrepôt* in favor of the United Provinces, making the Dutch spectacularly rich, while the Spanish, still obsessed with the treasure fleets, were in a process of marked national decline.[63] Conflict in the East Indies also served as the occasion of a bitter propaganda campaign, beginning in 1624 with *Newes out of East India* and John Skinner's *A True Relation of the Unjust, Cruell, and Barbarous Proceedings against the English at Amboyna in the East Indies*, in which the English accused the Dutch of falsely imprisoning and torturing English traders in Amboyna.[64] Accompanied by lurid woodcuts, these charges were reissued throughout the century to coincide with each of the Dutch wars, as well as in 1688 to warn Englishmen against William of Orange.

Fourth, as a consequence of these various conditions, the early 1600s witnessed the launching of a polemical debate among three figures whose names became, in the course of the century, canonical. These are Gerard de Malynes, Thomas Mun, and Edward Misselden. Drawing on Thomas Wilson, whom he does not acknowledge, and Jean Bodin, whom he does, Malynes issued, in 1601, *Saint George for England, Allegorically Described* and *A Treatise of the Canker of England's Commonwealth*, and in 1603, *England's View, in the Unmasking of Two Paradoxes*, couched as a commentary on Bodin. In 1622, he issued *Consuetudo, Vel Lex Mercatoria, or the Ancient Law Merchant* and, in response to Misselden, published *The Maintainance of Free Trade* (1622) and *The Center of the Circle of Commerce* (1623). Malynes is often dismissed as a regressive thinker because, as Joyce Appleby puts it, he sees the object of his analysis in terms of fixed points or "simples" (to use his term), namely commodity, money, and exchange.[65] He is a bullionist in that he thinks of national wealth in terms of accumulated bullion,[66] he is a strict balance-of-trade theorist, since the aim is to export more than you import,[67] and his entire argument is in the thrall of an unyielding aesthetic of harmony, ratio, and proportion, evidently expressing the great chain of being[68] – the dragon in *Saint George for England*, for example, "overthroweth the harmony of the strings of the good government of a common-wealth."[69] Unlike Mun and Misselden, he cannot see that a calculus of national wealth might involve some logarithmic relation among goods, currency, and credit. Like the Divine Right theorists of whom he is obviously aware,[70] frequently repeating that the King is *parens patriae*,[71] and like Bodin, who argues that a prime feature of sovereignty is the sovereign's control of coinage, his tract makes the prince the sole determinant of national value, answerable to God alone, so mounting a defense of sovereignty as such. He writes, "the valuation or alteration of money, concerneth only the sovereignty and dignity of the Prince or governour of every countrey, as a thing peculiar unto them."[72]

Although Andrea Finkelstein takes some account of the metaphors through which Malynes and other trade theorists pursue their arguments, most commentators ignore such metaphors as extraneous to the chief matter at hand, namely the development of economic analysis.[73] But this neglects the degree to which, when Malynes, Mun, and Misselden engage in vigorous debate in the 1620s, one explicit concern is the nature of economic model-making itself.[74] That is, the question is, now that new phenomena are breaking into people's consciousness, what kinds of metaphor help generate the most useful interpretive models of them? These writers are aware that they face a series of discrete and unarticulated symptoms in trade whose general pattern of behavior demands but yet resists systemic interpretation (what Mun calls "coherence"), so that though Malynes and Mun differ, they both seek to penetrate *"the Mystery of Exchange,"* or the "mysterie of Merchandizing."[75] The disagreement between Malynes on the one hand and Mun and Misselden on the other is partly fueled by Malynes's obsession with treasure, producing an anxiety about Mun's and Misselden's argument that flows of money are indications of flows of goods, and about the fact that though they still stress a positive balance of trade, their emphasis rests on the velocity of goods on the world market. The East India trade is no cause for alarm, Mun and Misselden agree, because to permit flows of goods in and out of the nation is to produce wealth. In his *Discourse of Trade* (1621), Mun writes that "money doth attend Merchandize, for money is the price of wares, and wares are the proper use of money; so that their coherence is unseparable";[76] and in his posthumous but profoundly influential *England's Treasure by Forraign Trade* (1664) – obviously issued to coincide with the second Dutch War – he writes that "the monies which are carried from us within the ballance of our trade are not considerable, for they do return to us again."[77] In sum, *"Money begets trade and trade encreaseth money."*[78]

Misselden's frustration with Malynes in his *The Circle of Commerce. Or, The Ballance of Trade, in Defence of Free Trade* (1623) proceeds in part from the fact that, unlike his rival, he recognizes the entirely heuristic and contingent nature of model-making in the face of the forensic obscurities accompanying economic life. Malynes's riposte to Misselden's tract is called *The Center of the Circle of Commerce*, the title of which alone explains his resistance. First, it is not enough to concede that Giotto could draw a perfect circle freehand – the fiction behind both titles – but it is important to imagine that he placed a point at its center, that center denoting a Platonic form of sorts, figured as "*gaine.*"[79] ("Even as the *Circle* of *Giotto*, was made without a *Center*," Malynes complains, "even so is [Misselden's] *Circle of Commerce*, without substance or *Center*, like unto a stone cast into a standing water.")[80] In reaction to Malynes's *The Maintainance of Free Trade*, Misselden accuses Malynes of outright misprision and of distorting "my Modell," reminding him that, like metaphors, models work only heuristically: "I layd a *Basis* or foundation only, for a more skillfull worke-man to erect a more stately building. Mine, was but a model or frame, rough hewen, slightly set up and pinn'd together; to try how the parts and joints thereof would trent [sic] and fit the square."[81]

The opposition between Malynes's fixed point and Misselden's circle amounts to an opposition between substance and process, between some moral essence and mere method, and, in the economic sphere, between bullion and the fluid processes of trade that more indirectly generate wealth. (Mun writes that "the current of Merchandize . . . becomes a flowing stream.")[82] We also observe a clear opposition between Malynes's Bodinian absolutism, by which the sovereign regulates coinage by fiat, and Mun's and Misselden's emphases on the accumulated prudence of merchants at home, the mutual experience of international traders, and a collaborative endeavor between the monarch, who can protect trade and provide grants of monopolies, and the self-regulating behavior of the merchant community.[83] This opposition between a singular and more dispersed view of authority translates into a literary and generic distinction between romance and some other, less determinate, way of writing and thinking. In fact, according to Misselden's and Mun's accounts, merchants act very much like the Ciceronian rhetor we will encounter in Chapter Two, since like the orator they determine value communally and circumstantially: merchants reach trading agreements "according to the circumstances of *time*, and *place*, and *persons*"; or in the trading community, "by a course of traffick (which changeth according to the accurrents of time) the particular members do accommodate each other."[84] Of the distinction between romance and rhetoric as modes of apprehending value Malynes is at least half-aware, since at the end of *Saint George for England* he draws attention to his vehicle – a mildly Spenserian allegory, in which the dragon is the monster of covetousnness or *"Politicall usury,"*[85] "the virgin is the kings treasure: [and] the champion *Saint George* is the kings authoritie, armed with the right armor of a Christian."[86] The Spenserian aura is extended to another tract Malynes published before Elizabeth died, because the title-page of the highly Bodinian *Englands View* (1603) reproduces the very emblem – *anchora spei* – that introduced readers to the 1596 edition of *The Faerie Queene*. Like Hobbes's parodic enemies in *Leviathan*, Malynes thus sets himself up for a kind of epistemological satire, since to invoke romance is to invite the charge of prestidigitation. Misselden abruptly dismisses Malynes as a quack, while Mun writes that the focus on specie boils down to alchemy, because Malynes seeks a process of turning mere money into gold, currency into bullion.[87] "This Exchange," Mun concludes, as if anticipating Hobbes's Kingdom of Fairies, "goes beyond *Conjuring*; I think verily that neither Doctor *Faustus* nor *Banks* his Horse could ever do such admirable feats, though it is sure they had a Devil to help them; but wee Merchants deal not with such Spirits, we delight not to be thought the workers of lying wonders."[88]

Although this account highlights the differences between, on the one hand, Malynes's and, on the other, Mun's and Misselden's view of knowledge, authority, and commerce, their debate, taken as a whole, contributes to an increasingly systemic analysis of economic life. First, as Appleby argues, the mere fact of entry into print itself comprises an activity of model-making of the kind that Malynes doesn't fully appreciate, since to engage in the public polemic of print is both to create an audience for this kind of argument and at the same time to force the protagonists to generalize and abstract from the disparate phenomena about which they disagree.[89] This reveals the extent to which – as we have seen in relation to political pamphleteering in the 1640s – a more secure grasp of disciplinary method can result, perhaps paradoxically, in more vigorous debates about terms within the discipline, producing the kind of internal dialogue Dryden associates, in drama, with the Fletcherian mode, an internal dialogue which assumes that drama is as much about print as performance. As Misselden remarks, the discourse of trade should alert the King to "the Theorick part of Commerce."[90]

Second, we have seen how, in all the writers that we have considered so far, the well-worn image of the body politic is almost second nature. But just as in *The Maid's Tragedy* the appeal to physiology is an attempt to anatomize the polity by reference to the human body,[91] so Malynes, Misselden, and Mun seek to render their arguments syntactical by depending on a Galenic model, often speaking of trade itself as a body. Even though there are times when the use of the physiological metaphor seems merely habitual – as when Malynes declares himself a good physician treating the canker of the commonwealth,[92] or writes that "in time of wars, moneys are called to be the sinews thereof, or *Nervi Bellorum*,"[93] or when Sir Robert Cotton speaks of the mint as the pulse of the nation,[94] or when Mun says that "Mony is the Life of Trade"[95] – the trope still puts pressure on the way the argument might go. This has several effects. Most obviously, physiology is once again an heuristic device to lend a sense of coherence or system to a series of features for which an explanatory model has yet fully to emerge. Unsurprisingly, the more Galenic the presumptions, the more archaic the model appears to us. Thus, having distinguished between barter, the sale of goods for money, and the use of credit, Malynes concludes that "the said three essential parts of Trafficke are properly the *Bodie, Soule, and Spirit of Commerce*, and have their operation accordingly,"[96] and the connections among these properties he imagines as sympathetic and qualitative rather than statistical or mechanical:

As the elements are ioined by Symbolization, the aire to the fire by warmnesse, the water to the aire by moysture, the earth to the water by coldnesse; so is Exchange ioyned to Moneys, and Monys to Commodities by their proper qualities and effects whereby it did appear unto them.[97]

Moreover, the appeal to the monarch to cure the ills of the state, the analogy between the microcosm and macrocosm, as well as the *topos* of the King as a father of a family, consistently translate the argument from the narrow concerns of trade in the direction of an embryonic version of political economy: like the affairs of the household, the *oikon*, matters of commerce, bearing on the body of trade, are also matters of the body politic. This, I would propose, is the effect of one rather curious metaphor Mun uses: "A Prince (in this case) is like the stomach in the body, which if it cease to digest and distribute to the other members, it doth no sooner corrupt them, but it destroys it self."[98]

And lastly, well before 1628, because it ostensibly imagines the exchange of credit over great geographical distances, and because Mun and Misselden emphasize volume, rates, and flow of goods and money in the creation of wealth, we see how an heuristic derived from a Galenic model experiences internal pressures, *avant la lettre* as it were, to produce a theory of circulation or "revolution." Misselden is already focused on blood as a metaphor for trade, and one can see his struggles to push the Galenic model in the direction of circulation: he writes, "There is indeed a *Fluxus* and *refluxus*, a *Flood* and *Ebbe* of the monies of *Christendome*, . . . it cometh and goeth, and whirleth about the *Circle* of *Christendome*."[99] Since his entire argument advertises the benefits of the velocity of worldwide trade, it is not entirely surprising that Mun, writing within a broadly physiological tradition of imagining the polity but seven years before *De Motu Cordis*, also conceives a theory of circulation, declaring that "these revolutions in Trades, hath and doe turn to the good of the Common-wealth."[100]

Given his essentialism, it is more surprising to observe Malynes migrating in the same direction. For all that he seems concerned to secure fixed values, he is also aware that national health is perhaps dynamic and himself has recourse to the fluid metaphor that comes more readily to his opponents. This emerges largely from a widely shared providentialism which argues that God orchestrates intercourse among nations by endowing them with different natural resources. This is not, for Malynes, an entirely self-sustaining economy, for the King must regulate the "vitall spirit of trafficke," whose effects depend on "the radical moisture of commerce."[101] Nevertheless, this providentialism permits Malynes to imagine what he calls "a kind of Revolution in buying and selling of Commodities: because the commodities of one countrie growing ranke and abundant, are transported into other countries, in whose steed [sic] needfull commodities of those kingdomes and countries are returned thither, which is a neighbourly lending betweene kingdomes and countries."[102] This conception of circulation he epitomizes as a "Revolution of Trade."[103]

We have seen that, owing to several discursive and political changes, for Dryden political theory has, by comparison with the early years of the century, become remarkably systemic. Whereas these effects are brought about by Harvey, the pamphlet wars of the 1640s following the summoning of the Long Parliament, and a greater philosophical precision about the question of sovereignty, similar changes occur in the discourse of trade. If anything, the Harveian revolution is more definitive, and its after-effects continue into the nineteenth century in Marx's *Capital*, whose prime heuristic is still physiology, not statistics, and which parses the motions of capital through a metabolic trope (*Stoffwechsel*). In this case, the decisive political events are less the revolution or civil wars than the Dutch Wars, particularly the first (1652–4) and second (1664–7), the Navigation Acts of 1651 and 1660, the decision of the Cromwellian government as well as the Restored regime to establish a Council of Trade, though that advisory body had languished by 1667, and the marked increase in the status of merchants in the second half of the century, as described by Perry Gauci.[104] The importance of trade as a state concern is already visible, Charles Wilson writes, in 1651, because "with the Navigation Act we have arrived at a fully fashioned conception of economic policy in an essentially national form."[105]

These changes also seem to accompany an ideological shift of the kind proposed by Tawney, Letwin, and Wilson, which means that the second half of the seventeenth century sees the full development not only of the state as an autonomic and self-defining entity, but, in tandem, of economic thought, involving what Wilson – in reference to Sir George Downing, chief architect of the second Dutch War – calls an "autarchic logic."[106] (We can infer this connection in Dr. Thomas Willis's *The Practice of Physick*, when it speaks of circulation as providing a "Natural economy or Government"; or elsewhere when Willis speaks of nervous activity affecting both head and heart as causing "Commerces in both Kingdoms.")[107] Thus Tawney writes that "After the Restoration, we are in a new world of economic, as well as of political, thought"; while Letwin writes that "Before 1660 economics did not exist; by 1776 it existed in profusion."[108]

These changes are registered at least three ways. First, Harveian circulation becomes an almost automatic *topos*, though more extensively at the end of the century. We have already seen how, during the first Dutch War, the dedication to *De Generatione* (1653) links the pioneers of global circumnavigation to Harvey's discovery, and how, in 1662, Dryden summons Gilbert and Harvey to justify English claims to seaborne trade. Writing in 1662, Petty, using a more broadly anatomical idea, argues that

money is but the fat of the body politick, whereof too much doth as often hinder its agility, as too little makes it sick. 'Tis true, that as fat lubricates the motion of the muscles, feeds in want of victuals, fills up uneven cavities, and beautifies the body; so doth money in the state quicken its action, feeds from abroad in the time of dearth at home; evens accounts by reason of its divisibility, and beautifies the whole.[109]

In *Annus Mirabilis* (1667), Dryden writes of "Trade, which like blood should circularly flow" (l. 5). And writing in 1672, and commenting on the analogy between "the *Body Natural*, and *Body Politick*," Petty asserts that "as *Anatomy* is the best foundation of one, so also of the other."[110] *A Description of the Office of Credit* (1665) defines money as a medium that "must needs lie dead, till it can go round."[111] In 1685, Nicholas Barbon states of London that "the Metropolis is the heart of a Nation, through which the Trade and Commodities of it circulate, like the blood through the heart, which by its motion giveth life and growth to the rest of the Body."[112] In *Taxes No Charge* (1690), Defoe declares, "Men that live by their Pay, generally spend it faster than it comes in, by which means the Money of the Kingdom, like the Blood in the Veins, has its regular, circular motion, and every Member in the *Body* is warm'd and refreshed by it, which gives Life and Motion in the whole."[113]

In *England's Glory* (1694), Sir Humphrey Mackworth writes, "Money in a Nation in Motion in Trade, is like Blood in the Veins."[114] In *A Review of the Universal Remedy for all Diseases Incident to Coin* (1696), William Freke imagines London as "the Heart and Spring of Life and Motion."[115] In *An Essay upon the Probable Methods of Making a People Gainers in the Balance of Trade* (1699), Charles Davenant expatiates on how "the late discovery of the circulation of the blood" has rendered anatomy "more plain and certain." In the same manner, he continues, "such as would understand the body politic" must study "its Trade, the current money (which is its flowing blood), the arts, labour and manufactures, and the number of its people; with many other things which altogether are the members of which the great body is composed."[116] And in his *Review* for 3 January 1707, Defoe remarks that any prospect of trade must involve "an Infinite and incessant Circulation."

Second, after the Restoration it becomes conventional to declare that trade is a concern that links private with public interests, necessitating state initiatives on behalf of its subjects. This corresponds well to Appleby's argument that classic mercantilism – the use of trade policy to cement central state power – does not typify seventeenth-century economic realities, which involved a complicated dance of government and private motives.[117] (Revising Hirshman's influential thesis that the harmony of interests is a later development, Pincus also argues that the new political economy could productively harness private interests to public concerns – an implication, I would argue, of Wycherley's *The Country Wife*.)[118] Many of the clearest calls for state action in relation to trade occur in the wake of the third Dutch War (1672–4) – in the decade in which drama most obviously flourished – though ironically the third Dutch War was not fought for trade but because Charles II, in the pay of Louis XIV, was willing to support the French absolutist's effort to destroy the United Provinces. Thus in a tract dedicated to Charles II in 1673, Samuel Fortrey declares that "Two things . . . appear to be chiefly necessary, to make a nation great, and powerful; which is to be rich, and populous," which in turn requires "a Prince, who above all things delights and glories in his peoples happiness."[119] In his *Discourse of Coin* (1675), Rice Vaughan, quoting Sir Robert Cotton, writes, "Estates stand *magis fama quam vi*, as *Tacitus* saith of *Rome*, wealth is one essential mark of a Kingdoms greatness."[120]

And we also witness a series of pamphlets that recommend trade either as the grounds for, or as an essential component of, public policy. These include Sir George Downing's highly propagandistic *Discourse* recommending war against the Dutch in 1664; Sir William Temple's more generous appraisal of Dutch success in *Observations upon the United Provinces of the Netherlands* (1673); Carew Reynel's *The True English Interest: Or an Account of the Chief National Improvements; In some Political Observations, Demonstrating an Infallible Advance of this Nation to Infinite Wealth and Greatness, Trade and Populacy, with Imployment, and Preferment for all Persons* (1674), in which Reynel writes, "Get first but Trade and People which will produce riches, and then pleasure will come of course. Riches are the Convenience of the Nation, people are the strength, pleasure, and Glory of the Nation. But Trade preserves both";[121] John Evelyn's *Navigation and Commerce, Their Original and Progress* (1674), which argues that England as an island is providentially ordained to become a sea power, that she should imitate the success of Genoa, Venice, and the Dutch, that trade is a "true, and solid Interest of State,"[122] and that to exercise sea power is to exercise sovereignty; *Britannia Languens* (1680), which declares that "*Trade* is either *National or Private:* The *National Trade* doth influence the Wealth and Strength of a *whole Nation*, and therefore is not the only Concern of *Merchants*";[123] and Sir Francis Brewster's *Essays on Trade and Navigation* (1695), which, for example, recommends the reestablishment of a Council of Trade.[124]

Third, the methodical status of the discourse of trade in neoclassical thought is suggested by the frequency with which, like the political pamphlets, key texts were republished, not only throughout the century, but during the Restoration. Malynes's *Lex Mercatoria*, published in 1622, was reissued in 1629, 1636, 1656, 1685, and 1686; though Mun's *Discourse of Trade* was only issued in two different impressions in 1621, his *England's Treasure by Forraign Trade* was first issued in 1664 and reprinted (in some cases under a different title) in 1669, 1698, 1700, 1713 and twice more in the eighteenth century. Lewes Roberts's *Treasure of Traffike* was only issued in 1641, but his *Merchant's Map of Commerce*, originally published in 1638, was reprinted in 1671, 1677, and 1700, when Mun's *Treasure by Forraign Trade* was incorporated into it. Misselden's *Free Trade* (1622) was republished in 1651. Writing in the 1690s, Locke clearly assumes that the debates of the 1620s are part of the stock-in-trade of trade theorists even after the Revolution. The strong impression is that having established itself as a discipline, the discourse of trade was restimulated at significant moments of political crisis. Moreover, and more crucially for our purposes, like the political pamphlets we have discussed, and like Dryden's mixed plots in drama, those moments not only solidified the writers' sense that they were engaged in a generally coherent activity – debating the distribution of powers in the state, writing and performing plays, addressing the nature of trade – but also reanimated at each turn conceptual problems it was the purpose of those activities to scrutinize.

At this point, however, we should recognize an important difference between drama and the political and trade pamphlets we have examined: because it is slightly abstracted from the polemical arena, rather than seeking to reject one vision of the world in favor of its own drama invites its audience (ultimately the King) to contemplate the relative value of different postulates embedded in the language and behavior of different plots and different characters. It is precisely the multiplicity of competing perspectives that Dryden so values in English plays, and we will see how Davenant's reforms of the English stage allowed for an intensified conciousness of perspective both as a condition of performance and as a limitation on human knowledge. The rhetorical purpose of seventeenth-century drama in general is thus more hortatory than polemical, since, rather than propagandizing, it seeks to persuade its audience by revealing how some postulates simply function better than others on stage.

To be effective, therefore, even as it is topically informed by the languages of politics and trade, it must develop some intellectual and psychological distance from them: what – in the struggle for ideological mastery – began as naked polemic is transformed, in a given play, into two dramatic modes. Since the prime trope of Restoration drama is on the one hand simile, drama experiments with the analogies and correspondences that link arguments about political authority with epistemology and with the discourse of trade, and it often does this by observing how the similitudes used by characters in specific circumstances succeed or fail, or appear to be apt or inapt. (Though, as we will see, the economy implicitly linking questions of knowledge to questions of authority to questions of value differs in different plays.) On the other hand, it also observes how the behavior of different characters – often driven by different generic presumptions about the world, presumptions with clearly differentiated views of knowledge and thus of the degree to which the world lends itself to manipulation – succeeds in surviving or controlling the plot. This is one explanation for the perceived amorality, even immorality, of many Restoration plays, since what is at stake is not metaphysical truth, but what, in a local sense, works; and we can cite many figures from both comic and serious plays who are irrelevant to the main action, fail to understand it, or are expelled from it.

Dryden brilliantly converts *Of Dramatic Poesy* into a dramatic example of the shift from the polemical to the experimental, for though it begins with a moment that looks at first like an unequivocal victory – the Battle of Lowestoft – which might serve as an occasion of endless bad panegyrics

to the victors, Dryden not only published his essay when the singularity of
the victory had been called into question, but shows how the knowledge
shared by the four friends is not demonstrative but contingent and open-
ended. The plays still function as parallels because in applying the lessons of
what is laid out before it, the audience is encouraged to approve the more
functional alternatives; and as Dryden argues, the entire process is best
served by tragicomedy or mixed plots because their relative generic inde-
terminacy allows them, apparently without prejudice, to square different
generic and epistemological postulates off against each other. Characters
thus find themselves in a fluid and competitive environment which requires
the audience to judge ironically and dialectically. This atmosphere is assisted
by the fact that of all genres, drama most resists revealing the activity and
views of the author: in this sense it is intrinsically skeptical and mediated,
and characters on stage are only knowable phenomenally, as the sum of
their observed speeches and actions, as public, not, despite the reception of
Hamlet, as a revealed consciousness. In this scheme of things, knowledge is
more important than sympathy, and Restoration drama is often at pains to
emphasize and enforce epistemological limits – of audience *vis-à-vis* characters, and of characters *vis-à-vis* each other – so after Margery has seen
Horner at a distance at the playhouse, we also learn that he is the mere
sign of a man, as if to underscore that we are all forensic tokens, especially
in a world populated by Jonsonian types. (Hobbes remarks that human
identity is only a *persona*, an actor's mask.) Wycherley never allows us to
know for certain what happens offstage. And Congreve is discussing the
same limitations when, in *Love for Love*, he presents us with a comic debate
about hieroglyphs and Chinese characters.

This pervasive skepticism has two related implications for my argument.
On the one hand, though the mixed play might at first appear agnostic
about the relative virtues of the different epistemic, generic, and political
postulates it launches, its own dispositions will treat as most credible those
dimensions of the play aligned with the skeptical, contingent, and public.
This means that, on the one hand, because its motives are rhetorical and
topical, Restoration drama serves as an important vehicle for proliferating
debates within political theory and trade theory in the later seventeenth
century. On the other hand, and for the same reasons, drama belongs to the
narrative career of political theory and the discourse of trade in ways that
have rarely been recognized. First, we have two rather different accounts
of what happens to political theory in the seventeenth century. Because
Divine Right theory appears philosophically archaic, and *Leviathan* and the
Two Treatises appear in 1650 and the 1690s respectively, the philosophical

account tends to present a highly teleological narrative, whereby the problem of sovereignty is resolved by 1650, or Divine Right gives way increasingly to contract theory in the course of the century. The political account, by contrast, is distinctly antiteleological, since, the argument goes, while competing visions of authority remained alive throughout the century, the problem of sovereignty was resolved only suddenly and fortuitously by the political events of 1688–9, for which Louis XIV was partly responsible.

Second, if Appleby is right, the story of the discourse of trade more or less reverses the Whiggish account of political theory, which presumes that communitarian ideas permeated more deeply in the course of time. If there is a *terminus ad quem*, it is the debates about recoinage that resurfaced in the 1690s. Because coins were minted from gold and silver, because they were stamped, not milled, and because the relative values of bullion fluctuated on an international basis coins were subject to clipping. This problem preoccupied trade theorists from the start and involved incommensurable ideas of how coins were deemed to carry value, ideas which migrated easily into anxieties about value more generally. By the end of the century clipping had considerably eroded the bullion value of coins, and new technologies at the mint now allowed for milled coins of even weight to be minted. A strident debate pitted those who believed that the new coins should match the old in weight and fineness, since specie had "intrinsick" value, against those who saw the value of money as symbolic (as "extrinsick") and as sustained by conventional, customary, and communal behavior, either in the nation at large or within the merchant community. In marked contrast to the Whig triumph at the Revolution, Locke was paradoxically the victor in an argument for recoinage which sustained the "intrinsick" value of coins, whereby an essentialist view of value prevailed over a more conventional and – we might say – more enlightened or skeptical one.

Because, I am arguing, plays served as an important medium of political and economic debate, while they play out the different positions available to political actors, their endemic skepticism predisposes them towards conventional and customary, rather than natural and foundational, views of knowledge, authority, and value. Thus an account of drama as a constituent feature of political argumentation in the Restoration revives the teleological narrative, though under an entirely different aegis: rather than parliamentary privilege having its own Hegelian thrust in history, this crucial discursive vehicle of political theory is always inclined to the skeptical and communitarian alternative. The preferences the drama expresses are governed by rhetorical motives, in an attempt to counsel the King and the political nation, so that its tendency to prefer one view over another has none of the triumphalism we associate with the Whig historians, since no one could have predicted the events of 1688 or their outcome. As we will see, the purposes of loyalist plays were more local, consistently advising Charles II against the incipient absolutism of which, from the beginning, many Englishmen suspected the Stuarts. Paradoxically, while the drama remained equally committed to extrinsic value in general, the result of the recoinage debate meant that that position had, at least temporarily, failed. The net result for the last decade of the century, as we will see in *The Way of the World*, is that because the political and economic order now seemed more settled, drama no longer served as the dialectical medium of debate it once did.

SOME DRAMATIC APPLICATIONS

Thomas Jordan and the Lord Mayor's Shows, 1671–1684

Like Davenant, Thomas Jordan began his career before the closing of the theaters in 1642. And like Davenant, Jordan seems to have remained an ardent loyalist from his entry as a young man upon the polemical scene in 1641 until his death in the mid 1680s. He also wrote a play called *The Walks of Islington and Hogsdon* which, licensed in 1641 and running (surprisingly for the modern reader) for nineteen performances, was only printed in 1657 and again in 1663. Most of his royalist effusions in the 1640s are largely conventional, promoting an Erastian vision of king and church, so that from our point of view the interest mainly lies in the series of Lord Mayor's Shows he wrote every year from 1671, when they resumed after the Great Fire, until 1684.[125]

What we see here is a remarkable system of analogies which repeatedly connects the affairs of the City to that of the nation at large, the Lord Mayor's magistracy to that of the King, and the promotion of trade to political prudence in general. Less explicitly, but equally persistently, Jordan's shows link City commerce to a worldwide system of arterial circulation, yearly enacted in the progress of the Mayor's retinue from the City to Westminster and back via the Thames, now imagined as a new Tiber, in a process in which the affairs of the City (a new Rome), of the nation, and of an emerging Augustan empire are simultaneously invoked. Since the Mayor's perambulations early in the festivities included the boat trip to Westminster to make obeisance to the King, and because often the King, and more commonly the Duke of York, the Duke of Monmouth, and Prince Rupert, were guests at the final banquet, it is clear that, because the

Lord Mayor rules vicariously on the King's behalf, the rhetorical purpose of the emblematic pageants is to create a model of ideal rule *per se*. It is true that Jordan's youthful pamphlets have a fairly clear conception of the state as such[126] and loosely employ the *topos* of the body politic, but by the time that Jordan stages a private masque, *Fancy's Festivals*, in the 1650s, the systemic implications of political theory and of the Harveian revolution are already visible. Since "We are members of one body Politick," and since the corruptions of the pulpit mean that only the stage can properly deliberate on affairs of state, it follows that the internal organization of figures in the masque produces a conceptual "Model" for the internal economy of the polity.[127]

These possibilities are played out in the Lord Mayor's Shows in part because the whole ideal is assisted by London's increasingly clear relation to world trade. The second, third, and fourth shows (1672, 1673, and 1674) occur against the backdrop of the third Dutch War, while those from 1679 until the early 1680s are equally preoccupied with the Popish Plot and its aftermath. Like Dryden's vision at the end of *Annus Mirabilis* it is natural to celebrate how "London *holds Commerce / With all the Regions of the Universe*,"[128] making her an "*Emporium* . . . Into whose lap is daily hurl'd / The various treasures of the World."[129] London becomes an emblem for a nation sated with peace and plenty, whose possibilities are realized in elaborate stagings of Moors, Africans, Indians, and Americans festooned with exotic products, especially in those shows celebrating a Mayor elected from the Grocer's Company. An hortatory purpose informs the idea that the Lord Mayor rules the City at the King's pleasure, such that the Mayor in himself represents "*the Justice-Seat of this* Emporeum,"[130] which explains how Pallas, goddess of arts and arms, and riding the camel in *London in Splendor* (1673), could occupy "a sublime Seat of Soveraignty."[131] The Mayor enjoys rule vicariously: the City is "the Seat of *Magistrates*; where, next to the *KING*, / You have a complete Power of Governing," partly because the visit to Westminster reveals how the Mayor's powers are "abstracted from the Kings,"[132] and partly because the company from which the Mayor hails represents a miniature state. Thus *London's Triumphs* (1674) features the Goldsmiths, whose patron Saint Dunstan celebrates

> London's LORD MAYOR, *whose Value has been try'd,*
> *And found intrinsically purifi'd*:
> *So are the* Company *of which you're free,*
> *For Truth and Treasure, a Societie*
> *In all Parts fitted to adorn* Great States,
> *And prove a* Nursery *for* Magistrates.[133]

Just as, Weston and Greenberg argue, by the Restoration the idea of mixed monarchy has become more or less habitual even for royalists,[134] so here we find that the correspondence among different bodies in the state also means that mixed government is held up as an ideal, whether expressed as "*th*' KING, *the* City, *and your* Companie,"[135] or "*the City, the Countrey, the Camp, and the Court.*"[136] As Minerva puts it in *The Triumphs of London* (1675), "*I guide all Bodies Politick, and rule / I'th'Court, i'th'City*, Countrey, Camp, *and* School."[137] And this temperate ideal of rule – producing the parallel between London and the Thames on the one hand and Rome and the Tiber on the other[138] – recommends trade, not the sword, as a medium of state policy. Of course, trade is imagined physiologically, as an activity nourishing the body politic by a process of circulation. In *London's Resurrection*, Orpheus addresses the Lord Mayor: "May you in Traffick no disaster know, / Your riches never ebb, but ever flow."[139] And *London's Joy* celebrates the effects of the East India trade, with Fructifera "the *Governess*" singing, "Our Trading is whirl'd / All over the World, / In vast Voyages, on the Ocean so curl'd."[140]

Not least because, like Ogilby's *Entertainment*, the shows are themselves theatrical events on a grand scale – a process linking London with Westminster via the Thames, and providing a kind of emblematic syntax for the City itself – for Jordan the vision of temperate rule recommended both to Mayor and King most depends on the theater as an instrument of political instruction. This is conveyed thematically in Jordan's reminders that the theaters were reopened at the Restoration, so reviving one example of moderation not exemplified in Cromwell,[141] and in the material stylizing of the theater in the first scene of *London's Joy*, where, mounted on a camel, "is the figure of a Royal Theatre, framed, formed, and loftily erected according to the *Ionick* Order of *Architecture*, where the elaborate hand of Art has been as accurate in the little Model of this Fabrick, as some others have been in the more magnificent dimensions of such greater structures."[142] That the theater has a universal application or appeal is suggested by the fact that this material emblem encloses figures representing the seven champions of Christendom as well as the five senses. But the effect of the liberal arts on the arts of government is perhaps most clearly displayed in two roughly equivalent moments in *London's Resurrection* (1671) and *London's Triumphs* (1676). The second pageant of three in *London's Resurrection* involves an exotic wilderness in which "two *Negro* Boys" are mounted on two panthers, the whole scene dominated by a stately structure, the first arch of which frames the figure of Orpheus.[143] Like Amphion, Orpheus, depicted with his lyre, is able to animate the world by his art, summoning civil order out of chaos. Just as the Restoration has ushered in a new era of peace, so he reminds his audience – the Lord Mayor and, by extension, the King – that he represents "The *Hieroglyphick* of good Government."[144] Orpheus assumes that the Mayor's and the King's (and implicitly Jordan's) indebtedness to Ben Jonson and Inigo Jones means that the moderns have recently surpassed the ancients in harnessing the theater to deliberative advice,[145] advice that, in recommending the pursuit of commerce, assumes a correspondence between the ethical effects of trade and the mediating power of equity in government.

In 1676, *London's Triumphs* begins by reminding Sir Thomas Davies of the analogies between his magistracy and the King's prerogative. The first pageant features Atlas holding the globe, then Minerva, another goddess of arts and arms, introducing a series of emblems representing the seven liberal arts. This parade culminates in the figure of Cicero, "a very grave Person representing *GOVERNMENT*," despatched, he reminds his audience, "*To personate a* Civil Government," in which, evidently, the passions and affections of the Mayor must be "*Confin'd within the bounds of Equity*."[146] The second pageant features Tamburlaine, whose career as a shepherd also makes him a fit symbol both of the Drapier's Company and of rule in general;[147] while the third pageant concludes with a speech by Fortune, who presides over successful merchandizing and reminds her audience that trade, like Cicero's equity, has a tempering effect on the nation.[148] The final pageant ends with a song in which diverse members of society contribute to the good of the whole. These include a lawyer, a physician, a Quaker, a gallant, a cit, a philosopher, and an actor.[149]

Sir Samuel Tuke's The Adventures of Five Hours *(1663)*

Acted in the third season of the revived theatre, one of the most successful plays of the 1660s, Tuke's *The Adventures of Five Hours*, was rehearsed in December 1662, acted in January 1663, and printed on 21 February 1663. Evelyn wrote that his kinsman's translation of Coello "took so universally, that it was acted for some weeks every day," earning the players a small fortune.[150] Reprinted in 1664, 1671, 1704, and 1712, the play had been acted at court by early 1663, and was also presented there on 3 December 1666.[151] The Prologue for the court performance remarks that the King had recommended the plot to Tuke, and the play concludes with a gesture to the King's powers in parliament, by which the audience desires the King's imprimatur, signaled by the phrase "Le Roy le Veut," to confirm its approval.[152]

Billed in the first edition as a tragicomedy in the Fletcherian mode
and read merely for its theatrical *frisson*, Tuke's play could easily be seen as
something of a French farce capitalizing on mistaken and hidden identities,
and on doors opening in and out of gardens, the street, and adjoining houses
belonging to two cousins and their sisters. There is no question that the play
works in that melodramatic register; but that itself exploits elements of the
plot and the possibilities offered by the newly revived indoor theater which
have a clear intellectual rationale. (The play was performed by the Duke's
Men at Lisle's Tennis Court, Lincoln's Inn Fields, where "Davenant first
used in a professional theatre movable and changeable scenery.")[153] The two
adjacent houses in Seville are occupied on the one hand by Don Carlos and
his sister, Camilla, and on the other by Don Henrique and his sister, Porcia.
The play is set, significantly, during the Dutch revolt against Spanish rule
in the sixteenth century, and Tuke obviously expects his audience to see
the parallels to tensions with Holland prior to the second Dutch War. It
transpires that Camilla, while in the Spanish Netherlands, has been rescued
by and fallen in love with Don Antonio, whose name she doesn't know;
whereas Porcia is the occasion of a classic love-and-honor plot, because her
lover, Don Octavio, has accidentally killed a kinsman of Don Henrique,
who is now bent on revenge.

These circumstances alone explain the dialectical series of doublings and
juxtapositions of which the action is largely composed, since they finally
amount to an opposition between a world dictated by absolute value and
a world mediated by contingency. As Octavio says, "Contraries compar'd
set off each other" (IV,i,42): like the opening scene of *The Rover*, which
clearly owes something to this play, the two heroines in Act I tell stylized,
slightly competitive stories of their different circumstances; we are asked
nevertheless to think of their relation as symbiotic when – alluding to the
two houses they inhabit – they insist that "No walls can sever us" (I,i,119);
in the middle of the action, in Act III, scene ii, the characters spill from
house to garden, implying the curious proximity of different worlds and
literary genres; in Acts IV and V in particular, Tuke insists on reminding
us of the doors that separate, yet open upon, one house and the other,
or a given house and the garden or street; and, recalling his adventures in
the Low Countries, like Almanzor, Antonio reports on the conundrum he
faces from within, as it were ("My Love awhile disputed with my Honor"
[II,i,233]), while he asks later, "What course shall my Distracted Honor
steer / Betwixt these equal, opposite engagements?" (V,ii,217–18). Quite
apart from a reference to "*Janus* with his double face" in an appropriate
context (V,ii,66), there are persistent allusions to doubling: Diego has heard

Geraldo "give / The [door] Key a double Turn" (V,i,31–2), the door is thus "double-lock'd" (V,ii,123), Diego invokes a "double Curse" on all lovers (V,iii,35), the Epilogue imagines the ladies' embarrassment were they to grasp the play's "*Double Sense*" (Epilogue, 31), and, as in *Amphitryon*, we are reminded of the two faces of a single coin ("Cross and Pile" [V,iii,74]). And these doublings seem to accompany equivocations about personal identity. Diego says of Octavio that "my Master is not himself" (IV,i,341); Octavio reports "I am not my self" (V,iii,102); and towards the end of Act V, Camilla and Porcia speak as one individual (V,iii,391).

For these reasons alone, the setting is more than merely decorative, since early in the action the play goes to some lengths to explain the "Mystery" of Dutch wealth (I,i,447) – to use the very term employed by the trade theorists – explained by her trading prowess and captured in the image of "a huge Ship at Anchor" (I,i,421). This ethos is associated with Don Carlos's side of the equation, while Don Henrique obsesses throughout about "Honor," a word that saturates the play, connoting to him a world of fixed social value to be policed by the draconian methods associated with "revenge." The unconstrained world of the Spanish recalls, we are reminded, the grandiosity of the Armada (Prologue, 26–8), so that Don Henrique's focus on honor and revenge acompanies an insistence on absolute sovereignty (I,i,67) bordering on tyranny (I,i,178), and at one point he insists perversely that "There's in Revenge a Balm" (I,i,97).

Don Henrique's cathexis on the fixed, absolute, and permanent values conveyed variously by honor, revenge, and barter (as opposed to trade [V,iii,231]) amounts to an antitheatrical prejudice of sorts because it fails to allow for meanings responsive to occasion. It is Don Carlos, associated vicariously with the Dutch, who embodies an antithetical range of virtues which combine a respect for mediation in general with a regard for law as a means of moderating social relations, which must be applied – like rhetoric itself – contextually and circumstantially, and must accordingly respond to the precepts of equity. Tuke allows Don Carlos some ringing declarations about these principles, which of course define the conditions of a dramatically feasible outcome – in other words, the one that prevails:

> 'Tis better that a business of this nature,
> (Chiefly 'twixt Persons of such Quality)
> Should rather be reduc'd by Mediation
> (If it be possible) to some fair Agreement,
> Than to a publique Trial by the Law,
> Or, which is worse, some Barbarous Revenge.
>
> (IV,i,330–5)

Later he apparently quotes a proverb: "He who the Rules of Temperance neglects, / From a Good Cause may produce Vile Effects" (V,ii,164–5). And as we might anticipate in the context we have considered at length, there is also a physiological dimension to this contest over what properly comprises "Civil Prudence" (V,ii,170). Whereas, for Don Henrique, *blood* denotes nobility and genealogy to be violently defended, for Don Carlos, *blood* recalls the local workings of the human metabolism, involving motion and flux. Reading himself as a Harveian machine, he remarks at one point, "Freed from this Fright, my spirits flow so fast / To the forsaken Chanels of my Heart" (I,i,326–7).

The political purpose of the play is suggested by the fact that it was acted before Charles II at Whitehall and shows how loyalists in the Restoration repeatedly sought to steer Charles away from what they feared was a Stuart disposition to admire continental absolutism at the cost of vernacular habits of rule. Tuke's play reveals the way in which dramatic principles in their way execute the values embodied in Don Carlos, values associated with contingency in general, with trade, with the rule of law, with law applied equitably, and with ethical and epistemological moderation. Tuke brilliantly captures these values in the very design of his play, a design which renders the activity of the play English (and implicitly moderate) rather than Spanish (and implicitly tyrannical) by claiming that, however indebted to a Spanish original, this is a "A NEW PLAY" (Prologue, 4) because it obeys the "*Five Hours Law*" (Prologue, 10), namely the English convention of the five-act rather than six-act play. By what Tuke calls "a kind of Contract" (V,iii,163), the English audience, including the King, is bound by "the Law of Comedy" (V,iii,500); and these inherited constraints, to which all are equally subject, Tuke intends as the dramatic representation of the mixed monarchy, whereby, having "*pass'd the Lords, and Commons*," the King is asked to confirm what the political nation has already approved. Le Roy le Veut.

William Wycherley's The Country Wife *(1675)*

Critics have long remarked that (like *The Adventures of Five Hours*) the most famous scene in Restoration drama denaturalizes the notion of honor. When Lady Fidget says that ladies of honor have never had china enough, "honor" denotes only those characters who, like Horner and Lady Fidget, have mastered the game, a game that depends on the kind of contract to which Tuke alludes and which is, in effect, the object of Hobbes's concern in *Leviathan*. Few have noticed, however, that while the delicious high-wire act that makes the china scene so enjoyable renders china into a metaphor for Horner's semen, it is also about the trade in exotic objects for which china is a perfect symbol.

There is something literal about Sir Jasper, blundering in on Lady Fidget tickling Horner in his chambers, asking, "But is this you buying china?" This is because the play is more or less predicated on an idea of circulation which, as we have seen, migrates from the physiological into ideas about trade and politics and back. The premise of the play, guaranteed by the quack, is that the rumor of Horner's impotence will circulate in town producing exactly the effects we witness. Recalling Jordan's shows which link Westminster to the City, Wycherley also places the actions of the play on a highly precise topographical grid, which links "business" in the City in the East End with "business" at Whitehall in the West End, with "business" at the New Exchange and the playhouses situated between them. That "business" includes a number of things: financial affairs (Wycherley alludes to the Goldsmiths who underwrote state concerns until the founding of the Bank of England in 1694); the trade in women – orange-women and actresses – in which the King is implicated; and foreign trade not only in china but also in other exotic products, like the oranges sold at the playhouses and with which Horner rewards the disguised Margery near the New Exchange. The success of the china scene depends on our seeing the value of contingent language games whose clearest political expression in the play is the equalization of sexual desire between Horner and the women he services. Like the functioning of bills of exchange on the world market, the purpose is not the satisfaction of one man's desire but the effect of communal and mutual agreements; and for this reason the play can be thought of as feminist in impulse, a fact suggested by Hart as Horner speaking the Prologue while Mrs. Knep as Lady Fidget speaks the Epilogue.

The rule of the play is that Horner's semen must continue to circulate, and the threat to the community's continued satisfaction comes of course in the guise of Margery, a peculiarly absolutist figure arriving (as so often in Restoration plays) from the wrong genre, namely pastoral. Although she is partly inducted into the powers of *écriture*, she fails to learn the basic lessons of humanist literacy, for her language remains a tool of reference alone, either categorically lying or referring, rather than a medium by which humans continuously fashion and refashion the meanings they crave and, taken as a whole, amount to civilization itself. Like Marlowe's lie to the

Intended at the end of *Heart of Darkness*, she must be forced to lie about Horner's potency in Act V, and for two, equivalent, reasons. The world Wycherley is recommending to his audience must reject the comforts of the absolute in favor of the relative discomfort of the contingent; and to allow Margery's impulse to prevail would be to ignore the institutional constraints of what Tuke calls the law of comedy.

CHAPTER 2

"This Mimic State": Cicero, Quintilian, and the theatrical scene of culture

When, in *Of Dramatic Poesy*, Dryden imagines himself as Neander (the new man), he implicitly links the peculiar ethos of English drama, specifically tragicomedy, to Cicero, the *homo novus*. Like Dryden, who, though outranked by all the other interlocutors in his dialogue, is related by marriage to Sir Robert Howard, Cicero (until his ascent) comes from a socially and politically minor family, so that, again like the poet, his political eminence must rest entirely on his stupendous gifts as a lawyer and speaker. By reminding his readers of his humanist credentials, and in aligning the power of Ciceronian oratory with a history of English drama, Dryden anticipates developments in English literary culture of which his own dicta are often catalysts. When he published his dialogue in 1667, Dryden could not have known, despite hints in his own utterances, that the Restoration period as a whole would achieve several things at once. In response to French precedents, it would develop a rich culture of theatrical criticism (Krutch lists ninety-six titles published between 1660 and 1700).[1] Within that culture, it would increasingly distinguish purely descriptive histories of English plays, which value indigenous peculiarities, from a largely neo-Aristotelian and prescriptivist mode of approaching drama. With the publication of Gerard Langbaine's *An Account of the English Dramatick Poets* in 1691, English drama becomes what Homer Brown calls an *institution* – as opposed to a *practice* – namely a coherent object of interest interpretable solely through its own history. With other succeeding histories, most notably John Downes's *Roscius Anglicanus, or an Historical Review of the Stage* (1708) and Charles Gildon's *The Life of Mr. Thomas Betterton* (1710), the Restoration appears recursively as a distinct period – and a bygone age – in its own right, marked by the set of theatrical conventions introduced by William Davenant. And finally, that historical view of drama becomes associated with a high humanist defense of the power of playwrights to deliberate on state affairs. Just as the central program of Cicero's *De Oratore*, *Brutus*, and *Orator* is to erode the distinction between literature and philosophy as media of the good, these histories argue that, in civil life, the stage competes fully with the courtroom, the forum, or the pulpit. On this view, drama is not simply philosophy on holiday. In an argument also elaborated at length in Jean Baptiste Dubos's compendious *Critical Reflections on Poetry, Painting, and Music* (1719; trans. 1748), we hear how Demosthenes and Cicero learned their oratorical skills at the hands of the actors who trained them, a view of the grounds of rhetorical education systematized in Quintilian's *Institutes*. And because the central criterion of effective oratory is the ability to speak on any occasion to any audience and on any topic, the alliance of actor and orator effectively results in a vindication of tragicomedy – or at least a union of comedy and tragedy – for two closely related reasons.[2] Its generic inde-terminacy, variety, and copiousness correspond to the orator's ideal capacity for infinite epistemological, ethical, and generic variation;[3] and the internal dialogue excited by tragicomedy corresponds to the dialectical principle at the heart of the rhetorical consciousness, *in utramque partem*, the ability to speak persuasively and publicly on both sides of the question. Finally, in the corresponding notion that the ideal orator can at any moment draw on any or all of the three styles, the high, the middle, and the low – which only became formalized in Roman rhetoric – the orator, whether Cicero or Dryden, claims to embody the political ideal of the mixed republic or the mixed constitution.

D'AUBIGNAC, LANGBAINE, GILDON, AND DUBOS

Although it only appeared in translation in 1684 as *The Whole Art of the Stage*, François Hédelin, Abbé D'Aubignac's *La Prâtique du Théatre*, written at Richelieu's request, was first published in 1657. For two major reasons, it is important for my argument. First, it amplified a standard *topos*, repeated frequently, that drama is an essential medium for deliberating on affairs of state. Thus ventriloquizing the recent translation of D'Aubignac in her Dedication to *The Lucky Chance*, performed in 1687, Behn writes that "Plays have ever been held most important to the very Political Part of Government," and "that Plays and publick Diversions were thought by the Greatest and Wisest of States, one of the most essential Parts of good Government," such that "The Phylosophy of *Greece*, and the Majesty and Wisdom of the *Romans*, did equally concern their Great Men in making them Venerable, Noble, and Magnificent: Venerable, by their Consecration to their Gods: Noble, by being govern'd by their chiefest Men; and their

Magnificency was from the publick Treasury, and the liberal Contributions of their Noble Men."[4]

Second, it seems likely that Dryden's spirited defense of the political benefits of the mixed English tradition in drama was aimed at D'Aubignac, to the degree that he represented an uncritical view of French statism combined with a rigid regard for the requirements of neo-Aristotelian precept. It is not difficult to imagine that D'Aubignac's failure is the exact inverse of what Dryden sees as the success of the complex and ironic forms of English tragicomedy, in their capacity to make their audience politically self-conscious. D'Aubignac's tone in regard both to the French monarchy and the achievement of the French stage is entirely admiring and celebratory: in stark contrast to *The Maid's Tragedy*, plays should avoid the Greek habit of showing disasters befalling kings since "the respect and love which we have for our Princes, cannot endure that we should entertain the Publick with such Spectacles of horrour; we are not willing to believe that Kings are wicked, nor that their Subjects, though with some appearance of ill usage, ought to Rebel against their Power."[5] The adulation directed at the French King extends to the theatre: the century has seen French drama reach a perfection challenging the ancients, and D'Aubignac even suspects that his treatise is partly redundant, for "The Glory to which the *French* Theatre is arriv'd, may perhaps make some think that this Discourse is useless."[6] This monolithic conception of the ideological purpose of drama is also expressed in the view that the laws governing plays should not be fashioned from "Custom and Example, but from Reason," to which all men must blithely submit.[7]

Further requirements for the drama more or less follow naturally: playwrights should use figures of speech to convey a transparent experience of the action to the audience,[8] since, as D'Aubignac puts it, "the Stage is but a Representation of things," and the plot is "a representative Being," so we must avoid violent passions on stage because they call attention to the vehicle rather than the plot itself;[9] stage action should accordingly reproduce as nearly as possible the movements of real life ("this sort of Poem ought to carry a sensible Image of the Actions of Humane Life").[10] Because D'Aubignac aims at a kind of internally perfect action, plays should function as if no general audience existed, as if they could and should have no outwardly directed rhetorical purpose. Playwrights must avoid spectacle that distracts from a purely logical account of human motive, and breaks between acts and scenes should be imperceptible.[11] Thus rather than being instruments of political suasion, plays serve in effect as objects of political surveillance, with characters encouraged to see themselves as monarchs in their own realm.[12]

Like rhetoric in general, tragicomedy and split-plot plays draw attention to their own artifice, so that D'Aubignac insists throughout on the unity of action, not least because "the Stage is but a Picture or Image of Humane Life."[13] The English translation of 1684 evidently seeks to highlight D'Aubignac's objections, because whereas the first edition of 1657 buries the chapter on tragicomedy at the end of Book II (of a total of four), the translation presents it as the final essay of the entire treatise.[14] D'Aubignac fears the generic incommensurability that Dryden sees, precisely, as the strength of the Fletcherian mode: if a playwright finds that a given story involves two actions, they should be incorporated in two different plays rather than suffered to remain "so independent or opposite to each other, as not to be reconciled."[15] D'Aubignac's central desire here is to quell all conceptual or generic competition on the stage, so that although a main plot may require additional features to enrich it, the principle is one of subordination to a single action:

A Dramatick Poem ought not to contain above one Action, but it must be brought upon the Stage entire, with all its Dependencies, and nothing must be forgot of those Circumstances, which naturally are appropriated to it.[16]

Consequently, whereas the action of *The Adventures of Five Hours* flirts extensively with the degree to which the proscenium stage allows us to imagine how related figures, for dialectical effect, are both separated and linked by doors and walls, D'Aubignac objects precisely to this potential dimension of the story of Pyramus and Thisbe. In some exasperation, he asks how we could properly imagine them occupying separate spaces on a single stage, whose boundary also, in the course of the action, proves somewhat permeable. D'Aubignac demands, "I would fain know, by what suppos'd means in one action it self, this Wall could become visible and invisible? and by what enchantment it was sometimes in being, and then ceas'd quite to be again?"[17]

Perhaps unsurprisingly, this queasiness about double plots is extended to Plautus' *Amphitryon*. Remarking that the term "tragicomedy" is itself a neologism with no true Roman pedigree,[18] D'Aubignac objects to the action of Plautus' play because it implicates stage action in the audience's response, it promiscuously mingles a Greek past with a Roman present, and it presents characters with double identities:

[Plautus] mingles the concerns of the Actors with the Interest of the Spectators, and makes an Interfering of *Romans* who were present, with those who were suppos'd to act in *Greece*, which certainly cannot be but very ridiculous, and must confound the understanding of the Spectators, by forcing them to imagine a man double, and to distinguish in him both words and sentiments very different, without any necessity or reason for it.[19]

Published in 1691, only seven years after the translation of D'Aubignac, it is almost as if Langbaine's *An Account of the English Dramatick Poets* serves as a rebuttal. But this is the unintended consequence of a project whose motives are essentially antiquarian and taxonomic. Langbaine seeks to deal with the problems of organizing a concrete history of English drama which involves theories of sorts – for example about temporality, genre, and motive – but theories very different from the kind inhabiting D'Aubignac, René Rapin – who was widely published in translation – and even natives like Thomas Rymer. As a rabid bibliophile, Langbaine faced the challenge of organizing a vast collection of almost a thousand plays printed from the sixteenth century on. Following William Winstanley's *The Lives of the Most Famous English Poets* (1687) – the first such comprehensive literary history in English – he presents his commentary on the history of English secular drama since its inception as an alphabetical list of authors; but his project is deeply informed by what we can only call a genealogical imagination. Langbaine approaches his texts with two main considerations in mind: how they comprise a virtual history of England since the reign of Elizabeth I; and how many plays are refashioned from earlier sources. His consciousness of the English dramatic tradition means that he is aware of how playwrights, by adapting earlier material, reveal their own place in literary history; and his intense hostility to Dryden in particular means that he sees Dryden as an unconstrained plagiarist,[20] often pointing to dramatic sources that still have value. His organic approach to dramatic history means that he treats as "ancient" those authors responsible for establishing the tradition, as when he speaks of Abraham Fraunce as "An Ancient Writer who liv'd in the time of Queen *Elizabeth*."[21] And he conveys a remarkably precise sense of which dramatic culture defines the output of a given author – whether Elizabethan, early Stuart, Carolean, or post-Revolutionary. (I follow the conventional distinction between Caroline, pertaining to Charles I, and Carolean, pertaining to Charles II.)

The complete absence of any prescriptive motive – itself unusual – results in a kind of phenomenology of dramatic experience over a century and a half: Langbaine confidently but rather casually assigns plays to different genres, typically of course tragedy, comedy, and history. But for our purposes it is revealing to see that of the total of 970 plays described, 149, or just over 15 percent, he describes as tragicomedies, including *A Winter's Tale*, and, one of the best, we hear, *The Adventures of Five Hours*. The implication is that tragicomedy was expected to comprise part of the regular experience of the average playgoer, since he would see a tragicomedy about once every six or seven times he visited the theater.

This genre has its own roots in the earliest times, since George Gascoigne's *The Glasse of Governement* (1575) is described on its title-page as "A tragicall Comedie."[22] Langbaine's entry on Gascoigne proceeds to discuss his translation of Euripides' *Jocasta*, which he believes to be the only Euripides so far translated.[23] In Langbaine's mind, there is arguably a close relationship between *The Glasse of Governement* and *Jocasta*, for at this point he launches on a digression concerning the central importance of the Greek tragedians, especially Euripides, to Greek philosophy, which emerges, in his account, from Euripides' training in rhetoric. Langbaine recounts how "*Prodius* taught him Rhetorick, after which he made a Voyage to *AEgypt*, with *Plato*, to visit the Learned Men there, and to improve himself by their Conversation. He was also a Friend of *Socrates*, and some have believed that this Philosopher assisted him in the Composition of his Tragedies."[24] Langbaine is anticipated in his looser argument linking drama and rhetoric by René Rapin, whose *A Comparison between the Eloquence of Demosthenes and Cicero* (1672) recounts how Demosthenes, lacking the natural graces of delivery that fell to Cicero, had to train himself by strenuous means, not least by employing "a certain Player whom *Photius* calls *Neoptolemus*," though Quintilian and Plutarch call him different names. This actor, "who understood his art very well, made him begin, as Plutarch tells us, with rehearsing some of Sophocles, and Euripides his Poems, but after he had done, this Player repeated them again with so much life and grace, that they seem'd quite another thing." The result was that Demosthenes held that "Action was almost the chief quality, wherein his Eloquence consisted: and he himself us'd to say, it was the first, second, and third part of it."[25]

If modern commentators on Euripides are right, then Gascoigne's own tragicomedy is likewise somewhat Euripidean. In the wake of developments in rhetoric in the fifth century BC, of the sort exemplified by Thucydides' history of the period, of all the great Greek playwrights Euripides is generally the most interested in reproducing the experience of stylized rhetorical conflict – a view adopted by Quintilian.[26] *The Glasse of Governement* is similarly inflected by the devices of humanist rhetoric – and correspondingly more interested in speechifying than action – and similarly, as its title suggests, determined to make its mark in the forum of political debate. In a long speech by Gnomaticus in Act II, Gascoigne makes it clear that the responsibility for political consciousness rests equally with the rhetoricians (primarily Cicero), the divines, the philosophers, and the dramatists. At the beginning of the speech, Gnomaticus cites Diotogenes, Erasmus, Solomon, Paul, Peter, Sophocles, and Cicero. He continues thus:

Tully in his *Tusculanes* questions recyteth one *Lascaena*, who when he received tydings of his sonnes death, whom he had sent into the warres in defence of hys countrey, answered: therefore did I beget him (quoth hee) that hee might be such an one, as woulde not doubt to dye for hys countrey. In his booke entytuled the dreame of *Sipio*, he affirmeth that there is a certaine place appointed and ordeined in heaven, for all such as defende their countrey. *Euripides* warneth that we shoulde never be wearye in those travailes, which tend to the restitution or defence of our countrey. *Platoes* opinion was, that wee are more bound to defend our countrey, then our own Parents. Like argumentes have beene defended by many Phylosophers . . . *Lycurgus*, when he had by extreeme diligence and travayle reduced the *Spartans* unto cyvillytie, by sundrie holsome laws and pollityke constitutions, and that they began to murmure, saying that his lawes were untollerable, hee feyned that he would go to *Delphos*, to consulte with the God *Apollo*, whether his lawes were to be observed or not . . .[27]

For our purposes, the Jeremy Collier stage controversy which broke out in 1698 is of limited interest.[28] Athough it focused attention on the English stage, the attack on Restoration playwrights and most of the defenses were conducted in a moral register – were the plays immoral and did they pay insufficient respect to the clergy? – which did not by and large revitalize theories about dramatic form or the historical importance of drama. When, for example, in *The Usefulness of the Stage* (1698), John Dennis does gesture in that direction, he uses by now conventional arguments about the primacy of drama in the creation of civilization. In Greece, Rome, France, and England, the arts and sciences begin to flourish with the theater. "And this we may affirm," Dennis concludes,

not only of the more Humane Arts, Poetry, History, Eloquence, of which the Theatre, is certainly the best School in the World; the School that form'd in a great measure, those prodigious Disciples, *Cicero* and *Demosthenes*; but we may truly assert it of all other sorts of Learning.[29]

With Gildon's *Life of Betterton* (1710), however, the death of Betterton spells the end of a theatrical era – the Restoration period – which now appears clearly defined; and Betterton's greatness as an actor becomes an occasion of an extended deliberation on the rhetorical nature and purposes of drama. These motives appear early in the text, which devotes only 7 out of 176 pages to the actual details of Betterton's life. The passing of the theatrical culture of the Restoration Gildon compares in the first line to the eclipse of republican hopes in Rome, for "As it was said of *Brutus* and *Cassius*, that they were the last of the *Romans*; so it may be said of Mr. BETTERTON, that he was the last of our *Tragedians*."[30] And by "tragedian" it rapidly becomes clear that Gildon means an actor unconstrained by genre, an actor whose effectiveness perfectly expresses the rhetorical ideals to be found in Cicero and Quintilian: in *De Oratore* Cicero often uses the term denoting "tragedy" to refer more largely to the histrionic in general. Indeed, whereas Cicero often compares the accomplished orator to his friend Roscius, Gildon finds in Betterton an even fuller manifestation of that ideal, since unlike Roscius, who excelled only in comedy, "our Player excelled in both *Comedy* and *Tragedy*."[31] In creating a recursive account of the Restoration as a coherent dramatic culture (with its own distinctive sociology, as *Roscius Anglicanus* shows by listing the members of the repertory companies), and in linking that culture to a humanist justification of the rhetorical and civic purposes of the theater, Gildon is aware of his debts to French criticism, like that of Rapin, who was generously and instantly translated in England. But he is also right to qualify the extent of his indebtedness by remarking that "I have borrowed many of [the precepts] from the *French*, but then the *French* drew most of them from *Quintilian* and other Authors."[32] For although in treatises like *A Comparison between the Eloquence of Demosthenes and Cicero* and *Reflections upon the Eloquence of these Times* (1672), Rapin claims to be guided by the methodical hand of Aristotle in his *Rhetoric*, the implied history of rhetoric since the Sophists and the express criteria for effective oratory – with action or pronunciation at a premium – are most heavily derived from Cicero's rhetorical theories and Quintilian's *Institutes*, with dashes of Longinus for good measure.

In fact, Rapin seems to provide something of a model for Gildon's argument. Rapin celebrates what he sees as the emergence of a true rhetorical culture after the Sophists – including Isocrates, whom we know influenced Cicero[33] – coming into maturity in the Roman world. Similarly, Gildon interprets the emergence of operatic and sentimental modes after Betterton's death, signaling the demise of Restoration drama as such, as a decline into a modern version of what their critics saw as the empty and spectacular formulae of the Sophists. In both cases, the moral objection is that sensation sells, with the arts of speech aimed at titillation rather than true political debate. The benchmark for both is the second triumvirate, when Cicero was still alive and the young Octavius might be thought to be open to his influence. The difference is that Rapin's pessimism about modern times is pervasive (so that his inclinations are still prescriptive in the

French mode), whereas Gildon associates the Restoration with a healthy and vigorous deliberative climate centered on the theater (an argument whose thrust is more historical and descriptive in feel). Thus Rapin complains that "we have much pain in these times to find any remainder of that Empire which [eloquence] exercised upon the Spirits of men, and whereof there appear'd so many glorious marks in those Ages and States where she hath rul'd."[34]

This complaint Rapin maps onto a history of ancient rhetoric. "The *Sophists*," he says, "whose Lives *Philostratus* and *Eunapius* have describ'd, establish'd in their publick places [a] false eloquence, which gives all to the exteriour part by aiery and wandering Discourse, and hath no other tendency, than to amuse the people." "All its Movements," he concludes, "are false; it touches not at all the heart, nor enters in any manner into the Spirit; all that it gives, is a pleasure superficial, and is no more than a simple pastime for the foolish and idle."[35] Between them, because they were embedded within a charged political climate, Demosthenes and Cicero lent substance to the art, with Cicero also providing theories on how best to speak, treading the line between the purely prosaic, which fails to excite audiences, and verbal flashiness, which merely entertains without instructing.[36] What in particular empowers the deliberative orator is an attention to his prime vehicle of appeal, namely his body, so that both in a practical and theoretical sense, rhetoric becomes not only a matter of speech but of bodily dressage. Seventeenth-century commentators seem aware that it is at this point that, although the Spartans and Athenians included gymnastics as part of education, and Xenophon recommends bodily discipline in training a ruler, Greek theories of rhetoric are somewhat deficient, for like Aristotle, they either do not address it at length or, in the case of the *Phaedrus*, which as we will see is so important for Cicero, Plato is not entirely comfortable with the carnal implications of falling in love with beautiful boys. It follows that Demosthenes' and Cicero's most signal contributions to the practice as well as (in Cicero's case) the theory of rhetoric are in the area of delivery – *actio* and *pronuntiatio* – one of the many Ciceronian influences on Quintilian. Thus already in 1644, in his *Chironomia; Or, The Art of Manual Rhetoric*, John Bulwer criticizes Aristotle "in his mistaken opinion of Action, esteeming these Chironomicall Notions as things of no great matter" and recommends consulting "the Oracle of Quintilian, about this Manuall pronunciation; whose institutions contain all those ancient subtleties that escaped the injurious Hand of Time," reminding his reader of the relation between Cicero and Roscius.[37] The importance of gesture, he writes, is sufficiently proved by the old emulation between that famous Oratour Cicero and Roscius the great Master in the Art of Action; for it is certain that most eminent Oratour would often contend and strive avie [sic] with Roscius whether he should more often expresse the same sentence in gesture; or whether he himselfe by the copiousnesse of his eloquence in a differing speech and variety of expression pronounce the same; which raised Roscius to that height and and perfection of knowledge, that he wrote a booke, wherein he compared Eloquence with the Art or Science of Stage-Players.[38]

This is almost exactly the argument we see in Rapin, which likewise culminates in an emphasis on the stage:

The Pronunciation, which is one of the most important parts of Eloquence, is yet one of the most neglected: It renders Eloquence sensible to the people by the composition of the exteriour part, and which hath the Art to impose by the appearances, when it wants the power to touch by its effects. If its virtue be so great, as to make impression in Subjects feigned and supposed, as it doth upon a Theater in a Comedy, what can she not do, when things true are her object?[39]

The same criticisms of the Sophists and the same admiration for the two greatest orators we have known inform *A Comparison between the Eloquence of Demosthenes and Cicero*. The merely verbal, and accordingly superficial, art of Protagoras yields to Demosthenes, who trained himself comprehensively as an orator, amplifying his voice by speaking at the sea-shore, disciplining his tongue by putting pebbles in his mouth, and acquiring gestural fluency from an actor. So similarly Cicero, equally a man of principle, and equally motivated by the public good, learned the art of delivery from Roscius.[40] In the final count, Rapin sees Cicero as the more perfect orator, for four reasons: he was more naturally endowed with an "Eloquence of the body"; the Roman world provided a more universal podium on which Cicero could perform ("*Cicero* found a far more spatious field, wherein to exercise his Genius")[41]; Roman civilization was more polished and coherent than Greek culture, which, if more sublime, was perennially subject to local constraints and political atomization, so that whereas Demosthenes spoke with fire, Cicero spoke with grace; and the greater political comprehensiveness of the Roman order meant that Cicero "had the advantage over [Demosthenes] of leaving no kind of Eloquence unpractised, and wherein he had not exercised himself."[42]

Whereas Rapin maps this Ciceronian ideal against the superficial verbiage of the Sophists, Gildon like Pope associates it with the stage over which Betterton presided, and which is now giving way to a theatrical, sophistic culture of instant gratification epitomized in Italian opera, on this view a musical, and so disembodied, art. This new mode is to be contrasted,

Gildon insists, with William Davenant's reform of the stage. Davenant's introduction of a greater range of effects, of moveable scenery, and of actresses in *The Siege of Rhodes*, for example, merely emulated the civic function of spectacle in Athens and Rome, since those "Ornaments or Decorations" were matters of state interest.[43] The death of Betterton, on the other hand, accompanies a decline of tragedy, owing "chiefly to a Defect in the *Action*, to which we may add the Sowerness of our Tempers" in a new political climate.[44] The national character is sapped by continental adventurism, and like the decay of Roman republican vigor, English culture is becoming enfeebled:

as War carries abundance of peccant Humours from a State, generated by the Corruptions of a long and luxurious Peace; so does it introduce a sort of Libertinism in our Diversions, contrary to Decorum and Regularity . . . Nor is there any greater Proof of the Virtue or Corruption of the People than their Pleasures. Thus in the Time of the Vigour of the *Roman* Virtue, *Tragedy* was very much esteemed.[45]

"Thus when the *Roman* Vertue decay'd, or indeed was lost with their Liberty," Gildon continues, empire was less a matter of extending Roman virtue than the thirst for gain:

then Effeminacy and Folly spread through the People, which immediately appear'd in their Sports or Spectacles; *Tragedy* was slighted; Farce on the one hand, with its *Mimes* and *Pantomimes*; and *Opera* on the other, with its emasculating Sounds, invade and vanquish the Stage, and drew the Ears and Eyes of the People; who now care only to laugh, or to see things extravagant and monstrous.[46]

Because it can deliberate on virtue in the state, the Ciceronian regime embodied in Betterton unites the functions of the bar, the stage, and the pulpit.[47] Acting is thus a matter of "the Oratorian art."[48] And since in rhetoric the virtuous effects of speech depend on the virtue of the speaker, "the Stage may properly be esteemed the Handmaid of the Pulpit."[49] (Here Gildon reflects the influence of the Collier controversy, in which virtue on stage was at a premium.) The alliances among different fora are best expressed by the care with which Demosthenes and Cicero trained themselves in delivery, without which oratory is stillborn, so that the bulk of Gildon's *Life* is a version of Book XI of Quintilian's *Institutes*, the single most comprehensive ancient account of gesture. But as in Rapin, Gildon implies a greater range and sophistication in Cicero, a copiousness expressed as a form of generic flexibility or hybridity: whereas Demosthenes depended solely on the actor Satyrus to train him, Cicero combined a knowledge of comic and tragic technique. By sitting at the feet both of Roscius, the comic actor, and of Aesopius, the tragic actor, Cicero legitimately comes to signify for Dryden the range and flexibility of tragicomedy, whose purposes are almost inevitably civic.[50]

Although it was only translated from the fifth edition in 1748, Jean Baptiste Dubos's *Critical Reflections* was originally published in two volumes in 1719, only nine years after Gildon's *Life of Betterton*. One of the most widely published European meditations on the general role of the arts in human culture, translated into English and German and reaching a seventh edition in 1770, the full title, as printed in 1748, is *Critical Reflections on Poetry, Painting, and Music. With an Inquiry into the Rise and Progress of the Theatrical Entertainments of the Ancients*. The title was truncated by 1770 – omitting the reference to the ancient theater – and editions after 1740 placed the deliberations on the theatre in the last of three volumes. These changes obscure the extent to which the strongly Ciceronian and Quintilianic arguments about the centrality of the theater not only to rhetoric, but to the entire symbolic order, served, despite Dubos's later asseverations to the contrary, as the inspiration for the project. A quotation from Cicero towards the end of volume one encapsulates the spirit of the *Critical Reflections*: "*All the liberal arts . . . seem to have one common chain of agreement, and to be connected together by a kind of mutual affinity.*"[51] These connections can be imagined several ways. Most obviously, since all arts involve a methodical relation to nature which they represent or mediate, we can deduce common principles: "Arts are nothing more than methods regulated by certain principles; and upon examining these principles we find them to be maxims formed in consequence of many observations made on the effects of nature."[52] In other words – this is the final note of the entire book, which concludes with a reference to Quintilian – though some elements of culture, like singing or gesticulation, might arise from a natural impulse, culture as such is meaningless without weaving those elements into an artificial syntax whose purposes are ethical and political. The arts consequently serve to reflect local historical and geographical conditions; and they also serve uniformly as rhetorical means for maintaining social order.

Dubos's comparisons among the arts ride on several related assumptions. First, Dubos places a premium on the way in which the different arts create sensation – to that extent his criterion of judgment is essentially pragmatic – so that, employing an Horatian *topos*, he constantly compares the related effects of poetry and painting. Using a Quintilianic and Ciceronian logic, he links that argument to a discussion of music, which, by transforming into a question of somatic rhythm and pulse and thus of gesture, culminates in the alliance between orator and actor, between Cicero and Roscius, with which we are familiar.

Second, though he begins with the view that the meaning of art depends on the sensations it creates, Dubos carefully avoids a purely private and impressionistic consequence. By themselves the search for those effects reflects a universal human appetite for sensation, which explains why a civilized society like the Romans' could indulge in gladiatorial shows and why it was easy to export them to Greece. But the value of any given work of art can only be decided over time, so that the mere fact that it locally generates a response signifies nothing unless that response is confirmed under different circumstances and over a sufficiently long time. The canon is the result of a long, public process of artistic sedimentation.

Third, Dubos assumes that the conditions of artistic production in the Greek and Roman world are likewise public and hence political in the most precise sense, so that even at their inception all media participate in the performative mode we most readily associate with theater, such that it becomes impossible to distinguish meaningfully between artistic and civic life. (By mentioning wrestling – as well as dancing – Dubos is also recalling the connection between the performative, the gymnastic, and civic participation which was the peculiar contribution of the Spartans to educational theory.) Behind any human activity, Dubos implies, lies a psychological imperative, a universal need for public validation, or what he calls *eminence*. Thus,

The opportunities of receiving the applauses and favors of great assemblies, were . . . very frequent in Greece. As we have congresses in our times, where the deputies of princes and states meet in order to terminate wars, and regulate the fate of provinces, and the limits of kingdoms; in like manner there were assemblies formerly from time to time, where the most illustrious personages of Greece rendezvoused, in order to decide the merit of the most eminent painter, the most moving poet, and the best wrestler. This was the real motive which induced the multitudes of people to flock to those public games that were celebrated in different cities. The public porticoes where the poets went to recite their verses, or painters to expose their pictures, were places where the better sort of company used generally to meet.[53]

Citing Pliny, Dubos says that as a result the arts *"were looked upon as jewels of the state and as a public treasure,"*[54] which also explains why he believes all arts – including the plastic arts – have a rhetorical role to play in governance. He writes that "those who in all ages have had the government of nations, have generally made use of pictures and statues, to inspire the people thereby, with religious or political sentiments."[55] And because art is a total expression of a given culture, and because Dubos hews to a synaesthetic approach to all media, which act as cultural thermometers as well as regulators of political health, two more things follow: it is in the interest of the state to foster the arts; and in what Arnold calls epochs of concentration all the arts – from politics, to history, to poetry, to drama, to rhetoric (on which they all depend) – tend to flourish simultaneously, to enter into competition, and to be mutually enriching. Dubos's presiding genius is of course Quintilian, as he himself states: "Have we ever an author to compare to Quintilian for the order and solidity of his reasonings?"[56] So it follows that for Dubos, because the orator has learned the art of delivery from the actor, the golden ages of the ancients are marked by an alliance between the theater and the state. On the one hand, the Greek kings "did not think it a dishonor to chuse players for their ministers."[57] On the other, Dubos presents us with an exemplary picture of Rome in the late Republican and early Augustan period:

Among the monuments of Roman sculpture we meet with nothing more exquisite than those pieces which were made in the reign of Augustus. . . It was under Augustus that the Roman medals began to grow fine; and ingraving is an art which generally follows the fate of sculpture. . . We may affirm the same of the Roman architecture, as has been now said of sculpture. . . Everybody knows, that the greatest Roman poets, except two or three, flourished in the age of Augustus. . . The greatest part of the above-mentioned poets might have seen Cicero, Hortensius, and the rest of the most celebrated Roman orators. They must have seen Julius Caesar as remarkable, when a citizen, for his eloquence and several other civil virtues, as famous, when a general, for his exploits and knowledge in the art of war. Livy the prince of Roman historians, Sallust an historian whom Paterculus and Quintilian dare compare to Thucydides, flourished under Augustus. They were likewise contemporary with Vitruvius the most illustrious of the Roman architects. Augustus was born before the death of Æsopius and Roscius the most eminent comedians mentioned in the Roman history. . . As Seneca the father observes, *the most eminent orators that the Roman eloquence had to compare or prefer to proud Greece, flourished about Cicero's time.*[58]

CICERO AND QUINTILIAN: THE ORATOR, THE ACTOR, THE LAWYER, AND THE MIXED CONSTITUTION

It is a truism that the humanist program, initiated by the end of the four-teenth century, and defining what it means to be literate and hence fully human, not only prevailed until the end of the eighteenth century and even survived into the nineteenth, but was almost entirely centered on the rhetorical treatises of Cicero and Quintilian.[59] Famously the complete text of Quintilian was discovered by Poggio in 1416, while Vittorino da Feltre styled himself "Quintilianus Redux." The complete texts of *De Oratore*, *Brutus*, and *Orator* were only discovered later, at Lodi in 1422, but *De Oratore* was the first book to be printed in the Italian Renaissance, in

1465, with three more editions published in fifteen years.[60] Though, more or less reflexively, it is today common to dismiss Cicero as unphilosophical, as embarrassingly eclectic, and as an empty paraphrast, he inspired in the key humanists an almost religious devotion, beginning of course with Petrarch who "discovered" Cicero's orations in 1333, and extending to Erasmus, whose *Ciceronianus* involves some self-satire: in his dialogue Erasmus mocks those who revere Cicero so much that they only use words to be found in Cicero himself. Nosoponus declares in a fit of enthusiasm, "there is no place in my library for anyone else at all but Cicero."[61] Anticipating a major strain in what is to follow, Erasmus shows how an attachment to Ciceronian ideals of literacy, and of comportment in general, completely disappoints the thematic, prescriptive, and mechanical approach suggested by that outburst, since Cicero denotes an entirely methodical and catholic attitude to the materials of speech. Bulephorus explains,

Did Cicero himself derive his wonderful eloquence from one single source? Didn't he rather scrutinize philosophers, historians, and rhetoricians, comic, tragic, and lyric poets, Greek as well as Roman, in short, did he not from all writers of every kind assemble, fashion, and bring to perfection his own characteristic and divine idiom? If we choose to imitate Cicero in every respect, let us imitate his example here.[62]

And in *De Utraque Verborum ac Rerum Copia* – a massively important text in the reception of humanism from the sixteenth century on – Erasmus embarks on a major meditation on Ciceronian copiousness, which for him means four things at once: variation, abundance, eloquence, "and the *ability* to vary or enrich language and thought." Apuleis sets an example by representing an Aesopic fable in a variety of possible styles, whose equivalence is Ciceronian copiousness in speech and Roscius's range of acting styles:

That Aesopic fable about the fox and crow which Apuleis narrates briefly with a wonderful economy of words, and also amplifies as fully as possible with a great many words, doubtless to exercise and display his genius, shows the same thing fully. But come, who could find fault with his study when he sees that Cicero, that father of all eloquence, was so given to this exercise that he used to compete with his friend, the mimic actor Roscius, to see whether the latter might express the same idea more times by means of various gestures, or he himself render it more often in speech varied through copia or eloquence.[63]

The preeminence of Cicero among the ancients, particularly as a guide to the active life, is likewise an assumption in Henry Peacham's *The Compleat*

Gentleman (1634). Writing that "all Vertue consisteth in Action," Peacham says that we should remember

First, *Tullie* (in whose bosome the Treasure of Eloquence seemeth to have beene locked up, and with him to have perished) [who] offereth himselfe as *Pater Romani eloquii*: whose words and stile (that you may not bee held an Heretique of all the world) you must preferre above all other, as well for the sweetnesse, gravity, richnese, and unimitable texture thereof . . .).[64]

If we consider these conditions alone – and the fact that one of the high points of classical education in Britain between 1500 and 1700 was the regime at Westminster under Richard Busby, Dryden's headmaster[65] – it seems unlikely that *Of Dramatic Poesy*, though a "Ciceronian" dialogue, was as narrowly governed by its relation to *De Legibus* as the California editors imply.[66] In fact, Dryden's dialogue reproduces the densely allusive quality of Cicero's great rhetorical treatises, and for closely parallel reasons. Like Cicero, whose concern is with Roman politics and the Latin language, Dryden's essay comprises a meditation on the genealogies not only of English drama but of English letters as a whole. Given the debt of all modern languages to the ancients, and given the power of the French state, the French theater, and French dramatic theory, how can we meaningfully speak of a vernacular tradition which does not simply reproduce the materials, and the attitudes they foster, upon which it inevitably depends? Dryden's implied responses almost exactly echo Cicero's, and at exactly the point where modern critics too often dismiss the conceptual sophistication of Cicero's method. For Cicero's apparent untidiness as a philosopher – even as he proclaims the complete union of oratory and wisdom – emerges from an entirely principled defense of something like *bricolage*, a defense that, at a conceptual level, separates Cicero from Plato and Aristotle, a separation Cicero stylizes at the beginning of *De Oratore*. (These distinctions, it is clear, were fully understood by the humanists.) For Cicero's – and Dryden's – main point is that the human condition is always entirely conventional, and our place in history, marked by fluctuating moments of experience, always has an element of the surprising and unexpected about it, so to approach the world with generic demands of any sort – including the genre we denominate "philosophy" – is to engage in a form of conceptual and even political tyranny. For Cicero as for Dryden, culture involves an endless weaving and reweaving of the dense forest of symbols by which we recognize ourselves as human in the first instance, and through which we must navigate to continue to realize ourselves as human, a condition most fully expressed in our lives as *bioi politikoi*.

For these very reasons, of course, Cicero – who spoke Greek like a native – begins *De Oratore* with an evocative allusion to the opening scene of the *Phaedrus*, a country setting, like Cicero's beloved Tusculum, unique in Plato.[67] This is the one dialogue in which Plato is willing to accommodate philosophy to rhetoric, and the entire discussion ends with Socrates apparently praising Isocrates, but in terms which have led many modern scholars to believe that Plato, who had reason to resent Isocrates' greater success as an Athenian teacher, is in fact being ironic.[68] In the *Orator*, written in 46 BC, some nine years after *De Oratore*, Cicero strategically treats this moment as unironic, since it appears to endorse his own extensive and positive debt to Isocrates. But by alluding to this moment at the beginning of the earlier dialogue, Cicero is remarking on his departure from Platonic and Aristotelian foundationalism by indulging a device he owes to Carneades and the New Academy.[69] If Plato meant to praise Isocrates, then Cicero merely amplifies that choice; if Plato meant to criticize Isocrates as too unphilosophical, then Cicero now defends Isocrates' ambition to unite rhetoric, wisdom, and political virtue. By acting both as amplification and riposte, *De Oratore* itself becomes an incarnation of that foundational Ciceronian principle – *in utramque partem*: any statement we make is only ever a question of relative probabilities and must at all times compete dialectically with alternative or contradictory points of view.[70] As Catulus states in Book II:

the activity of the orator has to do with opinion, not knowledge [*scientia*] . . . we . . . often take opposite sides, not merely in the sense that Crassus sometimes argues against me, or I against him, when one or the other of us must of necessity be urging what is false, but also because we both maintain different opinions at different times on an identical issue, in which case only one of such opinions can possibly be right. (*DO* II,vii,30)[71]

The mutual relation of the three great dialogues – Plato's, Cicero's, and Dryden's – executes this complicated dance of difference and analogy. For first, Sulpicius declares that Crassus' Tusculan villa comprises a "semi-rural [suburban] training quarters" whose usefulness at this moment exceeds that of the Academy or Lyceum (*DO* I,xxi,98). Second, just as the *Phaedrus* is structured around three speeches – Lysias' speech read out by Phaedrus at Socrates' insistence, Socrates' first speech in reply, and Socrates' great second speech, the repository of untold numbers of literary *topoi* in the Western tradition – so Cicero's dialogue occurs in three books, like Plato's comprised, loosely, of a *narratio*, a laying-out of the case, a *refutatio*, a response, and a *probatio*, a fairly definitive exposition of the main points at issue. Further, just as Socrates is Plato's *persona* – in the most precise sense – so Crassus is Cicero's, and to similar effect, since, like rhetoric itself, "Socrates" and "Crassus" occupy an ambiguous place between biography and fiction. And just as *De Oratore* subtly differentiates itself from Plato, so the dialogue takes place at a temporal remove from its moment of composition, set as it is in 91 BC, almost forty years before Cicero took up the stylus. Moreover, although there are four main interlocutors, namely Crassus, Antonius, Sulpicius, and Cotta, they are also joined by Scaevola (in Book II) and Catulus and C. Julius Caesar (in Books II and III). Cicero was prompted to lay out an entire theory of oratory and culture in the winter of 55 BC because he knew that, although he had been recalled from exile, his political career was not assured, so that, although he waited another nine years to write *Brutus* and *Orator*, the three texts cohere, standing as a rebuke to the decline of the republic for which Antonius' and Julius Caesar's powerful descendents were partly responsible: the conditions under which the *Brutus* and *Orator* were written echo the context of the *De Oratore*. (Cicero vainly pinned his hopes on Pompey to revive the senate and the power of the optimates, though he reached an accommodation with Caesar; and of course Antony was chiefly responsible for his assassination in 44 BC in a gruesome scene which Cicero predicts at the beginning of Book III. Crassus says that "you must cut out this tongue of mine" to prevent him defending the powers of the senate [*DO* III,i,4].) That the personalities in Cicero's dialogue invite such fleeting correspondences to bridge an earlier and later moment in the decline and fall of the republic itself serves to enact or embody the central conceptual feature of *De Oratore*, one that crucially distinguishes Cicero from Plato and Aristotle, one that determines the symbolic logic of the *Institutio Oratoria*, and one that anticipates Dryden's scheme in *Of Dramatic Poesy*, namely the entirely contingent nature of human experience. In Cicero, this contingency is marked in numerous ways, but none more painfully than in the sudden and unexpected death of Crassus from pleurisy.[72]

For Dryden as for Cicero, this sense of the contingent flows from the practical turn of mind the English mythically share with the Romans. So just as Dryden echoes Cicero in describing a setting some way in the past, imagining four interlocutors who only elliptically represent historical figures, dividing the dialogue broadly into three sections, with the author's *persona* concluding, so he sees the French much as Cicero sees the Greeks – a powerful, potentially more philosophically charged culture than his own, one whose historical primacy he must, however reluctantly, grant, but a culture much taken with its own intellectual hegemony and with the sonorous beauty of its language, and whose perfections more rugged languages like Latin and English will never match. This distinction is invisible in Greek itself, since *rhetor* means ambiguously a speaker or a theorist of oratory, whereas Latin carefully distinguishes between the *orator* – one who actually speaks effectively – and the *rhetor*, the Greek word denoting only the teacher or theorist of rhetoric. Indebted as he confessedly is to Aristotle and the Stoics, Cicero seeks to effect a disciplinary revolution: for Aristotle, rhetoric is that art associated with the contingent, with matters of persuasion, by analogy to logic, which has to do with demonstrative truth, such that the enthymeme – the rhetorical figure – is an implicitly less rigorous version of the syllogism.[73] Similarly Zeno famously captured the relation between logic and rhetoric by clenching his fist and then opening his hand.

Influenced both by Isocrates and to some extent Protagoras, Cicero's central point in his great rhetorical treatises is that logic is one form of appeal among potentially thousands generated by the copiousness, the fecundity, of language, that medium by which man marks himself out from the animals. (Smethurst writes, "*Logos* is the great civilizer, the one essential element of all knowledge.")[74] Unlike the logician, the Ciceronian believes that no single form of appeal can have practical priority over any other, which means, in turn, that no single genre of thought or expression can serve us reliably. The enormous fund of resources ideally available to the speaker at any given moment Cicero designates as *copiousness*, and the ability to bring to bear that entire armory locally to produce the right effect in the public realm, *aptness*, the Latin version of what Aristotle calls *to prepon*, or the timely. Even so, Cicero suggests, their love of theory means that the Greeks have an inadequately developed sensitivity to the apt, such that, unlike the speakers in *De Oratore* and those in *Of Dramatic Poesy*, where minute variations in tone and affect in the conversation or *sermo* register the complex social relations among the speakers, they are, properly speaking, *inept* or "tactless."[75] Cicero expands:

The Greek nation, with all its learning, abounds in this fault, and so, as the Greeks do not perceive the significance of this plague, they have not even bestowed a name upon the fault in question, for search where you may, you will not find out how the Greeks designate the "tactless" [*ineptum*] man. (*DO* II,iv,18)

This tone-deafness to the infinitely variable effects of speech betrays itself in Greek letters as the reproduction of endless panegyrics, a criticism in Book II of which it seems impossible, given the opening dialogue in *Of Dramatic Poesy*, Dryden was unaware. Cicero writes, "the Greeks themselves have constantly thrown off masses of panegyrics, designed more for reading and for entertainment, or for giving a laudatory account of some person, than for the practical purposes of public life with which we are now concerned" (*DO* II,lxxxiv,341). By contrast, Dryden's preface pretends that he only published his dialogue by accident of circumstance – he having discovered it lately among his loose papers – and at the end Neander's slightly obsessive panegyric to rhyme is cut short by the arrival of the boat at Somerset stairs, an interruption that – like death itself – appears similarly untimely. Dryden's opening stresses the occasional – the historically circumscribed – conditions of the discussion. The four friends listen in silence to the distant battle, and Crites – whose character is minutely rendered as potentially disruptive of mannerly, or apt, conversation – begins the discussion by saying that in some ways he fears the outcome of the day's events, for "he knew he must pay for it, in being subject to the reading and hearing of so many ill verses as he was sure would be made upon it"; and Lisideus agrees by attacking those who have inaptly or impertinently prefabricated their responses both to victory and to defeat: "There are some of those impertinent people you speak of . . . who to my knowledge are already so provided, either way, that they can produce not only a panegyric upon the victory but, if need be, a funeral elegy upon the Duke."[76] (The brilliance of Dryden's essay is of course to avoid those generic strictures altogether, since the mutual positions of the different speakers remain largely suspended, yet another reason for deflating Neander so completely at the end.) And just as Cicero sees the idle and talkative Greeklings as trapped inside a certain self-regard, that is exactly the final image Dryden presents – the airy French folk dancing, unaware of, and unconcerned about, the portent of the day's events. A further irony is that – as Locke stresses in his *Some Thoughts concerning Education*, and as Pope assumes in his comment about an achieved style ("As those move easiest who have learn'd to dance") – dancing is one of the gymnastic disciplines anciently meant to inculcate physical and mental coherence in the fully articulate and politically engaged individual.[77] Yet here dancing is merely a form of entertainment.

The sum of Cicero's ambitions for oratory centers on his determination to see the practice of oratory as fully enmeshed in political life, which for him, as for Isocrates, defines the possibilities for human satisfaction. This explains the central features of the conceptual reform he hopes to achieve, beginning with the idea that because politics can only respond to publicly scrutible knowledge, individual disciplines are only valuable insofar as they assist the orator in expanding his repertoire and range of appeal. For example, logic is essential to oratory, but it becomes useless, if not harmful, if it becomes the preserve of professional philosophers. Cicero thus admires the Stoics for their clarity of argument but distrusts their epistemology because the *katalepsis* limits the apprehension of truth to an elite. In Book I of *De Oratore*, Crassus speaks of his visit to Greece: "I perceived that the orator was driven from the helm of State, shut out from all learning and knowledge of more important things, and thrust down and locked up exclusively in law-courts and petty little assemblies, as if in a pounding-mill" (*DO* I,xiv,54).

Second, political life is only ever the product of history and convention, and political effectiveness, as we all know, depends on respecting, managing, and inflecting both individual and institutional habits. The effective orator must then have at his fingertips, as if on a palette, the entire range of knowledges implied or assumed by the circumstances he faces and must know how to orchestrate them relative to his own character and personality, the character and personality of his necessarily shifting audience, and the character of the subject he wishes to convey, recognizing too that that subject could be as much a matter of atmosphere and affect as of propositional knowledge. Meaning in this context is only ever a matter of space and time – of temporality and dimension – so that as he speaks, the orator must be aware that in appealing to the habits of his audience, his reception depends on what they have come to mean historically, on, in short, their genealogies. And – this is another point at which Cicero calculatedly departs from Plato and Aristotle – because meaning is never a question of the patently semantic or the purely propositional, its power issues from two modes of inflection that are always with us but of which we are often insufficiently aware: our bodies and the rhythms of our speech, both of which combine in *actio* and *pronuntiatio*, modes of delivery in the public realm (which therefore also require memory) to which neither Plato nor Aristotle pays much attention, though the Romans still confessed their debts to the Greeks by recalling the practical oratorical power of Pericles, Themistocles, and Demosthenes.

The force of inflection, emerging from the historical, somatic, and aural conditions of human experience – which in Cicero are indistinguishable from rhetoric *tout court* – reveals how his three great theoretical dialogues are of a piece. The dramatic argument of *De Oratore* can be said to reveal how the orator, fully fleshed out by Crassus in Book III, corresponds chiefly to the lawyer on the one hand and the actor on the other, as well as, for identical reasons, the doctor. Readers of Book II, like many readers of Quintilian, who knows what is at stake, may find Antonius' concern with the details of the law somewhat numbing, but the the very fact of that comprehensiveness plays the symbolic role of reminding the budding orator how much knowledge, even in one field, he must master. The chief point is not just to recall Corax and Tisias, who famously founded the art of rhetoric on legal practice in Sicily, or the sheer copiousness and variety of forensic knowledge, but how the lawyer acts almost instinctively and on the spur of the moment to influence the case, just as success on the stage is elusive and irreducible to precept, and just as the doctor, faced with multiple and obscure symptoms, seeks in a timely fashion to effect a cure. Cicero causes our experience of comprehensiveness to clash with rather feeble attempts at taxonomizing, for example the divisions of speech, in order to suggest that the Aristotelian taxonomies tend to ossify distinctions that in theory make sense but render the practice of oratory or the law impotent, even as Cicero for his own purposes adopts the three-fold categories of appeal – *ethos, pathos,* and *logos* – that reflect an Aristotelian influence on rhetorical theory,[78] on the recognition that in practice each entails the other, though often, in different circumstances, in varying proportion. In combining the elements of a repertoire for a given courtroom, so to speak, the lawyer reveals how his art, like that of the orator – embodied in Crassus, and depicted in Book III – and the actor – embodied in Roscius, to whom there are running references in all three books[79] – requires an appreciation of what Clifford Geertz calls local knowledge, so that, although Book III crowns Cicero's attempts at epitomizing the perfect orator, Book II already presents us with some basic principles:

Bring me a man as accomplished, as clear and acute in thinking, and as ready in delivery as you please; if for all that he is a stranger to social intercourse, precedent, tradition, and the manners and disposition of his fellow-countrymen, those commonplaces from which proofs are derived will avail him but little. I must have talent which has been cultivated, soil, as it were, not of a single ploughing, but both broken and given a second ploughing so as to be capable of bearing better and more abundant produce. And the cultivation is practice, listening, reading and written composition. (*DO* II,xxx,131)

If meaning is a question of minute and local inflections of speech and of gesture, then by definition it must be understood entirely historically – as the reflex of custom. Despite a tendency to see the *Brutus* as Cicero's defence of his copious "Asian" style addressed to an important representative of the "Attic" school, which included Caesar, Cicero's chief aim is to present a history of Rome through an account of how different oratorical styles succeed in different circumstances, and of how, as a result of such organic development, Roman rhetoric can now challenge the Greeks' (*Br* lxxii,254). Cicero's main point is that there is no single transhistorical criterion of effective speech. His implied objection to a single "Attic" criterion of plain style is that it represents a mechanical application of the principle of imitation, which should rather select from a smorgasbord of possibilities with local ends in mind, and ignores the difference between Latin and Greek upon which a number of modern scholars have commented. However plainly rendered, Greek retains a musicality lost when Latin seeks analogous effects, which, from Cicero's point of view, limits its general powers of inflection. If Cicero favors the baroque complexities of the Asianists, this serves several conceptual purposes at once. His own preferences are firstly circumstantial, matters of personal choice, implying no desire to impose a singular rule of style, since *ornatus* is itself permissive: the Greek synonym is the word *kosmos*. At a theoretical level, in any case, as Erasmus also remarks of the Ciceronian, Cicero approaches the implied opposition between the Asianist and Atticist from an ironic point of view, which allows him to see it dialectically. In his journeys in the Greek world, he was trained neither on the Peloponnese, nor strictly in Asia Minor, but on Rhodes, where Molo taught him to moderate his attachment to hyperbolic effects (*Br* xci,316). The geographical dispersion of the Greek world becomes a figure of *copia* itself, so that Erasmus writes that the true Ciceronian "may be free either to emulate laconism, if you wish, or to copy Asian exuberance, or to exhibit Rhodian moderation."[80]

This dialectical principle is evident in the history of rhetoric itself.[81] Great oratory, almost always acting under duress, rarely finds a single ideal expositor. Since Isocrates trained both Ephorus and Theopompus (*DO* III,ix,36; *Br* lv,203), we see time and again that great moments of oratory have invariably required two very different kinds of speaker. These may be almost any combination of personalities and styles, producing a dynamic balance or "*mediocritas*," or a neighborliness expressing mutual regard (*Br* xlii,156–7), such as Balbus and Gallus (*Br* xli,153–xlii,155), Sulpicius and Cotta (*Br* lxii,227; lv,201; *Or* xxii,73–4), Crassus and Scaevola (*Br* xxxix,146–xl,150), and Cicero's ideal pair, Crassus and Antonius, the chief interlocutors of *De Oratore* (*DO* III,viii,32; ix,34; *Br* xxxvii,139–xxxviii,145; *Or* iv,16–v,19; xxx,106).[82] Never shy about his own claims, Cicero treats Crassus and Antonius as promissory notes for his own eminence, one he shares with Servius Sulpicius, for example (*Br* xl,150–xli,153). In the one passage in the *Brutus* in which Cicero directly refers to the characters of style, we see how the range of stylistic variants implied by the tensions among the low, the middle, and the high styles (which began with an opposition between the plain and the figurative) find expression in the differences among practicing orators, and, because practical oratory is essentially histrionic, invites analogies to the stage:

Since . . . there are two distinct types of good oratory – and that is the only kind we are considering – one simple and concise, the other elevated and abundant, while naturally that is better which is more brilliant and impressive, yet everything which falls under the category of good, and is supreme in its kind, wins a just praise. But the concise orator must be on his guard against meagreness and emaciation, the abundant and elevated type against inflation and errors of taste. . . Sulpicius was of all orators whom I have ever heard the most elevated in style, and, so to speak, the most theatrical. (*Br* lv,201–203)

It follows that when, in the *Orator*, Cicero speaks of the ideal orator as only embodied in a Platonic idea (*Or* I,3;ii,7;iii,9–10;xxix,101), he means only that the single orator capable of universal knowledge lies at best in the future.[83] Plato in the *Phaedrus* offers metaphor (like beautiful boys) as a foretaste of knowledge lying beyond representation, but remains, at the moment when Socrates imagines the sphere of heaven (2146E–247D), suspicious of the theatrical image he invokes (truth lying beyond the theatre). But for Cicero the issue is meaning, not truth, and meaning is customary, local, variable, and histrionic, which requires at once a consciousness of the range of styles available to a speaker, the application of the fundamental principle of decorum in local conditions, and confirmation of the orator's effectiveness by public response, or at least a response not limited to professional elites like philosophers. As Cicero writes of this capacity, "not only is language soft, pliant, and so flexible that it follows wherever you turn it, but also the varieties in ability and taste have produced styles widely different" (*Or* xvi,52). This has several implications, which, echoing the Aristotelian category of *the mean [mesotes]*, are at once aesthetic and ethical and political. Hendrickson writes that the early orators like Gorgias had no theory of style apart from invention and arrangement,[84] that Theophrastus was the first to formalize the distinction among styles, beginning first of all with the idea that two styles distinguished between the nature of the audience and the subject matter (*DO* I,x,44),[85] and that he began to develop the distinction among the three characters of style, which first makes its formal appearance in the *Ad Herennium*.[86]

It is Cicero who fully embraces the characters of style – to which he devotes considerable attention in the *Orator* (vi-20–vii,24) – and he does so for three distinct reasons.[87] First, to retain two styles invites the possibility – as in the Stoics – of a simple conceptual antinomy between some non-rhetorical mode of knowledge (like logic), and a figurative, rhetorical, and potentially secondary mode. For Cicero the three styles denote the inevitably linguistic condition of all human aspirations, so that logic, for example, falls not outside rhetoric but comprises one among a number of possible rhetorical choices. Second, the three styles intensify our sense of the dialectical competition inhabiting the linguistic moment. And third, following the Isocratean introduction of history into the orator's curriculum,[88] since to be in language in this way is to be in history, the three styles are an expression of Roman history taken as a whole: our being in language and our being in the state are different ways of talking about how humans are constituted by the culture they inhabit, and how human fulfillment depends not so much on mastering as on endlessly refashioning the elements of language and politics. The encompassing syllabus implied in the Sophistic conception of things becomes for Cicero – as it was to become for Burke – a defence of the organic and historical conditions of Roman life and the Roman state. Smethurst writes that "the state, through the medium of its religion, laws and customs, is the great storehouse of ethics, morality, politics, and rhetoric."[89] And though Rome embodies for Cicero a political ideal, this is not a pattern laid down outside or beyond history, but a Rome whose historical past and whose legal institutions, especially the Twelve Tables, exemplify her best self.[90] Influenced at some distance by Isocrates and the Stoics and more closely by the Scipionic circle to which Polybius belonged, it is clear that for Cicero the three styles are a linguistic expression of the national character and of his ideal of the mixed republic, as expressed in *De Republica*.[91]

In alluding to Cicero and by employing an Academic and Ciceronian method of debate, and in forging a parallel between the mixed modes of native English drama and the organic nature of the mixed English constitution, Dryden is revitalizing this imaginative union between the varied characters of style and the complex balances among the powers of the English state. But, given that Dryden is writing in the context of the theater, the connections are yet more precise and subtle. For whether thinking as a "stylist" or as a "legal constitutionalist," Dryden echoes Cicero in seeing knowledge as mediated entirely by history and custom, so that human experience is only ever phenomenological, as the total sum of all forms of human behavior in space and time. The behavioral, and thus somatic, conditions of the human enterprise place delivery at a premium in Roman rhetorical theory, a change in the nature of rhetorical treatises intiated, according to Solmsen, by Theophrastus.[92] The close analogies between the orator, lawyer, doctor, and actor in Roman rhetoric follows from the primacy of the body as an agent of communication, a literal reading of how meaning is somatically and histrionically inflected that also entails two other ideas. First, the difference among the characters of style seems to have originated, or at least finds expression, in the differences among dramatic genres, which is a major reason why in Book II of *De Oratore* Antonius assumes three different *personae* in the pursuit of a law case (*DO* II,xxix,102) and why Cicero's theories of *copia* and *aptus* so gracefully fit Horace's *Ars Poetica*, a text which is entirely second nature to neoclassical writers like Dryden. Grant and Fiske argue for example that Ciceronian and Horatian decorum assumes the differences among dramatic genres,[93] and that for Horace tragedy, satyr plays, and comedy are instances, respectively, of the high, middle, and low styles.[94]

Second, Cicero is profoundly influenced by the Greek conception that language itself is somatic and can be parsed physiologically in its own right. Hendrickson remarks that the Greek names for style, *ischnos* and *adros*, refer to the human form.[95] Cicero's choice for the parts of a speech, *membrum*, is originally somatic in meaning, referring to the limbs or organs of the body, but resonates in ways of which Dryden cannot have been unaware.[96] For it also can mean, rather neutrally, merely a part or element of something, but more significantly, a chamber in a house, a clause in a sentence, and a member of the state. Coming in the wake of the Harveian revolution, it is almost as if, in the seventeenth century, Cicero's conception plays to the new role of the blood in the body, for he refers to the sap [*sucus*] and blood [*sanguinis*] of oratory in the *Brutus* (ix,36). This has important effects by which the arts of speech and politics become mutually constitutive. Cicero ends the *Orator* with a lengthy disquisition on rhythm in prose. This is no mere aesthetic fancy, for rhythm is that non-propositional dimension by which language marks itself out as somatic; and rhythm represents a central semantic which plays not to the special knowledge of professional philosophers but relies for its effectiveness on public recognition, a corollary to Cicero's affection – though his inclinations were always aristocratic – for the idea that the senate represented the popular will. When Dryden, referring to mixed plots as copious, invokes the Fletcherian mode as a symbol of the mixed constitution and as a device for engaging the political complexities of his age, he is assuming the Ciceronian view that the role of tragicomedy was not so much to reflect as mediate the world it confronted. As Cicero writes in *De Oratore* in ways that apply simultaneously to language and the state, "These three styles should exhibit a certain charm of colouring, not as a surface varnish but as permeating their arterial system" (III,li,199). Fjelstad concludes that "ornate speech is, in sum, emotionally transformative."[97]

Davenant

CHAPTER 3

"The Civility of the Stage": Davenant's critical royalism

William Davenant is rightly famous in English theatrical history. Not only, with Thomas Killigrew, was he one of only two theatrical patentees at the Restoration,[1] but in 1656, by permission of the Cromwellian regime, he mounted *The Siege of Rhodes*, which involved a proscenium stage, moveable scenery, music, and actresses. Viewed from the end of the seventeenth century – for example in 1700 Congreve incorporated allusions to Roxalana, one of Davenant's heroines, into *The Way of the World* – this moment constituted a revolution in the staging of English dramas whose effects are still with us. Thus Langbaine memorializes Davenant's reform of the stage by writing that "an Eternal Fame . . . will always accompany his Memory; he having been the first Introducer of all that is splendid in our English *Opera's*, and 'tis by his means and industry, that our Stage at present rivals the Italian Theatre."[2]

Part of the argument of the following chapters follows from attending closely to what is implied by Langbaine's language. Intentionally or not, most scholars of English drama interpret the term "opera" here to connote an implicitly evacuated experience of the stage, as in the *merely* melodramatic or sensational. This view of the meretricious effects of Davenant's stagecraft is confirmed by the assumption that to revise Shakespeare, as he and other Restoration playwrights did, betokens not only a gross failure of taste, but constitutes a form of cultural vandalism of the sort suggested by Eliot's dissociation of sensibility and still almost instinctually underwritten by many early Stuart literary historians. Thus in his two elegant and influential books on the early Stuart masque, we find Stephen Orgel largely uninterested in the history of the genre after Ben Jonson and Inigo Jones angrily ceased their collaboration in 1631, concluding *The Jonsonian Masque* with a brief note to the effect that the masque tradition led to modern stage conventions, and in both books entirely eliding Davenant's role in the last five early Stuart masques ever presented.[3] In his encyclopedic catalogue of Jones's designs (co-edited with Roy Strong), we are left with a slightly

93

different impression: the final introductory essay concedes that the masques of the 1630s were heavily orchestrated by Jones, involving more sophisticated machinery than ever before, but argues that the chief collaborator was the King, and the function of Jones's perspectivism was centrally, from a neoplatonic vantage, to amplify and propagandize the values of Divine Right kingship.[4] Davenant himself remains relatively unimportant in this story, for, as regards his role in *Britannia Triumphans*, we are told, "Davenant is unaware of the implications of much of his material."[5]

There is plenty of evidence, however, that Davenant's role with Jones in these late masques was collaborative, involving an important stage in Davenant's thinking about scenic design for all kinds of play. Quite apart from my contention that Davenant was intellectually highly sophisticated, it is hard to imagine any writer so lacking in self-regard as to submerge himself completely in another's project. And though Orgel follows a respectable critical tradition when he segregates the methods and intentions of masques from other kinds of drama, he creates the impression that Jones's stage design for *Florimène* (1636), because it is a play, is deeper than that of masques like *Salmacida Spolia* (1640), when both designs in the Lansdowne MS 1171 seem to show a depth of 16 feet (see figures 2–3).[6] Moreover, there is extensive evidence in the Blackfriars repertory, from *The Maid's Tragedy*, to *The Tempest* and Davenant's own *The Cruel Brother*, of vigorous cross-talk between the staging of plays and the idea of the masque.[7] Though, like Andrew Gurr, Keith Sturgess makes clear that staging in the private theaters did not meaningfully anticipate the proscenium stage,[8] and that the early Stuart period distinguished clearly between masques and plays,[9] he also records how the court ordered command performances in the 1630s, on one occasion attending a performance of Heywood's masque, *Love's Mistress*, at a private theater.[10] Thinking specifically of Davenant and Killigrew, Sturgess writes that the histrionic bent of the Caroline court meant that it "became a laboratory for theatrical development and experimentation and it inevitably affected the ideas and the ambitions of the professional theatre people brought within its ambit."[11] This impression is supported in scrupulous detail by John Orrell. In designing indoor theaters (especially the Cockpit, Drury Lane) as well as different kinds of theatrical scene in the Serlian manner (not only for masques), Inigo Jones and his collaborator after 1628, John Webb, thinking in theoretical terms derived from architecture, were moving towards the scenic reform of the public stage that Davenant, with Webb's assistance, effected: rather than the Restoration denoting the death of an entire theatrical tradition, it becomes, in Orrell's account, the culmination of ideas about the stage and about architecture

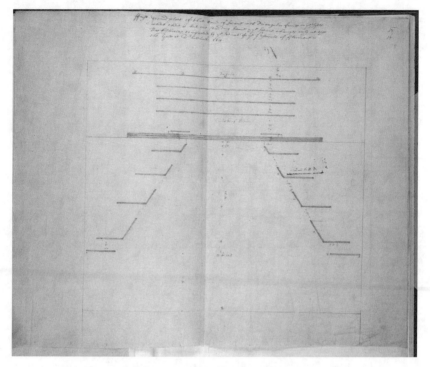

Figure 2: Stage designs for *Florimène* from BL Lansdowne MS 1171

that are implicit in Jones's and Webb's experiments in the last decade of the Caroline period.[12] This is exactly the argument Richard Southern pursues in relation to the designs in Lansdowne MS 1171. Citing William Grant Keith's view that several of the designs are not only in Webb's hand but involve plans for the Rutland House performances of *The Siege of Rhodes* (along with the plans for *Florimène* and *Salmacida Spolia*),[13] he writes that "the manuscript is evidence to us not only of masque technique, but is also presumptive evidence of the scenic system upon which the whole career of post-Restoration scenery (including, ultimately, our own) is based."[14] In sum, in collaboration with Webb and Davenant, it seems, Jones was free to pursue greater technical innovations in the *mise en scène*, innovations with distinct ideological implications of the kind that Davenant – who wrote only for indoor theaters – had debated from the inception of his career in the mid-to-late 1620s.

Langbaine's term *opera*, then, carries with it the Latin meaning of something wrought or produced, an honorific view of the artifice governing all

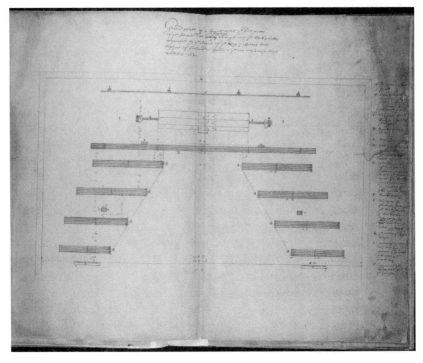

Figure 3: Stage designs for *Salmacida Spolia* from BL Lansdowne MS 1171

media which contribute admittedly to the sensationalism of the theatre but also to its overarching symbolic purposes, which cannot and should not – Cicero would have said – segregate the discursive and propositional from the rhetorical effects of bodies moving in space and time.[15] The histrionic, we have seen, necessarily inhabits any full description of how rhetoric works, so that *opera* has something of the effect of *Gesamtkunstwerk*. The discursive prejudice serves in virtually every discussion to canonize Jonson at the expense of Jones, almost despite the argument of the most widely cited article on the dispute, D. J. Gordon's "Poet and Architect: The Intellectual Setting of the Quarrel between Ben Jonson and Inigo Jones."[16] Gordon argues that the dispute was fueled by a major ideological disagreement about which art – the poet's or the architect's – best encompassed the scope of humanist learning.[17] Because (in contradistinction to the humanist tradition as expressed in Cicero and Quintilian, in which *actio* is supreme) Gordon treats invention as the most important of the five parts of oratory, he sees the effect of the quarrel as a stand-off. But of course – as I hope to show Davenant believed – if delivery is the necessary precondition of meaning in the public sphere, then Jonson must have known that the edge went to Jones, which can hardly have assuaged his anger and resentment. Indeed there is something disingenuous in his "Expostulation with Inigo Jones," for, associating poetry with sense and meaning as such, he denigrates the *mise en scène* by implying that its lowly media of representation (mere "slit deal" and "boards") render it incapable of symbolic action.

I will argue below that Davenant's career, which breaks into five phases, made him acutely sensitive to the degree to which meaning in the theater was mediated by the special, material conditions associated with dramatic representation. He began by writing in the Fletcherian mode for Blackfriars, wherein stage conditions, somewhat different from the outdoor public theaters, intensified the self-conscious artifice associated with tragicomedy.[18] All of Davenant's plays were printed from the 1630s on, under a new aegis when plays were printed soon after their original performance, anticipating an important feature of Restoration dramatic culture, where performance and text entered into some competition. Consequently, though *The Cruel Brother* and the *The Tragedy of Albovine* were performed in 1627 and 1628 respectively, as printed all the plays register the effects of the Harveian revolution: they can ask more insistently than *The Maid's Tragedy* how the private economy of the body – understood systemically – corresponds to the health of the body politic; and this question migrates neatly into issues of theatrical performance itself. We can now question the rhetorical relations between plays mounted in the private theaters like Blackfriars and the public matters they address, since the newly coherent space of the human body corresponds imaginatively to the enclosed space of the private theater. In contrast to Martin Butler's otherwise superb book, which argues that political dissent in the 1630s centered on the public theaters and playwrights like Richard Brome, I believe that the smaller and slightly better-heeled audience of the indoor theaters allowed playwrights a more precise sense that their plays could address the king and the political nation on an even footing, since the audience at Blackfriars was more elite than the "public" audience, and spectators seated on the stage would sometimes engage in banter with the actors. Andrew Gurr argues indeed that the prime difference between the public and private theaters was less the architecture of the stage, which remained relatively unchanged, than the fact that the wealthiest patrons in Blackfriars sat closest to the action.[19] Certainly, in his prologue to *The Platonick Lovers*, Davenant assumes that Blackfriars affords him a special rhetorical relation to the court unavailable in the public setting.

While continuing in that mode, which combined an epistemological critique of representation with a corresponding attack on the illusions and impossibilites associated with Platonic love (an official language of the Caroline court), Davenant began his collaboration with Inigo Jones on the masques. Despite the fact that scholars remain divided about their rhetorical effects – were they simply grandiloquent expressions of Caroline megalomania, or did they represent subtle forms of ideological critique? – for the very reasons I have mentioned, there is strong proof of a symbiotic relationship between Davenant and Jones, one underscoring, especially in the last early Stuart masque ever performed, *Salmacida Spolia* (1640), their desire to act as vehicles of advice to a court increasingly out of touch with the nation at large.

Though united in their commitment to the monarchy, both Davenant and Jones approach the task critically, and we can see evidence of that critique not only in Davenant's skeptical approach to representation and thence to authority, but also in Jones's relationship to the architectural treatises by which he bolstered his claims to cultural legitimacy: it is conventional to mention Jones's two trips to Italy, sometime before 1603 and in 1613–14, to explain the depth of his knowledge and sophistication about architectural theory, and his personal copies of the treatises with his annotations are still extant.[20] As Lily B. Campbell pointed out many years ago, thinking about stage design was founded on an intimate reading of the neo-classical tradition of architecture, beginning of course with Vitruvius, and conveyed in canonical texts like Leon Batista Alberti's *On the Art of Building*, Sebastiano Serlio's *On Architecture*, and Andrea Palladio's *The Four Books of Architecture*. John Orrell writes that the "neo-Roman" assumptions in this tradition were pervasive: "The persistence of the neo-Roman auditorium was doubtless due to the habit of Renaissance Courts of seeing themselves as resurrections of an ideal antique state."[21] Stage historians are fond of citing Book II of Serlio's treatise, which treats perspective and scenography and concludes with famous woodcuts of three designs for the stage, representing the tragic, the comic, and the satyric scenes respectively (see figures 4–6), while art historians show more interest in Jones's architectural designs, some of which are in fact scenes for masques, with a consciousness that Jones's neo-Palladianism is inflected by his understanding of the difference among the five orders of architecture. (As we will see in Chapter Four, Jones owned and annotated copies of Vitruvius, Alberti, two different

Figure 4: The comic scene from Book II of Serlio, *On Architecture*

editions of Serlio, and Palladio, as well as other treatises; and he tends to ignore Book II of Serlio, focusing most intensely on Books III and IV, which concern the remains of ancient architecture, and the five orders.) The Tuscan, the Doric, the Ionic, the Corinthian, and the Composite or Italic or Latin represent developing phases in civilization, an increasing refinement of manners, and the extension of the benefits of empire to

Figure 5: The tragic scene from Book II of Serlio, *On Architecture*

the known world. Importantly, for many theorists, these orders are to be contrasted with a primitive state represented by the rustic or Gothic,[22] subtle allusions to which (as well as to the Tuscan) all tend to enliven Jones's project, whose exact political equivalent is, I propose, the tension between English customary common law and the royal prerogative, since, following Vitruvius, any reference to the neoclassical orders infuses the entire discussion with a specifically Augustan motif. (Congreve alludes to this architectural tradition in *The Way of the World* – as we will see, an

Figure 6: The satyric scene from Book II of Serlio, *On Architecture*

immaculately neoclassical design – when Millamant dismisses Sir Wilfull Witwoud as "rustic! Ruder than Gothic!" [IV,95].)

Though Wittkower is rather disdainful of their general quality, the scholarly focus on Book II of Serlio has tended to blind us to the number of architectural treatises issued in England from the middle of the seventeenth century on and of course proliferating further after the Great Fire, which concentrate more on the architectural orders than on technical matters of perspective. In fact, just as Theophrastus formalized the distinction among the characters of style before Cicero, so it is Serlio who in Book IV, Chapter IX, adds the fifth, the Composite, to Vitruvius's original four orders, justifying it in the Ciceronian terms which had already influenced Vitruvius's entire approach to the relations between the elements of architecture and the selective use of them reflecting the local site and situation of a structure. And echoing the Harveian and Ciceronian climate we have already discussed at length, architectural theory in Vitruvius and Alberti also treats its art as biometric: just as for Cicero language can be thought of in somatic and thus histrionic terms, so the proportions of buildings in neoclassical theory rest on elaborate correspondences to the human body.[23] Thus a complex series of spatial analogies connect the body of architecture to the human body, to the body of drama, and finally to the body politic, which is invariably the final cause of humanist theory, whether in Cicero or Vitruvius.

Davenant's third phase is defined by his time in Paris and the writing of *Gondibert*, as well as its famous preface addressed to Hobbes. Though critics tend to be wary of the putative parallel between the planned five-canto epic and the five-act structure of English plays, both the preface and the poem – which we are fortunate Davenant never completed – comprise rigorous methodological discussions of the coherence among the various arts. The art of rule acts by analogy to rhetoric, poetry, and drama, and to natural philosophy as well as architecture, and they also enjoy a mutual interdependence, so that we cannot think about the one without considering the others. The various and arduous methods by which each of these disciplines achieves any internal coherence are, in the skeptical universe Davenant evidently shares with Hobbes, equivalent. These kinds of concern are more hospitable to the preface than the poem, since the forward momentum of narrative on which a poem of this length depends is constantly arrested by methodological excursus that finally comprise its main subject matter, so that most readers find it difficult to remember the characters and events to which the poem refers. Because the poem remains perpetually distracted by its own methods, it serves as more of an extension of the attitudes announced in the preface – which was published a year before the three surviving cantos – than we might normally expect; and it is in those terms that it reveals itself as a remarkably coherent intellectual exercise. Furthermore, since the poem was completed in 1651, as hostilities with the Dutch over the carrying trade seemed increasingly likely, we begin clearly to see Davenant developing the analogies between the processes of rule, the discourse of trade, and the language of physiology which for the Restoration, as we have seen, were endemic.

Davenant's fourth phase is summarized in the theatrical revolution for which he was later remembered. So we will consider at some length the implications of the staging of *The Siege of Rhodes* for the political argument of the play. The new arrangement, directly attributable to the Jonesian masque with which John Webb, Davenant's designer, had assisted, corresponds to two aspects of speech which are already visible in the earlier plays written for Blackfriars. Between 1656 and 1661, the opera develops an increasing self-consciousness about its own conditions of staging, extending, on the one hand, to the characters' inclination to spatialize, by summoning an architectural metaphor, their relation to their own bodies as vehicles of dramatic meaning; and, on the other, to reminding the audience of its assent to all the other artifices of production, such as their relative distance and proximity on stage. Whereas Orgel stresses the illusionistic effects of perspective scenery in the masques, Richard Southern argues that, in general, stage scenery was anti-illusionistic, an impression also conveyed by Evelyn's much-cited account of the Venetian opera in 1645, as well as by a later tract which cites Serlio and makes clear how the perspectives associated with scenography are entirely artificial, Joseph Moxon's *Practical Perspective; Or Perspective Made Easy* (1670). (Evelyn writes, "we went to the Opera, where comedies and other plays are represented in recitative music, by the most excellent musicians, vocal and instrumental, with variety of scenes painted and contrived with no less art of perspective, and machines for flying in the air, and other wonderful motions; taken together, it is one of the most magnificent and expensive diversions the wit of man can invent.")[24]

For Orgel the use of *perspective* – an idea that deeply engages Davenant – seamlessly reproduces the great chain of being, with the monarch supreme in the social order, but like Milton, Davenant seems much more aware of the way in which, in the wake of the Galilean revolution, perspective symbolizes the general problem of scientific instrumentation, as well as causing challenges to the stage designer, as Orrell shows.[25] Telescopes and microscopes ("perpectives") materially constrain what can be seen and how, even as they magnify objects at which they are directed, so that scientific "facts" are inventions of a sort, just as "perspective" meaning "point of view" connotes definite limits on knowledge. A general if contingent picture of things must emerge from multiple and competing perspectives, just as the Fletcherian mode (echoing Cicero's *copia* and Serlio's composite order) invites competition among different and often incommensurate genres. So similarly, even in his title, when Davenant stresses the effect of perspective, he is pointing at one and the same time to the raw fact of the staging as well as to its epistemological and subsequently political implications, since the spatial constraints on a given character on the proscenium stage limit his knowledge of the action, as well as the degree of his participation in other artificial orders like statecraft, Davenant's explicit subject.

The final phase of Davenant's career extends what he had learned into the Restoration proper, which had the effect of materializing the conditions of the Fletcherian mode. Killigrew and the King's Company had moved into a U-shaped theater in Vere Street by 8 November 1660, with performances echoing the early Stuart private court productions. After taking up temporary quarters at Salisbury Court, Davenant and the Duke's Company began playing at Lisle's Tennis Court, Lincoln's Inn Fields, on 28 June 1661, with an expanded version of *The Siege of Rhodes*, and began to extend the staging possibilities which had made it such a success in the Rutland House productions (though Orrell argues that Davenant in the late 1650s always had the Cockpit, Drury Lane in mind, which is where *The Siege of Rhodes* as well as *The Cruelty of the Spaniards in Peru* were performed in 1658–9).[26] Webb evidently continued to be involved, since he designed scenes for Orrery's *Mustapha*, an extension of *The Siege of Rhodes*, performed by the Duke's Company in April 1665. Harbage writes that

During the Commonwealth [Davenant] had used the proscenium arch, curtain, and scenes, such as he and Inigo Jones had worked with in Caroline court masques, and now he made these adjuncts, with further elaborations, a permanent feature of the public theatre. All his contemporaries recognized the importance of the step, and modern scholars see in it the birth of our modern picture-frame stage.[27]

Theater historians generally agree that Davenant established the conventions of staging that were to mark the Restoration as a whole: the proscenium stage projected at the front, and the proscenium arch framed the scenic stage behind it, which was raked from front to back and incorporated a series of slots for sliding shutters that would be drawn back in the course of the action (these shutters were the children of Jones's *scena ductilis*). The action would take place either on the proscenium stage or the scenic stage, or on both, which must have allowed for a certain fluctuating of effect.[28]

This means that the very architecture of the Restoration stage could have encouraged the Fletcherian mode, since part of the challenge would surely be to see how the entire stage – divided into two – could service a given action or series of different actions. Downes's account of the inauguration of Lisle's Tennis Court is highly suggestive, since having rehearsed *The Siege of Rhodes* before taking up residence, Davenant "Open'd his House with the said Plays, having new Scenes and Decorations, being the first that were e're Introduc'd in *England.*" Downes records the other plays that launched the season, including Davenant's version of *The Two Noble Kinsman* (a Shakespeare–Fletcher collaboration), entitled *The Wits; Hamlet; Love and Honour;* and *Romeo and Juliet,* which was soon revised as if purely to test the possibilities of the new stage: "This Tragedy of *Romeo* and *Juliet,* was made some time after into a Tragi-comedy, by Mr. *James Howard,* he preserving *Romeo* and *Juliet* alive; so that when the Tragedy was Reviv'd again, 'twas Play'd Alternately, Tragical one Day, and Tragicomical another; for several Days together."[29]

These were the conditions for which Davenant and Dryden collaborated in their revision of *The Tempest.* Performances began on 7 November 1667, five months before Davenant's death handed Dryden the laureateship. As we will see, the play shows the impress of the Fletcherian mode as well as the staging conditions which added to the spectacle, so that the doublings by which Ferdinand and Miranda gain a brother and sister are not some sterile neoclassical whim, but contribute to the play's determination to warn Charles away from some of his more regrettable tendencies. At the time that the play was performed, Davenant was already consulting with Christopher Wren for the design of a dedicated theater. Though his death prevented his ever seeing the outcome, the Duke's Company, under the guidance of Lady Davenant and Thomas Betterton, moved to the Dorset Garden theater, "a splendid new playhouse," according to *The London Stage,*[30] for the 1671–2 season, the same season in which Dryden's *Marriage a la Mode* was first performed by the King's Company, whose staging habits had been directly influenced by Davenant's innovations. This was only four months after the King's Company had lost the Bridges Street theater in Drury Lane to fire; but significantly again it was Wren who designed its replacement – the Theatre Royal, Drury Lane – which opened for business in March 1674.

We should consider Wren's role in this narrative (born in 1632, Wren was an exact contemporary of Dryden and Locke at Westminster). As we will see in the next chapter, theatrical design was intimately linked to Vitruvian and Palladian conceptions of architecture: Wren's move from astronomy to architecture involved the design of the Sheldonian theater, in dialogue with Renaissance editions of Vitruvius and Vignola, beginning in April 1663.[31] It thus becomes clear that, in addition to contributing to the texture of political debate, the theatrical culture to which Jonson, Jones, Davenant,

Webb, and Dryden belonged served as a chief vehicle of the transmission of neo-Palladianism from Jones to Wren, between whom there is, as John Summerson remarks, no other connection;[32] and this view is cast in quite concrete terms by Orrell, who argues that Wren modeled the Sheldonian, combining as it does a Vitruvian auditorium with a Serlian stage, on Jones's designs for the Cockpit, Drury Lane.[33] By the same token, the entirely Roman presumptions informing the distinctions among the five orders of architecture argue that the material practices and conditions of the theater contributed to specifically Augustan conceptions of neoclassicism in the middle of the seventeenth century.

THE LITERARY RECEPTION OF THE FLETCHERIAN MODE

I will briefly discuss two poems, printed forty-four years apart, that show how seventeenth-century authors believed that their varying debts to different figures in the theatrical canon involve two, related, principles of selection which are at once literary, conceptual, histrionic, and political. At the core, for both poets, a rereading of the literary history to which they belong amounts to an essay in constitutional theory to which they contribute. On the one hand, to imitate Beaumont and Fletcher or Jonson is, as these writers are well aware, to prefer more limited but focused writers to Shakespeare; and, on the other hand, to make this choice is also to refer to different conditions and traditions of production, whose implications, since they bear on the rhetorical relationship of audience to performers, are political. Thomas Carew wrote a dedication to Davenant's *The Just Italian*, a Fletcherian tragicomedy probably performed in 1629 but printed in 1630.[34] Aware of the conditions under which Davenant is operating – plays performed in the private theaters, and plays that soon occupy a different kind of "narrow room," namely that of the printed page – Carew argues that the audiences, distracted and inattentive because they still frequent the "Red-Bull and Cock-pit" ("that adulterate Stage"), contribute to the ills of the state. The fates of the "Stage" and "State" are intimately connected, so that the failure to respect the superior acting at Blackfriars corresponds to a resistance to "The tearser *Beaumonts* or great *Johnsons* Verse," whose equivalent is the rabble's failure to understand "men great and good." But the implication is not that the Fletcherian or Jonsonian modes amount to an uncritical adulation of those in power, but, because they represent a more concentrated experience than that of the public stage, the ability to challenge the audience's assumptions – just as Carew is now celebrating Davenant's implied "Satyre" – as well as providing advice to the political nation. Carew ends his poem with the hope that, while Davenant will awaken the audience to its public responsibilities, "thy Play, whose clear, yet lofty strain, / Wisemen, that govern Fate, shall entertain." Carew even suggests that the action of Davenant's play is dialectical: he calls it "a double Comedy" because the audience is implicated in the play's action; but the epithet also suggests a formally double action so typical of the Fletcherian mode, whose rhetorical purpose is to advise the political nation at large. The implication in part corresponds to Davenant's ongoing interest, from very early in his career, in the possible connections between various forms of perspective, which the private theaters intensify, and the emergence or creation of a discourse of civil society.

In 1674, in the Prologue to his and Davenant's revision of *The Tempest*, Dryden engages in a parallel method of allegorizing his debts to literary history. In Carew's poem, the general and unselective principle is located in the public theaters, by contrast to which the private theaters represent a principle of social and aesthetic selection and exclusion, with a corresponding heightening of rhetorical effect. In Dryden's poem, the generalizing or universalizing principle is associated with Shakespeare, who occupies a hallowed plot of literary ground. Shakespeare's semi-divine status means that whatever succeeds him is a mere grafting onto his stock, and by the same token he embodies the principle of sovereignty ("monarch-like, [he] gave . . . his Subjects Law"). But like the early Stuarts, Shakespeare, imagined as a great tree, has suffered a more or less inevitable diminution in his powers – though the root remains alive, the tree has been felled – so that his successors, Fletcher, Jonson, Davenant, and Dryden, must in the best sense imitate him, where imitation implies both dependence and selection ("If they have since out-writ all other Men, / 'Tis with the drops which fell from *Shakespear's* Pen"). That method of selection has implications at one and the same time for the constitutional metaphor Dryden has summoned, and for the sense that staging conditions are different from those of earlier times: Ancient superstition ("old Priesthood") makes "*Shakespear's* pow'r . . . Sacred as a King's," but just as Dryden believes that the powers of the King now depend on a mixed constitution (figured as the Fletcherian reform of the Shakespearean tradition), so the actors on stage are mixed in ways that was not formerly the case, since one of the changes Davenant and Dryden have made to Shakespeare's original is not only to have actresses play female roles, but in this instance to have "One of our Women to present a Boy." The audience is a fundamental feature of this new literary economy, since it must both grant grace to Shakespeare as monarch and to "our Theatre" as a mediator of his powers as revised for new staging conditions, which allow for the "transformation" of cross-dressing, as well as for the new age. Finally, it is clear that, for Carew and Dryden, because relying on the Fletcherian and Jonsonian modes rather than directly on Shakespeare involves a form of self-limitation in the service of political persuasion, the relation of Shakespeare to his successors is what, in Cicero, *copia* is to *aptus*: the possibilities of the discipline have to be applied locally.

"OUR FLESHY BUILDING": DAVENANT'S FLETCHERIAN PLAYS, TRAGICOMEDY, AND BLACKFRIARS

If we take four plays by Davenant performed between 1626–7 and 1636 – a period when the effects and costs of personal rule after 1629 became increasingly clear – we can see how Davenant uses the obvious epistemological limitations of the stage to expose the dangers of the unconstrained exercise of prerogative power.[35] These are Fletcherian plays, though not all billed as tragicomedies. Like the Fletcherian originals, they were performed at the Blackfriars theater, but they respond with even greater specificity to the confinement of the stage, involving precise stage directions and conveying a strong feeling for blocking, dimensions, the use of doors, traps, and the mutual positioning of characters (who often assume emblematic postures, such as kneeling before another character). Blackfriars also allows for a freer use of music of the kind we also see in Shakespeare's late plays.[36] Taken together, *The Cruel Brother* (1626–7), *The Just Italian* (1629–30), *Love and Honour* (1634), and *The Platonick Lovers* (1636) comprise a critique of the conditions of power in general, the first three concerned with the unstable balance between the arbitrary use of personal power, the legal application of force in ensuring justice, and the extent to which custom can supply a corrective to improperly conceived acts of "justice." (At one point Foreste in *The Cruel Brother* declares that "Custom . . . only gives us hope of certainty in justice" [III,ii,474a]; and the Duke inveighs against the convention of marriage as a barrier to his lust [III,v,476a].) *The Platonick Lovers* takes issue with the language of Platonic love cultivated by Henrietta Maria. According to Davenant, the neoplatonic cult is epistemologically naïve in seeking to elude the representational conditions which permit the fiction at all, whether the circumstances of the stage which give characters life in the first place, or the rhetorical conditions permitting examples to proliferate. Davenant stylizes the relation between the two by asking his audience to observe how characters respond to local examples, which depends on a careful choreography of stage space relative to particular moments in the action.

At the center of this political argument, then, is an epistemological concern expounded in this instance through matters of staging. Because in the nature of it we can have no independent narrator, drama always favors a skeptical over a dogmatic view of knowledge. For Davenant, with his eye clearly on the Caroline court, at the heart of the argument is a statement made by the Duke in *The Cruel Brother* (a figure subject to his most immediate instincts): "'Tis cheap and base for Majesty not to be singular in all effects" (I,ii,467b). This singularity connotes a fundamentally hermetic and centripetal thrust, an instant gratification of personal impulse and power, a disregard for the constraints of mediation, and (in this play) the dispensing of monopolies which had been a point of contention between the court and the nation at large ever since the reign of Elizabeth (perhaps a subtext in Davenant's dedication to Lord Weston, Lord High Treasurer).[37] The sense of singularity is executed in the main action, a sensitive reworking of *The Maid's Tragedy*: the Duke of Sienna commits a rape upon his "creature" Lucio's wife, Corsa, whereupon her brother Foreste, Lucio's "creature," sacrifices her to purge the stain. At first Foreste plans to kill the Duke but submits to arguments about the Duke's Divine Right, though poetic justice prevails: the Duke falls victim to a trap of his own making and bleeds to death.

Davenant's plays seem more or less exact instances of what Lee Bliss and R. A. Foakes depict as the central features of tragicomedy. Bliss writes that "English tragicomic authors locate the new forms' focus on love and private relations within satirically anatomized social and political worlds"; while Foakes writes that those impulses can be ascribed to the impact of lust (rather than love) and the related function of satire or the satirist, operating under highly self-conscious theatrical conditions which reflect both the experience of the private theaters and the masque form.[38] The overwhelming effect is a rapid fluctuation between passionate engagement and alienation and irony, perhaps intensified by the numerous different scenes in a given act (seven in Act V of *The Cruel Brother* alone), as well as the *Verfremdungseffekt* of having members of the audience on the stage proper, as Sturgess suggests.[39] For Davenant, this mechanism itself serves to reveal the entirely artificial quality of human relations – hence the reference to the "creatures" of those in power – as well as the state, imagined in *The Cruel Brother* as an "engine" (I,i,466a). Thus Castruchio, "a satyrical Courtier," aware of the experimental quality of political arrangements, declares, "When I dye, I dye a Martyr to the Common-weal" (II,i,471a). Though we experience all human relations from within, as it were, the play uses the "satirical" voice as a means to externalize and anatomize the workings of the "engine," so that the play opposes a public, spatial, and centrifugal tendency to the Duke's private, hermetic, and centripetal desires: typically Davenant combines a consciousness of the artificial concerns of the plot – like statecraft – with a reminder of the continuously artificial conditions of the stage itself. It is therefore natural for Foreste to imagine that under duress a person might "be scatter'd into Atoms" (V,iv,484b), as if identity can easily disperse into the original elements from which it was only strenuously assembled. Similarly, the Duke meditates on what it might mean to make a man *ex nihilo* (I,ii,468a), partly intended as a hit at the Stuart sale of titles (II,i,471b). As in Restoration drama, the precarious quality of institutions – of society, the state, the play – also emerges from the presence of characters who inhabit the wrong literary genre, in this case Lothario (a "frantick young Gallant" or "Court Baboon" [I,iv,468b]), accompanied by his rustic servant Borachio who is no more than "a bundle of Proverbs" (I,iv,468b): this anticipates Melantha in *Marriage a la Mode* and Sir Fopling in *The Man of Mode*, characters whose obsessions with French and with clothes denote, like pastoral as a genre, a generic fixity in a game demanding a much greater capacity for accommodation. Because, like the satirist, such characters are out of order in the world into which they are thrust, it is therefore significant that virtually by accident it is Lothario who stabs the Duke, thus allowing Davenant to preserve the Duke's prerogative and yet respect the demands of poetic justice.

The consciousness of the stage as space produces an effect that Dryden was to exploit in *Marriage a la Mode* and *Don Sebastian*, and is also a feature of Wycherley's china scene. The mere fact of stage space disrupts attempts to preserve the integrity of the private against the incursions of the public. Unless they are entirely occult, meanings in drama always occur as publicly mediated events, even if they are events that occur offstage. At the crudest level, the Duke imagines that satisfying private desire will have no immediate public consequences; and this attempt to cordon off these realms of apprehension produces frustration, for hearing "*A noise within*" in Act I, scene ii, he asks irritably, "Are we debarred all place of privacy?" (I,ii,468a). The public conditions of the stage have several consequences for Davenant's argument. A consciousness of the space of the indoor theater allows Act V to render both the murder of Corsa (in scene i) and the potential trial and execution of the Duke (scene vi) into coherent emblems, for the act begins with the chair in which Corsa is to sit placed carefully "*at the Arras*" in order to frame and stylize the event; and similarly the Duke "*is drawn forth*" on his bed at the moment of reckoning. That the placement of objects and persons on stage has potentially exemplary purposes and effects is itself an object of interest throughout, because, Davenent makes clear, the meaning of such things depends on the perspective of the viewer. Whether we think of *perspective* as point of view or *perspective* as instrument, it denotes the limitations of knowledge. Foreste declares that "Where sight is young and clear, there spectacles are troublesom; and rather hide than shew the object" (I,ii,467b); and he elaborates: "Faith's a Perspective; through whose narrow lane; little things (far off) seem so much too great, too near: that what was first unknown is more chang'd from knowledge than it was before" (V,ii,483a). Borachio concurs that "when a man sees things plainly, he need not buy Spectacles, till he grow old" (III,iv,475b); and as he is about to kill his sister, Foreste impugns the ability of the mob to educe proper examples from what it observes: "Their quick censure brings such effect as Spectacles, when used in haste; which then do rather aggravate the shape: then give distinction of the form" (V,ii,482a).

Though the play was performed before the publication of *De Motu Cordis*, this kind of specular fascination informs a proto-Harveian consciousness of the body as an object to be explored and anatomized, itself a space inviting interpretation, so that Foreste's murder of Corsa assumes the air of an anatomical experiment. He opens her veins to kill her, wishing that he could separate her defiled from her pure blood, and brother and sister seem almost equally rapt by Corsa's ebbing strength, so that as Corsa dies, Foreste comments on "A Convulsion in her Arteries!" (V,ii,483a). The succeeding indictment of the Duke laid out on his bed extends the metaphor, shortly after Foreste has told Lucio that only in the final hour of reckoning will he "behold my heart without a Perspective" (V,iv,484b). Only the most urgent expressions of royalist principle prevent the Duke's execution, a moment Lucio speaks of as "the surgery which I desire" (V,vi,485b); and as the would-be executioners leave, the Duke objects to being morally anatomized but demands that they perform on him physically:

> Duke. Lucio stay, Foreste stay awhile.
> Leave me not thus anatomiz'd.
> > He riseth from the Bed.
> Dissect me really with your good Swords.
> Behold my breast, take out my heart: and if you
> find your figures there, then use my fame with mercy.
> > (V,vi,486a)

The Harveian space of the body, the space of the private stage, and the perspectivilism of the masque play analogous roles in Davenant's political consciousness. The effect of anatomizing and distributing the elements of any system – plays, bodies, the state – draws attention to the effect of method, the artifice by which each of these, from a certain perspective, achieves functional coherence. At a crucial juncture, Davenant makes it clear that the arts of the soldier, the scholar, the statesman, the farmer, and the writer of masques for this reason play equivalent roles in civilization, so that in this ideological sense, Davenant is arguing that, for all their generic distinctness, masques and plays belong together (I,ii,468a).

Like *The Cruel Brother*, *The Just Italian* (a tragicomedy) asks us to consider the fine line between naked violence or acts of revenge and the legal application of force to achieve "justice" or the rule of law in the state. As he is about to kill his sister, by commenting that "I will be just yet cruel too" (V,i,481b), Foreste reveals how both titles bear a casuistical relation to the action: there are ways in which Foreste's "cruelty" could be construed circumstantially as a form of justice, just as Altamont's behavior in *The Just Italian* could appear more arbitrary and capricious than just. This, I believe, is Davenant's commentary upon the unsettled balance – especially in the years of personal rule – between common customs of rule, in which, for example, the political nation expected the King informally to consult on matters of policy, and the singular assertion of prerogative. Once again, the conditions of staging in the private theater become an important medium of political debate, since Davenant exploits the increasing association between the private theater and its female patrons.[40] Altamont is married to Alteza, whose similarity of name invokes a subtle correspondence echoed in the play's other interests in twins and doubling (ones rehearsed in *Love and Honour*): Carew calls the play a double comedy, Sciolto the libertine has sired forty-three twins, while Dandolo, a real fop, is also aped by Altamont's brother, Florello, in disguise, so that in Act IV, scene i, Davenant exploits the double doors at the back of the stage to contrast the false and the true Dandolo. Echoing the Stuart dependence on parliamentary goodwill for grants-in-supply of the kind that would finally issue in civil war, Altamont – a magistrate of Florence, hence of a republic – owes his fortune to Alteza, whose uncle has guaranteed her dowry. Davenant is capitalizing on the Caroline fiction that the loving relations between the King and his subjects are conjugal in nature, at a time when the court, under the influence of Henrietta Maria, preaches that "Wit doth reside / In Ladies subtle riots, and their pride" (I,i,443a). But does the language of love adequately address the realities of power? To Altamont's sentiments that "'Tis sympathy and love, that gives the world continuance and life," Alteza responds, "You preach of love, but your obedience would more pleasure me," which prompts the rebuttal, "This argues thy revolt, and is a strategem against Nature. Thou wouldst usurp the Charter of the Male" (I,i,444a).

At the beginning of the play, Alteza has withdrawn from conjugal relations – symbolizing her "revolt" (I,i,443a) – so that the main action of the play seeks to balance the husband's assertion of prerogative against the wife's distinctive claims within the society of marriage and hence the state. Altamont complains that "*Alteza* hath forgot the allegiance of a wife, she doth practise how with her riot not to impoverish States" (I,i,443b). The contest is explicitly over sovereignty, such that Alteza's claim to sovereignty, which Davenant purposes finally to modify in favor of the patriarchy, rests in part on her appeal to the female audience: Alteza claims that "This part o'th'house doth call me soveraign" (II,i,446a). (Later, speaking to her sister, Alteza remarks, "oft have I preach'd unto thine ear a Sov'raignty o're man" [II,ii,448b].)

While the central mechanism of the play involves the relations between Altamont and Alteza, two figures act as satirists, highlighting the artifices of statecraft involved in the resolution. One is Florello, Altamont's brother, but "A cast Souldier" as the *dramatis personae* has it, who, by donning an outlandish costume, assumes Dandolo's role: his parody of the world of manners allows him to approach all institutions, like states, in much the same ironical spirit, such that waiting at the gate, in his representation of things, is "A leash of German Dukes that walk in Rug-Gowns. I should consult with 'em about the subversion of a state or two; but I'm not yet at leisure" (II,ii,449b). The other satirical figure is Sciolto, whose lustfulness deliberately recalls the role of the satyr–satirist (III,i,449a), but whose reform into suitable romance with Scoperta, Altamont's sister, parallels the central resolution. The conversion of unbridled lust into seemly passion anticipates Davenant's concerns in *Love and Honour* and *The Platonick Lovers*, where a viable polity must reconcile human physiology (which is "hot") with a more philosophical or considered conception of things (which is "cold"). By contrast with the figure enthralled by desire or revenge, the satirist always remains conscious of the various genres he inhabits and among which he typically migrates, each entailing a different set of laws, so that Sciolto can rather coolly observe – what Altamont has more difficulty realizing – that "There is a trick of gravity i'th'State, call'd Law" (III,i,450a).

Indeed, we could say that Davenant's title is ironic insofar as Altamont takes time to differentiate a desire for revenge, and the theatricalism it encourages, from the equitable and less spectacular application of law or justice. In Altamont and Alteza's stand-off, the love of theatrical *frisson* is expressed by Alteza's threat to sleep with Sciolto – the rule of lust – with

Altamont feigning interest in his sister – the taboo of incest. This is a volatile world of unmediated or almost instinctual response matched by Altamont mistaking revenge for justice. This occurs twice. In response to his friend Mervolle's counsel to "Obey revenge," Altamont declares that "I'll give a strict and cruel justice to Revenge" (III,i,450b), which results in the stagiest moment in the play: Altamont appears before his sister smeared with blood falsely declaring that he has justly murdered Alteza. Law is cumbersome and operates altogether too casuistically – having to accommodate motive and circumstance – whereas justice has more gratifying effects: "The Laws are sinfully contriv'd. Justice should weigh the present crime, not future inference on deeds" (IV,iii,456b). In the second misapplication of law, Altamont vengefully substitutes a trial by combat for a legal proceeding against Sciolto, who has been bound and deprived of weapons. Altamont declares that "I will give thee fair and equal tryal" (IV,iii,457b), offering him a sword, and then attacking him. In a scene suffused with a Harveian fascination with blood, Sciolto is wounded and then carried off, but to his horror Altamont discovers that he too is wounded: "A sudden frost congeals my heart; I shrink like crooked age, as if my Veins were empty grown" (IV,iii,458b).

Only in the wake of this, in Act V, does Davenant permit a resolution between Altamont and Alteza, showing that their mutuality corresponds to the equitable and circumstantial dispensation of justice in the state, which also reflects Altamont's experience of his physical fragility. Believing Altamont dead from his wound, Alteza is now in a doubly uncomfortable position, which exposes her vulnerability: she is the public dispenser of justice, and she must execute a verdict laid down by Altamont. He has apparently condemned Sciolto and Scoperta, arraigned together, to death. Admitting that her own motives have hitherto been vengeful, Alteza realizes that she is hardly the proper instrument of equity. At first, Mervolle reminds her of her painful dilemma ("Justice hath laid her Sword within your reach: and you have power to sheath it so; that where you execute, you may a murder do, or sacrifice"), and she sees her weakness ("Sir, you have skill to know my womanhood is weak as ignorance or sleep. Why should you seat me here, thus to dispense of Law; that ne'er knew any justice but revenge?" [V,ii,460b–61a; 461b]). Able to acquit only Scoperta of the charge, moved by the lovers' plight, and blaming herself for their quandary, Alteza offers herself as a sacrifice. She is prevented by one of the two attendant mutes who, disrobing, reveals himself as Altamont, and they are mutually reconciled. The implication is that law will henceforth be dispensed by the restored patriarchy, and though Alteza, as befits the woman, expresses repentance and submission, the strong suggestion – which amounts to political advice from Davenant to Charles – is that the benefits of subordination accrue from using persuasion and dissimulation rather than force to secure sovereignty.

Performed in 1634, the year before Davenant began his collaboration with Jones in *The Temple of Love*, *Love and Honour* pursues the central questions raised by *The Just Italian*. Whereas in the earlier play, force and equity struggle for dominion in the breast of the chief character, now the ethos of cruelty, severity, and revenge defines the Duke of Savoy, while a new focus on "philosophy," denoting the mollifying and civil effects of humanist learning, is embodied in the hero, Alvaro, the prince. The play opens in an atmosphere of violence, since the Savoyards return from a successful military campaign against the Milanese, capturing Evandra, the Milanese princess, in the process (as well as Leonel, Prince of Parma and his sister Melora, while the low characters have captured a widow and her daughter). The naked power of military glory – untempered by "philosophy" – is embodied in the unschooled Prospero, a figure combining the ethos of lust with the role of the satyr (I,229), which once again becomes a device by which the artifices of the civil order are exposed and defended. (This effect is also assisted by the low plot paralleling concerns in the high plot.) In this play, those artifices are associated with humanist learning in general, as well as with the exemplary effects of drama in particular. The difference between Prospero and Alvaro emerges as a distinction between an unselfconsciously savage nature and a politic consciousness which, though accustomed to the arts of war, interprets them as constituting a genre whose laws then govern relations among individuals. The implication is that if we understand our place in any given order, the state of nature is always mediated into a syntax that modifies the effects of the savage condition: on the one hand, the interpretive effort alone provokes self-consciousness about the artifices of civility and automatically helps to sustain them; on the other hand, because the endeavor is strenuous and quite fragile, part of our interpretive energy goes into seeking examples of how best to exist within that order. Thus, coming off the field of battle, Alvaro says to Prospero, "This day thou hast begot much History," as if to remind him of that genre which, for humanists, epitomized the benefits of moral philosophy (I,228). The art of war that history records is masculine and violent, but its translation into history as an interpretable medium of human aspiration must take account of women who participate in it, which means that they should not be reduced – as Evandra is at this moment – into the spoils of war: in terms of the play's title, honor demands that the crudities of martial honor be tempered by love. As Tristan remarks in Act II, scene ii, "you are not

here / I'th'Camp, but in a Civil Commonwealth" (II,ii,238). And Alvaro
virtually provides a motto for the play in stating that "man should wear /
His courage in a dress lovely and soft, / As are a Virgins bridal Ornaments"
(IV,iv,262). In Act I, Prospero remains obtuse about what is at stake, for
when he parrots Alvaro's courtly capture of Leonel and Melora, he sees
his prize Evandra as a valuable object only, which prompts this instructive
outburst from Alvaro:

> O thou hast lost my heart: from hence proceeds
> This cruel act, that to thy savage courage,
> I could never joyn Philosophy.
> Hadst thou been learned,
> And read the gentler deeds, of nobler minds,
> Reason had checked thy rage, thy valour would
> Have been more pitiful, than to have led
> So lost a Virgin, into harsh captivity.
>
> (I,229)

The Duke hates the Milanese and seeks revenge because he believes they
have killed his brother (III,ii,242), so Prospero begins his own rehabilitation
by agreeing to hide Evandra, whom the Duke seeks to capture, in his house.
This produces a dramatic effect which associates certain stage spaces – the
trap and the balcony – with the women in the plot, since Evandra is soon
joined by Melora. They can thus punctuate the action in a stylized and
emblematic way designed to remind the audience of the general exemplary
aspirations of the drama, with Davenant seeking to underscore its three-
dimensional nature (we can almost sense his straining against the limits
of the non-scenic or perspectival stage). Thus in Act II, we encounter the
direction, "*The Stage opens*, Prospero *lifts* Evandra *up*" (II,ii,234), and a
little later, "*They put* Evandra *down into the Cave*" (II,ii,236). In Act III,
characters begin a new scene, with Evandra sitting to read, as if to point
the parallel between general literacy and the effect of dramatic examples
(III,iv,247); in Act IV and again in Act V, the stage doors are used as
framing devices (IV,i,254) or as a means of contrasting the women and the
men (V,iii,268). Most importantly, in Act V, Melora and Evandra appear
framed in the balcony, so that they serve at once as emblems – objects of
speculation from below – as well as, in their own right, observers of the
action. Davenant is arguing a parallel between a notion of humanist literacy
and not only generous statecraft of the kind Alvaro embodies but also the
civil arts more broadly symbolized by the feminine principle, expressed by
a metatheatrical interest in how dramatic moments constitute persuasive
examples both to the characters on stage as well as the audience more

generally. Thus the play engages in a pervasive commentary on how, in the way she is situated on stage, Evandra – the object of Alvaro's, Prospero's, and Leonel's desire – comprises an example not only to be contemplated but also to provide a proper logic for the political order, which has therefore to confess its dependence on artifice: only by this means can the waywardness of "fortune" submit to the discipline of "virtue," to cite the classic humanist distinction recalled at one moment by the Duke (III,ii,243). To assent to drama as an exemplary medium thus becomes an implicit agreement to reform the patriarchy, to the extent that the patriarchy feels licensed to act on its own. Davenant already sets an example in the Prologue, since he submits to what he calls "*Tyrant custom*" in hewing to the convention of the Prologue in the first place, so that the slight struggle between wishing to dispose of the convention and submitting to it enacts in miniature the literary politics of the play that follows.

The relationship between stage- and statecraft becomes entirely focused in Act V, whereby playing to the audience in the one exactly corresponds to consulting with the political nation in the other. The point is that until the very last moment, the Duke fails to do either, so inviting catastrophe. In Act IV, realizing that "Revenge is a most dangerous kind of lust," as Vasco puts it (IV,iii,260), Melora decides sacrificially to disguise herself as Evandra, but the Duke, in a rampage, on detecting the imposture, decides they both must die. The intellectual virtues of tragicomedy are here apparent, for, speaking at the close of Act IV, Alvaro, Leonel, and Prospero, now composing their own civil order in their joint love for Evandra, approach the forthcoming act as the audience of an impending tragedy, an image reinforced, early in Act V, by Vasco's joking allusion to the puppet show: "The show! The motion of Queen *Guiniver*'s death, / Acted by Puppets would please her as well; / The Jade has no more remorse, than a Bear / That wants his supper" (V,i,264). Observing the show additionally are two ambassadors (it transpires, the Duke's brother and the Duke of Milan in disguise), the first of whom begins the act by announcing a principle with unavoidable implications for Charles's personal rule: "Access and Audience, Sir, is all our hopes / Presume to get" (V,i,263). In scene ii, the conception of the audience is stylized by Melora and Evandra's appearance in the balcony ("Evandra *and* Melora *are seen in mourning at the Window*" [V,ii,265]). They in turn observe from above how the three heroes have become one, and as they are dragged from the casement to face trial, Alvaro cries out, "Love's great Examples stay! Leave us not yet!" (V,ii,266). Prospero and Leonel contemplate violence, but Alvaro reveals his statecraft by pointing to the soldiers' probable reaction to what they have all witnessed – if it acts

without regard to popular sentiment, power endangers itself, so that direct
action, strictly speaking illicit, is unnecessary: "we may best observe, / What
looks the Officers and Souldiers wear. / If they begin to grieve, their grief
will soon / To anger grow" (V,ii,267). The Duke should become aware of
the political climate ("Too long / My Father has my constant duty known;
/ And now may find the peoples change" [V,ii,267]), but by the same token
the rebel also risks creating pity for a fallen magistrate, as political events in
England were soon to prove. Becoming conscious of the prince's reaction to
him, the Duke remains resolute, confounding cruelty and justice, though
Vasco remarks that the prince's squeamishness reflects popular sentiment
(V,iii,268). As the Duke is about to pronounce sentence, Leonel reveals
himself as the prince of Parma, and now becomes the sole object of the
Duke's resentment, but the Duke relents when the two ambassadors reveal
their true identities, which precipitates the comic conclusion. That the
political argument is bound up with the specular possibilities of the stage
is incoherently sensed by the characters in the low plot, for Vasco now
determines to buy a telescope and study astrology (V,iii,271).

Combining a number of familiar elements from earlier plays, *The Platonick Lovers*, performed in 1636, affectionately spoofs the language of platonic
love associated with the court and with Henrietta Maria. As so clearly in
Love and Honour, the purpose is to advise the King to consult with the
political nation, but more specifically, to respect the customary institutions
of English political life, and above all to respect the rule of law. The prologue implies that the private playhouse allows Davenant a more intimate
connection with the gentry than the public theaters, so that he is satirizing
ideas to which the audience – which includes many women – may subscribe. The self-ironizing tendency of tragicomedy – to which Davenant
explicitly gestures – means that, by anatomizing what Platonism might in
fact mean, the play seeks to use the weight of the audience's knowledge
against itself. Put another way, tragicomedy tends, by juxtaposing them, to
exacerbate the differences among modes of proceeding, whether we think
of them as different genres or different ways of knowing more largely, and
so typically calls into question our unexamined prejudices. At the simplest
level, the play presents two young dukes, Theander and Phylomont, who,
in pursuing each other's sisters (Eurithea and Ariola), imagine their relations with their lovers in largely opposed terms. That they have recently
returned to Sicily after years of campaigning intensifies the question of
how civil institutions will emerge after a hiatus. As lovers, Theander and
Eurithea are the most obvious objects of satire, because, caught up in an ide-
alized, disembodied, and abstract neo-Platonism, they cannot marry or have

children, since these depend – like language or the stage – on mundane and material realities at odds with the transcendental order they prefer. In general, Phylomont approaches the business more realistically, which includes taking into account passion and desire as preconditions to marriage. But the purpose of the play is to bring into alignment the disparate elements of the human experience which, though existing separately in tension, combine to create the institution of marriage we recognize. Davenant expresses sympathy with Charles's (and Laud's) Erastian sentiments, since he clearly understands matrimony as the historical, legal, customary, and sacramental institution visible in the 1559 Book of Common Prayer, bonding the highest with the lowest elements of the human condition, reconciling body, soul, mind, and spirit: holy matrimony is an honorable state expressing first "the mystical union that is betwixt Christ and his Churche." It was instituted for "the procreation of children, to be brought up in the feare and nurtoure of the Lorde," and "was ordained for a remedy agaynste sinne and to avoide fornication." Like the civil order more generally, it distinguishes us from the animals, so we do not approach it lightly, "to satisfye mennes carnall lustes and appetites, like brute beastes that have no understandyng." In short, of all the Christian sacraments, it most fully reconciles in one institution the mystical, the carnal, the legal, and the symbolic.

Davenant heightens the dramatic tension between platonic abstraction and the mundane by introducing additionally three more key characters: the by now familiar lustful satyr–satirist (Fredeline), who embodies the carnal imagination and yet can comment ironically on how other characters behave, so that we are made aware of the conflict of genres that lends the play its dramatic force; the unschooled and illiterate soldier (Gridonel), whose failures as a humanist correspond to his militaristic fear of the feminine; and Buonateste, who combines the values of the classic humanist (the "Philosopher" schooled in Aeschylus, Diodorus Siculus, Gorgias, Empedocles, Euclid, and Archimedes [I,388b]) with the signature of the new Harveian physician, whose potions are the occasion of a physiological "experiment" (I,388b) that Fredeline sets in motion, and which brings about the final reconciliations. Fredeline, desiring Eurithea for himself, fails to participate in the compromises of civil society, as the play imagines it, both because on the one hand his ironic sensibility excludes him from participation, and because on the other his lust betrays his obligations to Theander whose "creature" he is. He serves as one example of a predicament also acted out by the play's interest in physiology, since the disembodied platonic postulate cultivated by Theander is comically unnatural, as well as blind to the legal implications of the carnal aspect of marriage, since having progeny is more a question of inheritance than of breeding ("How!" he cries in reponse to Phylomont's suggestion that he marry Eurithea, "marry her! Your souls are wedded, Sir, I'm sure you would not marry bodies too, that were a needless charge" [II,v,394b]).

On the other hand, Buonateste's potion might simply excuse fornication, so that we are to relish the absurd Harveian effects of the potion on Theander, who reports, "Such fire as this I have not felt before, it burns my heart, my blood runs flaming till my scorched Veins together curle" (II,v,400a–b). Fredeline applauds these lustful effects, but that Buonateste intends something more subtle is revealed by Gridonel's more gracious response to the drug, discovering the feminine, as it were, in the figure of Amadine, Eurithea's woman, the implication being that such assent to a different world signals an admission of the virtues of literacy as such, as well as the mixed constitution embodied in the *détente* between the masculine and feminine orders. Marriage as custom and as legal convention (I,388b) reconciles the inner and outer, spirit and flesh, so that Phylomont comments that "we are forc'd to keep our spirits warm in flesh and blood, must be content to live as other mortals do" (IV,i,403a). Consequently, the action of the play – the different effects of Buonateste's drug on Gridonel, for whom it is benign, on Theander, for whom it is equally benign but only after he has experienced a rush of passion, and Fredeline, whom it puts out of commission – turns the official Platonic language of the Caroline court against itself. Paradoxically, the language of pure Platonism adopted by Theander is a masculine fantasy, unwilling to negotiate with the world, even though in practice it was encouraged by the Queen. The actual Plato, we learn, by contrast to Gridonel, whose illiteracy betokens the state of nature, and Theander, who yearns for an instant pre-linguistic state of communion with his lover (IV,i,403b), defines the literate condition (he is revealed as "An odd Greek fellow that could write and read" [II,i,390b]). And similarly, whereas Gridonel and Theander's fears of language accompany a fear of women as bodies in space and time (I,385b), Plato was quite a womanizer: Buonateste warns the aged counselor Sciolto

not to wrong my good old Friend *Plato*, with this Court calumny; they father on him a fantastick love he never knew, poor Gentleman, upon my knowledge, Sir, about two thousand years ago, in the high street yonder at *Athens*, just by the corner as you pass by *Diana*'s Conduit (a Haberdashers house) it was (I think) he kept a wench. (II,iv,393b)

Davenant means us to notice the scenic setting of Plato's exploits, because, Buonateste avers, one of the consequences of his drug – like Plato's *pharmakon* – is to change the way we see things: our perspective, in short. This is a rhetorical function that language shares with the stage, involving, in Harveian physiology, harmonizing the spirit, flesh, and blood, and in the Aristotelian parallel between the family and state to which Davenant refers, a customary and legal balance of powers among the participants, even if the final arbiter remains the father. Indeed, only the convention of marriage – the "Nuptial Rites" – "doth advance the Husband's Government" (IV,ii,405b). The alternative is embodied in the mute condition either of Gridonel's state of nature or of the Platonic absurdities cultivated by Theander, and more pointedly yet for Davenant's art of the stage, in the figure of Antipheron of Oreus (II,iv,393). Evidently, Antipheron makes his sole appearance in history in Aristotle's *On Memory*. At this juncture, Aristotle is considering how different images or sudden ideas from the past affect us: at 45a, he writes that "from contemplating a mental object in itself, one changes his point of view, and regards it as relative to something else."[41] A powerful exception to this rule is, however, "Antipheron of Oreus and others suffering from mental derangement; for they were accustomed to speak of their images as facts of their past experience, and as if remembering them. This takes place whenever one contemplates what is not a likeness as if it were a likeness."[42] The warning to the dangers of Caroline self-regard could hardly be clearer.

CHAPTER 4

"The Vitruvius of His Age": Inigo Jones, the rhetoric of stage design, and architectural theory

It is my contention that we cannot understand the purposes and aims of the masques Davenant wrote in the 1630s unless we understand the arguments of the plays we have just considered, and unless we understand how Jones viewed his relationship to the tradition of architectural theory beginning with Vitruvius and extending, most importantly, to Alberti, Serlio, and Palladio. This recognition has a bearing on the nature of theater design of the kind that Davenant inherited directly from Jones and later from John Webb, who from 1628 worked closely with Jones on masques and architectural designs, who designed the scenery in *The Siege of Rhodes*, who continued to work on the Restoration stage, who inherited Jones's drawings and designs upon his death, and who naturally expected to succeed Jones in the surveyorship at the Restoration but was twice disappointed when it passed first to John Denham, who was unqualified for the position, and then to Christopher Wren.[1] I think it fair to say that the prevailing historiography on the Jonesian masque almost entirely ignores the probability that Jones's approach to that admittedly unusual theatrical mode was informed not by a neoplatonic iconology, for the purposes of reflecting and amplifying the perfections of Divine Right kingship, but by a classical and Roman conception of public architecture.

The assumption that the protocol of the masques was centrally neo-platonic, a view that has achieved something of an independent life in the scholarship, is of fairly recent invention.[2] It derives in large part from individuals associated with the Warburg Institute – figures like D. J. Gordon, D. P. Walker, and Frances Yates – who after the Second World War sought to emphasize heterodox, occult, and hitherto neglected aspects of Renaissance thought. But though varieties of neo-Platonism were undoubtedly abroad in the seventeenth century, they have little to do with the tradition of architectural theory stemming from Vitruvius, a tradition, as George Kennedy remarks, that, along with rhetoric, represents the only ancient art to achieve a fully fledged second-order discourse about its own conditions of possibility.[3] Thus we are faced with the curious circumstance in which the neoplatonic postulate finds only equivocal, local, and unsystematic expression in early Stuart masque texts, while we must suppress Jones's defining interest in architecture as conceptually prior to masque design if not from his Italian visit at the turn of the century, then certainly from his Italian visit of 1613–14, when he was accompanied by his own copy of Palladio, which, along with his notebook, we possess.[4] On this trip, Jones also met Vincenzo Scamozzi, who famously completed Palladio's design for the Teatro Olimpico in Vicenza, as if to express the Vitruvian point that theater design belongs to a more encompassing idea about architecture as the universal art. (Palladio was himself drawn to architecture partly by seeing a theatrical performance designed by Serlio, which became the germ for Book II of Serlio's *On Architecture*, devoted to perspective and scenography.)[5] It may be tempting to see the elaborate analogy between buildings and the human body as an expression of the neoplatonic correspondence between microcosm and macrocosm, or to presume that architectural criteria of proportion and symmetry must depend on some transcendental order, whether Pythagorean or neoplatonic, but as we have already seen, the somatic metaphor – with its accompanying ideals of proportion and balance – belongs, on the Ciceronian view of things, within an order of expression which is contingent and antifoundationalist, so that in rhetoric *membra* denotes those elements of an utterance which, taken together, result in persuasive – and thus aesthetic – speech.[6] And Aristotle also sees proportion not as dependent on some transcendental category, but as internal to the decorous functioning of language as such.[7] A central criterion is the category *décor*. Palladio makes it clear that the aesthetic effect of a building is local and essentially functional, an idea captured in Isaac Ware's term "commodious." Probably because Vitruvius and Alberti, and to some extent Serlio, have addressed questions of architectural theory quite thoroughly, Palladio only addresses theory briefly at the beginning of *The Four Books of Architecture*, writing:

AN edifice may be deemed commodious, when every part or member stands in its due place and fit situation, neither above or below its dignity or use; or when the *loggia's*, halls, chambers, cellars and granaries are conveniently disposed, and in their proper places. . . BEAUTY will result from the form and correspondence of the whole, with respect to the several parts, of the parts with regard to each other, and of these again to the whole; that the structure may appear an entire and complete body, wherein each member agrees with the other, and all necessary to compose what you intend to form.[8]

This is a functionalism we see in Jones's note in his Roman notebook made on his crucial second visit to Italy: "In all inuencions of C[a]ppresious ornaments on must first designe ye Ground, or ye thing plaine, as yt is for youse, and on that, varry yt, addorne yt, Compose yt wth decorum according to the youse, and ye order yt is of, as in the Cartouses I haue of Tarquino ligustri of Vitterbo."

In his book on the culture of the early Stuart court, however, Vaughan Hart postulates that since, evidently, we know that masques expressed a neoplatonic scheme, then we could detect neoplatonic principles in Jones's architectural designs.[9] The difficulty here is that Vitruvius – writing under and to Augustus in the early Empire – and the Vitruvian tradition are, as Vitruvius' most recent editors have argued, almost entirely Ciceronian in conception, as well as, for identical reasons, also influenced (in Vitruvius' case) by Lucretius.[10] Cicero, Horace, and Quintilian remain the central guides to the great Italian theorists,[11] with Alberti, famously, not only influenced by Cicero as cultural and ethical philosopher, but seeking like a good humanist to emulate his style.[12] (Joseph Rykwert writes, indeed, that "not Vitruvius but Cicero – the Cicero of the legal and rhetorical treatises – is the model to whom Alberti appeals.")[13] The French architectural writer Guillaume Philandrier was not only an acknowledged expert on Quintilian but wrote his treatises along Quintilianic lines.[14] Daniel Barbaro, whose 1567 translation of Vitruvius Jones owned and annotated, wrote dialogues on eloquence and a commentary on Aristotle's *Rhetoric*. And on a broader scale, describing what he calls "the discovery of pictorial composition" in early Renaissance Italy, Michael Baxandall argues, in *Giotto and the Orators*, that the plastic arts developed a language for their own methods and techniques only by appropriating Ciceronian categories originally meant to be applied to the fashioning and interpretation of speeches.[15] These facts betoken an epistemological position almost diametrically opposed to the mysteries supposedly revealed by neoplatonic emblematology, in which the obscurities of this world and the complexities of mediation vanish at the masque's climax, when the magic of Jones's stage machinery could simultaneously banish all figures of misrule, purging the last echoes of the antimasque, and by inviting the King or Queen (or both) to step into the action and exercise rule over chaos and discord.[16] Readings of the masques along these lines, one might remark, enact the properties of new-critical forms of reading, where the organic nature of the text as a whole is capable of absorbing any number of ironies and ambiguities into its formal action. It is unsurprising that this view of the masques has difficulty distinguishing between literature and outright propaganda, because it allows little room for the idea that the masque might – as I am arguing royalists invariably did – seek as much to advise the King as to celebrate his prerogatives, though it is fair to say that Orgel does allow for a certain exemplary effect in the hyperbolic praise lavished on the monarch. (Thus Jones responds to De L'Orme's adage that *"L'architecte devoir conseiller fidelement aux seigneurs."*)[17] Whether this is a proper assessment of masques prior to Jonson and Jones's altercation in 1631, I would argue – with the sole exception of *Luminalia,* which is piously conventional and addressed in any case to the Queen, not the King – that this fails to account for the rhetorical aims and conditions of the masques that followed, including *Coelum Britannicum.*

The reflection theory of representation embedded in the neoplatonic approach to the masques is thus contradicted by the intellectual and literary culture to which architectural theory belonged and to which it very substantially contributed. In the Vitruvian conception of the human order, buildings – which always expressly include theaters as one of the most civically important forms of public architecture[18] – are exactly like good speeches, made with matters of place, time, and circumstance in mind, and performing a rhetorical action designed to express and foster our deepest civic ambitions for ourselves and for our community.[19] Thus for Jones, architecture, like rhetoric, is best represented by the flexible abstractions of philosophy and the contingencies of equity, both expressed by the principles of eurythmia in architectural design, which is always local and fungible, as opposed, on the one hand, to the literalism of the grammarian, or on the other to the narrow prescriptions of law or "justice," involving a mechanical application of "proportion" to the plastic arts.[20] Even Plato, he remarks elsewhere, "saw ye soul of ye world to be not simpell nor vniforme," commenting further that though there is something heavenly about harmony, "no sort of harmony hath in it any absolute proprietye."[21] In fact, more than rhetoric – that other civilizing art – architecture represents the most material means for making and sustaining human societies that we can imagine. This may explain one cause, quite apart from matters of personality, for the rift between Jonson and Jones. For Vitruvius, it is architecture, not only the arts of speech, that most fully realizes the ends of *paideia* or a liberal education, since, as his most recent editors write, not only was a liberal education the essential Roman prelude to the study of law and rhetoric, but that conceptually, "the field of 'architecture' covers the entire built and mechanical environment and is an art of great complexity and one of the most essential of the arts of social humanity."[22] (Thus Henry Wotton at the end of his treatise on architecture, writing in 1624, plans also

"*A Philosophicall Survey of Education*, which is indeed a second *Building*, or repairing of Nature, and, as I may tearme it, a kinde of *Morall Architecture*.")[23]

Another way to think of it is that two media compose the human experience as such: language, which is the province of rhetoric, and the spatial environment, which even more obviously defines us as social animals, the province of architecture. Alberti could hardly be clearer on this point: "the security, dignity, and honor of the republic depend greatly on the architect: it is he who is responsible for our delight, entertainment, and health while at leisure, and our profit and advantage while at work, and in short, that we live in a dignified manner, free from any danger"; and later, "Everyone relies on the city and all the public services that it contains. If we have concluded rightly, from what the philosophers say, that cities owe their origin and their existence to their enabling their inhabitants to enjoy a peaceful life, as free from any inconveniences or harm as possible, then surely the most thorough consideration should be given to the city's layout, site, and outline."[24] For Palladio, correspondingly, "the counterpart to the virtuous architect was a barbarian."[25] And in his notes to Palladio, Jones writes, "The Citti a great house and ye house a littell Cittye."[26]

Either medium (language or architecture) on its own effectively saturates the human consciousness, which is why for Cicero and Vitruvius, writing in a knowingly Ciceronian vein, words and buildings constitute the human as such, since both present worlds that – rather than merely reflecting them – define and direct people's aspirations in such a way as to make the orator and architect equally kinds of social engineer, with ethical and civic responsibilities to match. Because – like the natural world and our bodies, the instruments of our apprehension of things – language and architecture both enfold and channel our energies, Vitruvius' appropriation of Lucretius is both apt and long-lived: just as for Lucretius, the cosmos is made up of atoms and void, so, he argues, we see the analogy to language, a dense fabric of meaning woven from a range of elements or letters, as well as to architecture, which permits an almost endless combination of materials and styles; so that it is almost inevitable that the cosmos itself is then imagined as a complex articulated fabric like a building.[27] These sets of mutually enforcing analogies also find expression in the Vitruvian argument – elaborated at length by Alberti and Serlio – that a building is a kind of body, and that because our most intimate experiences of the world are mediated primarily through our bodies, proportions in buildings should correspond to the proportions of the human body;[28] and that respecting those proportions is part of the architect's concern with health, also expressed in the proper selection of building sites. In his notes to Scamozzi, Jones encourages the architect to "Immitat nature in the boddy of a man," and remarks that "stairs [are] compard to the vaines in the boddy"; while in response to Vitruvius, he writes that "the boddi of man well proporsioned is the patern for proportion in buildings"; and later that "Ye boddy of man cause of perfection in the arts."[29] In his Alberti, Jones sees an "Edifice as an Animall."[30] The somatic metaphor – almost obsessively reworked by Alberti, for example[31] – allows for thinking about buildings both as structures and as themselves capable of imparting and sustaining our physical well-being, which itself corresponds to the ancient analogy between rhetoric and medicine.[32]

Furthermore, as Alina Payne shows, the relationship between texts and buildings, in which verbal compositions enact or model the ideal building, becomes a central *topos* in the Italian treatises, aware as they are of their own standing as printed artifacts. Payne argues for the increasing self-consciousness of architectural theory *as theory* by virtue of its capacity to scrutinize its prescriptions for building through the textual model embodied in the printed treatise, so that in the mere act of reading, the reader can reflect on the architectural principles being discussed.[33] Medieval guilds associated with Gothic architecture had been congeries of workmen who shared their knowledge orally and secretively;[34] whereas, because they are printed, neoclassical treatises project the implications of architecture into the public realm. Commenting on his own Latin style, Alberti expands his rhetorical and textual interests into the architectural subject of his treatise, recalling "the three conditions that apply to every form of construction – that what we construct should be appropriate to its use, lasting in structure, and graceful and pleasing in appearance."[35] It almost follows that when Jones created designs for rebuilding the Strand front of Somerset House, contemporary accounts referred to the façades as "frontispieces."[36]

Because architecture is a spatially encompassing and consequently a cognitively – and thus ethically – defining discipline, it is unsurprising that Marco Frascari can, on the one hand, argue that Scamozzi's text itself comprises what he calls an "imaginal" theater;[37] and that Robert Tavernor can, on the other, argue that the new printing and the new scientific conditions of the sixteenth century mean that Palladio's architectural imagination parallels Vesalius' finely etched illustrations in his medical treatises[38] (see figure 7). Those illustrations reveal the body as a kind of architectural space, which, like the theater more than any other kind of public edifice, comprises an arena within which human experience is not only represented but constituted, an apt expression of what we might call the

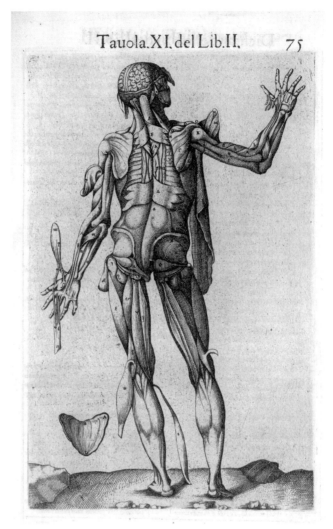

Figure 7: Diagram from Vesalius

phenomenological grounds of humanist rhetoric. Like our bodies which provide a kind of envelope from within which we register our experiences, the richly symbolic world of speech or of buildings constitutes our apprehension of the world at large. Thus the frontispiece to Scamozzi's treatise, which we can imagine as a portal or gateway, warns "Let no one enter here without knowledge of the liberal arts,"[39] to underscore the hermeneutic burden of embarking on the architectural enterprise. Echoing Vesalius' drawings, the cut-away representations of buildings in Palladio emphasize our experience of their internal as much as their external space, as if they were bodies dissected for our edification; so that Davenant coolly refers to the human body as "our fleshy building."[40] As Payne argues, the close relation between architecture and rhetoric is constantly rehearsed in the analogy that links buildings, bodies, and texts.[41] This connection is, one might remark, materially expressed in neoclassical designs for anatomy theaters, as well as in the fact that, in the process of becoming the greatest English architect, beginning with the Sheldonian theater, which was reputedly designed for "the dissection of bodies, and acting of plays," Wren also designed diagrams for important medical treatises in the Restoration.[42]

If buildings reflect the cosmos, the human body, and texts, then two principles central to Jones's understanding of himself as architect follow. These are, first, expressing the variety of nature and the complexity of the human form, buildings are made from a huge number and kinds of material. Second, reflecting the role of language, each element that the architect chooses for a given building contributes its own semantic weight to the total combined effect, whether we think of those elements as Lucretian atoms or the four Pythagorean elements.[43] (Thus Vitruvius more or less begins the *Ten Books* by reminding the budding architect of the distinction between signifier and signified, since the reader is being introduced to a universe of signifiers.)[44] Further, because at any given moment many and different such elements present themselves, the architect, like the orator, selects according to the principle of decorum. A building should suit the time and place in which it is built, and should comment on its prime function, as well as the social status and aspirations of its patrons or owners.[45] These architectural elements are physical and material manifestations of a function already fully expounded in the characters of style: though contributing meaningfully to the whole, each still retains something of its original symbolic distinctness, so that the analytico-compositive unity that results does not militate against a productive competition among styles. This representational and rhetorical economy is epitomized in Alberti's notion of compartition – the architectural equivalent of *partitio* – which he defines as follows: "Compartition is the process of dividing up the site into yet smaller units, so that the building may be considered as made up of close-fitting smaller buildings, joined together like members of the whole body."[46] Because those elements already represent very precise symbolic values, the architect thus serves as the most plastic kind of rhetorician, seeking in his edifice not blandly to reflect its temporal, physical, and social circumstances, but to comment on them for ethical and civil purposes. Payne writes that Alberti's views "are deeply embedded in social and political convictions of civic rectitude and consciousness on the part of all patrons and consequently in an understanding of architecture as a social and political act that both demonstrates and facilitates the harmony necessary to the well-being and prosperity of the state."[47]

It seems therefore that what is at stake between Jonson and Jones is not so much invention *per se*, but what invention signifies, namely the different senses in which the poet and the architect could claim to be true rhetoricians. Thus, whatever role neo-Platonism may have played in Jonson's conception of things, *Neptune's Triumph for the Return of Albion* (1624), juxtaposing the claims of a Cook and a Poet, clearly refers to Plato's attack on demagoguery in the *Gorgias*. Thus Jonson begs the question, which the masque does not – indeed cannot – resolve, about the extent to which the poet can distinguish himself from the orator. The process of invention is not formal and fixed, but pragmatic and contingent; so that because it is a diagnostic, strategic, and rhetorical mode, the embarrassing fact is that poet and architect must invent, that is, determine, what conceptual categories or *topoi* best fit the specific arguments required by the circumstance each faces, from within completely different media and traditions. It is not only Jonson who expresses discomfort at the resulting competition or misalliance, but, as early as 1610, Samuel Daniel, who in *Tethys' Festival* indulges in a backhand compliment to Jones, on the view that masque design is less substantive than writing: "But in these things whereof the only life consists in show, the art and invention of the architect gives the greatest grace, and is of most importance, ours of the least part and of least note in the time of the performance thereof; and therefore I have interserted the description of the artificial part, which speaks Master Inigo Jones."[48]

In accusing Jones of artifice – and so camouflaging the similar artifice of the dramatist – Daniel exploits the ambiguity in definitions of invention on which all scholars comment. But architectural theory shows how, for writer and designer alike, invention (discovering appropriate categories) and imitation (employing appropriate styles and materials for the occasion) are two sides of the same coin.[49] As expounded by Quintilian, stasis theory, for example, shows how in legal cases the theory can help the lawyer taxonomize the main issues under debate; but that faculty also points the pleader not only to the proper conceptual categories, but to the best examples, precedents, and styles for this particular case.[50] Thus, as G. W. Pigman and Thomas M. Greene have by now definitively demonstrated, humanist conceptions of imitation represented a highly flexible and imaginative approach to the cultural tradition of which any writer is inevitably part, and which he can only seek in vain to escape.[51] Rather than imitation representing the sterility of Roman culture represented both by Kitto and Kennedy, Vitruvius anticipates figures like Erasmus in seeing Ciceronianism not mechanically – the object of slavish stylistic imitation – but as a profound expression of the creative tensions inhabiting the difference between tradition and innovation.[52] Invention and imitation thus denote a combined discipline producing often surprising effects. Thus Vitruvius writes, "invention is the unraveling of obscure problems, arriving through energetic flexibility, at a new set of principles"; Serlio comments further by writing that "Diversity of invention sometimes leads the architect to conceive things which he would perhaps never have imagined"; and, because the elements with which the true architect juggles are products of the tradition, Alberti reveals the proximity of invention to imitation when he declares,

All the power of invention, all the skill and experience in the art of building, are called upon in compartition; compartition alone divides up the whole building into the parts by which it is articulated, and integrates its every part by composing all the lines and angles into a single, harmonious work that respects utility, dignity, and delight.[53]

Finally, Scamozzi's chapter on invention (I,I,XIV) provokes a flurry of annotations from Jones, revealing precisely Jones's understanding of the dynamic relations between invention and imitation, and the degree to which the combined sum of effects in a given building expresses a modular notion of design.

The orator invents both by reference to language as such, to the topics, and finally by reference to the characters of style, the distinctions among which were formalized by Theophrastus and only fully expounded by Cicero. In architecture, the key elements are the raw materials from which a building is composed and the symbolic distinctions among the five orders of architecture, representing the total sum of ancient styles anthologized in the Roman ruins: the three Greek orders which predominated in Vitruvius (Doric, Ionic, Corinthian, in order of complexity), and then the two Roman or Italic orders, the Tuscan (the simplest) and the Composite (the most complex), which were only fully formalized by Serlio.[54] Thus, inheriting and taxonomizing a fully formed tradition from which to imitate, the first book of Palladio's *The Four Books of Architecture* begins by discussing the raw materials of building – timber, stones, sand, lime, metals – and then rapidly proceeds to discussing the distinctions among the five orders.

Given the charged atmosphere of the Jonson–Jones debate, the nature of Jones's relationship to the great architectural treatises is significant, since it indicates not only his general attitude to invention and imitation, but how far the treatises must have provided him with the essentials of his own designs, as well as the extent to which we should read those designs rhetorically. Orrell in particular implies that the chief architectural influence on Jones as a designer of masques and theaters was Book II of Serlio's *On Architecture*, because, reflecting Serlio's own theatrical experience, it concludes with a famous essay on stage scenery, including the well-known woodcuts representing the comic, the tragic, and the satyric scenes.[55] What very substantial evidence of Jones's relationship to architectural theory we do possess, however, demonstrates that his relationship to architecture was much more complicated than such a preliminary picture suggests. Quite apart from the Roman notebook, a very rich source now at Chatsworth, he owned and obsessively annotated his personal Italian copy of Vitruvius (in a translation by Barbaro with illustrations by Palladio); an illustrated Italian translation of Alberti (1565); the first three books of the 1600 and the full seven books of the 1619 Italian editions of Serlio; his own copy of Palladio – an edition of 1601 which supplies an anthology of Jones's thinking about architecture and architectural theory especially from 1614 on; the 1567 edition of De L'Orme; and the 1615 edition of Scamozzi's *L'Idea della Architettura*. He also owned but did not annotate the 1617 edition of Vignola. (He frequently annotated his select but substantial library.)[56] His annotations to both his copies of Serlio show very little interest in Book II. Rather, his approach to Serlio – whose frontispiece to Book III includes the motto *"Roma Quanta Fuit Ipsa Ruina Docet"* – reveals a consistent interest in seeing his manuals as (like the Roman ruins) a storehouse of architectural *topoi*, to be imitated, combined, and refashioned, just as the orator – to whom Alberti explicitly compares the architect[57]–invents and imitates to create a persuasive speech (see figure 8). Hard evidence of Serlio as a rich repository of an architectural vocabulary appears in his 1619 edition, now at the Royal Institute of British Architects. Book III – describing the antiquities in detail – is extensively annotated. There are many implications in what catches Jones's eye, but a crucial moment occurs when, in contemplating mixed architectural forms, Serlio describes a simple arch. At this point, as so often in his annotations to Palladio, Jones feels compelled to remark, "to bee imitated."[58]

That Jones here adopts the language of imitation speaks worlds. For it reveals how far for him architecture was indeed a rhetorical art in its own right. (In his comments on Vitruvius, Jones notes the "Comparrason

Figure 8: Frontispiece to Book III of Serlio, *On Architecture*

betweene the orator & the Architect," and expresses his approval of the translation: "An exelent comparason of Barbaro consirne the Ourator and the architect.")[59] Given the history of the development of the five orders, this should not come as a surprise. For beginning in the ancient world, by the seventeenth century each order had become infused with an elaborate set of symbolic meanings to distinguish it from the other orders, meanings whose purpose was essentially a form of cultural commentary. Over time and in different contexts these meanings had become both richer and more varied, in such a way that Jones had at his disposal an immense arsenal of possibilities. There are some basic distinctions among the five orders, beginning with the obvious physical differences, which in turn supply different ways of representing distinct cultural histories, stances, styles, and values.[60] Thus, as we can see from the famous illustration in Serlio, the Tuscan, on one end of the scale, is squat, plain, and unornamented, whereas the Corinthian and Composite orders, on the other end, are more slender, elaborate, and more highly decorated, the Corinthian with acanthus leaves, a feature explained by an elaborate myth. This opposition in styles is echoed in the simpler Greek orders between the Doric – the plainer – and the Ionic – the more elaborate. Second, the shift from the Tuscan to the Doric also represents a shift in building materials from wood – the most primitive medium – to stone; so that although Tuscan, as we shall see, becomes an established masonry style, Tuscan designs were supposed still to remind the onlooker of wooden forms. (As the reader can see, the modern St. Paul's, Covent Garden, Jones's most systematic essay in the Tuscan, uses a mixture of wood and masonry.) (See figure 9.)

Third, whereas the Tuscan, and to some extent the Doric, represented solid and masculine forms of civilization, the Corinthian in particular represented more sophisticated, refined, and feminine forms, a gendering of the historical process.[61] This distinctive form of architectural prosopopoeia is most concretely expressed by the substitutions of human figures for columns to support the entablature: in the case of the male form, known as *atlantes*, the most famous example being the Greek temple of Zeus, Agrigento, Sicily; and in the case of the female form, *caryatides*, the most famous example being the Erechtheion on the Acropolis.[62]

Fourth, the analogy between architecture and rhetoric had already developed in Vitruvius a correspondence between the architectural orders and the characters of style,[63] an idea also expanded in Alberti's notion that his own textual style, modeled on Cicero, had an exact architectural equivalent.[64] Tacitus is a most vivid example of the alliance between the Ciceronian and Vitruvian conceptions. His *Dialogue on Oratory* represents the changing fortunes of rhetoric since the Augustan period in terms of architectural styles: defending the moderns, Aper denies that "the temples of the present day are weaker, because, instead of being built of rough blocks and ill-shaped tiles, they shine with marble and glitter with gold."[65] All Tacitus' interlocutors seem to agree that Cicero represents a benchmark, but Aper expresses his preference for the mature and polished Cicero by recourse to the by now familiar physiological and architectural metaphors. "Style," he declares, "like the human body, is . . . specially beautiful when, so to say,

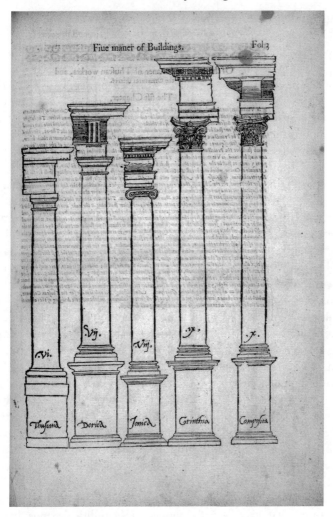

Figure 9: Serlio's diagram of the five orders of architecture

the veins are not prominent, and the bones cannot be counted, but when a healthy and sound blood fills the limbs, and shows itself in the muscles, and the very sinews become beautiful under a ruddy glow and graceful outline." Whereas Cicero's later accomplishments are graceful structures, his early attempts are rough-hewn: "There is nothing which you can pick out or quote, and the style is like a rough building, the wall of which indeed is strong and lasting, but not particularly polished and bright."[66]

Unsurprisingly, the most basic opposition between the prime Greek orders – the Doric and Ionic – corresponds neatly to the fabled distinction between Attic and Asiatic oratorical modes, with the additional connection being that the plainer and more disciplined mode in both cases is associated with the Peloponnese, while the more florid is associated with Asia Minor.[67] Indeed, in his annotations to Palladio, Jones habitually speaks of the Doric style as "attic." And since the organization and distribution of styles is always a matter of aptness and decorum,[68] the different orders of architecture denote different classes in society, or, as Onians puts it, a "material means of expression for communities, groups, and individuals."[69]

Ciceronian criteria of *ornatus* and *aptus* explain, first, that actual buildings are, like well-fashioned speeches, composed of the different styles available to the architect, as if to an orator; and, second, that architectural practice involves a highly flexible "modular system," involving an "awareness of a shared assemblage strategy" or "the combinatory potential of ornament," so that buildings can respond properly to the contingencies of place, time, and circumstance.[70] Alberti makes it clear that the distribution of elements in a building – whether by this we mean the different orders or different materials – will reflect and comment on geography and the political lives of the inhabitants.[71] It is important therefore that each element be distinct, lending to the completed edifice its own special range of meanings; and it is equally important that the ultimate combination of effects, like the well-made sentence, producing the final proposition, as it were, retain its own syntactical integrity. These are the two core principles of architectural design for Jones, for whom the Tuscan and rustic modes were particularly important, and yet for whom the combinations or juxtapositions of elements or orders were equally significant. For him, to imitate was to select from a range of architectural possibilities – like those best represented in Book III of Serlio – to speak to his own age.

Tuscan is of particular interest in this context, because it represents a cultural mode that was especially charged in the political atmosphere of the early seventeenth century. The meaning of the Tuscan becomes increasingly refined in roughly three stages. Though Vitruvius does not elaborate on the Tuscan or Composite orders, the Augustans saw Tuscan as a primitive form related on the one hand to the rustic mode, and on the other to the plain Doric, though it represents a further simplification of the Doric because the columns were never fluted. The vernacular aura of the Tuscan encouraged the idea that it epitomized the simplicity and ruggedness of early Roman republicanism. Tuscan and Doric were thus linked to the specifically Roman virtues of Stoicism, whose central values were *virtus* and *gravitas*, values recommended in Cicero's *De Officiis*.[72] Tuscan also harked back to even more primitive and originary times because it also recalled the Etruscans.[73]

All these ancient values were reworked by the Italian theorists, who added further features to the Roman story and used the Tuscan as their own way of recommending the virtues of the Italian vernacular. Thus because ancient Roman republicanism was associated with the virtue of political freedom, Tuscan, according to Serlio, was the order presented by town walls to repel potential invaders from the outside, thus executing a function that, in rhetoric, corresponds exactly to the deliberative, in which the orator animates his audience to defend the state. Moreover, Serlio treated rustication as such as an expression of political freedom because "country life was always thought to offer a greater opportunity for freedom."[74] The Tuscan order also became a means for the early Italian humanists – figures like Dante, Petrarch, and Boccaccio, whose native Italian was the Tuscan dialect – to legitimate the vernacular. Brunelleschi explicitly related the development of a Tuscan architectural style to Tuscan as a language;[75] and Alberti's nationalism was expressed in the fact that he was the first to write an Italian grammar, and that for him the two "Roman" orders – Tuscan and Composite – should be spoken of as Italic or Italian.[76] Cosimo Bartoli's translation of Alberti – which Jones owned – advertises itself as a translation into "Florentine," that is, Tuscan speech. Given the prevailing Ciceronianism of these foundational humanist figures, it is virtually predictable that they parsed Cicero's republican leanings in stylistic terms, holding that "Doric . . . in terms of Ciceronian morality, would be the highest of the orders and Corinthian the lowest, in complete opposition to established opinion."[77]

In a resonant passage, discussing the Roman relationship to the Tuscan, Joseph Rykwert writes, "To the Romans the Etruscans had seemed an unusually pious people: their antiquities were accordingly considered venerable, so that both 'Etruscan' and 'Tuscan' were extended to mean native and ancient generally, rather than specifically Etruscan. That more general sense may well be what Vitruvius meant by his *Tuscanicae dispositiones*: ancient, venerable, native ways of arranging things."[78] This language inadvertently but happily recalls the increasing tensions in the early seventeenth-century constitutional debates which we examined in Chapter One. On the one hand we see the – mythically – native, customary, vernacular habits embodied in the common law, associated with the Gothic tribes (after Tacitus) or with the Romano-Celtic aura surrounding Arthur, an idea appropriated by the Tudors to legitimate their Welsh ancestry, as well as the pre-Norman piety associated with Edward the Confessor. On the other, we have an increasing solidification of assertions of royal prerogative, which, recursively at least, and partly because they were associated with civil (that is, Scottish Roman) law, were interpreted to conflict with the vernacular principles and habits of the common law.

That, for the English, Tuscan could invoke Romano-Celtic and thus pre-Norman values is strongly suggested by the first English architectural treatise to appear, John Shute's *The First and Chief Groundes of Architecture* (1563), dedicated to the Queen. Like Vignola's *Rule of the Five Orders of Architecture*, published only a year before, and possibly the single most reprinted architectural treatise ever issued, Shute's book focuses almost exclusively on the differences among the five orders, accompanied by some astonishingly detailed engravings. (See figures 10–14.) Each order is advertised by a kind of frontispiece, representing the order both in columnar form and in relation to the appropriate *atlantes* (for Tuscan and Doric) or *caryatides* (for Ionic, Corinthian, and Composite). Inspired in particular by Vitruvius, Serlio, and Philandre, Shute repeats the truism that architecture is the most universal liberal art, beginning his treatise with reference to Cicero's *De Officiis* and arguing that since architectural theory in England is in its infancy, readers should first and foremost become acquainted with the five orders, for Shute the essential elements in architectural design.[79] That Tuscan is the most elemental order is argued by its association with Atlas (Doric, says Shute, is associated with Hercules, Ionic with Diana or Apollo, Corinthian with Vesta, and Composite with Pandora).[80] Atlas, one of the Titans, originally guarded the pillars of heaven, but later held the sky up himself. In Plato, he becomes linked with kingship, so that Shute can translate the cosmically primal idea of Atlas into a myth of primitive English kingship, for, Hart writes, Shute's personification of Tuscan shows a Romano-Celtic figure who evokes the Arthurian tradition generally, but more specifically serves to remind the reader of Brutus, after whom Britain is named.[81]

Tuscan – and the related motif of the rustic – thus serves to remind the onlooker of the grounds of civilization and of the foundations of royal legitimacy. But the other "Roman" or "Italic" order creates similar rhetorical effects in different ways. The Composite is the architectural expression of Ciceronian *ornatus* or *copia*, since it mixes aspects of the other orders for local purposes. (In this case, however, mixtures of effects had also a technical explanation, originating, according to Alberti, in developments in engineering, since the Romans learned how to combine wood and masonry structures.)[82] Like that principle, the mixed forms that result express the

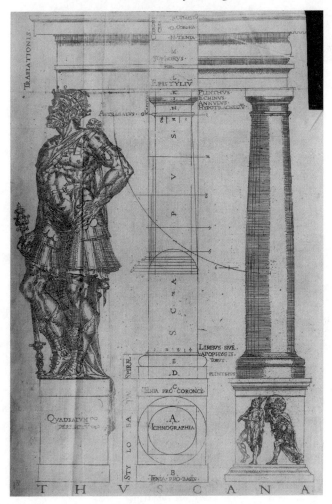

Figure 10: Representation of the Tuscan order from Shute's *The First and Chief Groundes of Architecture* (1563)

cosmopolitanism of the Roman imagination, the hybrid nature of Italian identity, echoing the geographical balance of Italy between north and south, a freedom of invention or *licentia* that echoes the liberty implied in that climatic image, producing in Alberti (echoing Cicero) a theory of the balanced or mixed nature of the Roman constitution.[83] So just as for Dryden mixed plots in drama are endemic to the English character, so mixed architectural forms epitomize the Roman sense of self. Vitruvius compares the

Figure 11: Representation of the Doric order from Shute's *The First and Chief Groundes of Architecture* (1563)

internal balances in the cosmos with the balances among different kinds of Italian, and so implicitly with balances within the state of the kind that causes Alberti to remark that just as there are "different parts of the state," so "each should be designated a different type of building."[84]

Since theaters are integral to public architecture, mixed modes partly derive from dramatic conventions and are exemplified in actual theaters.[85] Writing of the cube as a unit of design, Vitruvius says that "The Greek comic poets divided up the space of their plays by inserting a song by the chorus; defining the parts of the play by the principle of the cube they relieve the

Figure 12: Representation of the Ionic order from Shute's *The First and Chief Groundes of Architecture* (1563)

actors' speeches with these intervals."[86] Anticipating Serlio's division of the theatrical scene into tragic, comic, and satyric modes, he emphasizes that "Their ornamentation is unlike, and conceived on different principles."[87] And from Vitruvius on, the Theater of Marcellus – Wren's inspiration for the Sheldonian – is often cited as the classic example of the mixture of Doric and Ionic: in Vitruvius this represented the different social classes that made up the Roman audience.[88]

I would argue, then, that since the principles governing architectural design are humanistic and Ciceronian, they do not serve as outright forms of royal panegyric. The orator might support the magistrate, but his chief

Figure 13: Representation of the Corinthian order from Shute's *The First and Chief Groundes of Architecture* (1563)

duty to the body politic is to counsel him. When the early Stuarts were confronted by designs that incorporated the orders (or different genres) while presenting them in an articulated way, the architect was indicating that the monarch's powers were legitimate because they confirmed the ancient pedigree of the English royal house. But by the same token, by employing Tuscan and rustic motifs in particular, he was reminding the King of the customary and native traditions – epitomized in the common law – to which neither James nor (especially) Charles was fully sensitive or responsive. As we have seen, in the course of the century, royalists were increasingly enamored of the idea of the mixed constitution. This argument

Figure 14: Representation of the Composite order from Shute's *The First and Chief Groundes of Architecture* (1563)

had particular resonance in a climate where James was at loggerheads with Coke, and Charles decided to rule without summoning parliament. For this reason alone, it is a mistake to interpret Jones's neo-Palladianism as an admiring reflection of Divine Right. As Ackerman says, Palladianism migrated north because it was a style that suited the Protestant temper of northern Italy and was associated with country values, while Michelangelo was favored further south.[89]

A striking material expression of this entire architectural conception is embodied in the Tower of the Orders, in the Schools Quadrangle, Oxford. Resurfaced between 1613 and 1624, it plays on the five orders, placing Tuscan

at the base, and Composite at the summit. Hart correctly suggests that
the tower, providing an important gateway to the Bodleian library, serves
a didactic and mnemonic function for scholars, enacting as it does the
development of civilization from "rustic nobility to licentiousness."[90] The
benefits of this Augustan story are clearly meant to celebrate James I, who
appears in a niche between the Corinthian columns. But given the meanings
that the Vitruvian tradition had projected onto Tuscan and Doric, the
design must also have served to remind the King that his power depended
on a respect for custom and the vernacular. [See figure 15]

INIGO JONES, THE RUSTIC, AND THE TUSCAN ORDER

Because they must focus on matters of stage design, theater historians
naturally concentrate on Jones's experience in Vicenza in 1614, when he saw
the Teatro Olimpico, and on his response to Book II of Serlio's *Architettura*,
which discusses perspective and scenography. But those interests are rarely
interpreted in the larger framework of architectural theory as a whole, with
which Jones's library and notebooks demonstrate he was almost obsessed.
When we are looking for evidence of Jones's thinking about architecture
as such in the masques, Orgel and Strong's catalogue of all Jones's designs
for masques is revealing. First, probably for entirely accidental reasons,
the overwhelming number of designs are for costumes, and prior to about
1610 there are very few surviving scene designs of any kind. Thereafter,
there seem to be four related developments: the number of scene designs
proliferates; well over half involve architectural subjects (I count at least
twenty-nine); there is a stylistic shift from a fantastic and Gothic mode in
a distinctly neoclassical direction, so that at points we become conscious
both of the contrast of styles and their curious interdependence; and, as
a number of scholars comment, after 1609 the quality of draftsmanship
noticeably improves, truly maturing in the wake of his Italian visit of 1613–
14.[91] Thus Higgott argues that Jones's relation to scenic design achieved
greater discipline and coherence at the very time when he began his career as
a full-scale architect, involving a great advance both in Jones's practical grasp
of architecture and in his sophistication about architectural theory: most
historians see his design for the Queen's House, Greenwich as his first major
commission, beginning in 1616. (Higgott writes that "the Queen's House
has been recognized as the fount of the classical tradition in Britain.")[92] But
when we focus on the masques alone, given the fantastic quality of some
scene designs and the apparently casual nature of some of the architectural
designs – in which the default order seems to be the Ionic – there seems at

Figure 15: The tower of the orders, Schools Quadrangle, Oxford

first no clear expression of Jones's approach to the different orders, or any clear line of development.

Harris and Higgott show in detail, however, that the transformation in Jones as architect is profoundly connected with a heightened sensitivity to the orders, and a new appreciation of the importance of rustication, and of the Tuscan and Doric. This alone explains the significance of the single most requoted theoretical statement by Jones, in which Jones recommends a solid and masculine style in public architecture. Scholars often assume that Jones is advertising his shift to the neoclassical mode in general; but I think there is plenty of evidence that he has in mind, for ideological reasons, a preference for the vernacular and primitive orders over the later and more refined, or at least designs that are "mixed" in such a way as to show the debt of the latter to the former. This is a preference that, in the case of rustication, finds its way into building and masque designs, and in the case of Tuscan, informs his most ambitious town-planning scheme, as well as his final theoretical excursus, *Stoneheng Restored*, published posthumously by John Webb in 1655. I believe that as regards masques, these distinctions become somewhat clearer in the 1630s, when, as we will see, Davenant explicitly uses architectural motifs as part of the argument.

I believe, indeed, that the Roman notebook, combined with the annotations to Palladio, reveals that Jones experienced an imaginative and intellectual revolution in January 1614. As the designs to the masques suggest, hitherto, although Jones seems to have known the architectural theorists, his taste remained eclectic, mannerist, and even Gothic in inclination. In the late winter of 1614, while on tour in Italy, five changes seem to have occurred simultaneously, all of which are confirmed by Jones's annotations to the other major theorists, some of which could only have been acquired after 1614, and some of which include dates that suggest that Jones embarked on a binge which amplified and solidified the effects of his epiphany (in his Alberti, Jones writes, "16 July 1615!")[93]: there is a new discipline both in his approach to architecture and his draftsmanship; he seems to have clarified his view that architecture as a centrally civilizing activity is distinctively Roman and Augustan; he shows a remarkable interest in the way different styles express or are apt for different social classes (a more Roman than Greek conception of decorum); he shows a minute interest in different building materials; and his approach is infused with a respect for the distinctions among the orders.

All these changes inform the entire posture of the Roman notebook, beginning with the opening few pages, dated Tuesday 24 January 1614.[94] Here Jones comments on "The manner Of D[r]apery all antica," showing how different social classes in Roman society dressed differently, ranging from women, to consuls, to senators, to some deities, to common soldiers. Behind this interest lies a distinctively Roman and Horatian criterion of stylistic decorum, framed by the more general idea, expressed in Jones's Scamozzi, that "Architecture [is] but beginning in Augustus time."[95] This implicitly cosmopolitan and mixed approach to the ideological implications of style occurs within the context of a series of recognitions which have found expression the previous week, on 19 and 20 January, though historians are apt only to cite a few lines from Jones's notes made on the 20th. Part of the problem is that Jones, like so many artists with a sketchbook, flips around rather randomly, so that later entries often precede the earlier. That this is an artist's sketchbook has received inadequate attention, because we must begin here if we are to appreciate the full nature of the conceptual revolution we are witnessing. The entire sketchbook is filled with drawings of heads, limbs, torsos, lips, noses, and eyes with a few partial full-figure drawings. This in turn stimulates the biometric analogy between bodies and buildings, so that Jones is moved on 19 January to write,

As in designe first on Sttudies the parts of the boddy of man as Eyes, noses mouths ears and so of the rest to bee practicke in the parts sepperat can on comm to put them toggathear to make a hole figgure and cloath yt and consequently a hoole story with all [. . .] ornaments

So in Architecture on must studdy the Parts as logias Entranses Haales chambers staires doures windowes and then adorrne them with colloms.

That these primary elements of building also include the different orders is indicated by Jones's criticism – dated 20 January 1614 – of Michelangelo's licentious designs, which also implicitly distinguishes the northern Italian "Protestant" feel of Palladianism from its Catholic, southern competitor: "to saie trew all thes Composed ornamentes the wch Proceed out of ye aboundance of dessignes, and wear brought in by Mihill Angell and his followers, in my oppignion do not do well in sollid Architecture." And the statement concludes with an emphasis on the public – that is, rhetorical – face of architecture, again amplifying the virtues of solidity:

for as outwardly euery wyse ma[n] carrieth a grauiti in Publick Places, whear ther is nothing els looked for, & yt inwardly hath his Immginacy set free, and sometimes flying out, as nature hirself doeth often tymes Srauagantly, to delight, amase us sumtimes moufe us to laughter, Sumetimes to Contemplatio[n] and horror, So in architecture ye outward ornaments oft to be Sollid, proporsionable according to the rulles, masculine and unaffected

whears, within the Cimeras used by the ansientes the[y] varied and Compoced ornamentes both of the house yt Sealf and the mouables within yt ar most commendable.

I have mentioned that scholars often take the language of solidity to signify Jones's general commitment to neo-Palladian principles. But by focusing on the different emotions aroused in the onlooker or audience of a building, the statement implies at least two closely linked things: that the effects of buildings should *move* us, a persuasive or "gracious" power resulting from proportion and eurythmia; and that such effects are best secured by the proper mixture of elements or orders, so that we are always reminded of the dependence of more sophisticated on more primitive or elemental forms. Thus, in his Alberti, Jones writes that "excelens in buildings moufs the mind," a rational virtue guaranteed by the internal economy of nature herself, expressed for example in the various beauties of women, so that the architect, after "finding out the orders of the Collombes," reveals in his design that "In fair bodies the members are not alike, but not different but together gratious."[96] The chief principle of what Jones calls "composed proportion" is a degree of internal aesthetic and symbolic play, so that elsewhere in his Vitruvius Jones remarks that "order is ye Dispencing of things equall and unequale," and that order emerges from "comparason of inequalitie."[97] In his Scamozzi, Jones notes that "on thing accompanyn another gives more grace to Architecture."[98] He finds that the Vitruvian "Diffinition of proportion . . . is comparison of too quantities comprehended under on Genus," the principle being that "in all thinges is found great littell & middling."[99] Jones summarizes virtually the entire conception in response to his copy of Vasari, where he writes,

Architeture must be Masculine fearme [Sollid] Simpell and Inriched with ye grace of desine and of a varied subiecte in the Compossition that with nether too littell nor to[o] much alterithe ye Order of architecture nor ye sight of ye Iuditious.[100]

When we turn to Serlio we find that such an interest is expressed in the context of a commitment to the rustic and Tuscan, either representing a mixed mode in themselves or as signifying the stylistic ground upon which mixed architectural arguments could then proceed. For Jones, responding to Scamozzi, "Rustick is under no determinat order," just as earlier he comments, "essy and simpell Inventions best."[101] In Book VII of his 1619 *Architettura*, Jones would have read of designs for gates, by which we know from his own early designs he was fascinated, and which caused him also to consult Serlio's *The Extraordinary Book on Architecture* (1551), entirely devoted to rustic and rusticated gates. Ch. 38 discusses gates for fortified cities, and its opening paragraph reads:

Variety in things gives great contentment to the human eye and satisfaction to the heart. Hence the present gate; even though it is Tuscan mixed with Rustic – work which is perfectly suited to a fortress – the four exceedingly Rustic, unfinished columns give it the appearance of even greater strength and solidity.[102]

In his commentary on the transformation effected by the Italian trip on Jones's architectural imagination, Higgott makes clear how persistently

Jones seemed taken not only with the variety of the classical orders he observed or with the variety of textures permitted by different materials and methods of construction, but with a particular interest in forms of rustication. Thus, commenting on Palladio's Palazzo Thiene, Jones observes how the building involved brick for the rustication and stone for the details, and that there are two types of rustication, rough cut below and "a flat rusticke aboufe or rather a [sw]eet rusticke to be imitated." In fact Jones's Palladio is full of references to brickwork, as well as its relation to the rustic mode, just as he also expresses an interest in wood and the Tuscan mode. That Jones followed his own advice is clear both from a series of designs, inspired by Serlio and dated to 1617, for rusticated gates for Oatlands Palace, Surrey, and from the Queen's House, Greenwich. Of Jones's relation to gates, John Harris writes, "Jones was perennially fascinated by the variety of architectural display possible in gateways. This variety is shown in his surviving designs [and] they would often be used as vehicles for the exposition of the orders of architecture."[103] (See figure 16.) Plans of the Queen's House from 1616 show two floors of equal height, "a ground floor treated as a rusticated basement and an upper floor with shared features such as pulvinated friezes and a blocking course above the entablature."[104]

I am arguing, in short, that Jones's designs express the depth of his engagement with architectural theory, and that his major buildings – the Queen's House, the Banqueting House, and St. Paul's, Covent Garden – represent uses of building textures and the orders whose purpose, like the Tower of the Orders, was perhaps to legitimate his patrons, but also to remind them of the mixed nature of the English constitution. Thus the Queen's House is more or less an essay in rustication, both on the entire lower floor of the house and owing to the fact that the house involves also a basement, and a series of archways below the body of the house, again provoking a festival of rustication: the house had to span the road out of town, thus troping spatially on the relation between the common and customary and the prerogatives of the court, a tension of which Jones cannot have been unaware, and which informs, I believe, the symbology of his design. (The heavy emphasis on rustication is also visible in the King Charles court, by John Webb, Jones's disciple, and also part of the complex comprising the Royal Naval College, Greenwich, the other buildings being by Wren.) (See figures 17–19.) The Banqueting House is expressed in three major drawings: two architectural drawings now at Chatsworth, and a design for a masque now at the Pierpont Morgan Library. (See figures 20–2.) The Chatsworth designs obviously occur in sequence in 1619: the first is a preliminary design, while the second introduces heavy rustication on the

Figure 16: Jones, Design for rusticated gate

basement. No one has commented extensively on the drawing for *Time Vindicated to Himself and to his Honors* (1623), especially its most obvious feature, which juxtaposes the neoclassical Banqueting House with minutely rendered drawings of the Gothic and Elizabethan buildings abutting it. The structural variety of orders in the House itself is amplified by a kind of historical vocabulary, so that the King, if he so wished, could see both in the House and its setting the dependence of newer and more cosmopolitan modes on a native, vernacular, and rustic apprehension of the world. Moreover, as several historians have pointed out, the Banqueting House was an essay in different building textures and materials, not the more monolithic Palladian edifice we see today. Harris writes that "the Banqueting House looks today very much as completed in 1622 – except for one important

Figure 17: Jones, Queen's House, Greenwich: front view

fact: it is now all faced with Portland stone, a process which was begun by Sir William Chambers and completed by Sir John Soane. In the seventeenth century its basement was of honey-coloured Oxfordshire stone, the upper walls of a brownish Northamptonshire stone, and white Portland for the enriched details. It was a subtle essay in the art of polychromy."[105] For numerous reasons, therefore, Jones's masterpiece is no simple celebration of a grandiose neoclassicism: like the Ciceronian oration, it serves to remind

Figure 18: Jones, Queen's House, Greenwich: rusticated basement

us of the various and mixed elements from which our lives proceed, above all our civic lives.

Given the overwhelming evidence that architectural design was semantically charged in the ways we have examined, it is also remarkable that very little has been added to John Summerson's suggestive discussion of Jones's design for the Covent Garden piazza. In his own commentary on Jones's

Figure 19: Webb, King Charles Court, Greenwich

plan, for example, John Harris agrees that Jones sought systematically to expound the Tuscan order, revealed in its entirety in volume II of Colen Campbell's *Vitruvius Britannicus* (1717), but only visible to us in the church – a centerpiece of the design – though modified by fire and rebuilding in the eighteenth century. (See figures 23–4.) In choosing the simplest order available to him, Jones was obviously not motivated by questions of cost or

Figure 20: Jones, Design for the Banqueting House

mere aesthetics, since the choice of orders, as we have seen, was profoundly ideological. We could read this proposition from the building with which we are today confronted, which is uncompromising in its severity, but there are at least two points from which such a reading gains independent support from Jones himself. The first emerges from Jones's clear conviction – expressed in his Scamozzi – that whereas "secular buildings [should be] more svelte," "sacred buildings [should be] more solid,"[106] a commitment to the simple orders in church architecture visible, according to Harris, citing Summerson, in the renovations for old St. Paul's Cathedral, where

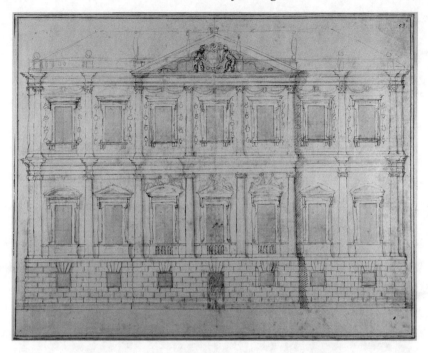

Figure 21: Jones, Design for the Banqueting House

the plan "was no haphazard application of a classically ornamented skin, but a profound learned exposition, where each part of the cathedral was seen to be expressed in an architectonic mood, Tuscan for the nave, Doric for the aisles and doorways there, Ionic for the portals in the transepts, and culminating in Corinthian for the tremendous portico."[107] Harris sees the portico as a gift from Jones to the King, which is an unobjectionable idea, so long as we recall that the Corinthian in this progression self-consciously emerges from the more primitive orders. A more cryptic clue is provided by Jones's annotations to his Vitruvius. In the middle of a discussion of the Tuscan order he seems to be complaining that Barbaro and others don't fully understand what materials are most appropriate to the order, but that though he understands the issue more clearly now, his Covent Garden design was properly committed to the "plaine" style.[108]

Jones must have intended the ecclesiological implications of his choice. For, as some commentators suggest, Tuscan may well have been an exact equivalent to the ideals of the primitive church which infused the religious

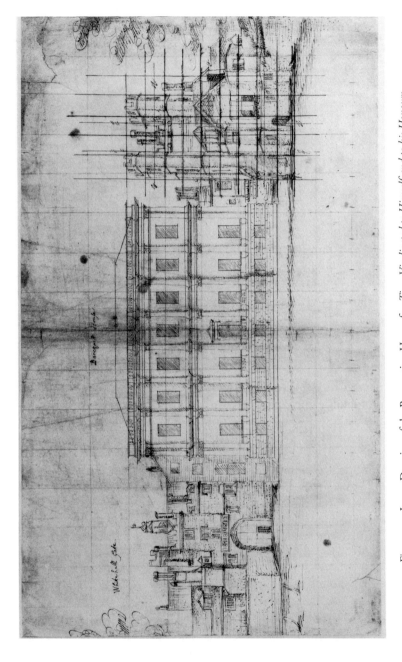

Figure 22: Jones, Drawing of the Banqueting House for *Time Vindicated to Himself and to his Honours*

polemics leading to the Civil War. The simplicity of the hall church itself reinforces the idea that, as in the primitive church, the sacred is available to all worshipers, who together constitute the priesthood of believers. The complexity of Jones's entry into the discussion is that its political implications are highly equivocal, for the appeal to the primitive church lay behind both Erastian defenses of the Anglican church and the demands of the reformers. On the one hand the moderate skepticism of William Chillingworth's *The Religion of Protestants the Safe Way of Salvation* (1638) permitted Chillingworth – Laud's godson – to claim that Anglicanism was as good a means for Englishmen through which to express their faith as any other. In this, the single most important religious polemic of the century, Chillingworth wrote, the truths of scripture, though not cast-iron, were sufficient for our purposes; Anglicanism was permissive since, like the primitive church, it preserved the essentials of the faith; and attempts to legislate further (like demanding believers' baptism or Marian doctrine or other "inessentials") was beyond human capacities to know and a political imposition on the faithful. The reformers, on the other hand, could claim that the governance and liturgy of the Church of England contradicted the simplicity of the primitive church, and that those abuses should be excised root and branch. Jones's decision to engage the first great town-planning scheme in London in the Tuscan mode has all the appearances of deliberation, as if the architect as rhetor were seeking to remind the nation of the very grounds of political contention.

That Jones intended his engagement with the Tuscan as a commentary on the state of the nation at large is confirmed, I believe, by his speculations on Stonehenge, published in 1655 as *The Most Notable Antiquity of Great Britain, Vulgarly Called Stone-Heng* by John Webb, who was to work a year later with William Davenant on *The Siege of Rhodes*. This is a curious document which argues that Stonehenge was not Druidic, for example, but a Roman temple dedicated to the god Coelus. But at its core, it is a Vitruvian defense – backed up by references to Alberti, Serlio, and Scamozzi – of the centrality of Roman (not Greek) architecture to the exercise of the "liberall sciences," themselves the precondition of "civil conversation" or "*Roman* civility," namely a viable polity.[109] The argument proceeds in roughly four movements, beginning with a lengthy consideration of the antiquarians who have speculated on Stonehenge before, often offering mythical explanations for its existence. Jones discusses such figures as the Venerable Bede, Geoffrey of Monmouth, William of Malmesbury, Polydore Vergil, and Camden, but, as Jones puts it, "*Architecture* depending upon demonstration, not fancy, the fictions of *Mythologists* are no further to

Figure 23: Jones, St. Paul's, Covent Garden

be embraced" (96). The second section analyzes the numerous geometrical proportions of Stonehenge, which supports his view that, since architecture is the most encompassing humanist art and geometry is endemic to the liberal sciences, neither pre-Roman societies nor the Saxons, who were illiterate or partially literate at best, could have cultivated this highest of human sciences. They even failed to construct significant funerary monuments

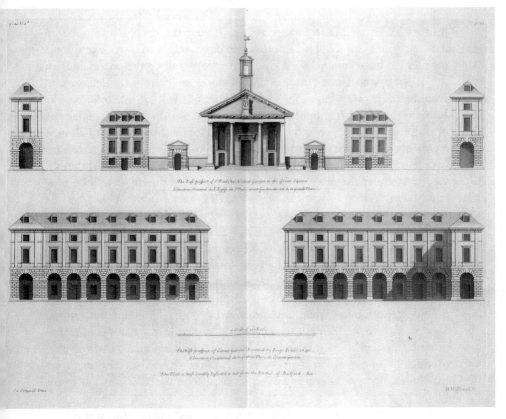

Figure 24: Jones, St. Paul's, Covent Garden; Covent Garden Piazza, from *Vitruvius Britannicus*

to great national heroes like Boadicea. Given Roman achievements in engineering, the size of Stonehenge poses no obstacle, and significantly this is best represented in the Circus Maximus and the Theater of Marcellus in Rome. The introduction of these public places of display subtly sets the stage for the rest of the argument, because by associating the Circus specifically with Augustus, Jones is remarking on the fact that it was that emperor who initiated the custom of consulting popular opinion in the Circus, the theater, and the Colosseum. At first, the final two sections of the argument may seem a departure from this theme, because Jones then argues that Stonehenge is chiefly in the Tuscan mood, and that it is a temple dedicated to Coelus. They are, however, intimately connected to the idea that public edifices like theaters or temples signify an appropriate balance of power in the state and most perfectly symbolize the civil order. Roman achievements in architecture expressed the deeply cosmopolitan nature of their empire, which on the one hand sought to introduce subject peoples by the art of analysis to the distinctions among the orders, and on the other, by the art of synthesis and obeying the precepts of decorum to accommodate given buildings to the temper of the local inhabitants. The Romans thus import enlightenment, discipline, and an aesthetic of balance or proportion: If we "consider the *Art*, and elegant disposition [of Roman architecture], all *Arts* and *Sciences* (we must know) were in full perfection with them, and *Architecture*, which amongst the *Greeks* was youthfull only, vigorous; under the *Romans* their *Empire* grown to the full height became manly and perfect, not in *inventions, and elegancy of forms alone, but also in exquisitenesse of Art, and excellency of materials*" (66–7). The ruggedness of Stonehenge means that it is primarily an exercise in the Tuscan, "a grave and humble *Order*" (101), which corresponds to the nature of the inhabitants. The style agrees with "the rude, plain, simple nature of those they intended to instruct" (68); but since like all arts architectural design must be governed by the principles of decorum, Stonehenge no more expresses a single genre or style than any other work of art. Though based on the Tuscan, Stonehenge obeys the neoclassical principle of balanced or mixed modular design: it "is mingled of *Greek* [Corinthian] and *Tuscan* work," producing "*one common composure*" (76). Architectural invention, Jones concludes, necessarily commits you to such "composed" or mixed forms (78).

In his final section, Jones selects Coelus as the figure to whom Stonehenge is dedicated because, being an open design, Stonehenge seems to gesture towards celestial and universal knowledge. Some commentators stress that Coelus is implicated in astronomy and astrology as further proof of Jones's neoplatonic bias; but this ignores the extent to which Jones contrasts true geometrical calculation with mythology, on the one hand, and the extent to which Coelus, on the other, represents the founding of civil society by gathering different groups together into a complex whole, of the kind announced in the composite architectural forms of Stonehenge itself. Though Coelus does also become a cosmic knower of sorts, his origins lie in orchestrating the emergence of political society from disparate groups, so that he is clearly intended as a functional magistrate of the kind Charles, by 1640, had patently failed to be: "*he which first reigned over the* Atlantides *was* Coelus, *and . . . he invited men living dispersedly before throughout the fields, to convene, and dwell in companies together, exhorting them to build Towns, and reducing them from wild and savage to the conversations of civill life: Taught them to sow corn and seeds, and divers other things belonging to the common use of mankind"* (104). Read as a Roman monument, and sited as it is in the center of Salisbury Plain, Stonehenge stands as a subtle rebuke to the failures of the early Stuarts.

DAVENANT'S MASQUES AND ARCHITECTURE

In a typically judicious assessment of the prevailing criticism of early Stuart masques, Martin Butler argues that currently we have three main lines of argument: an established notion that the masques are neoplatonic celebrations of Jacobean and Caroline power; Kevin Sharpe's view that the Caroline court harbored a vigorous culture of dissent; and Butler's modification of Sharpe's position, which holds that only the public theaters permitted true political criticism, and that whatever strains we detect within court culture echo the increasing tensions of the nation at large in the years of personal rule.[110] While agreeing that Sharpe somewhat overstates his case, I submit that a knowledge of the architectural tradition we have just considered reveals how Davenant's masques from the 1630s not merely incidentally but conscientiously express a form of dissent by reminding the King that the customary grounds of his power limit his prerogative. Pointed criticism of royal policy is already visible in Thomas Carew's *Coelum Britannicum* (1634), originally published anonymously before being included in *The Works of Sir William Davenant* (1673); but it becomes closely associated with architectural motifs from *The Triumphs of the Prince D'Amour* (1635) to *Salmacida Spolia* (1640). The appreciation of architecture as a public rhetorical medium strongly distinguishes Davenant's masques from *Love's Welcome at Bolsover* (1634), Jonson's last entertainment, whose verbal prejudices accompany a disdain for architecture as nothing but a mechanical trade and correspondingly permit the masque to culminate in a neoplatonic fog of the kind the architectural mode cultivated by Davenant and Jones calculatedly sought to dissipate. Further, that not all of his masques were mounted in collaboration with Jones indicates not only that Davenant had independently developed an appreciation of architecture as a symbolic medium, but that these late masques are not – as is often implied – productions of Jones in close collaboration with the King, a position for which I have seen no hard evidence.

Mistaken as it is, the association of *Coelum Britannicum* with Davenant is useful because it initiates a tradition of political advice in the late masques that, in Davenant's own texts, becomes systemic. Set on Shrove Tuesday 1634, Carew's masque exploits the possibilities of the feast of misrule by introducing Momus, a satyr–satirist set against the more conventional Mercury. It is possible, though unlikely, that Carew is drawing on architecture for his argument, since the scene is set – like the frontispiece of Book III of Serlio's *Architettura* – amidst the Roman ruins, and the masque culminates in praise of Charles as a British Hercules, a figure associated (as would be apt) with the Doric order. However, the strain of dissent in Momus's behavior is marked by an oratorical manner associated with satire, and to which Mercury can only respond in the most pinched and conventional terms. A series of charges against political mismanagement lurk barely below the surface: the political climate discourages true statesmanship; legal processes are under threat; Momus asserts his rights as a "free-born god" within the "politique state of heaven"; Momus recalls abuses behind the King's fiscal policy, involving monopolies and taxes; he alludes to the contentious Book of Sports; an "Amazonian mutiny" and flight to New England remind the King of disquiet at home; and most importantly, Momus puns on the decorated space of the Banqueting Hall as "the Star Chamber."[111] Performed on 18 February 1633, Carew's masque must be commenting on an event which occurred exactly four months and a day before, when the Star Chamber restricted the freedom of the press in response to Spanish and Austrian complaints that English reports of the Thirty Years' War were prejudiced. (By way of riposte, Carew thus reminds his audience of the events of 1588.) Even given the striking catalogue of Momus's complaints, none resonates more than this reference. The Star Chamber originated as a Privy Council to the King and served as the seat of equity; but by this point in history it had become associated with Stuart autocracy, so that the Long Parliament abolished the institution in 1641 as the perfect symptom of Caroline abuses.

Though the masque does indeed culminate in proper panegyric to the royal couple ("CARLOMARIA"), the resolution does not, significantly, occur by quelling or answering Momus's protestations. Rather unaccountably, he bows out after serving as master of ceremonies to a series of less threatening allegorical figures (wealth, poverty, fortune, pleasure) who are accorded their own antimasques, having, he says, "grown so weary of these tedious pleadings" (375). So Carew's entertainment ostensibly succeeds in its propagandistic aim while raising, without resolving them, issues that were later to drive the nation to war.

The strained relation between the King and the law is the central focus of Davenant's *The Triumphs of the Prince D'Amour* (1635). The barely disguised argument that the King must respect his place in the mixed monarchy, distilled in the common law itself, is conducted by two devices. First, the masque was hurriedly produced in the Middle Temple as an entertainment for Charles Louis, Elector Palatine, the second son of Frederick V ("the winter king"), who had married James I's daughter Elizabeth; and the master of ceremonies emphasizes that though the purpose is not to undermine his authority, this event requires the King to remove himself from his native surroundings in Whitehall, as if to make a topographical issue of the need for the King to defer. The exordium, though seeking a modification in the King's powers, is carefully clothed in dutiful language, so that the speaker insists he is no "easie Traytor, no Ambassador," to be treated "As if my words would pull his Empire down, / Shorten his Scepter, and contract his Crown."[112]

But the argument of the masque as a whole unequivocally favors a mixed constitution, because it parses the entire action in terms of the differences among the architectural orders, the movement of the presentation occurring as a shift from order to order, from the rustic and (implicitly) Tuscan to the "composita" (400). Each scene comprises a kind of architectural vignette, the main action being announced when "there was presented to sight a Front of *Architecture* with two Pillasters at each side" (396). The rhythm of the piece generates two allegories simultaneously, for, reflecting the metamorphosis of the orders from the rude and masculine (Tuscan, Doric) to the polite and feminine (Ionic, Corinthian), it argues ambiguously that Charles has either caused the wonders of love to transcend the martial values of war, or that he should do so; and it also, by culminating in that distinctively Augustan order, the composite, equally ambiguously argues that Charles's power either expresses or should respect customary constraints on his prerogative. The effect is that by subscribing to the official court language of love, Davenant implicates his audience in a constitutional exercise whose connotations are advisory as much as panegyrical.

The first antimasque is thus set in a scene closely resembling Serlio's model for the "satyric," featuring a rural village with alehouses and tobacco shops, where "Before each door were often seen old Logs, and Trunks of hollow Trees" (396). By populating the scene with rough and begging soldiers as well as Dutch seamen, Davenant prepares us for the next, dominated by a temple of Mars "of the Dorick Order" (397). Priests of Mars, "cloathed in Crimson Robes, of the Antick shape" (397) approach the state before being succeeded by the masquers in martial dress of "the old Roman shape" (398), meant also to allude to the Knights Templar, but the descent of Cupid heralds a transformation into the second antimasque, whereby war gives place to love. This also occurs in two scenes, the first set in a Venetian piazza (implicitly in the Ionic order), and populated now by Spanish,

Italian, French, Dutch, and English lovers; and this in turn culminates in the erection of a temple of Venus in the Corinthian mode, signifying "a more soft and Courtly change" (400). After the priests of Venus have also addressed the audience, the scene transforms for a final and dramatic time: the silver age of love now gives way to a golden and Apollonian age at one and the same time intended to flatter the audience, to unite arms and arts, and to celebrate, reflecting the Virgilian tenor of the moment, the mixed nature of the Augustan achievement. Thus,

> The Scene wholly changing, strait was perceiv'd in a Grove of Lawrel Trees, the Temple of *Apollo*, being round and transparent, of the order of Composita, the Columnes and Ornaments, being heightened with Gold, his Statue of Gold, standing in the middle of the Temple, upon a round Pedestal: behind and between the Columnes did appear a prospect of Lanskap. (400)

After the priests of Apollo have sung, twelve rudely clad "Labourers on a fruitful soil" (401) celebrate the natural fecundity of the land, the masque concluding when they "conjoin" with the priests of Mars, Venus, and Apollo in prophetic song (402), a conjunction which confirms the culturally collaborative implications of the architectural motifs that cement the whole event.

   None of Davenant's remaining masques before 1640 is so clearly designed around an architectural device in this way. Instead, architecture serves to punctuate and secure arguments conducted in different registers. The very title of *The Temple of Love* (1635) recalls Book V of Serlio, dedicated to temples; but the masque remains slightly obscure unless we pair it with *The Platonick Lovers* (1636), since they share the same target, namely the degree to which the courtly cult of Platonism encourages an aura of abstraction and unreality which rejects the particularities of human existence. Thus one of the magicians in the masque describes the new fad:

> They raise strange doctrines and new sects of love,
> Which must not woo or court the person, but
> The mind, and practice generation not
> Of bodies, but of souls.[113]

Like *The Platonick Lovers*, then, for which it serves as a dry run, *The Temple of Love* hypostasizes a series of oppositions engendered by the neoplatonic challenge to the ordinary, some of which are broadly epistemic (body vs. mind or soul; hot vs. cold, a physiological expansion of that idea) and one of which is more emphatically political (the opposition between land and sea, signified by the appearance of Dutch sailors on stage). As in the later play, the purpose is, in respecting empirical realities and promoting a political desideratum, to engineer a reconciliation of elements – like the four Pythagorean elements Davenant mentions (602). In celebrating the Queen as the beauteous Indamora, and uniting her with the King, the masque culminates in an architectural emblem, raising the *"true Temple of Chaste Love"* (604), in which the differences among the orders are harmoniously displayed. The basic order, corresponding to the Tuscan or rustic,

instead of columns had terms of young satyrs bearing up the returns of architrave, frieze and cornice; the further part of the temple running far from the eye was designed of another kind of architecture, with pilasters, niches and statues, and in the midst a stately gate adorned with columns and their ornaments, and a frontispiece on the top, all which seemed to be of burnished gold. (604)

This background frames the conclusion, in which Sunesis and Thelma first unite in "one virtuous appetite," "mixed" of thoughts, actions, will, and reason. They are joined by Chaste Love (who descends in a machine), Divine Poesy, Orpheus, and a cluster of poets, and they too celebrate their "union" as a "mixture" (604). The grammar of the architectural setting tropes on the distinctions among the orders in two ways: it distinguishes the "satyric" from the more disciplined neoclassical orders with which it is implicitly contrasted by a perspective device; and the gate in the middle of the arrangement seems to anthologize the different orders in the ways that Jones's extant designs for gates invariably do. The kinds of reconciliation the masque embodies at the end, therefore, are jointly celebratory and advisory, since they occur emphatically not as a neoplatonic singularity, but as a Vitruvian mixture: an aesthetic balance of powers, in short.

As most commentators have written, *Britannia Triumphans*, performed in 1637, is set against the ship money crisis; and as a royalist, it is fair to say, Davenant sees one of his major purposes as to justify the King's right to raise taxes in the interests of national security. The King is allegorized therefore as the virtuous "Britanocles, *the glory of the Western world*";[114] and the masque is full of echoes of various political troubles, from agitation about church reform to the central issue, ship money. Britanocles inevitably triumphs at the end over all the various blocking figures in the antimasques, a victory anticipated in the mock romance curiously inserted in the action after the arrival of Merlin. But however clearly the masque serves as a vehicle of legitimation, it is equally clearly a form of advice to Charles about how most prudently to project his power. Again, this occurs through architecture, and in two somewhat different forms. First, the entire action is predicated on a preliminary emblem and the first scene. After the Queen was seated on the state, the spectators were presented by a tableau signifying jointly "Navall

Figure 25: Jones, Scene for *Britannia Triumphans*

victory" (3) and "right government" (3), the entire ornament comprising a descant on a maritime theme. Then,

> A curtaine flying up discovered the first Scene, wherein were English houses of the old and newer formes, intermixt with trees, and a farre off a prospect of the Citie of London, and the River of Thames, which being a principall part, might be taken for all great Britain. (3–4)

We possess two versions of this scene, both of them at Chatsworth. (See figures 25–6.) The finer is of course by Jones himself, the cruder by Webb, and the difference is revealing. For Jones the contrasts between styles of architecture, and between the neoclassical suburb on the South Bank and the City of London on the North, are symbolically significant. Webb seems slightly to have missed the point; for the contrast between "older and newer formes" of architecture, and between the neoclassical foreground and the background dominated by the old St. Paul's Cathedral, once again gestures to the tension between customary and other forms of power in the state. Orgel rather casually asserts that the background to the scene features St. Paul's with Jones's additions, but I am inclined to agree with David Howarth that in this design "Jones's cathedral remains resolutely northern and gothic."[115] Davenant's directions make clear that this vernacular mode

Figure 26: Webb, Scene for *Britannia Triumphans*

represents the interests of the country, the unavoidable implication in this moment of crisis being that the King, in exercising his prerogative in matters of taxation, should also respect conventions of advice from the political nation.

This double consciousness is rehearsed in the penultimate scene of the masque, when Jones conjures up the Palace of Fame, which incorporates both the Doric and Ionic orders:

When this Palace was arrived to its height, the whole Scene was changed into a Peristilium of two orders, Doric and Ionick with their severall Ornaments seeming of white marble, the Bases and Capitals of gold. (20)

Before the masque concludes with a maritime vignette, the action returns to the opening scene we have just discussed, now spoken of synecdochically as a "Scene . . . of Brittaine" (22).

The implication of all that we have discussed for the final early Stuart masque ever performed, *Salmacida Spolia* (1640), should by now be clear. Critics have long recognized that this masque addresses a moment of great national crisis, and that it represents an appeal to the King to placate the forces of criticism with which he was confronted. In her wonderful essay, "The Last Masque," C. V. Wedgwood also shows how some participants in the masque were allied with interests that were soon to resist the King.[116]

But this posture of appeal is not, as is usually thought, an exception to a tradition of artistic flattery, thrust upon Davenant and Jones by the turn of events. It is, I have been arguing at length, endemic to the architectural imagination that Jones had been cultivating at least since 1613. So *Salmacida Spolia* virtually concludes in the following way:

The second dance ended and their Majesties being seated under the state the scene was changed, into magnificent buildings composed of several selected pieces of architecture. In the furthest part was a bridge over a river, where many people, coaches, horses, and such like were seen to pass to and fro. Beyond this on the shore were buildings in prospective, which, shooting far from the eye, showed as the suburbs of a great city.[117]

CHAPTER 5

"This New Building": Davenant's last phase

GONDIBERT (1650–1651)

Though no one wished it longer, the coherence of *Gondibert*, I would argue, depends on the biometric metaphor that the architectural imagination fostered. For this poem is a scrupulous Hobbesian deliberation on the artificiality of civil life, an idea to which Davenant immediately commits himself when, at the outset of his preface to Hobbes, he speaks of his poem as "this new Building."[1] The architectural trope is not merely incidental but constitutes Davenant's method, poised to proliferate into a series of other concerns. It not only plays an important role in the poem proper, but it provides the essential skeleton not only for his entire preface, nor only for Hobbes's reply, but also for the final gesture of the published text, the postscript to Book III, Canto vii, where the architectural image reemerges for a final time, yet under very different compositional circumstances from the Parisian leisure that prevailed a short year before, Davenant now finding himself imprisoned by the Cromwellian regime (250). Even one of the affectionate satires on the poem printed with the second edition in 1653 touches on the importance of architecture to the argument, for the writer accuses Davenant, in having published the preface and no poem, of having supplied "A Preface to no Book, a Porch to no House" (273).

We should remember that the Paris Davenant visited was a hotbed of speculation about atomism: Hobbes was a close friend of Gassendi, and Margaret Cavendish was in the process of contracting her enthusiasm for the new cosmology. Thus it is no accident that like *The Blazing World*, Book II of *Gondibert* engages in a lengthy anatomy of different scientific societies, which almost certainly reflects Davenant's French sojourn. As we have seen, Lucretius is as central to Vitruvian conceptions of architecture as Cicero; and we could say, for the purposes of this chapter, that imaginatively all engage a similar conundrum. First, the question is, from what elements and from what arrangements of elements does the natural world proceed?

Second, by what similar structural principles do we read the human body, itself a composite of members and – like the natural world in general – apparently driven by processes and laws that remain hidden, though medicine purports to teach the physician to interpret symptoms? Third, the Lucretian analogy between the atoms comprising the material world, the letters of the alphabet upon which language is founded, and the elements of a building produces the concern that absorbs *Gondibert*, and which explains both its connection to Hobbes and why Davenant had no need to continue the poem beyond Book III. For Davenant is asking in numerous different ways, first, what foundational elements produce the possibility of civil society and what principles inform their perceived coherence. He is also asking how poetry in general and his poem in particular structurally enact the artifices of the polity and contribute to its function by serving as a species of political rhetoric, since civil society palpably makes poetry possible, and depends equally on the moral effects of literary and suasive examples.

This is the main issue that has occupied commentators; but Davenant's full concerns are much broader. The overarching demand for coherence in all relevant arts – whether the art of statesmanship, the art of war, the art of natural philosophy, including medicine, or the art of poetry, whose rhetorical power links it once again to issues of governance – is imposed from without, as it were, in that a prescription for civil society is that it should secure peace; and Davenant endlessly worries at the internal dynamic that might explain how primary, hidden, occult or "private" categories of experience generate or explain the scrutible, legible, and "public" aspects of human endeavor: the terms "private" and especially "public" appear dozens of times in Davenant's poem, always within this larger framework of inquiry. This tension between public and private, with the accompanying question of how we are to think about their connectedness, is also, throughout the poem, given additional weight by reference to the Cartesian distinction between the mind and body: this imports a corresponding puzzle about how these different modes may or may not be causally related, as cause, for example, to effect, to adopt yet another set of terms in Davenant's text.

It follows that the poem's vacillation between the idea of art and the idea of nature is neither banal nor casual, for the poem perennially circulates between these two entirely conventional *topoi* for conceptually profound reasons. On the one hand Davenant is committed to the idea that all major human or "liberall" arts – reflecting the architecture of the cosmos and the human body – are purely artificial, functional constructs for the purposes of what is humanly possible and rewarding. Indeed, human life is only feasible within the "public" categories to which even the most constructive skepticism limits us, so that like his friend Hobbes, Davenant is sketching out a proto-Wittgensteinian view that to adhere to a private language is to inhabit a contradiction in terms. On the other hand, and at the same time, just as the architectural theorists see glimmerings of a divine or natural order in the principles of eurythmia or proportion that regulate the relations between the material elements that make up a given edifice, so Davenant imagines that though we inhabit a necessarily skeptical universe, we are still drawn to the ontological postulate that responds most ardently to those artifacts that somehow, without transparently representing them, adumbrate the proportions and relations of nature herself. The suspicion that the structure of the world might still find expression in our representations is conveyed by the language of alchemy that populates *Gondibert* (I,iv,4–5; I,v,29; II,ii,87; II,iii,24; II,iv.11), so that the connection between the occult and the visible, like Newton's attraction at a distance, remains itself rather mysterious, though perhaps driven by some principle of sympathy. Thus two virtual mottos for Davenant's entire method occur in the course of the poem proper, the first in Book I and the second in Book II. The first argues that "Nature calls for Art to make life stay" (I,v,82), to indicate the extent to which what is socially recognizable is by definition artificial; and the second argues that "Arts are weak that are of Scepticks shy" (II,I,58), to reveal that the integrity of any postulate within the human realm depends on some representational order.

Part of the failure of the poem as a poem results from the extent to which Davenant is focused on the second-order questions I have sketched, so that its forward impulse, feeble enough as it is, is constantly marooned on a self-reflexive obsession which Davenant expounds in the preface. In migrating from the poem as building, to the human body as "our fleshy building" (8), to the parallel between the poem and drama, as well as the *topos, ut pictura poesis*, Davenant has in mind the degree to which "Art" – one of the most frequently used words in the poem – involves the contingent harmonizing of different materials, elements, and effects, and whose tendency is more centrifugal than centripetal. The product of all human activities, whether politics, science, architecture, or poetry, follows from bricolage, a temporary juxtaposition or melding of elements in a certain tension. Davenant combines his interest in the relation between the artificial and natural with a fascination not only with the variety of nature herself, reproduced in the complexity of the human form and thus of buildings, but with the inevitable consequences of literary imitation in which different genres and materials are differently combined for different purposes. Thus Davenant rather archly chastises Homer for "intermixing" fables with his "Story" (3); describes the chiaroscuric and differentiating effect of perspective in painting (4); talks of how painters become sorts of historian by "assembling divers figures in a larger volume" (5); and speaks of the English language as the effect, not always happy, of endless grafts upon some original stock:

Language (which is the onely Creature of Man's creation) hath like a Plant, seasons of flourishing and decay, like Plants is remov'd from one soile to an other, and by being so transplanted, doth often gather vigour and increase. But as it is false husbandry to graft old branches upon young Stocks: so wee may wonder that our Language (not long before his time created out of a confusion of others, and then beginning to flourish like a new plant) should (as helps to its increase) receive from his hand new grafts of old wither'd words. But this vulgar exception, shall only have the vulgar excuse; which is, that the unlucky choice of his *Stanza* hath by repetition of Rime brought him to the necessity of many exploded words. (7)

All life is characterized as a mixed affair, and this idea informs several related arguments that follow. As in *The Platonick Lovers*, soul and body, cold and hot are mingled in the human constitution, whether we think of that constitution physiologically or politically (9; 14). The complex harmonies and balances in the body (echoing the new Harveian conception) become a figure for the liberal state, an idea which also receives support from Davenant's epistemic resistance to neo-Platonism, here figured locally in the Jewish repugnance to things of the flesh, so that separating yourself from the corporeal becomes an expression of an antisocial, hermetic, and melancholic habit of mind. (The Jews cultivate an "uncivill disdaine for the imagin'd contagiousness of others" [10].) There are two alternatives, it seems. On the one hand, Muslim society "drew all Nations together," but in this case only "in the vaine pride of Empire"(10); whereas the "Christian Religion hath the innocence of Village neighbourhood, and did anciently in its politicks rather promote the interest of Mankinde then of States; and rather of all States then of one" (10), and, Davenant glosses,

for particular endeavors only in behalfe of our owne homes, are signes of a narrow morall education, not of the vast kindnesse of Christian Religion, which like-wise ordain'd as well an universall communion of bosoms, as a community of Wealth (10).

This is less an expression of bigotry than might at first appear because the imagined distinctions among different forms of social organization are for Davenant heuristic, a kind of thought experiment in political and representational desiderata which it is the purpose of his poem to explore.

This is suggested by a further extension of the argument, where the mixed nature of architecture, the human body, and civil society becomes embodied specifically in the theater.

According to Davenant's conception, poets are a more effective species of rhetor than divines (38), creating organisms that, because they combine different elements, enact the properties of a "liberall" polity, inviting participation by persuading readers or audiences by their handling of proportion, an architectonic principle confirmed by Solomon's role as a divinely inspired architect (22). So since by implication any art form can manifest these principles, Davenant almost casually recalls the importance of Italian theater for the practice of drama of the kind on which his poem – which was to have five books or "acts" – is modeled. The Italian theater apparently mediates between comedy and tragedy, and between the sexes (11–12), a melding of different properties and values that echoes the conjunction of body and soul in human experience (14), and anticipates the hybrid "method" of *Gondibert* (again spoken of as an edifice) and more pointedly English drama *per se* (15). The architectural language also allows Davenant to stress the extent to which all these constructs supply not precise descriptions of reality, but constructive *ways of thinking* about the world, which explains his recourse to the language of "forme," "designe," and "Modell," the effects of a poet who "make[s] my surveys as one that travail'd not to bring home the names, but the proportion, and nature of things" (21).

The ongoing and barely suppressed parallel between architecture, poetry, the theater, and nature also issues in the resurfacing of the biometric metaphor, which begins to move us from hermeneutic to political issues. If poetry and drama, as well as history, model rather than reflect our apprehension of things, we can think of literature as having its own "Body," which like Homer's epics to later ages is an assemblage of "scatter'd limbs" (27): the result is an entirely artificial but nonetheless meaningful form, articulated as a patterning or *ars combinatoria* of the kind that drives the organization of narrative in *Gondibert* proper. Davenant is arguing that these patternings are the basis of the rhetorical appeal of poetry, which, he says, is essential to statecraft, comprising its own art like drama, poetry, architecture, or natural history. (Indeed, we learn, "the lastingnesse of Government . . . is the principall worke of Art" [40]; and even religion herself is "our Art towards God" [42].)

Critics have often assumed that Davenant's royalism means that the suasive force of poetry serves to control popular appetite, but this is only partly true. The more central principle, as we should expect from the masques, is that the magistrate must consult popular opinion and so steer it, if we are to navigate between complete autocracy and mass insurrection. The local adjustments in the polity echo the influence of equity in the exercise of law, so that, Davenant writes:

Judges (the Copies of *Law-makers*) differ from their Originalls: for Judges, like all bold Interpreters, by often altering the Text, make it quite new; and *Statesmen* (who differ not from Law-makers in the act, but in the manner of doing) make new Lawes presumptuously without the consent of the People, but *Legislators* more civilly seeme to whistle to the Beast, and stroke him into the Yoke (32).

Echoing Demosthenes' use of parable (41), in engaging their readers with their fictions, poets are modeling the proper relationship between the exercise of prerogative power and popular opinion, so that Plato, by banishing poets from the republic, proved "an absolute Monarch over Arts" (43). All the arts, denoting any product of human activity, or any construct permitting civil society, thus play out in their different ways the ideal relations between authority and counsel, a form of counsel realized, in the case of poetry and drama, in the customary engagement and implicit judgment of the audience. It almost follows that Davenant sees the sacrifice of Charles I not as the exercise of custom, but as its subversion (I,iii,77). Thus, like the plays which it emulates, *Gondibert* is an instantiation of the ideal polity, which Davenant, writing as hostilities over trade with the Dutch are developing in the early 1650s, now begins explicitly to align with an early form of political economy: if a poem, like a building, is a kind of (post-Harveian) body; if that body models the body politic; and if the health of the body politic now depends on commerce, then, Davenant writes, using a metaphor that was soon to become stock-in-trade, "Mony is the life blood of the People" (34).

Hobbes's famous reply to his friend has all the signs that he fully understood and approved of the implications of Davenant's argument. Recalling Serlio's distinction among the tragic, the comic, and the satyric scenes – though Hobbes calls these the "*Heroique, Scommatique,* and *Pastorall*" (45) – he instantly politicizes the artistic capacity to reconcile these modes, as signifying a balance between "*Court, Citty,* and *Country*" (45), which themselves echo the cosmic balances among the three regions, the "*Caelestiall, Aëriall,* and *Terrestriall*" (45). The artifices that make this palpable and thus functional for civil society are grounded in an architectural conception, so that building appears first in the list of civilizing arts – including engineering, astronomy, geography, horology, and navigation (49). But it transpires that since fancy makes these possible with the help of philosophy, and since fancy is best imaged in the discipline of architecture, guided as it is by philosophical principles, architecture like poetry perfectly represents the conjunction of material and abstract principles ("body and soule, colour and shadow") that imbue civilized activities with force and meaning (50). Hobbes's ready appropriation of the architectural *topos* means too that the biometric metaphor returns equally readily, so that we are reminded that language is a body of sorts (53). Since the civilizing arts reconcile or contain different principles and impulses, they are like the plains of Lombardy, lying between the Po and the Adice, which shows how, in the post-Harveian world, the conceptual territory Hobbes alludes to "hath the same resemblance also with a mans veins, which proceeding from different parts, after the like concourse, insert themselves at last into the two principall veynes of the Body" (50).[2] More explicitly than in Davenant's longer preface, the *topos* of variety is grounded in Ciceronian *copia*. Hobbes writes, "From *Knowing much*, proceedeth the admirable variety and novelty of metaphors and similitudes, which are not possibly to be lighted on, in the compasse of a narrow knowledge" (53). It almost follows logically, that, in arguing that Davenant's strangely theatrical poem encompasses and balances a series of different impulses – thereby serving as an expression of Hobbes's own artificial polity in *Leviathan* – Hobbes concludes with the famous allusion to anamorphic perspective:

I beleeve (Sir) you have seene a curious kind of perspective, where, he that looks through a short hollow pipe, upon a picture conteyning diverse figures, sees none of those that are there paynted, but some one person made up of their partes, conveighed to the eye by the artificiall cutting of a glasse. I find in my imagination an effect not unlike it from your Poeme. The virtues you distribute there amongst so many noble Persons, represent (in the reading) the image but of one mans virtue to my fancy, which is your owne. (55)

The clear implication is that the work of the poet, like the product of the anamorphic artist (and like the liberal polity itself), can display dramatic distinctions among different perspectives and yet provide a device or frame within which they can be balanced and even reconciled.

We are now on the brink of the poem whose details are easy to forget. But it can – indeed should – be approached along the methodical lines introduced in the exchange with Hobbes, namely as a question of how the spatialization of meaning, assumed in the architectural metaphor and Hobbes's anamorphic perspective, serves to describe the arts of civil society. Consequently, the essential outlines of the plot are relatively simple and few, amounting to about four movements which together flesh out an argument about the polity that made it redundant for Davenant to continue. The story is set in Lombardy, ruled over by King Aribert, who only appears in Book III. His two lieutenants are Oswald and Gondibert, who are rivals, not least for the hand of the princess, Rhodalind. At first encamped with their followers at Brescia and Bergamo, respectively, the two rivals engage in battle when Oswald ambushes Gondibert. Oswald is killed, while Gondibert is eventually badly wounded. Book II involves two movements: the first transports events from the country to Verona, which allows Davenant to introduce his specifically civic concerns; and these are developed in the second half, where the wounded Gondibert is tended by the physician and virtuoso, Astragon, whose daughter, Birtha, catches Gondibert's eye. The third book ends inconclusively, because to thank Gondibert for his services Aribert decides to bestow on him the hand of his daughter Rhodalind, and though Birtha is willing to relinquish Gondibert to her for reasons of state, Gondibert presents Birtha with an emerald as an enduring pledge of their love. We never learn whether their love is consummated or not.

Since, however, the motives of the poem are more conceptual than narrative, the actual fate of the lovers remains merely academic. For Davenant's entire thrust is to consider the relationship between the hidden and occult processes of nature herself, as well as the equivalent impulses informing human agency – in the essentially Hobbesian guise of ambition, power, desire, and love – and the legible institutions that both express and contain them. Critics are thus right to point out that at some level the poem anticipates the dynamics of heroic drama by deliberating on the tensions between private desire (love) and public demands (honor), so the poem loses direction once Davenant reveals – as we will see – that the institution of marriage, which also informs the Aristoteleian basis of monarchy, comprehends both, so echoing the resolution of *The Platonick Lovers* and anticipating that of *The Siege of Rhodes*.

The three books form a neat triptych in this scheme. Book I begins on the field of battle, which it stylizes in two ways: the hunt in Canto ii serves as an emblem of Charles I's fate, and, more importantly, the oppositions between the two camps encourage Davenant to engage in balanced arrangements of characters whose effect is a fundamental feature of the poem. It is fascinated by the sense in which civil life can be conceptualized as an aesthetic, as falling into patterns or what at one point Davenant calls "civil shape" (III,ii,41), visible constructs whose legitimacy depends in large part on how they are viewed from without by spectators or an audience, just as Davenant's own poem enacts those very formal properties whose force depends on his reader. Book I is concerned with one particular expression of the civil order involving the containment of the most primitive impulses to violence, a Hobbesian enterprise that Burckhardt calls "war as a work of art," a "purely rational treatment of warlike affairs" that was only possible after the fourteenth and fifteenth centuries in Italy; this is one aspect in what Burckhardt generalizes as the "systematization of outward life."[3] Thus, at the outset, war is King Aribert's "study'd Art," the reason being that "To conquer Tumult, Nature's sodain force, / War, Art's delib'rate strength, was first devis'd" (I,i,3–4). Later, we hear that because the characters we meet are civilly conscious agents, "War, the worlds Art, Nature to them became" (I,ii,75); and in Canto iv, war itself occurs as a choreographed ballet:

> Calmly their temper did their art obay;
> Then stretch'd Arms regular in motion prove;
> And force with as unseen a stealth convay,
> As noyselesse Howres by hands of Dials move.
>
> (I,iv,40)

The opposition between Rhodalind – the virtuous princess – and Gartha – Oswald's dubious sister – encourages Davenant to raise anew the question he raised in his preface, namely how we recognize when we are moved by moral examples. We respond to examples, it seems, while we remain conscious of the distinction between innate virtue and its expression, so that Rhodalind, who serves as an example of the exemplary, at least contingently reconciles the Cartesian divorce between mind and body, the softness of her female form better capable than the male of retaining traces of an essential mental or spiritual core (I,i,17–18). But we are moved by examples for reasons we have already encountered: they appeal to our aesthetic sense, to the way in which formal arrangements (whether in war or poetry, and thence of politics more largely, which are metaphors for each other) have their own logic and appeal. Thus, when we are first introduced to the main characters we are asked to see them not so much as internally motivated beings as figures whose meanings depend on their mutual juxtaposition:

> *Oswald* the great, and greater *Gondibert*!
> Both from successful conqu'ring Fathers sprung;
> Whom both examples made of Warre's high art,
> And far out-wrought their patterns being young.
>
> (I,i,27)

Here it is the reader to whom Davenant is directly appealing, whereas the account of the battle that ensues in Canto iii and its aftermath involves participants who stand in – by appearing conscious of the spectacle of which they form a part – for that readerly and ocular activity (see for example

I,vi,59–60). The beginning of Canto iii converts Gondibert, as well as the poet, into just such a "spy" (as the text has it on numerous occasions), seeing the field of battle as its own kind of text:

> The Duke observ'd (whilst safe in his firm Square)
> Whether their front did change whom *Oswald* led;
> That thence he shifts of figure might prepare,
> Divide, or make more depth, or loosely spred.
>
> (I,iii,1)

Later, in Book III, Davenant generalizes about what we might call the pageant of power expressed in the aesthetics of war, as Ulfin instructs Ulfinore in the arts of statesmanship:

> Thy greatness be in Armes! Who else are great,
> Move but like Pageants in the People's view;
> And in foul weather make a scorn'd retreat;
> The *Greeks*, their painted Gods in Armor drew.
>
> (III,vi,9)

The battle continues in this way much like a spectator sport, with participants (indeed spoken of as "Spectators" [e.g. I,iii,39]) always conscious of how the arrangements comprise patterns to be observed, however deadly their effects. Thus as Oswald is to Gondibert, so Orna (Gondibert's sister) is to Gartha (Oswald's), so Hubert to Hurgonil, Paradine to Arnold, Dragonet to Hugo, Borgia to Goltho, and Vasco to Tybalt. Death is experienced by both sides in parallel, as it were, the major difference being that whereas Oswald is killed, Gondibert is wounded, so preparing us for Book II. In rallying his troops, Gondibert explicitly compares the scene with the theater, with, in this case, a specifically female audience:

> Think now your valor enters on the Stage,
> Think Fame the eternal *Chorus* to declare
> Your mighty mindes to each succeeding age,
> And that your Ladys the Spectators are.
>
> (I,v,19)

That we, the poet, and the characters observe and deem significant these arrangements calls up consistent allusions to the Lucretian notion that atoms or elements comprise the building-blocks of any viable human experience (I,v,17; I,vi,30). And the ongoing question too is what mysterious power or force, if any, explains their appeal, so that along with the alchemical postulate – which may explain how occult properties inhabit publicly mediated forms of knowledge – Davenant also begins to conjure with another opposition, reflecting the historical moment as hostilities with the Dutch became palpable, and so naturally derived from the discourse of trade. (The Navigation Act, which was to result in the first Dutch War, was passed in October 1651.) How, the question asks, are we to assess value in general, since for Davenant, evidently, the nature of literary effectiveness, the nature of political authority, and matters of national wealth all run in parallel and can be debated with shared vocabularies? How, locally, does the distinction between "intrinsick" and "extrinsick" value in the discourse of trade, that is, bear on the larger framework of inquiry? There are at least eleven points in the course of *Gondibert* where that analogy comes to the fore, five of which are in Book I (I,ii,18; I,ii,31; I,iii,17; I,iii,82; I,v,9). So at one point, how do we endure life, Davenant asks, once the mysterious animating principle in love has evaporated?

> If we call living Life, when Love is gone,
> We then to Souls Gods coyne vain rev'rence pay;
> Since Reason (which is Love, and his best knowne
> And currant Image) Age has worne away.
>
> (I,ii,18)

If, here, Davenant seems to preserve some core principle – reason as God's coin, for instance – later he implies that such an innate guarantor of value must submit to convention. What was current in one sense is now current in a different sense, so that the poem seeks to effect a change of perspective in our sense of the root meaning of "currency." The consequence is that *Gondibert* itself becomes an exercise in customary behavior, because what appears to be an established principle of meaning changes in the course of time to reflect the altered circumstances of an utterance. For all its allure as an item of worth, it transpires that money, like language, depends on how it is used not on a single source of authority but on the community within which it is embedded; and Davenant seeks to cultivate that consciousness in the various observers within the poem, as well as in the observers of his poem, namely his readers, so that the reader's relationship to the poem translates in course of time into a defense of custom *per se*. Thus viewing the dead Oswald, Gondibert laments the loss of intrinsic value in his peerless rival, regrettable but inevitable, comparing him to those that remain:

> In these we the intrinsick vallew know
> By which first Lovers did love currant deem;
> But Love's false Coyners will allay it now,
> Till men suspect what next they must contemn.
>
> (I,v,9)

The poem naturally settles after Book I, because for all that war is, in the ways we have seen, a civil institution like any other, its effects are nonetheless chaotic and destructive. The poet bids farewell to the field of battle both by aestheticizing it once more, rendering it into an artifact (viewed recursively, the events comprise the pattern of history itself [I,ii,26]), and by anticipating the wounded Gondibert's sojourn in the house of Astragon which, because it is a building, is a more permanent artifact. Because it is also the occasion of scientific activity, as the Book closes we are reminded that, like trade and alchemy, indeed poetry herself, natural philosophy inculcates a regard for the dynamic principles that link the hidden operations of nature with the visible and material world.

Book II now decisively shifts the scene to Verona, which figures an historically sedimented consciousness and a socially multifaceted world. This in turn raises the issue of how the populace in general participates in civil affairs, which initiates a series of meditations (expanded in Book III) both on the danger of popular opinion (consistently spoken of as "fashion") and the corresponding corruption of court life ("luxury"). Inasmuch as the rhetoric of custom seeks to subvert law, to resist the King's prerogative to raise taxes, and to justify resistance to authority on religious grounds, Davenant criticizes the "vicious vulgar" (II,i,59); but at the same time he begins to postulate an altogether more latitudinarian approach to the polity, partly imagined through the reconciliation of body (signifying popular materialism) and mind (II,i,61). The test case must have appealed to Hobbes, because it directly reflects the position taken by members of the Tew Circle, especially Viscount Falkland himself. The view is that the state should not directly regulate all matters of faith but rather supply an umbrella for the exercise of conscience. Conscience mediates between the rigors of the law and the ambiguities of custom, and accommodates the fact that "Faiths so sev'ral be, that few are those / Can chuse right wings when they to Heav'n would fly" (II,i,63). If custom is potentially subversive, for its part the law is associated with pomp and the exercise of violence (II,i,66–8), and has no right to dictate religious practice by force. For Davenent as for the latitudinarians, all Englishmen should enjoy the shared "Rites" of religious practice (implicitly the Anglican communion), offering a public forum for social engagement, but one which nonetheless allows individuals to exercise their private conscience (II,i,72). Echoing the precepts of the Tew Circle, the argument to Canto vi will read, *"Religion's Rites, seem here, in Reasons sway; / Though Reason must Religion's Laws obay"* (II,vi,Arg.).

Canto ii expands these concerns even more explicitly, first by recourse to the architectural ideal we have already explored and then by direct discussion of the relation between the exercise of prerogative and counsel. Hurgonil dispatches Tybalt to the palace, which Davenant carefully describes. Tybalt goes

> To that proud Palace which once low did lie
> In *Parian* Quarries, now on Columes stands;
> *Ionique* Props that bear their Arches high,
> With ample treasure rais'd by *Tuscan* Hands.
> (II,ii,6)

The dependence of the Ionic on the Tuscan (like the conjunction of soul and body, cold and hot [II,ii,12–13;25;51]) rapidly migrates into a disquisition on the symbiotic relationship between the King, the people, and sources of counsel which it symbolically denotes. Aribert's wisdom is expressed by his listening selectively to popular opinion (II,ii,8) and by grounding his power in the organs of counsel:

> He wealth nor birth preferred to Councels place;
> For Councel is for use, not ornament;
> Soules are alike, of rich and ancient Race;
> Though Bodies claim distinctions by descent.
> (II,ii,12)

While it implicitly castigates Charles I for having immured himself in court culture (II,ii,14;23;30), the narrative also intensifies the problem of false counsel by introducing Gartha, Oswald's sister, who intends no good (Canto iii), and Hermegild, an unreliable source of advice (Canto iv). But Davenant clearly sees the challenge as a question of statecraft, an art, like good counsel and like Davenant's own poem, which can channel and control the effects of naked power, conceived as a force of nature (II,ii,20;74). As Hermegild puts it in Canto iv,

> We are the People's Pilots, they our winds;
> To change by Nature prone; but Art Laveers,
> And rules them till they rise with Stormy Mindes;
> Then Art with danger against Nature steers.
> (II,iv,32)

The idea that the world is contingent and in flux, and that the magistrate must accordingly constantly navigate among political shoals – so requiring counsel – is developed in the other motif of Canto ii. The beauteous Rhodalind, smitten with Gondibert, must come to terms with the fact that his recovery is unsure and that she cannot secure his response. Fame or rumor also signify the impermanence of the human lot (II,ii,54). The point is that affairs of the heart – lying in the realm of the private – have, like woman's beauty, at best a tangential relationship to the movements of history in the public realm. And, apart from extensive troping on the difference between public and private (II,ii,79;86–7;91), Davenant reintroduces the metaphors of trade and coinage as if further to dilute the suspicion that woman's beauty can secure permanence of any kind. The problem is intensified because Rhodalind's beauty is fully matched by that of Laura (who also desires Gondibert), so that neither enjoys a monopoly in that relation; and the erosion of value proceeds further when, in Canto iv, Hermegild falls for Gartha because she too is beautiful. In any realm, the implication goes, the original perceived value of an object is merely notional and must, like currency proper, yield to its "currant price" (II,ii,52;66).

Cantos v through viii shift the scene to the house of Astragon, where similar arguments are differently pursued. The entire conception is predicated on the threefold correspondence between the new science, the political order, and poetry. These are all linked by what we might call a dual "Lucretian" conception of the arts, since, first, the art of scientific inquiry, the art of government, and the art of poetry all operate under the aegis of some dramatic distinction between cause and effect, or what Boyle and Locke speak of as the difference between primary and secondary qualities. Importantly, all these activities take place in an architectural space – the house of Astragon – that, though it apparently embraces both Art and Nature, is defined by the extent to which even natural philosophy is one among several arts that seek to inquire into the inner workings of nature. Obeying the second "Lucretian" principle, science is just one of many searches into the truth of things, none of which has epistemological priority, because in a shared, skeptical universe no single art is descriptively adequate. Different activities run in parallel: truth is merely a matter of what works, or, as Milton was soon to argue, an attempt to save the appearances; so that Davenant compares numerous different traditions and disciplines, beginning with an allusion to cosmology and the new astronomy, both of which (like architecture) picture the motions of nature rather than penetrate to its essence ("Here Art by such a diligence is serv'd, / As does th'unwearied Planets imitate" [II,v,7]). Thus the preliminary gesture is followed by references to alchemy, attempts to plumb the depths of the sea and earth, and astronomy, whose Copernican structure encourages the postulate of the plurality of worlds. The erosion of the qualitative distinction between sublunary and superlunary worlds allows, by analogy, the notion that there may be numerous worlds elsewhere like our own, which in Davenant's conception itself serves as a model of the liberal order:

And wisely *Astragon*, thus busy grew,
To seek the Stars remote societies,
The judge the walks of th'old, by finding new;
For Nature's law, in correspondence lies.

(II,v,18)

We then approach a kind of research academy whose purpose is in effect to textualize nature, to render her operations public and legible. Davenant pursues the argument three ways, first by listing the pursuits involved – zoology, ichthyology, ornithology, and botany – before, second, describing a virtuoso's cabinet, whose contents, it transpires, make it "The Monument of vanish'd Mindes" (II,v,36), by which he means a kind of anthology of earlier cultures, all of which are distinguished by a commitment to occult and secret forms of knowledge, whereby intellectual elites seek to control the world around them. All previous societies have lost sight of the forensic and hermeneutic task of drawing out knowledge for public consumption and debate, whether we recall the Egyptians, Chaldeans, Persians, Hebrews, Greeks, or Romans. Becoming enmeshed in some form of esoterica, each tradition has relinquished a responsibility to nature as a primary text to be openly read and interpreted.

This brings Davenant to his third point. The humanist ambition, we could say, is to treat numerous disciplines as tending towards the same end, on the view that they all inhabit the language arts, and that their highest motive is finally civic. So, rehearsing the relative virtues of philosophy, ethics, history, and medicine, the Canto concludes with a celebration of poetry as – in the figure of David – an art allying the figural values of language with political purposes, which echoes the way Aesop succeeded in making morality digestible in his fables (II,v,59). Since poetry absorbs all the virtues of the other disciplines, Davenant trumpets it as a "hyreless Science! and of all alone / The Liberal!" (II,v,68).

If Canto v expatiates on the artificial virtues of natural philosophy that correspond to the artifice of statecraft, both symbolized by the poet's endeavors, then Canto vi applies the same principles to an Erastian view of the church, signified again in an architectural motif. Astragon has built a triangular apartment, indicating the threefold importance of praise, penitence, and prayer (II,vi,4). To each of these spiritual exercises Astragon has erected a temple, as if to objectify the religious life, so converting it into a matter of public property, just as Books III and IV of *Leviathan* argue that the magistrate should serve as the public arbiter of scriptural interpretation. Visits to the three temples essentially structure the Canto, which also weaves a commentary on science and trade into the view that we must approach religious observance as a matter of public concern rather than private enthusiasm. The actual practice of natural philosophy and the operations of trade reveal how healthy human activities of all sorts are mediated, whether by that we mean that we only have access to second causes in nature or that wealth in world commerce emerges surreptitiously from the activities of trade carried out over great distances. The general principle is that "*Astragon* makes Nature last by Art" (II,vi,24), and accordingly our knowledge of creation only occurs as a panel in the Temple of Praise:

> The great Creation by bold Pencils drawn;
> Where a feign'd Curtain does our Eies forbid,
> Till the Sun's Parent, Light, first seems to dawn
> From quiet *Chaos*, which that Curtain hid.
>
> (II,vi,53)

Similarly, we understand nature as a design upon Astragon's cloak:

> Lord *Astragon* a Purple Mantle wore,
> Where Nature's story was in Colours wrought;
> And though her ancient Text seem'd dark before,
> 'Tis in this pleasant Comment clearly taught.
>
> (II,vi,76)

And in one of his poem's most elaborate discussions of trade, Davenant pursues a parallel argument (II,vi,31–40). The discovery of the loadstone – which Dryden celebrates in the "Epistle to Charleton" – modernizes the *topos, translatio studii et imperii*, since it prompts hitherto coast-bound vessels to make long ocean voyages into the west. Like a proper appreciation of our mediated knowledge of the divine, the effects of trade have an only tangential relation to some guarantor of riches, like the "wretched Gold" that deluded traders seek to obtain (II,vi,36). Davenant associates an obsession with such unequivocal sources of value with the kind of ignorance that seeks to penetrate the divine mysteries, such that an Erastian expression of churchmanship, in which all religious knowledge is accommodated to social coherence, finds its corollary in a vision of worldwide trade of the kind that Dryden was to indulge in *Annus Mirabilis*:

> . . . when this plague of ignorance shall end,
> (Dire ignorance with which God plagues us most;
> Whilst we not feeling it, him most offend)
> Then lower'd Sayles no more shall tide the Coast.
>
> They with new *Tops* to *Formasts* and the *Main*,
> And *Misens* new, shall th'Oceans Breast invade;

Stretch new Sayles out, as Armes to entertain
Those windes, of which their Fathers were afraid.

Then (sure of either Pole) they will with pride,
In ev'ry storm, salute this constant Stone!
And scorn that Star, which ev'ry Cloud could hide;
The Seamen's spark! which soon, as seen, is gone!

'Tis sung, the Ocean shall his Bonds untie,
And Earth in half a Globe be pent no more;
Typhis shall sayle, till *Thule* he discry,
But a domestick step to distant shore!

(II,vi,37–40)

The Canto closes by, among other things, suggesting that the "discordant" interests expressed in the activity of trade might be curiously reconciled by providential action. Men's prayers are perennially in mutual competition, blindly launched onto the ocean of supplication, but of course they achieve an inscrutible coherence in the pattern of the divine order (II,vi,85). This is clearly an early version of what was to become Adam Smith's invisible hand.

Cantos vii and viii record the arrival of Birtha and her effects on Gondibert's sense of things. While maintaining the poem's tensions between inner and outer, private and public, occult and representational, the mutual sympathy between Birtha and Gondibert prepares the way for the poem's effectual resolution in Book III, for Davenant is experimenting with the possibility of a multiple economy – affective, somatic, literary, and political – that could, echoing such thematic correspondences in his own poem, at least contingently promote desirable balances in the state. The key point occurs in Goltho's complaint in Canto vii that Gondibert now prefers love (in the form of Birtha) to honor (in the form of war): "the Duke," he claims, "shuns Empire for a Bride" (II,viii,59). But Davenant reminds us that Birtha's attraction to Gondibert has to do with the fact that though he is a product of courtly culture, she represents the country, a point already anticipated in Hobbes's reply to Davenant's preface, where he imagines the ideal balances among court, city, and country. In Goltho's jaundiced view of it,

> *Birtha*, (a harmless Cottage Ornament!)
> May be his Bride, that's born himself to serve;
> But you must pay that blood your Army spent,
> And wed that Empire which our wounds deserve.
>
> (II,viii,57)

The implicit symmetry within the polity pictured here alone explains why Gondibert resists creating a monolithic state of the kind his father (presumably representing Charles I) attempted: "For could I force all Monarchys to one," he asserts, "That Universal Crown I would not weare" (II,viii,34–43).

Canto vii makes it clear that Birtha represents a kind of natural postulate with which Gondibert is now taken, even though the closer alliance between inner truth and outward manifestation remains vexed; so that the fact that they are now in love is a truth only testified to empirically by Astragon the natural philosopher ("Nature's wise Spy" [II,vii,73]). Accordingly, although Birtha's arrival invites a rapprochement between the world of Nature that she embodies and the courtly Arts in which Gondibert excels (II,vii,11–16;37–8;55–63), knowledge of occult processes, echoing the method of the new science, remains strictly experimental and symptomatic. The experience is rendered, for example, in entirely physiognomic terms:

> Her Face, o'recast with thought, does soon betray
> Th'assembled spirits, which [Astragon's] Eies detect
> By her pale look, as by the Milkie way,
> Men first did the assembled stars suspect.
>
> (II,vii,69)

Davenant's prevailing phenomenalism is such that the commercial expression of the lovers' newfound position, though allying hitherto opposed terms, retains the critical distinction between coins as the visible tokens of trade and the hidden world of credit which allows the system to operate at all:

> That she the payment he of love would make
> Less understood, then yet the debt she knew;
> But coynes unknown, suspitiously we take,
> And debts, till manifest, are never due.
>
> (II,vii,66)

As we conclude Book II, the same phenomenalism displaces the desire to distribute value across a range of incommensurables from the various thematics of the poem (representing the mixed constitution), to the poem itself as a species of arrangement or patterning of the kind we saw – in relation to the order of battle – in Book I. At stanza 82 of Canto viii, Davenant freezes the forward movement of the poem so that both he and the reader once again look back on our experience of the text as if from some elevation in a landscape, or as the kind of epitaph he mentions in the penultimate stanza (II,viii,90). (He repeats this move in Book III, Canto iii.) Recalling *Cooper's Hill*, this topographical gesture stands in for the pattern of history considered recursively, but Davenant wants to conscript the moral force conventionally associated with history for his text, both because the balanced patternings in the poem adumbrate the balances described in other terms and because he sees poetry, like history and moral philosophy, as a species of rhetoric, as recommending what it describes. Because this mechanism requires that rather than being coerced, the reader assent to what is proposed, once again it is the reader who occupies, relative to the poem as an aesthetic proposition, the structural place of counsel itself.

It is conventional to argue that Davenant never completed *Gondibert* because, as the published poem has it, Book III was "Written by the Author During his Imprisonment" (191). However, I believe that because Davenant's project concerns establishing certain conceptual (as well as formal) equilibria whose implications are invariably political, he had in effect found his answer in the balance between Birtha and Gondibert, so that Book III struggles, eventually in vain, to continue. This book only adds one further element to the mix, and one clearly anticipated by the conclusion of *The Platonick Lovers*, in which marriage, combining private desire with a public institution, and custom with law, stands in for the mixed constitution. Thus, though it is quite clear that Birtha and Gondibert, despite temporary obstructions, will get married, that marriage is already figured early in Book III in the union of Hurgonil and Orna.

By contrast with the occult and magic arts of the evil counselor Hermegild (III,i,3), on the one hand, and the purely formal exercises to which court life is prone, on the other, marriage is that civil and religious rite that at least notionally reconciles private passion with public institutions. To reiterate, marriage is a point at which prerogative and custom meet, because it is a customary institution bestowing pleasure, but one nevertheless regulated by law, so marriage becomes the perfect symptom of the mixed monarchy. Behind that institution is of course the Aristotelian analogy between family and state, as Davenant reminds us:

> A King you are o're Subjects, so as wise
> And noble Husbands seem o're Loyal Wives;
> Who claim not, yet confess their liberties,
> And brag to strangers of their happy loves.
> (III,iv,22)

But since "Degree is monarch's Art, Love, Nature's Law" (III,v,28), the project in Book III is to harmonize both impulses, something Orna and Hurgonil, not Gondibert and Birtha, have already achieved. This is why Aribert's determination to bestow Rhodalind on Gondibert for reasons of state will almost certainly fail, since the decision plays purely to the public side of the equation. Failure to achieve the right kinds of equilibrium invites, we are reminded, civil war; so that the answer comes in the extent to which Gondibert and Birtha can reconcile their mental states with their bodily desires (III,ii,47), the extent to which the king respects counsel (III,ii,73), and the extent to which custom unites form (or "civil shape") with pleasure: "Custom, which all, rather than Law obay, / For Lawes by force, Customes, by pleasure last" (III,i,39). As elsewhere in the poem, the dynamic connecting public and private, the state and the individual, is also imagined consistently in terms of the new discourse of trade, and the Harveian conception of the body on which by now it relies.

THE SIEGE OF RHODES (1656; 1658; 1661)

Following established precedent, I have argued consistently that *The Siege of Rhodes* represents a watershed moment in the history of English drama. Now that Davenant had received permission to mount an "opera" in a private residence – Rutland House – he was in a position to test the kinds of argument he had in *Gondibert* developed thematically – involving for example the relationship between the biometric metaphor embedded in architectural theory, civil society, the artifices of poetry, and trade – against the possibilities afforded by actual performance spaces. In this section, I argue that the ideological and technical revolution that might harmonize Davenant's ideas with the new proscenium stage and actresses took considerable time. It began with the 1656 performances at Rutland House, which did not really comprise a theater proper; it extended to a further performance in 1658 of what later came to be known as the first part of *The Siege of Rhodes*, this time at the Cock-Pit, Drury Lane, which had served as a theater in the early Stuart period; and it culminated in 1661 in an expanded version of the first part of *The Siege of Rhodes* supplemented by an entirely new second part, this time performed in Davenant's own dedicated theater in Lincoln's Inn Fields, itself a refashioned tennis court. (The theater opened with performances of the opera on 28 June 1661, some time after Killigrew's King's Company had already begun acting at Gibbon's Tennis Court Theatre; and the delay resulted from better scenic arrangements that Killigrew was soon forced to redress by restoring the Theatre Royal.) The developing history of Davenant's opera, therefore, perfectly describes the translation of the perspective stage from its inception in the Interregnum, where it remained more an idea and a potential, to the Restoration proper, in which, in the second part of *The Siege of Rhodes*, the new space of the theater clearly fashions the conditions of the symbolic argument being pursued at the level of plot.

Given our experience of *Gondibert*, it should not surprise us, however, that Davenant's ambitions for the new medium were from the outset of the highest order. Just as his Preface to Hobbes announces the aims of the poem in the most sophisticated terms, so his *First Dayes Entertainment at Rutland House* and *The Cruelty of the Spaniards in Peru* represent methodological investigations into the implications of the new staging conditions for the 1656 and 1658 performances respectively, especially the former. *The First Dayes Entertainment* instantly commits itself to civic humanist ends, since it is, we are told in the title, *"after the manner of the Ancients."*[4] By protesting against the restrictions of the indoor space, the prologue paradoxically emphasizes its immediacy and potential, as if we as audience are reminded how the walls of the house both press upon us as spectators and force the action of the play in a given direction. The theme of doubling and dialectical debate with a rhetorical thrust which is so central to the Fletcherian mode is now materialized in the fact that in Rutland House the two halves of the audience face each other (341); and this dialectical model is carried out by two further devices: *"two gilded* Rostras" front the scene (342), while the entire action, anticipating that of Dryden's *Of Dramatic Poesy*, is occupied with declamatory debate between, first, Diogenes the Cynic and Aristophanes, and, second, representatives of the rival cities of Paris and London. Here, as we should expect, the urban landscapes, situated on the Seine and the Thames respectively, represent opposing views of the political order and the role of trade within it. The "liberal" or rather haphazard civic space of London anticipates Dryden's view of the random nature of English drama; and so the town in which the performance occurs thus reflects back on the spatial organization of this new dramatic economy.

Though the Athenians represent the public to which the speakers appeal, the central conception is clearly Roman, figured here in the rostra, and in the Ciceronian action of the debate, where Diogenes and Aristophanes disagree about *"Publick Entertainment* by *Morall Representations"* (342). Diogenes represents the asocial tendency to withdraw from public life into his tub, a laconic view of language contradicted by the fact of debate in which Diogenes is forced to make concessions which both implicitly criticize the Cromwellian regime and prepare us for Aristophanes' eventual triumph: the Athenian mob ("Beasts of *Athens*") is too easily swayed by windy rhetoric; it too readily ostracizes dissenters; and as a body it has a habit of devouring its "Governours" (343). Diogenes ridicules the claim of Aristophanic "*Opera*" to inculcate civility by dismissing civility as a mere matter of "external behaviour" (344), which, we have already seen, is precisely the point, since the public conditions of representation in any medium trump the lure of the private and magical that seems to have seduced him.

In his riposte, Aristophanes pursues these arguments further. Descanting on the evils of solitude, he reminds the audience that humans are social animals, depicting their condition in strongly Hobbesian language: "Other creatures of the most pacifique species incline to society, that they may delight in each others safety, whilst they are protected by their conjunction of strength" (346). The assembled spectators here at Rutland House to whom these orators appeal *in utramque partem* stand in for public assemblies of all kinds, especially those that gather at the forum; and just as emulation is the basic psychological motive of public strivings after excellence, which presupposes a proper display of "external glory" (347), so this audience will only respond to patterns of virtue if they come larded with "the Ornaments of a publick *Opera*, Musick and Scenes" (349). Evidently civility – as Jones had argued twenty years before – depends on the entire gamut of histrionic machinery at the dramatist's disposal (349).

The debate between the Parisian and the Londoner pursues similar arguments in a different vein. Here the device of *in utramque partem* is more readily in evidence, since in both cases we are forced to infer Davenant's positive argument from the mutual criticisms that emerge. This method itself stands in for Davenant's obvious dislike of French absolutism in favor of a more mixed political and fiscal economy expressed in the winning chaos of the London streets and the centrality of the Thames to the world of commerce and trade. Here the correspondence between public architecture, urban and social variety, and conceptions of political liberty could not be more explicit:

The commodity and trade of your River belongs to your selves; but give a stranger leave to share in the pleasure of it, which will hardly be in the prospect or freedom of Ayr; unless prospect, consisting of variety, be made up with here a Palace, there a Wood-yard, here a Garden, there a Brew-house: Here dwells a Lord, there a Dyer, and between both *Duomo Comune*. If freedom of Ayr be inferr'd in the liberty of the Subject, where every private man hath Authority, for his own profit, to smoak up a Magistrate; then the Ayr of your *Thames* is open enough, because 'tis equally free. (352)

Predictably, in the Londoner's account, though it is more clearly laid out, the architecture of Paris – expressing the self-regard of the absolutist state – is given to size and grandiosity rather than use and custom. And given the unbridgeable divide between the great and the humble, dissent in this world can only manifest itself in the violent effusions of rebellion:

Your sons you dignifie betimes with a taste of pleasure and liberty; which perhaps breeds in them (that they may maintain the vast expences of high pleasure) too hasty and violent an appetite to such power as makes them, when they are Men, soon turbulent to Supream Authority. (357)

The disordered "rudeness" of London life thus contrasts with the "frequent insurrections" of Paris (357); and whereas the bustling activity of the Thames – whose energetic watermen anticipate the setting of Dryden's *Of Dramatic Poesy* – expresses the productivity of the one, the ferryman on the Seine "stands as sullen as an old Dutch Skipper after shipwrack" (356), by which single gesture Davenant cocks a snook at England's chief rivals in the political and economic spheres.

The topical concern with the conditions of civil life is, as we will see, also pursued in *The Siege of Rhodes*, whose first performance in 1656 *The First Dayes Entertainment* was evidently designed to introduce. The second performance in 1658 is similarly introduced by a different play, *The Cruelty of the Spaniards in Peru*, whose purpose is, like *The First Dayes Entertainment*, to deliberate on the distinction between civil life (an artificial and public concern) and a state of nature (governed mainly by "private" interests): now the state must be clearly distinguished from the tribe. At this juncture, we are entering a realm we could properly call political economy, for a commentary on the centrality of trade to the civil order and the relative political valences of different ideas about wealth accompanies the broadly Hobbesian motif, since the emergence of the state from the tribe is marked by the arrival of trade, an idea irrevocably connected to the incursion of Europeans into the new world. Although the state is in any instance – whether expressed by the Spanish or English – a kind of fall from primitive simplicity, it is nevertheless the best means of securing human ends. Thus whereas Hobbes indicts the state of nature for failing to provide the stability of the civil order, here the natural innocence of the Incas allows Davenant a subtle criticism of the Caroline regime: just as the Incas are incapable of politic thought because they are too entrenched in the immediate satisfactions of private life, so Charles I was often accused of uxoriousness. And though the lure of the primitive and private is great, it is also responsible for the outbreak of civil war among the Incas. The moral is that

Kings who move
Within a lowly sphear of private love,
Are too domestick for a throne.[5]

The innocence of the Incas renders them vulnerable to invasion but, occupying a crude barter economy where "none were rich by bus'ness made"
(5), they remain delightfully oblivious to the veins of gold and silver with
which the Spanish, "Idolators of Gold" (8), are obsessed. It is not perhaps
as clear as it could be, but the later arrival of English mariners, who free
the Incas from Spanish oppression, opposes a mercantile economy and
mentality to Spanish bullionism. English trade is thus associated with liberty, Spanish bullionism with a tyranny that results in an unintentionally
comic scene involving two Spaniards, "the one turning a Spit, whilst the
other is basting an *Indian* Prince, which is roasted at an artificiall fire"
(19).

The first version of *The Siege of Rhodes* was presented at Rutland House
(1656) and then at the Cock-Pit, Drury Lane (1658). Expressing frustration at the physical limitations of these theatrical spaces, Davenant actually
seeks to justify a new theatrical protocol, which again we could call loosely
Fletcherian in mode. Because the events to which the play refers are "in
story very copious,"[6] he looks forward to a time when better funds will
allow a "larger Room" (Sig. A2r), but at present, though assisted by John
Webb's designs (Sig. A3r) (see figures 27–32), he must squeeze the action
into a space "confin'd to eleven foot in height, and about fifteen in depth"
(Sig. A2v). Therefore, he writes, though the story is "Heroical," "you cannot expect the chief Ornaments belonging to a History Drammatically
digested into Turns and Counter-turns, to double Walks, and interweav-
ings of design" (Sig. A2v). The restrictions of space Davenant exploits,
however, by paring the dramatis personae to seven in total, so creating
a minimalist method of representing the counterturns and double walks.
This is achieved three ways: by opposing the values of the Christian and
Muslim worlds; by opposing the politic *virtù* of Solyman and Ianthe (who
harmonize private and public motives for civic ends) to the overly private
instincts of Alphonso in particular; and finally by converting the chorus
into what – in *Marriage a la Mode* – Dryden was to make the low plot of
the split-plot play, involving contemporary men and women of the town,
so that the opera begins usefully to exploit the presence of actual women on
stage, as if to emphasize their difference from the men. As in the later play,
the implied opposition of the sexes finds expression in the heroic plot, in
the figure, most palpably, of Alphonso's sexual jealousy, which threatens to

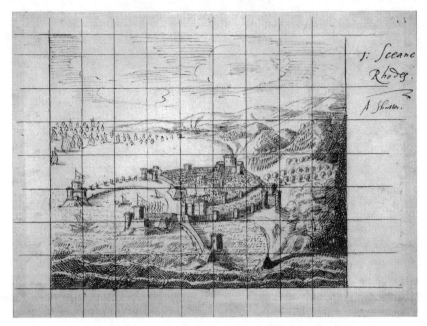

Figure 27: Webb, Design for *The Siege of Rhodes*

obstruct properly political solutions to the plight of the besieged Rhodians. The implication is that the behavior and assumptions of the fashionable world – apparently caught up in private matters like love affairs and sexual jealousy – have metaphorical resonances at the level of affairs of state, and vice versa.

Solyman almost becomes a transcendental signifier for the ideal monarch, able smoothly to move between the private world of affection, passion, and response to female beauty, and his public charge to the state; and in that capacity he also becomes a figure for the audience itself, since, as with Rhodalind in *Gondibert*, Ianthe embodies the very idea of theatrical example. Indeed the key action of the entire plot hinges on Solyman's principled response to Ianthe's beauty and virtue, which results in an invitation to stay in his camp and an offer of safe conduct to her and her betrothed Alphonso. The latter misinterprets the offer as a sign that Solyman might have, during the night, enjoyed her sexual favors. But just as (in both parts as performed in 1661) Ianthe remains true to herself, so Solyman is governed only by reasons of state, so that, in that later version, Davenant works with a chiasmus: Alphonso and Ianthe are the Christian, while Solyman and Roxolana are the Muslim, pairs; and Solyman and Ianthe remain true to

Figure 28: Webb, Design for *The Siege of Rhodes*

the civic implications of their actions, while Alphonso and then Roxolana become, at crucial points, distracted by sexual jealousy. These arrangements of characters indict the absolutism of Ottoman rule, as Solyman remarks himself, because his subjects are effectively slaves, so that the action of the opera, in seeking to balance public effects with private motives, and husbands with wives, establishes a model of healthy patriarchal rule.

Already in 1656 it is clear that this argument is advisory in intent, since the stage is framed by an architectural device as follows:

The Ornament which encompass'd the Scene, consisted of several Columns, of gross Rustick work, which bore up a large Freese. (1)

That we are talking about a debate on the grounds of the state in a context of considerable political chaos is strongly implied by the fact that, from the outset, Rhodes is defended by an uncoordinated consortium of Christian powers: Austrians, French, Spanish, Germans, Italians, and English. This untidy circumstance is reproduced at the level of plot because the Rhodian admiral at one point becomes entranced by Ianthe, raising fears, briefly, that he might seduce her or betray Alphonso, though he disciplines himself

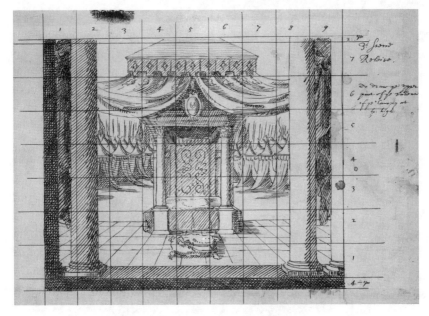

Figure 29: Webb, Design for *The Siege of Rhodes*

to become an effective political agent rather than a pining lover. A striking architectural image in Part II of *The Siege of Rhodes* – first performed in 1661 – confirms what the reference to the rustic order should imply, namely that drama plays a rhetorical role in affairs of state, and that Davenant's loosely Hobbesian conception of the state is fundamentally Roman, since it was the Romans who introduced the arch to architecture. Whereas the Rhodian defenders are a loose association of elements, the true state – as embodied in Solyman – like the arch becomes firmer as greater pressure is brought to bear. In Act II, scene i, Villerius says:

> Pow'r is an arch which ev'ry common hand
> Does help to raise to a magnifick height:
> And it requires their aid when it does stand
> With firmer strength beneath increasing weight.[7]

The two parts of the revised version of the opera, it must be said, play out the argument more systematically than the original first part taken on its own. The original plot ends with the Rhodians briefly repulsing the Ottoman forces, the main agent being Alphonso, whose courage is spurred by the belief that Ianthe has been false, so acting in the interests of love

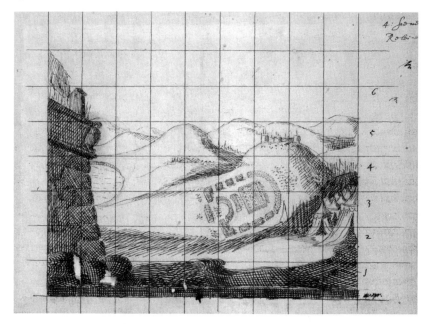

Figure 30: Webb, Design for *The Siege of Rhodes*

rather than honor. Because he thinks in these private terms, he has rejected
Solyman's offer of safe conduct. He is wounded in the process; and Part II
addresses the inevitability of Ottoman victory, so that Ianthe is once again
despatched as an ambassador, which again imperils her reputation. The
danger this time issues from Roxolana, Solyman's wife, who, like Alphonso
in Part I, mistakes Solyman's politic behavior for something more dubious;
and to intensify the chiastic patterns among Solyman, Roxolana, Ianthe,
and Alphonso, the expanded Part I in 1661 adds scenes devoted to Roxolana
to prepare us for Part II.

Part II is devoted to a kind of therapeutic action, whereby Alphonso
now sees his relation to Ianthe both in affective and civic terms, and that
implicitly Aristotelian model for ideal relations in the state is also the point
to which Roxolana is drawn. By the end, both pairs, Christian and Muslim,
serve as ideal models for the proper distribution of power and obligation
in the state, the harmonization of private desire with public ends, and – as
Dryden was similarly to argue in his Muslim play, *Don Sebastian* – a balance
between the Christian and Muslim orders, which in Dryden reconciles
soul and body, to use symbolic terms he almost certainly inherited from
Davenant.

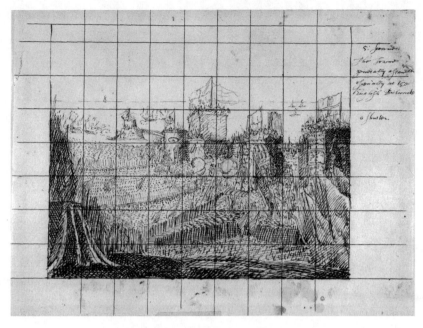

Figure 31: Webb, Design for *The Siege of Rhodes*

But Part II is also important because – finally under more generous staging conditions in Lincoln's Inn Fields – the space of the new proscenium stage could play its own symbolic role in the transformations to which the opera is committed. The first versions of *The Siege of Rhodes* trumpet the fact that now we have "the Art of Prospective in Scenes," and of course we have Webb's designs reproduced here. But although the limitations of the indoor theater have the effects we described above, the scenes remain largely thematic and decorative. It is clear, however, that Davenant understood – probably from the outset – that stage space could play its own role in the action, because the key scene in which Roxolana realizes that Ianthe's virtue is intact, and that she is no threat to her charms in Solyman's eyes, is orchestrated both at the obvious level of plot and, more significantly for the history of English drama, in the choreography of the stage itself. And since the stage stands in, forensically, for the invariably public conditions of dramatic action, our consciousness of the stage as such a medium corresponds to the political thrust of the plot: for it is here that, seeing Ianthe as a staged figure of virtue, Roxolana is suddenly persuaded to assume her full civic position as Solyman's consort.

Figure 32: Webb, Design for *The Siege of Rhodes*

This is a catalytic moment that occurs in Act IV, scene ii, to prepare for the *dénouement* of Act V. Scene i closes with Alphonso's adage that "Honour should no Leader have but Love" (51), precisely the proposition that the entire action is designed to revise. The next scene, redolent of the full possibilities of perspective staging, reads:

> *The Scene is Chang'd*
> Being wholly fill'd with *Roxolana*'s Rich Pavilion, wherein is discern'd at distance, *Ianthe* sleeping on a Couch; *Roxolana* at one End of it, and *Haly* at the other; Guards of Eunuchs are discover'd at the wings of the Pavilion; *Roxolana* having a *Turkish* Embroidered Handkerchief in her left hand, and a naked Ponyard in her right. (51)

Roxolana's view of Ianthe corresponds to the audience's because Ianthe, carefully framed by the deep perspective, is an emblem of vulnerable virtue. The spatial and public conditions of the stage themselves intensify the debate about how this image of Ianthe is to be apprehended: at first Roxolana is driven by private motives at odds with the staging, for the eunuchs look on from the wings, so converting the space of the action into a kind of experimental arena. Similarly, Haly and Roxolana occupy opposite sides of the stage so that Roxolana cannot proceed with her determination to kill Ianthe without protestations from Haly, who enjoins pity, so that the action is obstructed, as it were, by the requirement to debate it.

Because drama is an inevitably public mode of apprehension, Davenant seems to say, the theatrical itself reveals the impolitic nature of revenge, like jealousy an expression of private and inscrutable passion. Even in the early movements of the scene, this is argued in at least three different but related ways. The new Harveian physiology, as well as the more ancient biometric metaphor, lurks behind the idea that the body, site of numerous competing passions and desires, comprises a kind of theatrical space of its own, one which the inhabitant can herself observe and comment on as if spectator of her own sensations. (At one point, for example, Ianthe exclaims, "The Great live all within; / And are but seldom seen / Looking abroad through the Casements of their Eyes" [52].) The heady instincts of revenge are thus held in check, because the urge to unreflective action is prevented or delayed by the individual who, now an observer of her own internal motions, becomes entranced by the activity of interpreting the drama of her own passions, just as Haly's commentary from a different portion of the stage serves to ironize Roxolana's primitive impulses. Second, there is a looser sense that the ethical and political implications that these deliberations invoke, being matters of external behavior, must be thought of as belonging to the drama or theater of politics, as if the spatializing of agency itself encourages a more considered approach to human affairs.

Third, the moral and political transformations to which drama aspires are played out half-way through this scene. Haly agrees to wake the sleeping Ianthe, underscoring the histrionic nature of his action: "I go to draw the Curtain of a shrine. – / Awake! Behold the pow'rful Empress here" (52). Ianthe, awake, instantly transforms Roxolana's envy into shame, and the shifting political implications of the transformation are, throughout the scene, marked by Roxalana's tendency to weep, as if in response to what it is – a moment in a play – and by a running language of distance and proximity, which reminds us how the semiotics of the proscenium stage depend on the relative positions of characters, and the position of characters relative to the audience. Solyman's arrival is heralded as just such a staged – and stagey – event, which signals an impending resolution in which affairs of state will prevail over private and arbitrary sensation.

THE TEMPEST (FIRST PERFORMED 1667; FIRST EDITION 1670)

We conclude briefly with *The Tempest* because this "operatic" version of the Shakespeare play, first performed on 7 November 1667, five months before

Davenant's death, was jointly "revised" by Davenant and Dryden. It reveals the extent to which the various experiments in *Gondibert* and *The Siege of Rhodes* had, by the end of the 1660s, become more or less naturalized in the drama; and in the preface to the printed version of the play, dated 1670, only a year before the first performance of *Marriage a la Mode*, Dryden expresses his debt to Davenant as a pioneer of the restored drama, since he can now see that this is a moment when Davenant's authority on the stage has passed to the new poet laureate.

For all its numerous allusions to the Shakespearean original, this is a different play with very different commitments.[8] Whereas Shakespeare's original is obviously governed by profoundly political concerns, this new version is more frankly a direct exercise in political theory, asking, once again, how the civic order might arise out of a primitive and unschooled relation to human affairs. Just as, in *The Siege of Rhodes*, Solyman embodies the ideal state, so the Davenant/Dryden Prospero acts as tutor to the young people in his charge, who are now not just Miranda and Ferdinand, but Hippolito ("one that never saw Woman, right heir to the Dukedom of *Mantua*"), and Miranda's sister, Dorinda, who is even more naïve in her relations to the outside world than Miranda.[9] Whereas the legitimacy of Shakespeare's Prospero is complicated by different accounts of his authority on the island and by an unexplored affinity to Caliban (who is now assigned a sister, Sycorax), here the two plots operate in parallel, both pursuing similar arguments, with Prospero as a kind of master expositor.

Three interrelated features of the Davenant/Dryden version show how the revisions have, for all the damage done to Shakespeare's original, a combined intellectual purpose. In general, the "operatic" quality of the play, on which Pepys comments, contributes to what one might call the objectification of value to which Davenant and Dryden are committed. The machinery of the perspective stage – only in embryo at Blackfriars before the war – reveals how our apprehension of stage character is a purely public and artificial affair, as if the play were enacting Hobbes's observation that the word "person" derives from the Latin *persona*, meaning a mask, so that human identity only depends on how we are perceived from without. Second, that the semiotics of the stage depend on purely conventional recognitions corresponds to the argument that a viable polity must eschew our most primitive and immediate responses to things: much of the magic has gone from the Shakespeare play, because statecraft requires a disciplined rejection of the lure of the "natural," whether figured in the elemental impulses to power, sex, and drink in the low plot, or the naked response to the erotic in the high plot. Another way to think of it is that if, in Shakespeare, romance is an engine of the narrative, in Davenant and Dryden the mysterious nature of romance has, for political reasons, become an object of suspicion. And third, at a point when the enthusiasm of the very early Restoration had waned – Charles's womanizing was now known to be a political problem, the court had shamed itself in response to the plague, and the second Dutch War had ended in national humiliation – the play clearly seeks to advise the King to direct his energies from private matters to the public concerns of the state.

Davenant's prevailing skepticism is already visible in his version of *Macbeth*, where the poet's authority over metaphor, which gestures, however ambiguously, to the possibility of a transcendental order, must yield to a world in which all truths are a matter of characters' local perception. Thus, whereas Shakespeare's witches execute a poetic function that corresponds to that of the playwright in declaring that "fair is foul and foul is fair," Davenant's witches are confined to a purely phenomenal universe: "*to us* fair weather's foul, and foul is fair," they declare, so that discussion of the weather now substitutes for the hint of cosmic subversion.[10] Similarly, Shakespeare's *Tempest* begins with an opening scene in which mariners and passengers find their world turned upside down by the violence of the storm, in which they have little leisure to respond, the effect of Prospero's magic, and Miranda's anguished reaction to what she witnesses. No doubt conscious of what the perspective stage affords, Davenant and Dryden also convert Act I, scene i into a disquisition on the technical aspects of good seamanship, so we watch the mariners handling the storm with a high degree of precision, able in the midst of things to distinguish different types of sail, sheet, yard, and so forth (at a typical moment, Trincalo calls out, "Loose Fore-sail! Haul Aft both sheats! trim her right afore the Wind. Aft! Aft! Lads, and hale up the Misen here" [I,i,60–1]). But this is more than fun and games with staging, because agency in this world is entirely mundane: it is solely shaped by human efforts in space and time, in response to local circumstance, expressed by a premium on a technical control over our own vocabularies.

The same view of things determines Miranda's entry into the plot, for now the entire storm scene is objectified and aestheticized as the theatrical event it is, with a consciousness of how her sister might be a co-observer of what they – as well as the audience – experience. Prospero provides the frame of discussion, to indicate his tutorial role in the plot, whose purpose is to create in the young folk an ironic sense of their circumstances, with the chief aim of making them truly politic because properly artificial agents.

Prosp. Miranda! where's your Sister?
Miran. I left her looking from the pointed Rock, at the walks end,
　　on the huge beat of Waters.
Prosp. It is a dreadful object.

(I,ii,1–4)

The kind of perspective afforded by the proscenium stage becomes part
of a larger symbolic argument in the entire play. The addition of Hippolito and Dorinda to Shakespeare's cast of characters allows Davenant
and Dryden greatly to amplify the theme of the woman (Miranda) who
has never before seen any other person than her father and to intensify the
sexual aura surrounding the original Miranda–Ferdinand plot. Prospero
has kept Hippolito under wraps the entire time on the island, so he has
no idea what women are; and by the same token, though Miranda and
Dorinda know what other women are like, they too have never seen a man.
Much as Rochester's poetry is given over to the proposition that sex in the
human realm can never remain a raw matter of animal satiety, and much as
Wycherley in *The Country Wife* shows that there is no such thing as a neu-
tral apprehension of commodities apart from the systems to which objects
belong, so Davenant and Dryden exploit the perspectivilism of the stage
to show that our approach to the opposite sex is overdetermined, already
redolent with ideology. Thus later in Act I, scene ii, Dorinda and Miranda
debate what kind of animal they have seen leap from the foundering vessel –
could it be, asks Miranda, that "Which you have heard my Father call a
Man"? (I,ii,317), as if the patriarchy could somehow be detached from masculinity. That sex is a matter of ideology becomes even clearer in Act II,
scene iv, where Prospero tries to compensate for protecting Hippolito from
exposure to the outside by catechizing him about the nature of women,
a discourse infused with the most shop-worn and effectively antifeminist
truisms about women as both dangerous and fair. In the following scene,
the solitary Hippolito becomes in turn the object of speculation by the two
women. As the stage direction has it, "*Enter* Miranda *and* Dorinda *peep-
ing*," an experimental moment of observation reproduced so frequently
elsewhere in Restoration plays. All three remain curious and puzzled about
what it is they face, but the intoxication of the encounter proves for Hippolito so overwhelming that he decides that he wants not one woman but as
many as he can get, at one point suggesting two thousand (IV,i, 273). Once
sex is in the air, things go potentially haywire for both pairs – Prospero soon
introduces Miranda to Ferdinand – so that Hippolito's enthusiasm threatens Ferdinand, whose jealousy is hardly assuaged by Miranda declaring for

greater variety too (see III,vi; IV,i,100–11). Much plot space is devoted to the consequences of their duel, during which Hippolito swoons, is feared dead, but is finally revived by Ariel.

The point is that, like statecraft, the laws of monogamy, which harness sexual desire to culturally productive ends, belong to a highly artificial code designed to guarantee stability. Thus, just as the play opens with a technical language of seamanship, which may have reminded the audience of the issues fueling the second Dutch War that had ended in the Treaty of Breda signed that July, so the low plot in particular (also more heavily populated than in Shakespeare) engages an explicit second-order language of political analysis which one cannot imagine being readily available before Hobbes. (These characters are driven, we are told, by "their thirst of Government" [IV,iii,267].) As if in response to the wounds of civil war (II,iii,79; II,iii,141), there is a running debate about sovereignty (I,ii,65; II,i,17; II,iv,28), an inquiry into the nature of government *per se* (II,v,44; III,i,196; IV,ii,20; IV,iii,267), into the corresponding nature of subjecthood (at least six references), an interest in what comprises a dominion (II,iii,99–100; III,iii,82; V,ii,149), and reflections on the royal prerogative, including the dispensing power in particular (IV,ii,65; V,ii,11). The taboo against which the youth in the high plot as well as Caliban rebel is that larger principle of exogamy, which would stabilize monogamy in the one, while it would prevent Caliban sleeping with his sister, at which the plot briefly hints (IV,ii,110). Monogamy and the taboo against incest – as Dryden was to argue in *Don Sebastian* – belong to the fabric of what he and Davenant call "civill Nations" (IV,ii,22).

Whereas in Shakespeare's play the deep threat is posed by Caliban, here the difficulty is Hippolito, who has – like Charles II for the first thirty years of his life – been in political deep freeze until the storm. The two plays are thus starkly different, because one is about the possibility of real evil, the other about the dangers of political immaturity. Like the King, at whom this figure is pointed, we are meant to attend to Hippolito. In theory, in Act V he begins to divine the principle of monogamy as a civil institution, but that his grasp on the politic world is tenuous is strongly suggested by Prospero's introducing him to his future in the civil and civic order, whereupon he asks whether his subjects will be both men and women, and whether he will now enjoy a larger cave. The political future in this play is no more certain than Shakespeare's, though for different reasons. It may be that Davenant and Dryden, in showing how Ariel obtains drugs to free Hippolito from the swoon induced by a primitive response to a challenge, had in mind a different model of political conduct from the one that, many loyalists feared, currently obtained. The Dutch Wars had reinforced the possibility of trade as a largely impersonal basis of state power. Echoing Satan's voyage in *Paradise Lost*, the first edition of which also appeared in 1667, but to a more benign effect, Ariel recalls how

I prun'd my wings, and, fitted for a journey, from the next Isles of our *Hesperides*, I gather'd Moly first, thence shot my self to *Palestine*, and watch'd the trickling Balm, which caught, I glided to the *British* Isles, and there the purple Panacea found. (V,i,51–5)

PART III

Some Restoration plays from Dryden to Congreve

CHAPTER 6

Instituting empiricism: Hobbes and Dryden's Marriage a la Mode

Dryden's *Marriage a la Mode* has always teased its critics with the problem of interpreting its double plot. Accordingly, the formal and ideological relations between the low (comic) narrative and the high (heroic) narrative have been the focus of a number of increasingly sophisticated readings by, among others, Laura Brown, J. Douglas Canfield, David Rodes, and Eric Rothstein and Frances Kavenick.[1] And in the most ambitious reading yet, Michael McKeon argues that the terms of the two plots do not resolve easily into a preference for one mode over the other, but remain mutually destabilized, and thus reveal a dialectical tension between an aristocratic and a more proto-bourgeois ethos emerging during the late seventeenth century.[2]

Marriage a la Mode evidently tests our ability to conceptualize and interpret doubleness as an aesthetic feature that has a kind of peculiar life in the Restoration, and as a way of thinking about how different rhetorics might coexist in a given text. This problem has of course been very largely the formal and ideological core of earlier chapters; and what I have called the Fletcherian mode seems to me to explain in large measure the difficulties we have had in interpreting all the works discussed below. I link them largely because though we are now turning to analyses of individual plays, it is useful for what is to follow to see how Hobbes fits the pattern, both because *Leviathan* is so crucial to seventeenth-century philosophical arguments about sovereignty, and because after 1650 this text seems to have entered the bloodstream of any writer interested in the nature of political argumentation.

Readers will remember that Dryden's Preface to the *Fables* (1700) constructs a literary canon whose aesthetic values we have largely endorsed: after all, it is here that Dryden pronounces Chaucer the father of English poetry, and here that Chaucer, Spenser, and Milton are given a mutual lineage. There is, however, considerable irony in our modern approval of Dryden's choices, for these selections signify for Dryden no self-evident criteria of value but courageous expressions of personal taste which, in the preference he gives to Chaucer over Ovid, chooses a Modern over an Ancient, and in the preference he gives to Homer over Virgil, confesses a character more "violent, impetuous, and full of fire" than the Roman poet. There is a further irony embedded in Dryden's strategy, because although he aligns his own character with Homeric violence, implying that such a posture befits a writer denied true access to public life, the terms in which he does so recall not so much Homer as the "quiet, sedate" Virgil he describes (274).[3] The double-edged rhetoric by which Dryden pledges allegiance to one author while pleading in the habit of a rival is a striking feature of his late years, for he does much the same thing, though more pointedly, in his earlier "Discourse on the Original and Progress of Satire" (1693). The "Discourse" appeared as a preface to Dryden's (and others') translations of a number of Latin writers, including Juvenal, in which he admits his identification with Juvenal in a prose marked paradoxically by the Horatian values of discretion and privacy. It is those very values that so infuse his last great essay with an autumnal and elegiac beauty.

   Dryden's construction and use of a literary canon, then, in no way reinforce some simple ratio between power and the aesthetic values it might prefer. For he creates a double rhetoric by selecting Juvenal, then Homer to represent his anger, while nevertheless conducting his argument in an Horatian and leisurely manner. Thus he establishes an ironic perspective on the very motives – political and personal – that legitimate his peculiar identifications. That those identifications are apt is proven by the degree to which, in the actual exercise of translating Juvenal, the ex-poet laureate could fully inhabit Juvenal's alienated vision and rugged idiom. Who better than Juvenal could express the condition of life in the midst of a new regime governed by cultural and political imports, and operating in the baleful shadow of tyranny (in Juvenal's case Domitian's and Nero's)? By contrast, the late prose is marked by rounded periods, maintaining a series of extended analogies and qualifications, which provide an ethos of delay and retrospection rather than Juvenalian attack (an ethos one might legitimately call Horatian). Consequently, we witness the old poet showing his anger as a member of a religious minority, but able perhaps more than ever to observe himself dispassionately in that guise. This alone might explain the attraction to Juvenal's Satire III, where satiric authority is deflected from the poet to Umbricius' complaints about modern life, made as he stands at the city gate ready to depart. Dryden's construction of the canon – an act

which may in hindsight seem to us a moment of literary authoritarianism –
has therefore the character of an act of dissent. What is at issue is less the
construction of a canon, than the forms of discrimination brought to an
exercise that (we are now relearning) is an inescapable cultural fact. Canons
will come and go, but what marks the politics of each movement is the
conditions by which they do so, and the motives that we remark within
them.

By establishing a canon and yet exposing the terms by which it does so, the
Preface to the *Fables* calculatedly reveals the ideological work that Dryden
wants the canon to do. It also suggests that, for Dryden, empiricism itself
may also play a role in that ironic economy. For there are two other figures
with whom Dryden identifies in his late critical essays, namely Milton
and Hobbes. Dryden identifies with Milton in the last stage of his career
because, like his present self, the Milton he knew after the Restoration was
a remnant from a different political age. Dryden's use of Hobbes, on the
other hand, supposes that a given philosophical position – involving certain
attitudes to knowledge and language – bears no necessary or single relation
to the values with which we endow different political views. In the Preface
to the *Fables*, Hobbes stands in part for the translator of Homer that Dryden
himself would like to have been, although he criticizes Hobbes as too old
to have embarked on translating the *Iliad* (275). But more significantly,
Dryden believes that his relaxed habit of moving among a series of related
topics confirms "Mr. Hobbes['s]" view that "thoughts . . . have always some
connection" (271). Dryden is alluding to the early chapters of *Leviathan*,
in which Hobbes analyzes the human powers of perception and speech. In
contrast to a prevailing modern assumption that the Hobbesian system is
both politically and epistemologically authoritarian, Dryden takes Chapter
3 of *Leviathan* to denote a kind of mediated and negotiable knowledge
whose corollary in Dryden's text is his own highly rhetorical and often
digressive method. In fact, Dryden calls on Hobbes's cognitive theory to
excuse the very digression on which he just embarked. Because digression
does not command but rather invites attention to its own artifice, it reveals
the extent to which Dryden's admission of the violent nature attracting him
to Homer is, precisely, delivered by an act of confession, and mediated so
that it can become a local object of critical observation. If Dryden thinks of
Hobbes as the apostle of the authoritarian state whose powers are secured
by a stable epistemology – what I have called lyric knowledge – it is clear
that he is reading Hobbes against himself, because Hobbes also justifies the
waywardness of language itself.

Dryden's view and use of Hobbes does not, it seems, accord with most modern readings of *Leviathan*. Put simply, Hobbes studies have traditionally been dominated by political science or philosophy, such that most major books on Hobbes in the last half century have concentrated on the possibilities and difficulties offered by Chs. 13 to 18, those chapters which famously begin with the state of nature and conclude by enumerating the powers of the sovereign. Great energies have been directed to particular problems that those chapters have raised: the supposedly false philosophical slide from "is" to "ought"; or alternatively the conundrum by which the law of nature might be binding on the individual before the advent of the sovereign, in the context of an argument in which law appears to bind only when expressly issued by a sovereign. A more recent book has tried to construct a comprehensive Hobbesian analysis of politics almost entirely out of the concerns introduced by Books I and II.[4] There are readings which do not have that analytical urge, like Quentin Skinner's essay arguing that *Leviathan* should be seen as only the most articulate of a series of tracts issued in response to the engagement controversy, and, uniquely, J. G. A. Pocock's essay urging us to read the whole of *Leviathan* rather than concentrating on Books I and II.[5] But even very different kinds of approach, like that taken in Steven Shapin and Simon Schaffer's *Leviathan and the Air Pump*, stress the demonstrative and implicitly authoritarian force of the Hobbesian world. Indeed Shapin and Schaffer confirm rather than challenge a long-held assumption about Hobbes when they argue that Boyle's defence of vacuum against Hobbesian plenism is a proper metaphor for a newly emerging Restoration ideology of contingent social and intellectual relations – propounded by Boyle and the Royal Society – which successfully displaced a rhetoric of authority symbolized by Hobbes.[6] Boyle's commitment to the hypothesis of vacuum as inhabiting the structure of matter provides a metaphor of the voluntarist ethic he sought to foster. So Shapin and Schaffer's argument must suppose a secure analytical ratio between the Hobbesian cosmology (plenist and materialist), an authoritarian reading of the civil politics in *Leviathan*, and Hobbes's own rhetoric, which they treat as if it were functionally geometrical, even in the case of the dialogue that Schaffer translates as an appendix to the book. Because this argument places Boyleian and Hobbesian empiricism in conflict, Shapin and Schaffer's view of Hobbes finally amplifies the widely held conviction that Hobbes is only or primarily systematic, and that that system is given to largely prescriptive ends. Appropriately, Shapin and Schaffer rely on J. W. N. Watkins's *Hobbes's System of Ideas* for their interpretation of Hobbes.

We might ask what has happened at this point to the digressive Hobbes that Dryden exploits. The opposition between Boyleian and Hobbesian empiricism should suggest that there are various empiricisms at play; and I will argue that the Restoration (including Hobbes himself) held that a skeptical (contingent) empiricism necessarily qualified the epistemic claims made by an apparently more dogmatic (positivistic) form of empiricism. In so doing, it provides an analysis of the terms by which we might assent to certain dogmatisms, including the dogmatisms that allow institutions of all kinds to exist.

The kinds of reduction I describe thus seem to simplify the political implications of Hobbes's ideas and, more important, his method. The most famous political allegorizing of *Leviathan* occurs in C. B. MacPherson's *The Political Theory of Possessive Individualism*. Here MacPherson treats Hobbes's state of nature as representing the world that Hobbes finally approves: men are naturally competitive, which produces a highly ener-gized social economy, one that only requires the sovereign to supervise. Hobbes thus becomes willy-nilly an apologist for a capitalist world of free market relations, in which the sole function of government is to secure peace in order to maximize trade, so that "Natural man is civilized man with only the restraint of law removed."[7] Later readers have pointed out the obvious weakness of this Marxian interpretation, the chief being the notion that we can describe any aspect of Hobbes's environment as meaningfully "bourgeois." It is argued that if proper attention is paid to *Leviathan* itself, and to Hobbes's close relations with the gentry, his allegiances seem to vary-ing degrees to favor certain aristocratic ideals. *Leviathan* does not symbolize in any simple sense the "bourgeois mind," which, MacPherson goes on to assert elsewhere, finds its objectification in "mathematical thinking" and "materialist metaphysics."[8] Keith Thomas points out that *Leviathan* never discusses capital, assumes many features of feudal societies, and betrays signs of Hobbes's closeness to the aristocratic circle which employed him.[9] Hobbes also shares certain assumptions with the rather rarified and quite un-bourgeois atmosphere of the Tew Circle, a fact which in part accounts for the theological nature of Books III and IV, and its proximity to Angli-can polemics in the Restoration, even when the materialism of *Leviathan* angered many Anglican apologists.[10]

To justify the political allegories they wish to derive from *Leviathan*, Shapin and Schaffer and MacPherson equally must create stable the-matic correspondences between Hobbes's epistemology, his method, his cosmology, and, finally, the logic connecting the state of nature to the sovereign. I have mentioned how this criticism applies to Shapin and Schaffer's argument, which purports to attend to Hobbes's rhetorical gestures. For them, Hobbes is as much an epistemological as a political authoritarian, a single, totalizing entity. Flying in the face of general Restoration protocols of reading, they therefore deny that Hobbes's use of dialogue might express a contingent, negotiable epistemology rather like Boyle's experimentalism. In fact, like many political scientists, they fail to see that Hobbes is deeply interested in the degree to which theories of language must establish the conditions of political analysis. What relates language to politics is their common institutional base, and this is in large part one of Hobbes's descriptive aims. Just as Dryden sees that literary canons are unavoidable cultural facts, so Hobbes sees that humans inevitably create and inhabit institutions: like Cicero he assumes, first, that language is the primary feature of being human; second, that language underwrites other social institutions (figured in the contract); and, finally, that human life is conducted within a network of power relations. That Hobbes argues positively for the absolute powers of the sovereign can be taken – as indeed it was in the early 1650s – as a requirement that Englishmen should engage with the Cromwellian government. But Hobbes's hortatory rhetoric (say in Ch. 18) only follows on an entirely hypothetical picture of the state of nature. This dooms the attempt to treat the state of nature as anything more than an heuristic fiction, which therefore cannot provide a stable analytical point for deriving the conditions by which the sovereign either is or must be created. Michael Oakeshott's response to Hobbes's numerous analytical contradictions is to suggest that he has two different audiences in mind, a technical and a general audience, which explains why Hobbes's rhetoric seems to engage two different logics at once – what he calls "a core of discrepancy."[11] I would like to suggest something similar: Hobbes is both trying to persuade Englishmen to act at a particular point in history and, most significantly, trying to show that no member of any society can ever escape the institutional conditions which allow us even to imagine social life. Therefore Quentin Skinner is partly right to say that *Leviathan* is a tract in response to the engagement controversy, but he fails to see that his own argument is motivated by a more elemental fascination with *Leviathan* as a masterpiece of sorts whose descriptive power calls for explanation. The geometrical rhetoric reveals what Hobbes believes we must mutually agree to contain a state of war; but the argumentative terms which frame that prescription have made *Leviathan* endure as a descriptive analysis of the human condition. Hobbes's epideictic motive is contained within a forensic frame that supposes that human knowledge is not as certain or as absolute as readers of Chs. 13 to 18 have usually thought.

We can see the power of Hobbes's descriptive project when we take seriously what Hobbes says about how we should read it. Political scientists have tended to treat the early chapters in *Leviathan* as defining man as a self-motivated and selfish atom driven by passion and fear. But this is not what Hobbes says, or at least not all he says. Indeed, Hobbes's most paraphrased political argument is in its essentials anticipated by Lucretius' famous description, in *De Rerum Natura*, V: 1028–1160, which begins by describing the emergence of human language from animal cries and gestures, the emergence of society after the invention of fire, and the arrival of a state of civil conflict, which is only properly resolved by a contract to establish a commonwealth. Thomas Creech – who translated *De Rerum Natura* in 1682 – imagines this final moment thus:

> Those former *Kings* now murthered, they or'ethrown,
> The glory of the *Scepter*, and the *Crown*
> Decreas'd; the *Diadem*, that sign of State,
> Now wept in drops of bloud, the *Wearer's* fate,
> Spurn'd by the *common feet*, who fear'd no more:
> *Tis sweet to spurn the things we fear'd before.*
> Thus *Monarchy* was lost. –
> That *Sun* once set, a *thousand* little *Stars*
> Gave a *dim* light to *Jealousies* and *Wars*,
> Whilst each among the *many* sought the Throne,
> And thought no head like his deserv'd the Crown.
> This made them seek for *laws*, this led their Choice
> To *Rulers*; Power was given by *publick* voice.[12]

Book I of *Leviathan* (itself a kind of Epicurean text) similarly begins by analyzing humans' ability to think and use language before it describes the state of nature which the contract seeks to regulate. Further, the syntax of that argument finds a much more architectonic expression in Hobbes's entire approach to his reader, which marks a vital point at which Hobbes's pervasive skepticism drives his argument. Books I and II do indeed work by a kind of geometrical rhetoric, but in his Introduction Hobbes has already exposed the purely contingent terms by which any agreement to define words can proceed. Here Hobbes emphasizes the entirely artificial nature of the commonwealth he will describe and outlines the purpose of the four books of *Leviathan*. Hobbes proceeds to gloss the conditions that produce human wisdom, which he defines centrally by using the metaphor of reading. "*Wisedome* is acquired," he says, "not by reading of *Books*, but of *Men*."[13] Hobbes is admittedly trying to warn us against casual reading by producing a distinction between claims to read men which merely mask "uncharitable censures of one another" (82) and an ability to read which scrutinizes the conditions and circumstances of the activity itself. We have to begin, says Hobbes, by examining the text at hand, namely ourselves. Only then, and only by analogy, can we begin to infer the relations between ourselves and the minds of others. The choice of textuality as the metaphor for self-knowledge already resists a view of Hobbes as committed to a metaphysic of the logos, whatever he might do later in Books I and II to regulate his own text by a geometrical method. Any such move to secure knowledge by agreement depends on a prior stage, of revealing the purely conditional nature of our relations with the world, and the equally conditional nature of the reader's engagement with Hobbes's text. The precept that one should read oneself exists

> to teach us, that for the similitude of the thoughts, and Passions of one man, to the thoughts, and Passions of another, whosoever looketh into himself, and considereth what he doth, when he does *think, opine, reason, hope, feare,* &c, and upon what grounds; he shall thereby read and know, what are the thoughts, and Passions of all other men, upon the like occasions. (82)

The language of identity – where "the similitude of *Passions* [are] the same in all men" (82) – occurs within a rhetorical economy which already treats such forms of identity as only *functionally* identical, and is immediately questioned in any case by Hobbes's admission that even if passions as such are the same in all individuals, the way they articulate themselves as desire varies widely. Desires "do so vary, and they are so easie to be kept from our knowledge, that the characters of a man's heart, blotted and confounded as they are, with dissembling, lying, counterfeiting, and erroneous doctrines, are legible onely to him that searcheth hearts" (83). Since only God can read our desires, it is "solely by mens actions wee do discover their designe sometimes," but we cannot make anything of the actions we observe "without comparing them with our own, and distinguishing all circumstances, by which the case may come to be altered. [It] is to decypher without a key, and be for the most part deceived, by too much trust, or by too much diffidence; as he that reads, is himself a good or evil man" (83). This comparative form of knowledge underwrites the entire fabric of Hobbes's argument, for though a magistrate must "read in himself . . . Man-kind," that apparent identification between governor and the governed can only be secured by the method enacted in the reader confronting Hobbes's text. The relationship between reader and author depends on a mere analogy between the way minds work, an analogy that Hobbes leaves to his reader to deny or confirm at will: so, he writes, "when I shall have set down my own reading orderly, and perspicuously, the pains left another, will be onely to consider, if he also find not the same in himself" (83). Only if we admit this analogy as valid will we later find ourselves logically forced to accept the sovereign's authority. In a society bonded by the originary wills of the individuals who compose it, and maintained by the expressive will of the sovereign, it is essential that all parties to the contract be registered, visible, and accountable, and so Hobbes's final gesture in the Introduction textualizes the author as cultural agent, a phenomenon potentially contracting with other analogous phenomena.

Thus Hobbes, at the threshold of his argument, establishes the conditions by which we must understand its truth claims. These are not absolute, and for good cause: although definition secures a stability and continuity of argumentation within Books I and II that might and often does appear absolute, that kind of science occurs under conditions which treat all knowledge as probable at best. In fact, it is useful to see *Leviathan* as making four simultaneous propositions: that cultures are artificial; that they can only be understood as a network of external signs or symptoms; that they are produced by voluntary acts on the part of individuals; and that paradoxically they are also coercive. These propositions forge a close identification between the politics of *Leviathan* and its linguistic concerns, since the way we approach Hobbes's text symbolizes the conditions under which culture as a whole illustrates Hobbes's analysis. For *Leviathan*, like all texts or all other features of the world we try to interpret, reminds us constantly of the contingencies of human knowledge: the text is filled with moments of hyperbole and sardonic irony that remind the reader of the pleasure of reading, a mediated pleasure to which Dryden alludes in the Preface to the *Fables*. Yet Hobbes also offers another pleasure provided by the attempt to build a geometrical knowledge of political life, what one critic has called a "fiction of self-evidence."[14] In this sense, *Leviathan* is an internally conflicted text, since at moments it seems to prefer what Hobbes calls "science" to the more compromised and compromising forms of "prudence." But that doubleness is established in such a way as to enfold the geometrical within the prudential, the contingent. Even in Book I, Hobbes continually insists that our actions should be "voluntary," a fiction of local agency to some extent belied by the force of absolute sovereignty. Hobbes's analytical point is in part that the constructions of ideology are at once voluntary yet coercive: we are asked to confirm the seductions of Hobbes's early analogies, so experiencing a sensation of choice, but find ourselves later coerced by a demonstrative rhetoric whose articulations move us inexorably from axioms or definitions to their logical entailments. (The latter mechanism is also reinforced by typology, where capitals and italics visibly secure the junctures within the larger logical fabric.) But we remain at the same time uneasily conscious that the voluntary and the coercive coexist. So Dryden establishes one kind of institution – a literary canon – while at the same time revealing the conditions and motives that promote it. Similarly, Hobbes establishes the ultimate human institution – the state – which, figured as a geometrical construct, he treats as an inescapable condition of culture. At the same time he shows that it is the product of a complicated network of motives and desires, figured as a very different kind of rhetoric both conditioning and inhabiting the geometrical.

Precisely for this reason, Hobbes urges us to treat Books III and IV as integral to his entire argument: they are emphatically not mere theological appendages to Hobbes's primary concern to establish civil sovereignty. The failure to read Hobbes's entire argument, indeed, invites a political danger that Hobbes alludes to in his introduction: the temptation to suspend the rigors of purely analogical reasoning is often the product of too great a trust in or too pressing a fear of authority. To leave a text only partly read is to misconstrue it, to the extent that what is omitted cannot qualify earlier propositions that might by consequence be abstracted as axiomatic and used for arbitrary purposes that Hobbes does not approve. Consequently, Hobbes prefers the displacements implied in uses of analogy (where what is unlike is as important as what is alike) to the illusion of natural and unmediated identification between terms.

Hobbes's warning to us to complete our reading of *Leviathan* as a whole – a kind of formalist imperative – occurs as the final paragraph of Book III. He writes:

> . . . it is not the bare Words, but the scope of the writer that giveth the true light, by which any writing is to bee interpreted; and they that insist upon single Texts, without considering the main Designe, can derive no thing from them cleerly; but rather by casting atomes of Scripture, as dust before mens eyes, make everything more obscure than it is; an ordinary artifice of those that seek not the truth, but their own advantage. (626)

This passage applies to all texts, for which scripture is the master metaphor, and explains the major purpose behind Books III and IV. The sovereign in Books I and II comprises the public and visible site of civic interpretation;

in the last two books, he becomes the public site of scriptural interpretation, a hermeneutic court of last resort. The nature of the sovereign's decisions in this sphere may be arbitrary, inasmuch as they mark the final point beyond which hermeneutical indeterminacy will produce political chaos. But he stands in distinct opposition to the Papacy, where the forensic conditions of textual interpretation remain occult, and thus genuinely totalitarian. The distinction again is between those modes of knowledge and representation which are analogical in nature and some other way of thinking about knowledge which tries to obscure or subvert the workings of language as we have it. Like the Anglican apologists who also owed a great deal to the Tew Circle, not least William Chillingworth, one focus of Hobbes's assault on Catholic absolutism is the doctrine of transubstantiation, which Hobbes associates with an Aristotelian epistemology and attempts to legislate the nature of matter despite appearances, or to inspect the conscience of the believer. For Hobbes, "a sign is not a sign to him that giveth it, but to whom it is made; that is to the spectator" (401). Like character, which must perform dramatistically, a sign is only a sign by virtue of its public, externalized constitution; and so, anticipating Locke, Hobbes abolishes *mens rea*: "of Intentions, which never appear by any outward act, there is no place for humane accusation" (336). Hobbes therefore defines character by recourse to a theatrical metaphor:

The word Person is latine: instead, whereof the Greeks have [*prosopon*], which signifies *Face*, as *Persona* in latine signifies the *disguise*, or *outward appearance* of a man, counterfieted on the Stage; and sometimes more particularly that part of it, which disguiseth the face, as a Mask or Visard: and from the Stage, hath been translated to any Representer of speech and action, as well in Tribunalls, as Theaters. So that *Person*, is the same as an *Actor* is, both on stage and in common Conversation; and to *Personate*, is to *Act*, or *Represent* himself, or an other. (217)

To read scripture, we must engage in what was commonly called the "comparing of places," just as to understand the significance of character, we must see it both externally and contextually: in both cases the method is analogical. Neither texts nor character can be known essentially. Thus in Ch. 36 Hobbes writes that "the *Word of God* " is not "*Vocabulum*," an utterance with a stable kind of reference. If it creates meaning, it does so by placing its utterances into a context which continually qualifies them: scripture illustrates that language does not mean by referring, but by becoming a form of symbolic action. It is "*Sermo*, (in Greek [*logos*]) that is, some *Speech*, *Discourse*, or *Saying*" which "a perfect Speech or Discourse, whereby the speaker *affirmeth, denieth, commandeth, promiseth, threateneth, wisheth*, or *interrogateth*" (451). Jesus is not some direct signifier for God the Father: he is "called the *Word*, because his Incarnation was the Performance of the Promise" (455). Similarly, prophecy is not some special form of knowledge but a mode of public cultural performance whose significance is determined by local context (457), just as the (culturally determined) utterance that states that God spoke immediately to his instruments actually alludes to the complex of circumstances by which men come to know God's will (459).

Books III and IV thus comprise an analysis of the conditions which endow all cultural expressions with meaning. Even prophecy usually occurs "by mediation of second causes" (466). Hobbes's commitment to mediation in this sense also has a distinctly satiric purpose, because Book IV develops into a series of vivid analogies comparing the Catholic Church to the Kingdom of Fairies which by the end almost overwhelm the reader. By this time Hobbes's agency as a rhetorician palpably dominates: he celebrates the wicked power of his own verbal artifice, and in so doing has denaturalized the illusion that his geometrical method is anything but itself an artifice. To finish reading *Leviathan* entire is to experience in narrative form the doubleness that inhabits Dryden's construction of the canon: the institution (the canon, the state, the text) itself appears inevitable, but we become conscious of our role in making it possible.

Leviathan, then, perplexes the kinds of analysis it has often suffered: it is unsystematic in the analytical sense, such that philosophers have often concluded that it does – according to philosophic decorum – what it ought not to do; it does not represent class interests in any simple way, and certainly not in terms which allow distinctions between "bourgeois" and "aristocratic" values, since the category of "bourgeois" does not really apply; and its skeptical commitments compromise the urge to treat its geometrical rhetoric as Hobbesian nostalgia for an unmediated form of knowledge. It is a fundamentally ironic or critical document, in that it also plays a descriptive off a prescriptive urge, with the net result that Hobbes reveals that what he recommends as necessary (an institution invested with power) is also the inevitable condition of any society. Nor should we treat the various dualities that critics have postulated (analytical-contradictory; aristocratic-bourgeois; demonstrative-analogical; unmediated-mediated; prescriptive-descriptive) as dialectical in any simple sense, nor any given pair as a stable allegory of the next.

Put another way, *Leviathan* treats the fact of reading as an inevitability which itself denotes three things: first, a recognition that the activity entails a contingent epistemology – reading is the exercise of inference and analogy whose equivalence is a probable, empirical approach to the world, or other minds; second, a definite kind of pleasure, whether the pleasure we take in Hobbes's geometrical or analogical rhetoric; and third, a kind of pleasure which involves certain political costs – within the geometrical world of Books I and II, the sacrifice of political opposition, and within Books III and IV, the sacrifice of Catholicism. Reading in *Leviathan* exemplifies for the reader the institutions that Hobbes recommends. Hobbesian self-irony makes us observe life within the institutions that make it possible and meaningful, without invoking the liberationist implications often attached to self-consciousness as a textual or political posture. To that degree, it is scrupulously honest.

MARRIAGE A LA MODE

Marriage a la Mode similarly prefers its empirical to its romantic plot, and, as with *Leviathan*, it recognizes that one pole of the play's rhetoric (the skeptical-empirical) describes the epistemologically constrained conditions of literary – here dramatic – performance better than the other (the romantic or lyric). Hobbesian simile and irony denote the skeptical terms by which any reader might ever assent to the geometrical dimension of his argument. The low plot of Dryden's play likewise signifies the conditions under which any audience assents to knowledge on the stage. Insofar as the high plot as a theatrical performance tries to resist the purely conditional modes of knowledge involved in judging stage character, it tends to perplex itself or invite contradiction. That is, the romance forms of knowing adumbrated by heroic *topoi* are finally unavailable to ordinary human cognition, which is what dramatic knowledge must seek to satisfy. Unlike Rothstein and Kavenick, I therefore consider it significant that the low plot involves four Restoration stars (Mohun, Hart, Marshall, Boutell) and the high plot only one (Kynaston). Rather than the two plots engaging parallel lines of desire and performance, the play actually debates the terms by which desire and performance themselves obey the epistemological conditions assumed more consistently by the low plot. It also serves to reveal that dramatic pleasure entails a political as much as a cognitive economy which, in being committed to end in a way dictated by genre and by the stage itself, involves certain sacrifices. In this play, as in *The Country Wife*, it is primarily the female characters who pay to maintain these social and dramatic decorums.

Dryden's own ambivalence towards simple oppositions is immediately registered in his dedication. Dryden evidently sees himself as a professional writer, but one who still courts Rochester's patronage. His uncertainty about the nature and value of patronage emerges as he addresses an aristocrat who represents a certain access to power. But when Dryden depicts that court as morally dubious, supplying "much of Interest, and more of Detraction" (221), we could speculate that Dryden is alluding in part to Rochester's vexed relationship to it. Dryden thus makes himself Rochester's moral peer on the basis of their shared ability to discriminate, while at the same time he calls upon Rochester's "favour" for "Protection and Patronage" (222). That this protection involves its own threat to a writer's autonomy, however, is also suggested by Dryden's playful promise to sacrifice his play to the gods as "the Firstlings of the Flock" (221), where Dryden might find himself playing Abel to Rochester's Cain; alternatively, in his final sentences Dryden can imagine Rochester sliding from patronizing wit to "become its Tyrant: [to] Oppress our little Reputations with more ease than you now protect them" (224).

This little moral drama – created after the play had been performed – comments rather neatly on the play's own skepticism about noble values, where noble values might treat themselves as self-evidently to be read, unqualified by the universal constraints on knowledge. Even though we may finally endorse the fact of social hierarchy – Dryden still dedicates his play to Rochester – we must do so while recognizing the system's potential for victimage. To admit Rochester's power too readily might be fatal; to submit at all is still a threat. The point comes across too in the prologue, where the historical space in which the play is being performed occurs after the "civil war" (although Dryden is only indirectly alluding to the English Revolution) and during a "dead vacation" created by the absence of those fighting the third Dutch War, as if to emphasize that the play is performed in a culture bounded, like Hobbes's, by different forms of violence. Like Hobbes's sovereign, Dryden's play represents a space that holds off and so civilizes wider forms of conflict.

The entire plot of the play is activated by a simple forensic condition, namely the discovery of jewels and a letter which suggest that Polydamas might find his long-lost child in this corner of Sicily. The high plot recalls *Oedipus*, where Oedipus' curiosity about the past finally undoes him. But although Oedipus pursues the signs that lead to his destruction, the action of unfolding also suggests a mechanism beyond the King's control. Dryden places more pressure on the forensic moments which lead towards the *dénouement*. For example, Amalthea recounts the condition of the evidence that has set Polydamas on his search:

> . . . some few days since, a famous Robber
> Was taken with some Jewels of vast price,
> Which, when they were delivered to the King,
> He knew had been his Wife's; with these, a Letter,
> Much torn, and sulli'd, but which yet he knew
> To be her writing.
> *Arte.* – – – Sure from hence he learn'd
> He had a Son.
> *Amal.* – – – It was not left so plain:
> The Paper only said, she dy'd in childbed:
> But when it should have mention'd Son, or Daughter,
> Just there it was torn off.
>
> (I,i,287–96)

Polydamas speaks of the epistemological problem of interpreting scattered clues about the past as "the dark riddle" (IV,iv,144). This signifies the general condition of the play. The only unequivocal point at which a different, romance form of knowledge seems to provide a secure relation between signs observed and what they signify is the conviction held by all that Palmyra and Leonidas are much too beautifully formed to be children of peasants (even then, Polydamas says that their beauty makes "it seem suspicious / They are not what they seem" [I,i,306–7], as if to amplify the seemingness of it all). But that transparent knowledge fails to describe the workings of the play, since so much arises from Polydamas's ignorance about whether Palmyra or Leonidas is his true child. Hermogenes acts as a kind of playwright, determining the direction of the plot, by informing Polydamas first that Leonidas is his child, then changing his mind and telling the truth. And when he exclaims that "I had 'em from the Gods" (I,i,344), that utterance has no explanatory force whatsoever: we know that he is engaging in mystification for his own motives, much as the language of the divine used to refer to love in the low plot strikes us as self-deluding. The point is also made, slightly differently, in the failure of torture as a forensic instrument. Under torture the robber has revealed no more than is already circumstantially evident. Hermogenes too is led away to torture which "Will teach him other language" (I,i,357), but Polydamas promptly learns more than the rack would produce, for when Hermogenes's wig falls off, he recognizes him for who he is. The low plot raises its own skeptical issues, but the high plot must also make forensic deliberations on the evidences that prompt Polydamas's search for his child.

The most obvious sense in which this principle operates is that Dryden emphasizes the staginess of the play in a way that recalls, for example,

Wycherley's use of off-stage action in *The Country Wife* and *The Plain Dealer*. Thus Wycherley highlights the audience's inferential condition by asking us to guess what happens offstage when, for example, Horner goes off with Margery behind the hedge, with Margery returning laden with fruit. Dryden, by contrast, emphasizes the fact that no audience can know who a new character is until informed by someone else: the high plot emerges as a condition of the low plot, whose terms have already been established for us in Act I, when Argaleon appears. We depend on Rhodophil and Palamede to tell us who Argaleon is, just as Polydamas is subsequently introduced by Amalthea's account of the jewels and letter. Amalthea is in the high plot, but the role she plays as a spectator means that she has already been translated into a stage character who watches and supplies information, like Rhodophil and Palamede. Similarly, important forms of knowledge are supplied to Polydamas because Argaleon acts as a spy. When Palmyra and Leonidas engage in a kind of operatic pastoral duet (II,i,406), the possibilities of seeing their dialogue as a lyric and unmediated transaction are already compromised by the fact that the entire scene is observed by Argaleon. For the audience, this renders specious the distinctions governing Leonidas's opening complaint that "So many of [my] hours in publick move, / That few are left for privacy, and Love" (II,i,413–14). The opening scene of Act III reenacts the argument in different terms, for Rhodophil and Doralice play at marital affection for the benefit of Artemis, who looks on. As soon as Artemis leaves, they revert to the language of *ennui*. The difference between high and low appears in the degree to which the characters in the low plot understand themselves *as* stage characters, even in Melantha's case, where she practices her postures and engages in an imaginary dialogue with Rhodophil (III,i,219ff.).

Derek Hughes has very neatly parsed *Marriage a la Mode* as involving a series of such contrasts between private and public knowledge: the "private" is, precisely, a fiction made possible under terms established by the public.[15] This admittedly creates some ironies and disappointments in the low plot; for the would-be lovers are driven by the rather conventional pseudo-libertine axiom that when passion has decayed, it is time to seek partners outside conventional marriage. Their attempts to seek a point at which passion might be consummated only produces comic mistakes: all four make separate assignations to meet in the same private place in Act III, scene ii. The scene in and around the grotto translates a potentially private space into a place for a series of intensely stagey effects.

The resistance to the public condition of knowledge in the high plot creates more internal tension, because characters aspire to be self-defining in ways that resist how stage character can in practice be known and how stage plots must move. The lyric knowledge apparently shared by Leonidas and Palmyra involves certain internal contradictions: where the intensity of emotion combines with the unthinking quality of the play's pastoral formulations, it supplies a fiction of an unmediated bond between the lovers; yet they can't help thinking of each other in slightly different terms, also drawn from pastoral convention, which remind us that character is realized always as a kind of representation. Thus, Leonidas recalls the purity of the pastoral world he and Palmyra earlier shared by speaking of sucking "in Love, as insensibly as Ayre" (II,i,430) and concludes the scene by insisting that even in public,

> Our souls sit close, and silently within;
> And their own Web from their own Intrals spin.
> And when eyes meet far off, our sense is such,
> That, Spider-like, we feel the tender'st touch.
>
> (II,i,501–2)

We should remember that neoclassical spiders are given to spinning self-pleasing webs, the ultimate figure for a self-regarding knowledge. By contrast, Palmyra recalls herself rather as the May Queen, which reconverts that world into another stage (II,i,431ff.). This, it transpires, is the stage of politics itself, because the public manipulation of images of the kind played out in the May festival predicts the device by which Polydamas will publish Palmyra's presumed treachery:

> First, in her hand
> There shall be plac'd a Player's painted Sceptre,
> And, on her head, a gilded Pageant Crown;
> Thus shall she go,
> With all the Boys attending on her Triumph:
> That done, be put alone into a Boat,
> With bread and water onely for three days . . .
>
> (III,i,300–6)

It is almost as if Polydamas confirms Hobbes's and Davenant's view that politics has to be conducted by example or public spectacle (a "Triumph"). Leonidas continually attempts to frustrate those conditions by declaring that he is an epistemic law unto himself: not unlike Milton's Satan, he declares in one soliloquy, "I have Scene enough within / To exercise my vertue" (III,i,477–8). Later, he asserts that "I have a Kingly Soul yet" (IV,i,22) and argues that "Duty's a Name; and Love's a Real thing" (IV,iv,46). His attempt to identify himself is twice dramatically cut off by

Argaleon, so that he never defines himself directly: his quasi-Cartesian assertion "I am–" (V,i,422) significantly ends in a gap. His self-discovery, when it occurs, takes place in Amalthea's report of his escaping arrest (V,i,438–47).

Dryden is attempting a critique of knowledge in the assertion that knowledge of character, including oneself, is dramatistic. That is partly why the masquerade, which regulates the purely inferential nature of social knowledge, serves to distinguish the high from the low. Of course there are important parallels. Palamede asserts – to Doralice – that he would know his mistress "in any shape" (IV,iii,54). And Doralice can quietly mock him by asking whether he would make a loadstone of his mistress. But the assertion of some stable and self-evident knowledge is more urgent in the high plot and, rather than a local comic irony, produces the possibility of violence. Because lyric or demonstrative knowledge treats its claims as self-evident, the dangers of romance are very real: unlike dramatistic knowledge, which builds up propositions by exposing multiple points of view, it tends to sweep aside or disregard competing kinds of claim. Thus Leonidas glibly assures Amalthea that he will know Palmyra

> by a thousand other signs,
> She cannot hide so much Divinity.
> Disguis'd, and silent, yet some graceful motion
> Breaks from her, and shines round her like a Glory.
>   (IV,ii,11–14)

That possibility of knowledge is belied by Argaleon's ability to impersonate Leonidas and so glean potentially fatal knowledge from Palmyra.

The equivalent in many ways to Leonidas in the low plot is Melantha. Like Leonidas, Melantha attempts to create a private language by fabricating an identity from French, which she learns by rote. Dryden is making several points at once: that there can be no such thing as a private language; that language is more than a mere vocabulary – it comes attached to an entire grammar of behavior; and that Melantha's urgency to Frenchify herself is an expression of any woman's fragile political circumstances. Like other women in Restoration comedy – Millamant above all – Melantha is trying to create a kind of leisure which suppresses the fact that women in this culture cannot afford to engage in the same fictions of self-definition as men. As opposed to the vernacular, French stands for the world of romance or lyric figured in the high plot and in the world outside Sicily: Palamede has just returned from a sojourn in "*Spain* or *Italy*, or some of the hot Countreys" (I,i,49). But Palamede is returning to Sicily – a type of England – in response to another condition that also stands in the wings: his father threatens his inheritance unless he marries. The same applies to Melantha, for she too is threatened by her father; and Palamede reengages with the world of the vernacular at the beginning of the play, just as Melantha must drop her defenses at the end. That is, if, like Doralice, women can play for a while, they must return to those institutions that regulate their social being: marriage both for Doralice and Melantha, and the vernacular for Melantha.

Leonidas perhaps experiences a momentary lapse of identity on stage because Argaleon strong-arms him, but he recovers both his identity and the kingdom. If he remains deluded about the kind of knowledge available to him, the consequences to him are minimal. Melantha experiences a more genuinely tragic collapse when Palamede sings her French into silence: Palamede overcomes her and she weeps, but the figure of this conquest is, significantly, taken from theology. Melantha and Amalthea play out similar roles in the low and high plots respectively: the high plot is constructed as a chiasmus of power (Polydamas–Leonidas; Argaleon–Palmyra), the low plot as a chiasmus of desire (Rhodophil–Melantha; Palamede–Doralice). Amalthea figures the pure exercise of desire within the high plot, and so she is reduced to silence in soliciting for Leonidas and finally retiring to a nunnery. Melantha similarly wants unmediated access to the world of the court – what Doralice speaks of as "the Presence," an idea Dryden might well have inherited from Book II of *Gondibert* (III,i,110). Amalthea's desire results in an obvious cost: she must sacrifice herself to Leonidas; but Melantha's desire is figured not only as her comic French (also a possible bequest from Davenant), but a series of equally surprising rushes from the stage into the wings in pursuit of the court offstage. When she too collapses into silence, it propels her into, not out of, social relations. This move, Philotis explains to her, occurs because Palamede "does but accommodate his phrase to your refin'd language" (V,i,147–8).

Melantha must submit, that is, to the vernacular, the terms of the comic ending, to marriage, which are institutions that resist the attempt to treat knowledge and language as unmediated expressions of desire. Like other institutions, language involves a series of accommodations. Shortly before she finds her French fails to protect her from Palamede, Melantha remarks that in one exchange she has not used all the words in her armory: "*Naiveté* should have been there, but the disobedient word would not come in" (V,i,89–90). And Melantha's final utterance expresses frustration that "our damn'd Language expresses nothing" (V,i,495): language has failed to protect her from her own impotence. This recalcitrance at the heart of language – its refusal to bend immediately to our will – is what also reveals the self-delusions in Leonidas, and indeed the instabilties of the entire high plot. The very body of Melantha as agent in the plot – itself a tactile and negotiable fact – serves as a dramaturgical figure of that recalcitrance. "*Naïveté*" will not submit to Melantha at the one point where she tries to engage Palmyra directly on stage. Palmyra asks "What is she?" – which curiously objectifies Melantha, as if she is a physical obstruction – to which Artemis replies, "An impertinent Lady, Madam" (V,i,91–2). Melantha's impertinence is of course a lapse of social decorum, but it is also an impertinence of the kind that bothers Manly, Olivia, and the Widow Blackacre in *The Plain Dealer*, namely the tendency of the actual, the empirical world to break into the romantic fictions by which we might like to define ourselves. It is unlikely that the two plots in *Marriage a la Mode* can operate independently for five acts without intruding upon and qualifying each other: the conventions of the stage themselves figure the resistance of the actual, empirical world to the romantic and ideal world. But nevertheless the high plot still resents the intrusions of the low.

Leviathan asserts the necessity and inevitability of power, the product of the seemingly inescapable logic of Hobbes's geometrical rhetoric. But the larger frame of *Leviathan* presents a different, more voluntaristic rhetoric which accords with Hobbes's linguistics, as if to expose the pure artifice of power that we both construct and inhabit. Similarly, for all that the high plot of *Marriage a la Mode* finally recommends the restoration of a rightful prince, the terms of that institution are examined by its relation to the low plot. The low plot inscribes the inevitability and desirability of marriage; the high plot the inevitability and desirability of the lawfully constituted state. But where the exchange of value in the low plot occurs finally as an empirical recognition of certain realities, whose consequences for women are potentially tragic, the value of monarchy in the high plot is still to some extent the outcome of its romance premises which lead Leonidas to think of his claims as self-evident. But because Leonidas is a man, he can afford not to scrutinize the epistemological grounds of his power. Dryden wants us to observe the discrepancy between the empiricial and self-evident, the dramatistic and the lyrical, as if to scrutinize the gap between the institutions that govern and the terms by which we agree to obey them. One of those institutions is the play itself, whose generic conventions demand an ending after five acts, but again – as in *The Country Wife* – our pleasure is purchased at a visible cost to some of the characters. Dryden always recognizes the necessity of institutions of all kinds, but always makes us conscious of the mediations that make them possible: even in *Astrea Redux* he warns us against seeing Charles's restoration as a natural and unmediated event, for if we do, we might fail to remind the King that his rule must follow the precepts of "method," the most valuable product of his experience in exile, which might serve to check the potential excesses of power. If Hobbes and Dryden defend the status quo, they also denaturalize its ideology: their double rhetoric shows that it may be inevitable, but it is not to be treated as transparent.

CHAPTER 7

Equity and exchange – or trade and contingency – in The Plain Dealer

It is a standard *topos* in the criticism on Wycherley's difficult play, *The Plain Dealer*, that the standard conundrum is posed by its chief figure, Manly. As Helen Burke remarks, we are commonly asked to consider whether we sympathize with his anger at the world, or whether his bluster alienates the audience, or whether, in readings like Peter Holland's, we can parse "the shifting way in which nearly all the characters – especially Manly – waver in and out of the audience's sympathies and moral approval."[1] And there are numerous different accounts as to how or whether he develops as a character in the course of five acts: part of the problem is accounting for the terms that – after almost an entire play in which he is obsessed with desire for Olivia, with whom he at first believes he has an unshakeable alliance and, when apprised of her infidelity, whom he seeks to humiliate – he seemingly suddenly embraces his future with Fidelia, a character whose name suggests that she has entered the play from the pages of romance.

Most critics apparently see their task as solving the problem of Manly in characterological terms. Thus Derek Cohen writes that "the problem of characterization in *The Plain Dealer* is the problem of styles of speech"; and later, "the key to Wycherley's meaning lies in Manly's character."[2] Laura Morrow writes, "the most significant and diverse critical disputes concerning William Wycherley's *The Plain Dealer* arise from the complexity of Manly, Wycherley's rudely wise but darkly great protagonist."[3] And Robert Bode writes that "it is and always has been a difficult play, and that Manly is its most difficult character."[4] More nakedly yet, Anthony Kaufman and Gerald Marshall find Manly either the epitome of narcissistic rage or a means of taxonomizing madness on the stage.[5]

A related tack assumes that the play is a satire and that therefore Manly – still occupying the center of attention – is either the ground of Wycherley's satirical perspective or is the object of satire, or occasionally both. Thus – taking account of the relationship between the Manly and Widow Blackacre plots, an important and surprisingly infrequent move – Bode finds in Manly a hinge between the two plots: he is angry at injustice in the world and angry at the maladministration of justice in the law courts.[6] But part of the aim of this chapter is to argue that a focus on character in drama also represents a failure in understanding satire, since both plays as a genre and satire as a mode represent an entire universe of value which it is the purpose of literature to explore.[7] We should remember that Aristotle insists that characters in plays are functions of the plot, not the other way around.

By recourse to three of the best assessments of the play in the last twenty years, namely those by Derek Hughes, Ronald Berman, and Peter Holland, I want to suggest that there are different ways of approaching the problem of the play which have got a good deal to do with the way that Restoration drama works in general, as well as with the rhetorical role drama was thought to play in the late seventeenth century.[8] What Hughes, Berman, and Holland have in common is the view that the play – like most Restoration plays – is about a problem. It is a response to an hypothesis about the nature of the world which we can only frame by reference to the entire action of the play, and by reference to the entire set of symbolic relationships implied in the mutual juxtaposition of characters, as well as the juxtaposition of characters with different circumstances. Holland extends this view of the structural relation among different kinds of plot in the play by focusing on how the roles were cast. The confluence of Hart as Manly and Mrs. Marshall as Olivia suggests that here we have players typically associated with heroic and romance modes projected into a comic plot which they cannot fully understand or control. Holland thus shows how casting choices had what we might call Fletcherian consequences, because typecasting drew attention to the incommensurable genres of which the play is composed and which cause both the characters themselves and modern critics so many problems. In this sense, we could perhaps oppose a notion of symbolic action to the essentially psychologistic habits of interpreting plays whose usually unconscious genealogy, I have argued, is the nineteenth-century cult of reading Shakespeare. Given the preeminence of Beaumont and Fletcher on the Restoration stage, it is no accident that, like *Marriage a la Mode*, *The Plain Dealer* is a double-plotted play, and whatever we may think about Manly individually, Wycherley is asking us to interpret the symbolic relations between the two main plots, and, for example, between Manly (originally played by Hart though probably later by Mohun) and Freeman (played by Kynaston).

Berman holds, however, that, like the late Rochester, Wycherley in *The Plain Dealer* attacks "those things that have sustained [his] early work,"[9] whereas I would argue that the play comprises a brilliant anatomy of the prime elements of the social and philosophical hypothesis underwriting *The Country Wife*. A connection is suggested in the mere fact that the figure of romance epistemology in both plays (Margery and Fidelia) was played by Betty Boutell. Here I am closer to Hughes, because he nicely deflects the psychologistic problem of character into Wycherley's typically philosophical interests, which usually center on questions of epistemology which then lead to matters of political philosophy, or – another way to put it – engage questions of genre in order to ask which implied way of organizing the world corresponds best to a functional society. Thus Hughes writes that the play deliberates on "the perplexed relationship between man's instinctual and social selves."[10]

Here I depart from Hughes's otherwise excellent piece on what may at first seem a small point, since Hughes throughout deliberates on what he calls "man's biform" character, which could be exemplified in the fact that Manly seems himself to issue from the state of nature and has nothing but disdain for the forms and ceremonies of civil society.[11] Though critics like Holland, Bode, and Burke rightly emphasize what Holland calls "the double nature" of the play, and while Bode remarks too on how fluently the Manly and Widow Blackacre plots are woven together, I would argue that the play is not finally governed by dyads or oppositions of the sort to which Hughes refers.[12] On the one hand, most critics engaged with the question of satire – a fair number – fail to see that satire as a mode is not solely or even primarily about objects or vehicles of moral outrage, but just as often and more interestingly about the problem of the epistemic grounds from which the self-declared satirist proceeds: this is surely one way of finessing the perennial problem of seeing a mote in your brother's eye but having a beam in your own. That is, too great a focus on Manly as character has the effect, within this discussion, of limiting the range and topics of satire itself, of rendering satire into a conceptual dyad (Manly as satirist or Manly as object of satire). It is true that the Westminster Hall scenes encourage the view that satire in the play rests on Manly expressing disdain for each of the communities that present themselves as vignettes in public spaces; but I would argue that the play as a whole seems largely *about* the question of the grounds of knowledge in society, and so we should notice that those points at which either Manly or Olivia rail at society, and so act as outright satirists, are both intellectually and dramatically inadequate to the play's total effect. In fact, in Act V, Manly himself asks the pertinent question: "is railing satire?"[13]

On the other hand, no critic to my knowledge – including Hughes and Holland, the two most astute – has recognized the importance of the play's

setting during what Leo Hughes calls rather vaguely the Dutch Wars, by
which, it transpires, he intends the second Dutch War (69, note). (By Leo
Hughes's own calculations, if the Widow was born by her own claim in
1636 [II,836], and Jerry her son is of age, the play must actually be set not
during the second but during the third Dutch war – in fact precisely in
1674 – though the fiction is clearly that this war, like the others, is centered
on trade.) Like so many plays in the Restoration, this plot echoes that
of *The Tempest*, almost certainly in the Dryden–Davenant version. And
like two plays performed the following season, *The Rover* and *All for Love*,
and like *Love for Love*, this play asks how an individual cast up from the
sea might alter the economy of landlubbers: as we will see, in *The Rover*
Willmore and his companions seriously disturb the honor-bound world
of the Spaniards as well as Angellica's heretofore confident control of the
sexual marketplace; while the sterile and self-absorbed world of Antony and
Cleopatra in Dryden's greatest play depends on suppressing disturbances
to their self-regard which issue from the Mediterranean world to the north,
whether in the guise of Ventidius, who appears on stage, or Octavius, who
offstage proves the victor in the implied contest of value.

I have already argued at length that Restoration plays have a close and
symbiotic relationship to the political and commercial changes in England
that accompanied, and were the result of, the three Dutch Wars, especially
the two last. The second Dutch War, we may remember, provides the
occasion for the magnificent opening of Dryden's *Essay of Dramatic Poesy*.
And as we have seen, the Battle of Lowestoft is not merely an occasion for
the piece: it is also constitutive of Dryden's argument aligning dramatic
form with different kinds of constitutional and political arrangements.
And prologues and epilogues to numerous plays especially in the 1670s
descant on the effects of the third Dutch War, particularly on the make-
up and disposition of audiences. In *The Plain Dealer*, Wycherley seems
to be working especially hard to underscore a relationship between the
Dutch Wars and the play's design, since the ship that Manly has sunk
has been participating in the third Dutch War, involving matters of trade
and mercantile power to which there are at least twenty-eight pointed
references, when the climate of political debate in the play is also informed
by the ideological and economic consequences of the Dutch Wars. Thus
in Act III, the alderman complains ambiguously that "this war spoils our
trade" (III,705–6).

One way of getting to the argument of the play would be to remain with
the fact that Manly has sunk his ship. Even though, as Holland points out,
the sailors have different accounts of the implications, Wycherley seems at

some pains to emphasize that the circumstances are perverse, since sinking the ship prevents both the nation at large and Manly personally from benefitting from the war, whose purpose is to ensure British participation in the circulation of goods on a worldwide scale and so to rival, if not displace, the Dutch. So, early in Act I, the first sailor complains that "our bully tar sunk our ship: not only that the Dutch might not have her, but that the courtiers, who laugh at wooden legs, might not make her prize" (I,98–100). Two other comments to this effect (I,111ff.; IV,ii,142), as well as his naked hostility to money as a figure of social relations (IV,ii,254), reveal that Manly represents a curiously fixed rather than mobile economy, so that there is something paradoxical about his past as a sea captain. Like the sea monsters referred to in Act IV, indeed, Manly's association with the sea echoes Caliban's general hostility to the niceties of civil society (IV,i,39).

By stark contrast, I have already argued that the rule that upholds the conclusion of *The Country Wife* is that Horner's semen must continue to circulate. At the end of that play Wycherley is saying that the political arrangement that can secure the most satisfaction for the greatest number of parties is entirely contingent and depends on the lie that Margery is forced to tell: as at the conclusion of *Marriage a la Mode*, where the lovers engage in *détente*, the implication is that all viable institutions, perhaps epitomized in the comic necessity of a five-act play, are meaningful and socially authoritative without being true in any definitive sense. And the problem that links Margery and Manly is, precisely, that their world makes no allowance for contingency – that epistemological space between a foundationalist view of truth, and the effects of seeing it crumble. For dramatis personae like Margery and Manly and for disappointed referentialists like Paul de Man and Stanley Fish, when reference evaporates we are driven as much by psychological despair as by a philosophical commitment to treating the alternative as either a kind of hypocrisy or as merely at best a matter of "ceremony" (as Manly calls it). Thus Manly either condemns all forms of civil society as falling short of some moral ideal he espouses or becomes entirely Machiavellian in his scheme to exact revenge on Olivia; and the erosion of reference in this context is such that critics still engage in a minor debate about whether he actually copulates with Olivia offstage or not. It is no accident that Manly dismisses circulation itself as a metaphor of what he sees as the inevitable hypocrisy of social life, attacking those who "tread 'round in a preposterous huddle of ceremony to each other" (I,305–6). And in Act I, in the midst of Manly's polemics against the hollowness of social forms, Wycherley very precisely recalls the discourse of trade we have examined at length, in order to reveal exactly where Manly goes wrong. In a speech suffused with the language associated with the various coinage crises of the century, Manly opposes people's "intrinsic worth" to what he calls "counterfeit honor" (I,80); but of course we know that that is a false alternative, for the antonym of the "intrinsic" in this debate (denoting an ontologically fixed realm of value like gold or bullion) is not the counterfeit, but the "extrinsic," a kind of perfectly dependable value which, rather than being implicitly evacuated, simply depends on communal agreements, on knowledge of the rules of the game, of the kind that underwrite the china scene in *The Country Wife*.

To ask whether Freeman represents a golden mean on the other hand is to ask a question that conflates different kinds of response to dramatic character. Critics often consider the possibility in order to dismiss it on the grounds that he is neither morally especially savory nor all that likeable. But this, I would argue, is beside the point. Holland remarks quite properly that "The audience's doubts over the acceptability of Freeman's success are small in comparison with their doubts over Manly."[14] As with the ending of *The Country Wife*, the issue is not whether we like it, but whether it works. Like Manly, we discover, Freeman too has come from sea (II,932), but he is quite unlike Manly, whose name suggests a fixed order of nature, which he insists upon by opposing masculine and brutish courage, of a raw animal kind recalling Hobbes's state of nature, to the taint of effeminacy of the character that was soon associated with the mollifying effects of trade on the habits and sensibilities of the nation. Freeman, by contrast, represents what his name implies, namely what that play at one point explicitly describes as a "liberal" alternative (V,ii,59).

In fact, Freeman is the only character capable of seeing the world empirically. The first three acts are devoted, respectively, to Manly, Olivia, and the Widow Blackacre, all of whom represent an epistemologically absolutist or an absolutely superficial engagement with the world: for Manly, the world either disappoints or presents a phantasmagoria of illusion and deceit, so to get what he wants once he is disappointed can only involve hypocrisy. For Olivia, it is solely a space for the exercise of hypocrisy; and for the Widow, it represents the free play of the legal signifier, best expressed in the autonomic and ingrown formulae of law-French. That most of the characters cannot see what is in front of them is epitomized in Olivia's misreading of the china scene from *The Country Wife*. For her, Wycherley's scene has forever sullied the decorative item itself, whereas the real point is to reveal the fundamental contingency of all human institutions, so that characters who know the game can make temporary agreements that are viable and even yield a degree of pleasure and satisfaction. And the connection between the two plays is also forged by the fact that *The Country Wife* creates a parallel between the exchanges such agreements involve, the circulation of Horner's semen – the medium of so much important exchange – and the consequences of the new worldwide economy of circulation involving exotic objects like china and oranges.

By contrast, Manly, Olivia, and the Widow are not so much psychologically as epistemologically self-absorbed, committed to a fixed order of things of their own invention. Holland has remarked that the key word in the play is "world"; but this obscures the extent to which, like the persistent references to the third Dutch War, there are a series of words – or more properly complexes of words – that Wycherley is equally at pains to stress, which when considered in relation to each other lead us to the play's central set of arguments. These happen in turn to be closely connected to the historic setting. There are three main such groupings: the first involves a term also central to *The Country Wife*, namely "business," which, like "commerce" in Locke's *Essay*, migrates between conceptions of general social intercourse and the fiscal meaning with which, today, it is most readily associated (about forty-one instances); the second involves the idea of friendship, since an ongoing debate in the play concerns the degree to which an attention to social forms (of the kind Manly and Olivia disdain) fosters true friendship, which by their logic is impossible (about twenty-five instances); and third, we have a habit of deep resistance in the dogmatic characters – Manly, Olivia, and the Widow – to any perceived disturbance from without. Just as Melantha's curious obsessions, in *Marriage a la Mode*, with access to the court and with French cause her to be perceived as an "impertinent" person, since she so often speaks and acts out of order, so these three characters treat any sudden and unplanned demands on their attention as, variously, a similar impertinence, impudence, or interruption (about forty-four instances).

Friendship, business, and impertinent interruptions create resistance in Manly, Olivia, and the Widow because in their different ways each conception, which amounts to a fact in the world, represents an unwelcome burden on these characters' different forms of monomania, as Hughes calls it. (Olivia's general objection is that "'Tis a very impertinent world" [II,22].) This is because, at core, each is a way of talking about or symbolizing what Kuhn calls paradigms or Wittgenstein forms of life or Huizinga the ludic principle, for, like "friendship," each man's "business" represents a communal way of approaching human experience which, to function at all, must involve certain contingencies, compromises, and forms of dissimulation of the kind expounded in *The Country Wife*. But anticipating Kuhn, Wittgenstein, and Huizinga, Wycherley's point is that, for all that social activity of any kind might be morally tainted, it also expresses an inevitability about the texture of human life, which is that, like language itself, it is conventional and rule-driven. Berman is right to say that Manly's anger is directed "against the limits of language"; while Holland reminds us that by contrast Freeman "is in part the voice of social ideals."[15] Thus we are intended to remark on the moral simplifications that inform both Acts II and III: in Act II, Olivia indicts as inevitably corrupt numerous social forms of behavior, ranging from clothing, to dancing, plays, masquerading, walking in Hyde Park, engaging in marriage or love affairs, or attending court; and Manly uses the setting of Westminster Hall similarly to indict, from a Juvenalian vantage, numerous different individuals and professions.

Precisely because drama is one of those kinds of activity, Wycherley intends his own play to become yet another example of the very world that Manly, Olivia, and the Widow reject. This argument is carefully laid out in Act I. Early in the act, Manly declares that "I can walk alone" (I,9), and, proclaiming that he is an unmannerly seaman, concludes the entire act with an expressed preference for something remarkably like the Hobbesian state of nature, an honest world where "barbarity is professed, where men devour one another like generous hungry lions and tigers" (I,616–17). Wycherley is aware that, on Hobbesian grounds, this is repellent; and, on Rochesterian grounds, functionally unsustainable, since the very arguments by which the libertine seeks to propound his views depend on the very conventions it rejects, not least language as such. Thus, for Manly, friendship is already a compromise he disdains, and he accuses Freeman of being a "latitudinarian in friendship," to which Freeman responds, recalling the kind of Erastianism endemic to Davenant and Hobbes, "no professing, no ceremony at all in friendship, were as unnatural and undecent as in religion" (I,214;220–1). That Wycherley's own play becomes a symptom of all Manly abhors – namely the forms of behavior which comprise civil society – becomes clear in the ensuing conversation. In response to a Manlian outburst against courtiers, lawyers, officers, poets, and religious women (I,247–93), Freeman remarks, "Well, doctors differ. You are for plain dealing I find. But against your particular notions I have the practice of the whole world" (I,294–6). For Manly, however, the inevitable corruption of all these activities is proven by their correspondence to the theater, the implication that the dramatistic nature of human endeavor involves moral – rather than merely epistemological – compromise. Thus, all these communities "seem to rehearse Bays's grand dance" (I,299).

But the theater in general, and this play in particular, represent constraints on the dogmatic characters, since, as Holland shows, the casting alludes to the heroic drama and romance modes which seem to fit ill with comic conventions. Thus Manly expresses his distaste for the social round seen as a theatrical performance, and at the same time embodies a determination to perplex or frustrate the comic plot, as if he wishes he did not find himself in the play of which he is a chief character. It should not surprise us, therefore, that Wycherley assigns monologues only to Manly and Fidelia, as if they seek an oasis, a moment of respite, from the mundane forward momentum of the narrative. And in improbably recognizing Fidelia as a soul-mate at the end, Manly anticipates Don Sebastian by absenting himself from a plot in which he has always seemed ill at ease. Already in the 1620s and 1630s, we have seen, Davenant was experimenting with the notion that the limits of the private theater might themselves serve as a symbolic constraint on unfettered power, which he also associates with a kind of feminine principle. Wycherley most clearly exploits this possibility in Act IV, when Vernish makes an attempt upon Fidelia. Three things happen simultaneously in this scene: the raw fact of staging, the sudden arrival of a servant from offstage, serves to interrupt Vernish's purposes, as if the playwright were intervening (Vernish exclaims at his impudence: "You saucy rascal" [IV,ii,413]); the interruption implicitly modifies the political language of tyranny in a more desirable direction (Vernish claims, "I am lord here," which Fidelia revises: "Tyrant here" [IV,ii,402–3]); and since the servant seeks merely to announce the alderman with his cashier, this moment of political revisionism occurs as the unwelcome arrival of money, which Vernish, echoing Manly, resents: "Damn his money! Money never came to any sure unseasonably till now" (IV,ii,419–20).

This is exactly a point where Freeman differs from the other characters, for he is comfortable in handling and lending money in ways the others are not. To understand money, we must already understand the larger system of which it is part and which endows it not only with fiscal but social and representational value: like language which underwrites social institutions, its value is not intrinsic but extrinsic, dependent on the way it is customarily used. For these reasons, that system entails an appreciation of the fluid world of circulation to which Manly, Olivia, and the Widow are opposed, a world newly animated by commerce in the wake of the Dutch wars, a world in which monetary behavior corresponds to sociability as such, and therefore a world in which language and money play a similarly socializing, public, and centrifugal role. The Widow is symptomatic for three reasons: she is the object of Freeman's machinations through much of the plot; caught up in the autotoxic world of the law, which notionally involves money, like Manly and Olivia she will not deal with the world around her; and her behavior at law confounds the critical difference between law and equity, which should provide for just exceptions to the rigid application of law, even though she has spent much of her career in chancery, the notional seat of equity (II,852). Freeman confirms a principle expressed by Ascham: custom makes law and custom makes words (59).

For all that Freeman's treatment of the Widow is regrettable – she rightly objects that, in others' estimation, she is not a being but a gap – his activity is predicated on two priorities: freeing Jerry from the web of factual and legal deceit spun by his mother, a repossession of his own will expressed by release into the world of commodities and a parallel world of sociability; and breaking into her completely autonomic legal conception so that it produces effects outside the narrow world of the law itself. The Widow and Olivia are cousins, and their shared sterility is epitomized in Olivia's letters to Novel and Plausible – the same letter with only the name changed, an utterance unresponsive to particular differences in the empirical world. The Widow, we hear, is like Manly "at law and difference with all the world" (I,407), and, to her, empirical demands are an impertinence: she will not "listen" or "hear," so that Major Oldfox is compelled to tie down the Widow so that she will hear his suit. Freeman capitalizes on this moment by trumping the Widow at her own legal game: she has manipulated the evidence about Jerry; and Freeman exploits the language of contract to argue that releasing her from an obligation to marry her is a "consideration," requiring her to pay his debts and promising him £300 a year.

While Freeman detaches the Widow from her cathexis on the law, we witness Jerry experiencing a parallel liberation through three devices: as we will see, Freeman twice appeals to custom to modify the effects of the law to which the Widow appeals; Jerry is curiously insinuated into the world of commodity, arriving in Act III laden with trinkets (III,430–42); and he becomes absorbed in a round of sociability, represented only in part by bawdyhouses and access to women. The Widow objects that he deserts the Inn of Chancery and Westminster Hall for "coffeehouses and ordinaries, playhouses, tennis courts, and bawdyhouses" (IV,i,277–8).

Whether we approve of the content of the arrangement or not, Freeman succeeds with the Widow where Oldfox does not, and that is because, as a good trader, he is also a good rhetorician. If, as Holland argues, Freeman is the Horatian satirist to Manly's Juvenal, that is because he is both sociable and rhetorical. Trade and rhetoric are alike in that they oppose mobility and the contingent to the fixed and absolute, so that it is characteristic of Manly, who has sunk his ship, that he also declares against rhetoric: rhetoric for him is mere rhetoric, a sophistical juggling of forms (III,131), just as society for him is merely theatrical. Manly forgets or ignores what Cicero, Quintilian, and Burke would have us remember – that human affairs are like drama precisely because they are only a dense series of habits and customs through which and by which we move, and in which we see and reflect our humanity. So whereas Manly thinks it something of an insult both to Freeman and friendship to call Freeman a latitudinarian, Freeman more or less embraces the idea. In this context, I think it significant that modern readers betray the same squeamishness towards Quintilian as they do towards Freeman. Freeman loses credibility because his arrangement with the Widow appears so utterly venal and unromantic; but on the other hand, we have to remember that he springs Jerry out of servitude to his mother by showing that he has reached the age of maturity and that his mother has lied about his bastardy. Quintilian for his part is not above regularly recommending dissimulating to the judge even when you know your case is without grounds; but he is also the most notorious ancient theorist to declare that only the good man can be the good speaker. The Ciceronian principle binding these precepts is the anti-foundationalist notion that human institutions are life-worlds, and that the closest we ever get to a moral axiom is to make our reality of what is to hand, whether at the coffeehouse, the theater, the Exchange, in Westminster Hall, or at Whitehall, so that the Ciceronian criterion (obeyed by Horner and Lady Fidget in the china scene) is the joint one of *copia* and *aptus*.

The endlessly shifting contingencies of the local as a philosophical and Isocratean principle in Roman rhetoric mean that Cicero and Quintilian see the activity of rhetoric as providing the occasion for the mediation of law by equity. Like Manly, Olivia (in her way), and the Widow Blackacre, law is fixed and apparently epistemologically unassailable. Equity on the other hand endlessly seeks to make exceptions for the particular case understood contextually and thus always runs the risk of appearing altogether unprincipled. So just as Freeman seems to understand the causes and purposes of the Dutch wars, so he sees himself as representing the power of that peculiarly English repository of equity, namely custom. In Act II, the Widow dismisses the idea that being a second son should be of interest to the law, asking "by what foolish custom" that might be so, to which Freeman sardonically replies, "By custom time out of mind only" (II, 845–6). And in preparing to provide Jerry with his own rights, Freeman declares, "I understand no law especially that against bastards, since I am sure the custom is against the law" (IV,i,394–6).

I will close by briefly returning to the question of satire. In the author's apology to *The State of Innocence*, Dryden proudly refers to his friendship with Wycherley, writing that *The Plain Dealer* is "one of the most bold, most general, and most useful satires, which has ever been presented on the English theatre." Rather than assuming that Dryden was thinking of Manly, like Rose Zimbardo I would like to believe that he was speaking etymologically of the word *satire*, as deriving from the Latin *satura*, denoting a mixed dish of foods, or an *olio*, exactly the term Dryden also used to describe English tragicomedy. By referring at once to satire as an ironic device and by implication to the tragicomic mode lurking behind *The Plain Dealer*, I think he could see that the play acts as an anatomy of political affairs, so that, like him, Wycherley is warning the Stuarts away from their own inclinations to absolutism.

CHAPTER 8

Merchants and bullionists in Behn's The Rover

Not enough has been made of the fact that Behn's early plays in the 1670s were Fletcherian in inspiration. And I have argued at length that the Fletcherian mode, throughout the seventeenth century, was an important vehicle of political deliberation and advice, as well as an instrument of taxonomizing altogether incommensurable ways of approaching the world. As a result, in both cases because she is a woman writer, Behn has suffered from the charge that she is either insufficiently political in her commitments or that, to the extent that she engages in politics, her arguments prove to be internally conflicted. I thus disagree with Maureen Duffy's estimation that since affairs of the heart are the peculiar province of a woman, it follows more or less obviously that, for her, *The Rover* "is, quite simply, about sex in its several manifestations from prostitution to romantic tenderness"; and she expands further, to write that the play "isn't a vehicle for social criticism although critical comment does form part of its imagery. It's about something much more permanent than transitory fashions of dress or behavior: human beings in search of a temporary or lifelong mate."[1] For his part, writing mostly about the second part of *The Rover*, as well as other plays, Robert Markley essentially accuses Behn of, for ideological reasons, suppressing the conflicts around her: "The appeal of Behn's Tory comedies," we are told,

depends ultimately on the audience's accepting a socioideological framework that represses and mystifies the causes of political strife in seventeenth-century England. Class relations, religious discontent, the upper class's monopoly on property, and the economic problems of trade, mining, and agriculture are violently effaced from her plays, replaced by her invocations of a golden age that paradoxically can be represented only in the refracted images of her heroes' exile and dispossession.[2]

I believe that Behn palpably engages with many of the most important political issues of her day, but casts them in the language of knowledge, representation, authority, and trade which were meaningful to her and her audience; but in entering the debates surrounding these issues, which Behn treats as related, she avoids two anachronisms informing Markley's charges against her inadequacies. On the one hand, she may appear insufficiently aware of the laundry list of ills that are more visible to us than they were to the Restoration, but I deny that she censors political issues that were, in the wake of the third Dutch War, immediate and pressing to Englishmen in 1677. On the other, as with a number of other critics, the play is taken as a reflection of or response to a specific ideological formation, treated in almost all cases as a given or singularity. In Markley's case – repeated elsewhere – the plays reflect "a Royalist ideology"; and by the same token they seek to subvert "the Puritan ideology of self-denial," as if either the nature of royalism or of Puritanism was, in the mid 1670s, a settled affair.[3] Heidi Hutner even more sweepingly indicts what she calls "the Puritan ideology of rational thought," as if a proper feminist politics of the kind I believe Behn is propounding either need not be rational in inclination or should (disturbingly) embrace irrationalism as an apt political response to the evils of the patriarchy.[4]

It is equally common to accuse Behn of some form of nostalgia, not least in part because modern critics suspect that Behn's Toryism was some form of bad faith.[5] Contemporary anti-establishmentarianism lurks behind the suspicion that her feminism must be compromised by her Stuart loyalism, as if an attachment to Stuart legitimacy blinded her to the difficulties faced by her sex. Again, we will see how in Willmore in particular Behn is capable of advising Charles against difficulties of his own making and yet proposing an economy in which women can at least contingently negotiate their own position. The accusation of nostalgia also implies that the play was belated in its response to contemporary realities at best, or, at worst, that it indulges in fantasy to stave off the painful actualities that Behn refused directly to confront; whereas I have argued at length that the dialectical habits of the Fletcherian mode made it fully capable of answering to local circumstance and of deliberating on the complexities involved. Finally, it is equally common for critics to imply that Behn's own positions are internally conflicted or contradictory. I take this gesture partly as an expression of sympathy by the modern critic for the difficulties women suffered in the late seventeenth century: the often unexplored logic here seems to be that the degree to which women were excluded from educational, cultural, and political advantages in the period aroused in them contradictory impulses, for to speak at all about their condition they were forced to appeal to shared modes of apprehension which were innately patriarchal in inclination and thus somewhat at odds with women's deepest desires.

The impression that Behn is internally divided in her commitments also flows from the assumption that the play is governed, or should be governed, by a coherent approach either to the men – as representing the patriarchy – or the women – representing the feminine position in general. The tendency is, first, to obscure the distinction between private and public forms of politics, to treat the patriarchy as a single formation to be resisted by the joint force of the female characters in the play and the critics themselves; and, second, systematically to distinguish between the female and male characters, so that plot and language (which Aristotle thought should govern dramatic conception) yield to character and psychology as a locus of significance. But we must recall that when the play was first performed in March 1677, Behn's play was a revision of Killigrew's *Thomaso, or The Wanderer*, written in 1654. Faced with a loose ten-act drama, Behn engaged in numerous revisions and changes, but none more important at this point than the decision – only commented on at length by Derek Hughes and Taylor Corse[6] – to displace the action from Madrid to Naples.

In shifting the action of *The Rover* to Italy, in a period when southern Italy was dominated by the Spanish, Behn invests her plot with an obviously Fletcherian dynamic, because this now allows the play to explore fundamental differences between the Spanish – rulers in Naples – and the English sailors cast ashore during carnival, yet another replay of the plot of *The Tempest*, which like both 1677 plays I examine in this and the next chapter – *The Rover* and *All for Love* – is set in the Mediterranean. (Willmore depicts the situation in charmingly iconographic terms, saying to Hellena, "I am come from sea, child, and Venus not being propitious to me in her own element, I have a world of love in store" [I,ii,153–5].) The opposition between these two communities is real even if it is not entirely diagrammatic. Rather than all the men in the play representing the patriarchy as such, the Spanish and English, and implicitly the Italians, embody different conceptions of the political order, and correspondingly different generic ways of conceptualizing human behavior, involving, for example, such matters as personal honor of the kind that easily results in dueling. The effect of squaring the Spanish against the English in an Italian setting allows Behn to create a highly palimpsestic effect, because both groups, as well as different individuals within a group, especially the English, play out their fortunes in a fluid environment saturated with carnival, an environment into which both the Spanish sisters and the English sailors enthusiastically launch themselves, since it seems to offer both freedom and possibility of a kind hitherto unknown and, it transpires, not always savory.[7]

Behn's selection of Naples as a locale suggests that she knows the history to which she appeals and its appropriateness to what I believe are her central concerns in the play. We should consider both the political history of Italy in the sixteenth and seventeenth centuries, and its rather eccentric relation to the decline of both Italian and Spanish economic fortunes in the same period. First, the Treaty of Câteau Cambrésis in 1559 established the overwhelming power of the Emperor in Italy, by which the Spanish, not the French, remained effective masters of most of Italy for well over a century, providing the peninsula with an unusual period of peace as well as, in the practical management of affairs, a high degree of local autonomy.[8] Thus, though Charles V was natively a Spaniard, he preferred to address his subjects in their own languages, most of which, apart from German, he spoke, and viewed his power as an extension of the ideal of universal monarchy, an expression of the *corpus christianorum*. The period involved a number of attempts by the French to gain a foothold in northern Italy, but for the most part without permanent success not least because early in the seventeenth century Richelieu was preoccupied with Protestant revolt at La Rochelle.

This period can, then, be celebrated as ushering in an era of political stability, but the picture shifts when we consider the changing role both of Italy and Spain not only in Mediterranean, but in world trade. Spanish power heralded a dramatic decline in Italian commerce, such that by the first half of the seventeenth century, though Italian hopes had been pinned on the spice trade, which seemed so promising in the sixteenth century, the Dutch East India Company now enjoyed a monopoly.[9] The status of merchants reflected these changes, for merchants now sought – as they were later to do in northern Europe – to enter the ranks of the landed nobility.[10] Put simply, the Mediterranean was a key theatre for the emergence of the Dutch and English as the prime trading powers in the seventeenth century, an activity in which they engaged with Spanish permission. Sella writes,

In the area of maritime transportation foreign competition . . . had already taken its toll in the late sixteenth century. It intensified after England in 1604 and the Dutch Republic five years later made peace with Spain and their merchant ships could now sail undisturbed in Mediterranean waters. English and Dutch mariners, it was reported with a growing sense of alarm and envy in Venice, offered faster services and cheaper freight rates thanks to the better design of their ships, lower construction costs and lower rates of pay for their crews. No wonder, then, if a growing share of the traffic in the harbours of Genoa, Venice and Leghorn came to be handled by ships of the North Atlantic.[11]

The apparent political health of the system disguised serious problems in Castile herself, and these problems could be interpreted as fatal versions of what the English had experienced in the seventeenth century, culminating most recently in Charles II's damaging Stop on the Exchequer in January 1672, the difference being that the Spanish remained addicted to infusions of bullion from the Indies:

> The Spanish position was much more dire than an impression drawn from the map would indicate. Castile declared bankruptcy in 1627, 1647, 1652, 1662 and 1663, each occasion wreaking havoc in financial circles. The monarch altered the coinage and debased the currency in an attempt to avoid paying his debts. Almost none of the silver still arriving from the Indies in 1660 finished in the crown's coffers, having been mortgaged in advance to the daring bankers who kept the finances afloat. There were similar suspensions of payments in Naples in 1632, 1645 and 1646 . . .[12]

The two main male communities in Behn's play thus operate in very different registers. On the one hand the Spanish represent a set of entirely archaic and dysfunctional values, ones associated with exotic sources of wealth operating in the background – we hear variously of the Indies, Gambia, and Peru – and an attitude to an exchange of value that is likewise primitive, recalling more the activity of barter than of trade.[13] (Thus Hellena archly speaks of Don Vincentio as "Don Indian," who would "barter himself . . . for your youth and fortune" [I,i,140–2].) Though notionally caught up in questions of family honor (itself an archaic set of values), the Spanish represent the patriarchy in crisis and suffering internal confusion and conflict. Don Vincentio, enormously rich from his dealings in Africa and the Indies, and therefore intended by her father as a husband for Florinda, never appears. Equally and markedly absent from the action are the other chief representatives of the Spanish patriarchy, namely the Viceroy and Don Pedro's, Florinda's, and Hellena's father, who is, throughout the play, to be in Rome, though always pending, while his commands are supposedly to be executed by Don Pedro, acting as his representative. Angellica Bianca's former keeper, the Spanish general, is dead, and that is why, once again, she is on the market, offering her favors for one thousand crowns. Because Don Pedro thinks of Angellica as a desirable possession – the degree of overtly sexual interest remains obscure – rather than obeying his father's injunction he seeks instead to interest Don Antonio in Florinda his sister, because he fears that otherwise Don Antonio will compete with him for Angellica. That this is an entirely self-defeating economy with little long-term future is also implied by the fact that Don Antonio is wounded and cannot therefore fight Don Pedro over his honor, and he has to rely on Belvile's services, as if his masculinity as such were now in doubt. Hobbes opposed dueling as an expression of some pre-civil apprehension of the political order; and dueling is therefore equivalent to revenge, of a kind that motivates Angellica in later acts, since its purpose is to reduce the world to some absolute, final conclusion whose implications are opposed to the contingencies of plot and narrative itself, of the kind that Behn emphasizes further by steeping the entire action in masquerade. Dueling and revenge have some interesting cousins on the one hand in barter and on the other in incest and homosexual relations (of the kinds of which Don Sebastian is indicted in Dryden's play), since the thrust in all cases is to create a closed social, commercial, or sexual economy governed by seemingly perfect equivalences of value. Thus when the men draw swords to see who will enjoy Florinda in Act V, Don Pedro's success brings him dangerously close to incest with his own sister (V,101–16).

That disaster is avoided in large part because three of the four English sailors cast rather arbitrarily ashore by circumstance are the beneficiaries or victims of generically entirely conventional plots, by which I think Behn is stressing the marked difference between the archaic world represented by the Spanish (and also, we will see, by Angellica) and the unavoidable fact of convention in the literary universe, which, as Davenant constantly argues about the convention of marriage as such, offers as many possibilities as drawbacks. Most obviously, whereas the Spanish men seek to act competitively and vengefully, resulting in a duel, the English, for all their flaws, subscribe to a world of mutual co-operation and expansiveness. It is after all Belvile's decision to return to help Willmore and also the wounded Don Antonio that results paradoxically in his arrest, and he can only in effect ameliorate his condition by becoming an instrument of revenge in Don Antonio's hands. For all that Blunt is foolish, his companions do not rebuke him for his faults, expecting little less from a country squire; and whereas in Act III Belvile is irritated that Willmore quits the scene of the skirmish with the Spanish and is more angry at Willmore's attempt on Florinda, Willmore's actions never appear openly malicious, being motivated by the overwhelming intoxications of drink and lust, which actually appear as a curious form of generosity, for all that they threaten danger. This admittedly charged atmosphere of co-operation picks up rather interestingly on Behn's prologue, in which she recognizes that the literary world is infused with unfortunate sentiments like envy (in the play a Spanish weakness), but that a new play and playwright depend on a certain generosity from other authors and the audience, a generosity from which Behn had, at the hands of Dryden among others, benefitted.

Critics have often, and rightly, objected to the fact that two of the three major English plots – those involving Belvile and Blunt – reduce women to the status of virgin or whore. But they are mistaken in thinking that these problems are endemic to the patriarchy as a whole, and almost none notice that though the Spanish treat women as commodities or ciphers, in all the English plots, involving Florinda, Lucetta, Valeria, and Hellena supremely, the women get exactly what they want, and in three cases can be said to have planned the outcome from the beginning. (The Frederick–Valeria resolution follows the convention by which a marriage of a confidante or minor companion merely shadows resolutions in more major plots.) All three major English plots comment very precisely on the idea not so much of the marriage market, which is the preferred view of critics, but of the market relations informing not only any correspondence between men and women, but between people and nations more largely. This occurs in a context in which, as she does in other plays like *The Feigned Courtesans*, Behn consistently alludes to important terms derived from the discourse of trade: quite apart from the conventional opening discussion which introduces the notion of a woman's value on the sexual marketplace and deliberates on potential suitors' wealth and fortune (see for example, I,i,79–92), the play, as we have seen, refers to exotic sources of wealth, speaks of the sequestration of royalists' estates by the Cromwellian regime, introduces the idea that Blunt has acted as the group banker and moneylender, discusses the distinction between credit and retail, mentions Jewish moneylenders, alludes to the coinage crises that occurred in the course of the century, and cites the bills of exchange that created such conceptual difficulties for trade theorists.

Although there is no denying that some of this language is a dead metaphor, such as when Lucetta refers to whoring as a trade, I would argue that the persistence of an ideologically loaded vocabulary means that each of the three major English plots is constructed to comment differently on the world of trade which, especially in the wake of the third Dutch War, was an immediate reality to political writers like Behn. In fact, the entire behavior of each plot is predicated on its distinctive relation to this idea. As in *Oroonoko*, whose Frenchman guarantees Oroonoko's sensitivities to the world of romance, so the Belvile–Florinda plot, initiated we are told at the Siege of Pamplona (Belvile being colonel of the French horse), follows a classic romance pattern. Belvile secures Florinda's honor in Spain, and, unlike relations between Willmore and Hellena, their mutual satisfaction is permanently guaranteed not by endless negotiations of the kind that distinguishes that other pair, but by the fact that they never enter the commercial order, for their mutual commitment is secured in Act V not by such venal concerns, but by the rings they have earlier exchanged, tokens of unimpeachable value. Though there are potential obstructions to their happiness, this has nothing to do with the epistemological equivocations which Willmore and Hellena must confront, but classic romance threats to Florinda's virginity (and similar situational misunderstandings, like the effects of disguise), once in the shape of the drunken Willmore and once as a result of Blunt's anger at Lucetta, which almost causes Don Pedro to commit incest with his sister. But the romance features of the resolution – Belvile has already recognized Florinda's token – make it highly unlikely that Florinda will suffer harm, which is one among many reasons why the scenes of potential rape in the play seem at once so disturbing and yet slightly grotesque or comic: in fact in performance it is hard at those moments for the audience to know how to respond, because a degree of titillation clashes with our fears for Florinda.

The essential irrelevance of the world of romance to the commercial world surrounding it also informs the Angellica plot, as we will see, but romance is the exact inverse of the Blunt–Lucetta plot, in which, for Blunt, relations with women are merely a matter of sex for money. As a bit of a bumpkin, Blunt is unlikely to be very successful, and his future humiliation at Lucetta's highly professional hands is more or less guaranteed when, prior to embarking on his adventure, he resigns his role as group banker and restores the money to its owners. Here relations between people are imagined in almost mute and material terms, so that Blunt rather wistfully imagines that his body alone will serve to persuade Lucetta; and this dynamic endows the farce with an unusual degree of symbolic purchase, because farce is so often itself – as Dryden remarks of Shadwell's *The Virtuoso* – an activity without apparent sense apart from the mere sensation of, for example, watching Blunt being dropped into a sewer. This would be merely stupid and funny if it weren't such an apt theatrical expression of Blunt's own unselfconsciousness as a sexual agent.

The very great complexities of the Willmore plot – which involves both Angellica and Hellena, and, more incidentally, Florinda – are at the center of Behn's concerns; for it is here that the implications of trade as a metaphor for the moral and political order are being worked out. First, I appreciate Derek Hughes's reminder that *The Rover* was performed the season after *The Man of Mode*, for it is clear that Dorimant and Willmore are cousins, since, in performance especially, they firmly occupy the center of theatric interest.[14] This unavoidable dramatic fact, which both Etherege and Behn harness, creates some immediate interpretive problems, for both Dorimant and Willmore inevitably draw our sympathy with our interest because they are the performers to watch: if for Dorimant the deep play is now in private houses, for Willmore it is on the street. (One hears an Etheregean echo in Angellica's description of Willmore: "thou'st a tongue / That would persuade him to deny his faith" [IV,ii,305–6].) In both cases the sheerly performative fascination that grips us comes at the cost of subscribing to a blithely amoral ethic, since both characters exercise their athletic and verbal energies at the expense of virtually any and all women they encounter, so we are intended to remain skeptical about Dorimant's future in Hampshire, just as Hellena must wring concessions from Willmore. Though the theatrical genealogy of such players must include Richard III, the closest cinematic equivalent is the Jimmy Stewart character in Hitchcock's *Rear Window*: part of the argument of the film is that the audience's engagement with the chief character as chair-bound spectator implicates us, as co-participants in the visual scene, in a general amoral fascination with what Jimmy Stewart observes, even though it may amount to a ghoulish interest in Miss Lonelihearts's potential suicide. The Hollywood film is, however, more sentimental than the Restoration plays because it transforms into a detective story about a murder across the way, which Jimmy Stewart helps resolve, while a question mark hangs over the reliability of Etherege's hero at the end, and Willmore is subject to a hardly less ambiguous conclusion.

For all its dangers, then, which Behn is at pains to stress, Willmore's role holds the center of attention. This is because of all the male characters, indeed of all the characters apart from Hellena, he is most attuned to the carnivalesque atmosphere. Behn carefully juxtaposes two scenes in Act I, the first devoted to the two sisters' determination to break out of their prescribed roles as object of an arranged marriage (Florinda) and captive in a nunnery (Hellena). Spanish custom would enslave women, Florinda remarks (I,i,66–8), while Hellena's response is that "I'm resolved to provide myself this Carnival" (I,i,38–9), the festival representing that amphibious cultural moment in which pagan excess and indulgence temporarily stave off the temporal rule of the Christian and, in its way, patriarchal or phallic order, figured in Lent and then Easter. At the end of the scene, the sisters and Valeria launch themselves into its "innocent freedoms" (I,i,182).

It is important, for our understanding both of Willmore and of Angellica, as well as of Willmore's treatment of Angellica, to recognize that carnival reveals culture itself as a serious fiction, a necessary artifice which both determines human possibility and remains open to negotiation. In Act I, scene ii this fluid and artificial climate is rendered through several devices: as in so many scenes in the play, the action now takes place in "*A long street*" (15) in such a way that, like Manly in Westminster Hall, so many Horatian satires, and the frontispiece to Dryden's translation of Juvenal X, we are reminded of the way that public space frames a series of different social vignettes upon which the dramatist is implicitly commenting. The proliferation of scenes within acts (Act III has six, Act IV has five scenes) and scene changes within scenes also emphasize the artifice of the stage itself and underscores the extent to which stage meaning so often depends on vigorous juxtapositions of characters and groupings. As Richard Southern argues of stage design in this period, and as I have argued at length earlier in this book, I believe that these effects are not so much illusionistic as anti-illusionistic, as if to mark the extent to which cultural competence depends on an antinaturalistic vision of our social environment. This explains why in this scenic context the two sisters pass themselves off as gypsies, figures both comprising cryptic signs in themselves – a fact that catches Willmore's attention – and figures associated with the skill to interpret the occult. Moreover, this scene is suddenly populated by collocations of Italians who, "*with papers pinned to their breasts*," and some cross-dressed, themselves comprise hieroglyphic symbols (18).

It is in this context that Behn begins to align the English – as opposed to the Spanish – with the world of commerce and trade. First, just as in *All for Love*, where the action is set against the invisible actions of Augustus either on or across the Mediterranean, in this case, whereas the Spanish patriarchy is moribund or in crisis, Charles II (or more ambiguously James Duke of York, hero of the Battle of Lowestoft) is depicted as a kind of Neptune. This image nicely brackets the entire action. In Act I, scene ii Frederick asks where the prince is, to which Willmore replies, implying that his own shore leave will last only a day or two, "He's well, and reigns still lord of the wat'ry element" (I,ii,67). Almost at the end of Act V, Belvile returns to the idea. The cavaliers, he says, "are gentlemen, and ought to be esteemed for their misfortunes, since they have the glory to suffer with the best of men and kings. 'Tis true, he's a rover of fortune yet a prince aboard his little wooden world" (V,509–12). Willmore's arrival in particular is cast in the general language of "business" that informs *The Country Wife* but animates very specifically the language of merchandizing, linking the Englishmen to the fluid environment of Neapolitan masquerade. In Act I, Willmore declares, "Love and mirth are my business in Naples, and if I mistake not the place, here's an excellent market for chapmen of my humor," an observation Belvile confirms by pointing to the Italian masqueraders: "See, here those kind merchants of love you look for" (I,ii,76–9).

When in Act II Angellica admits Willmore to her boudoir, one running debate in the conversation is exactly what kind of transaction buying her favors might comprise, with Moretta, as Willmore puts it, "forewoman of the shop" (II,ii,29). It is my central thesis here that for all that some transaction is undoubtedly involved, this is closer to barter than to trade, since Angellica can only think in terms of some absolute exchange: her full favors for a thousand crowns, nothing more or less on either side. Willmore cannot afford this sum, nor does the absoluteness of the proposition strike him as a proper form of commerce, for, he objects,

'Tis very hard, the whole cargo or nothing. Faith, madam, my stock will not reach it; I cannot be your chapman. Yet I have countrymen in town, merchants of love like me; I'll see if they put up for a share. (II,ii,43–6)

Critics have been tempted by the correspondence in the initials to see Angellica Bianca as a type of the author Aphra Behn, so that female authorship becomes neatly equated with prostitution, but I think the logic of Angellica's position in the plot makes this equation unlikely. Angellica is as far from being the virtual playwright and plotter in this drama as Mirabell, in *The Way of the World*, is as close to his creator, Congreve. Indeed, whereas Act I launches first the sisters and then the rovers onto the adventure of carnival, Act II is given over to Angellica, to reveal two equal and opposite faces of how she resists the prevailing economy: on the one hand, to protect her heart, which she claims has never suffered, and out of fear of impermanence, she sells her body for gold. As she puts it, "inconstancy's the sin of all mankind, therefore I'm resolved that nothing but gold shall charm my heart," though the point is that gold has never truly penetrated her emotions (II,i,145–6). This is the scene in which her bravos place three pictures below her balcony. In an influential article, Elin Diamond argues that when Willmore helps himself to one of the pictures, this comprises an example of the Brechtian *gestus*, the logic being that this action punctures the illusion fostered by the effects of the proscenium stage – Diamond stresses the dreamlike quality of having both the stage and audience bathed in the same candlelight.[15] This presupposes an ideological, at root Marxian, need to shatter the illusion of bourgeois consciousness through a *Verfremdungseffekt*; but this ignores the degree to which stage effects in the Restoration were, one might say, *schon verfremdet*, already known to be artificial. Indeed, the placing of the three pictures becomes a sophisticated commentary on the tension between the artifice involved in the naked proliferation of signs, implying the experience of temporality, and the religious possibilities of the triptych, so that Willmore, aware that it is only a representation, in taking a picture irritates Antonio, who views it, it seems, with a degree of reverence.

The contrast here between the purely representational and the religious comments on the structure of the act and anticipates the nature of Angellica's eventual tragedy. For whereas, in scene i, Angellica self-commodifies to protect herself, like Blunt seeing the world of sexual exchange as a raw matter of barter, in scene ii, she seeks to escape that world altogether in favor of some epistemologically privileged – religiously imagined – sphere. In fact she is captivated by what Willmore and the audience know to be the most vapid and conventional protestations of love: "See here," he cries, "The only sum I can command on earth: / I know not where to eat when this is gone. / Yet such a slave I am to love and beauty / This last reserve I'll sacrifice to enjoy you" (II,ii,61–5). And from the point where Angellica declares "His words go through me to the very soul" (II,ii,76), she begins rapidly to lose her purchase on the plot, resigning the strategic advantage increasingly to Hellena, precisely because strategy is not within her purview. Already Act III, scene i is much more Hellena's than Angellica's moment, for all that she confronts a Willmore freshly out of Angellica's arms. The contrast between Hellena as mistress of theatrical, material, and contingent effects of the kind that will eventually win Willmore, and Angellica's abstracted and absolute consciousness already appears: Hellena interrupts the action by slapping Willmore violently on the back, while Angellica sees her erstwhile lover entirely differently: she "would have raised the man above the vulgar, / Made him all soul, and that all soft and constant" (III,i,172–3). In Act IV, scene ii, Angellica must compete more directly with Hellena; but because Angellica bids farewell to her virgin heart (IV,ii,151) and Hellena can describe Angellica's conundrum perfectly, control of the plot passes unequivocally to Hellena, while Angellica, in a rare monologue, can only resolve on revenge (IV,ii,413).

In the original production, Angellica was played by Mrs. Quin, but in later productions by Mrs. Barry, the tragic actress who had played Loveit in *The Man of Mode* and, much later, was to play Marwood in *The Way of the World*. Like Malvolio, their ancestor in part, these are all figures who, because they cannot play the game, seek revenge not only on others, but on the plot: because the revenger thinks in the wrong generic terms, he or she is in fact at war with temporality itself, of the mundane kind represented, in Shakespeare's play, by the clown's slight but moving conclusion:

> When that I was and a little tine boy,
> With hey ho, the wind and the rain,
> A foolish thing was but a toy,
> For the rain it raineth every day.

Hellena is aptly named because her name alludes to a figure – like the gypsies – who plays havoc with the masculine certainties so often projected onto military glory, signifying an archaic regime of value. Like the business of carnival, like the mercantile economy, like Willmore, but crucially unlike Angellica, we discover in Act V how her imagination is mobile, contingent, and negotiable. Angellica only reappears to put a violent stop to the action, and at this point we see a striking contrast between her and Willmore. Just prior to the critical exchange with Hellena, confronted with Angellica's absolutist rage fueled by her broken heart, a painful figure from romance, Willmore remarks that his heart is an altogether different affair, namely a Harveian engine: undaunted by Angellica's threats, "My blood keeps its odd ebbs and flows still" (V,225). He is already anticipating the terms of the final *détente*. Whereas Angellica's innocent, literal understanding demands, like the bullionists, the "constancy" of things, that term now becomes the ironic basis of the elliptical trade between Willmore and Hellena. This exchange involves a dynamic disequilibrium echoing the difference between the diastolic and systolic movement of the blood in the Harveian system. When Behn shows us Robert the Constant doing a deal, on her insistence, with Hellena the Inconstant, she has not only warned Charles II against his sexual excesses, but at the same time reminds him that true national health depends on trade.

CHAPTER 9

The political economy of All for Love

Like theatergoers from 1677 until the end of the eighteenth century, I believe that *All for Love* is Dryden's greatest play. A measure of its greatness is that it is not only powerful theater in its own right, but perfectly expresses a series of decisions by its author, for entirely local political reasons, to shape the play deliberately to mark its departure less from Shakespeare (despite Dryden's hints to the contrary) than from the Fletcherian and tragicomic tradition that Dryden had inherited from William Davenant, his predecessor as poet laureate. I believe that it is precisely the metatheatrical possibilities of Davenant's reform of the stage that Dryden brilliantly adapted in his serious plays, whether *Marriage a la Mode* (1671), *All for Love* (1677), or *Don Sebastian* (1689; pub. 1690); and it is for these reasons that Davenant's reputation survived until the end of the century. Moreover, at no point can we argue that though, from Davenant on, this is clearly loyalist drama, it represents anything but a skeptical view of the romance of Stuart Kingship. It is as though loyalist playwrights consistently urged their royal audience to examine and so justify, rather than merely assert, the grounds of their power.

Thus in the split plot and the on- and offstage business in *Marriage a la Mode*, Dryden's use of perspectives provided by the proscenium stage urges us to view ironically the machinations of the high plot, in which Leonidas and Palmyra rehearse the romance delusions that Davenant mocks in *The Platonick Lovers* – also a play set in Sicily – so that the play serves as a meditation on the conditions and limitations of Stuart power. The moral is also rendered comic in Melantha's determination to impress her French credentials on the court. The implication is that power can never operate in the belief of its own self-evidence – that is both an expression of epistemological naïveté and the urgency of power itself – but must emerge, Hobbes- or even Burke-like, from within the highly mediated conditions of institutions, in this case represented by the patently material conditions of drama. In *Marriage a la Mode*, one of those generic conditions, inherited from the tradition of English tragicomedy, is the double plot, which allows Dryden to reveal the terms of the outcome as the effect of internal competition and most of the political arrangements at the end as the consequence of *détente*, as essentially contingent. Similarly, in *Don Sebastian* Dryden was to return to the double plot as a means both to defend Stuart legitimacy and yet reveal his dissent from what moderate Catholics saw as James II's abuse of power. *Détente* and a respect for the mediating force of institutions seem also to be the key to settlements at the end of major comedies from the 1670s: Margery is silenced at the end of *The Country Wife* to preserve the brittle contingencies of the game enjoyed by Horner and his paramours, as well as to secure the ending of that established institution, the five-act play; and in *The Rover*, Hellena and Willmore engage in an ironical exchange of terms – Robert the Constant for Hellena the Inconstant – that for the time being at least denotes their mutual satisfaction, while, given Willmore's tendencies, we remain aware of the unsettled nature of such agreements.

Because the play engages with the various generic traditions I have described, *All for Love*, probably performed at the end of 1677 and printed the following spring, similarly expresses a skepticism about the self-regarding tendencies of those in power. It does so, however, by calculatedly abjuring the kinds of generic compromise embedded in *Marriage a la Mode* and *Don Sebastian*, and by purifying and intensifying its neo-Aristotelian commitments to the unities of place, time, and action, unities towards which Dryden had expressed deep ambivalence in *Of Dramatic Poesy*. The play was performed at the height of Danby's preeminence as a politician, at which time, the end of 1677, having displaced the influence of the CABAL, he formed, according to his biographer Andrew Browning, a member of a triumvirate, the other two members of which were the King and the Duke of York. The setting of *All for Love*, representing the final dissolution of the most famous political triumvirate in ancient history, already serves to spotlight the difficult balancing act facing Danby. The nature of Danby's success as a politician, the policies he sought to promote, and the parallels between Dryden's literary allegiances and Danby's political allegiances are all vital to understanding both the argument of *All for Love* as a whole and the relation it bears to the dedication included in the printed version of March 1678, at which time Danby's plans for the future and security of the monarchy were already at risk. Dryden's dedication is full of approving allusions to Danby's signficance in the revolutions in British institutional history which mark the entire late Stuart period, and of which Danby's success at the Treasury and creation of party politics constitute a watershed, even though their broader scope and, of course, their outcome cannot have been visible to any political agent during 1677. Though it is sometimes suspected of being overly Whiggish in the tradition of S. R. Gardiner, David Ogg's splendid account of the late Stuart period is germane, though rendered more particular in Danby's career.[1] In some ways, Ogg's thesis could be reduced to two principles against a common backdrop, that being that Charles II was naturally inclined to a certain absolutism, both expressed and encouraged by his cousin Louis XIV, with whom he had secret treaties and from whom he was essentially receiving bribes to dissolve parliament and return the country to the true – that is, Catholic – faith.

These two principles are, first, that the business of government experienced a shift in the economy of scale and complexity, such that the proceedings of the Privy Council, for example, depended increasingly on the advice of technicians and experts and less on personal allegiances; and second, that in the wake of the second and third Dutch Wars, with the application of the Navigation Acts, with Pepys's revolutionary reforms of the Royal Navy, and with the acquisition of the remnants of a vast Portuguese trading empire in outposts like Bombay, after 1674 Britain dramatically experienced the results of her de facto control of world trade that followed less from the defeat of the Dutch at sea than from their exhaustion through war. In some ways the larger contrasts of Ogg's story are implicit in Figgis's account of the career of Divine Right theory, since, paradoxically, the theory achieved its most elaborate expression under Charles II – who cured more people of scrofula than any other English monarch – while his personal predilections, his indolence, and his womanizing made him a poor personal example of regal sanctity.[2]

Commentators agree that the period between 1660 and 1677 represents a rapid decline in Charles's reputation: the joy of the Restoration was rapidly tempered by plague and fire, and by the Dutch destroying some capital ships of the Royal Navy at their moorings at the close of the second Dutch War; in 1672 Charles scandalously put a Stop on the Exchequer, driving many of his creditors to the brink of bankruptcy and calling the moral as well as fiscal credit of the government into question. Neither of Charles's most powerful mistresses was popular, and the fact that the second, the Duchess of Portsmouth, was French, made more nervous a nation whose Protestant sympathies rightly suspected Charles of improper dealings with Louis. By 1677, moreover, anti-Dutch feeling stimulated by naval rivalry had subsided in favor of the more familiar dislike and distrust of the French – in this case, we now know, well justified. In their different ways, accordingly, Danby and Dryden's loyalism incorporates an element of dissent; for Dryden had rarely been properly paid for his post as Poet Laureate and Historiographer Royal – James Winn's biography merely confirms the shoddy treatment Dryden received from his Stuart masters;[3] while Danby's preeminence in the mid 1670s arose, first, from his highly professional role at the Navy Board; and, secondly, from his genius at the Treasury. Dryden's major literary enemies had coincidentally proven to be Danby's political enemies. Although Danby owed his start to Buckingham, by 1677 Buckingham had become a faded but still dangerous rival whose final moments at the centers of power eventually undid him; and by an entirely different march of events, Danby, like Dryden, had fallen out with Sir Robert Howard.

When Dryden addresses his dedication to Danby, therefore, its carefully chosen analogies place a critical distance between Danby, the professional public servant, and his master, such that, while Danby is said to express the virtues of Charles, Dryden's purpose is hortatory, in an attempt, through Danby, to recall Charles to his own best self. The point can be cogently made in Browning's summary of Danby's lifelong political aims, all of which deviate significantly from Charles's inclinations, and all of which, at this point, exactly coincide with Dryden's implicit prescriptions for a healthy polity: "Protestantism at home and abroad, the maintainance and extension of the Triple Alliance, and observance of rigid honesty and economy in financial matters."[4]

We can take three moments in Dryden's dedication to show his appreciation for Danby as a professionally competent politician, his implicit criticism of Charles as something very different, and his elaboration of what we can only call a theory of political economy, in which the power and interests of the state are judged relative to its commercial viability, a commercial viability fundamentally associated with the sea, and a commercial viability already recommended many years before in the closing stanzas of *Annus Mirabilis*.[5] Thus, Dryden writes, Danby had first to rescue the Treasury from the wreckage of financial mismanagement: "All things were in the confusion of a chaos, without form or method, if not reduced beyond it even to annihilation, so that you had not only to separate the jarring elements but (if the boldness of expression might be allowed me) to create them."[6] Dryden's subtle Lucretianism, for which he pretends to apologize, carefully objectifies and materializes Danby's fiscal reforms in such a way as to prepare us for the next analogy, one opening directly onto political theory proper. Charles's virtue is expressed in his choice of servants, as body expresses soul, but the moderation embodied in Danby then emerges as an obstruction to two opposing forces in the affairs of state. He becomes, in Dryden's vivid metaphor, "an isthmus betwixt the two encroaching seas of arbitrary power and lawless anarchy" (6); and I think there is enough evidence of Dryden's political sophistication here and elsewhere to argue that he is referring to Danby's management of an embryonic government party in parliament, because, like Clarendon and like the Dryden of this Dedication, Danby's loyalism was Cavalier and Anglican, and his management of the House, which anticipated – indeed required – the creation of something like a government whip, effectively imagined parliamentary processes themselves as distinct from, on the one hand, the government in the person of the King and his immediate servants, and on the other, the demagoguery of the emerging opposition party led by Buckingham and Shaftesbury. By the end of 1677, Browning writes, "Not merely had [Danby] obtained for the King one of the largest grants of supply ever accorded him in time of peace, but he had almost contrived to establish a genuine reconciliation between King and Parliament on the basis of a truly national policy."[7] In passing, Browning also remarks that the failure to develop such a national policy owed much to "the essential selfishness of Charles" and that in trying to develop it Danby appeared "to regard Parliament as a third interest which cannot be identified with either King or People."[8]

From a theoretical point of view the shifts in political attitude associated with Danby are thus very significant, a significance not lost on Dryden, whose final analogy promotes the view of England as a maritime and commercial power, whose interests do not include continental adventurism of the French kind – at this point William of Orange was in a merely defensive position and was being courted, with the assistance of Sir William Temple, by Danby to marry James's daughter Mary. Having declared his distaste for republican principles, Dryden then writes: "The nature of our government, above all others, is exactly suited both to the situation of our country and the temper of the natives, an island being more proper for commerce and for defense than for extending its dominions on the Continent" (7).

All for Love as a play, by contrast, operates in a world clinically divorced from these values: compromise, political negotiation, concern for the national interest, the political power of commercial seaborne processes, all are dramatically purged from the main action of the play, but purged in such a way as to make us conscious of their absence, even without the assistance of the printed dedication. We might begin our analysis of the play by asking how Shakespearean it is. Max Novak's commentary in the California Dryden argues that the Shakespearean element emerges only from Dryden's commitment to blank verse;[9] and I agree that Dryden's references to Shakespeare are otherwise something of a red herring. In Shakespeare, Caesar appears as the ultimate victor, which is also the point at which Sedley's version of *Antony and Cleopatra*, published in 1677, begins. In his play, Shakespeare posits a language which can legitimate and mediate the world of practical politics, because the Augustan chemistry is able to manufacture contingent fictions out of Antony and Cleopatra's discrete and self-serving metadramatic habits of speech: it is as though the incantatory speech of Richard II were to encounter in the same plot Henry V's Ciceronian pliability. Taken together, the Shakespearean and Sedleian versions represent Octavius in some explicit contrast to the autotoxic world inhabited by the eponymous pair. In Shakespeare, Octavius presents a largely positive assessment of the Augustan enterprise; whereas Sedley's aristocratic libertinism permits him to expose all his chief actors as corrupt: Octavius is clearly a version of Louis XIV, already bent on the expansion of France at virtually any cost to others, including (in Octavius' case) his sister; and Antony is equally clearly, as well as by association, both effeminated by the East and unable to model himself on any image of proper rule, since even Julius Caesar offers no clear precedent for his circumstances.

In contrast to the untidiness of Sedley's play, the action of *All for Love* is essentially Racinian. It is physically isolated from any image of action, whether in Egypt or the Roman Empire. Caesar or Octavius never appears, though the action is marked by the inevitability of his appproach; and no individual coming from "outside" approximates a verbal protocol which might signal the nature of rule and speech in the Early Empire under Augustus. Cicero, the figure of rhetoric, has been murdered by the connivance of both Octavius and Antony.[10] Ventidius and Dolabella are extensions of what Antony might be if he were to choose a certain course of action, and that is because they represent features of his past and try to recall him to those forgotten or elided aspects of his personality. Octavia is no stand-in for Octavius – the future Augustus – for she becomes the occasion of a verbal and gestural rhetoric of the sentimental family, even though she does hint at the possibility of some public world of value: her proposal of an arrangement with Antony alludes to the public conditions of Restoration comedy since it aims less to preserve their putatively private love than the public image of her "reputation."

The entire action in any case describes a complete political vacuum. The Battle of Actium has occurred and supplies one boundary; the other is provided by the betrayal by the Egyptian fleet, which acts seemingly autonomously without regard to the action or speeches of the chief characters. And Antony's main action, if it warrants that epithet, is to watch the betrayal occurring from Pharos, and so this itself becomes an emblem of Antony emblematizing knowledge.

The dynamic of the play is brilliantly if inadvertently described by Roland Barthes's *On Racine*,[11] and we should notice that Dryden rather backhand-edly admits the influence of *Phèdre*, while referring to Shakespeare as, I think, a smokescreen. The action moves obsessively towards the construc-tion of vignettes, emblems, and icons conceived fundamentally in visual terms, so that its vocabulary is more or less saturated with references to the face, to the eyes, to sight. In their exchanges – or what passes for exchanges – characters tend to try using verbal devices that function as discrete visual counters in order to do one of two things: either obsessively to discover and rediscover the self or the other in some visually imagined past, just as Leonidas and Palmyra fantasize about their past through a stylized pas-toral haze; or to persuade their hearers, as if their hearers were a dramatic audience moved as much by what they see gesturally as what they hear verbally. This in turn produces a paradox, since the play's wordiness arises as a result of the degree to which verbal persuasion *per se* is bankrupt. The situation is exacerbated – by contrast with Shakespeare or Sedley – by the fact that no representative of a functional view of language appears; and the closest equivalent is Alexas, whose uses of language to persuade are perverse and cause Antony's and Cleopatra's deaths almost directly. Great effort is accordingly expended on the verbal construction of almost reified narratives which tend to leave the speakers stranded in the midst of the putatively dramatic situation.

Shakespearean poetry moves fluently among an enormous range or vari-ety of potential metaphors, any or all of which, as it were, are waiting in the wings at any given moment. Speakers can thus appropriate any metaphor or analogy at will without fixating on the need to complete, caress, or polish any single one. Rather than destabilizing the moment of utterance, the fecundity of Shakespearean metaphor tends to stun the hearer with its aptness to the situation – or, if ironic – exactly the reverse. The effect is that of stabilizing representation, such that the plurality of metaphor is, as it were, "the mind of Shakespeare."

The marked thinness of Dryden's analogical protocol, by contrast, derives in large part from three causes: first, from the fact that the semantic of the dramatic moment, at any given point, can draw on all the resources of the proscenium stage, with its capacities to create spatial distinctions between the front and back stage, and to materialize the various perspectives that distinguish characters from one another, and the audience from the stage action; second, from the clarity of the relations among the chief terms of the governing analogies (for example, the analogy between "stage" and "world"), and the degree to which an already selected metaphor of this kind is the methodical key to an entire play; and third, given that in *All for Love* only one side of the analogy is visible – "play" as opposed to "world" – figuration appears as a continual repetition of only one side of an analogy whose empirical application or aptness we cannot judge: all we see is people talking and people constantly conscious that they are talking.

Dryden's play is thus precisely *about* the evacuation of force from the act of speech: the world of words operates at an almost complete remove from the "business" of the world, whether everyday life, love, or politics. There are several features of the play that expound this concern. First, as in the case of Dolabella and Ventidius' commenting on Octavia's possible effect on Antony in Act III, Dryden presents a sequence of hidden or partially hidden viewers who transform the scenes they watch into stylized tableaux of the irrelevance of action in the world. Second, we witness the "discovery" or stylization of Antony and Cleopatra as one among a number of emblems, whether it is Antony surrounded by statuesque Roman soldiers in Act II (Charmion relates, "I found him, then, / Incompassed round, I think, with iron statues, / So mute, so motionless his soldiers stood / While awfully he cast his eyes about" [II, 48–51]), or Cleopatra in her monument. In both cases, the effect is to monumentalize the characters and to suggest that they seek so to monumentalize themselves and each other. Third, in a parody of the living protocols of the Stuart masque, Cleopatra finally monumentalizes Antony by dressing him up in state, so that what was once the theater of relevance becomes the theater of irrelevance, for there is no true audience for the image so presented, or at least an audience we must imagine as sentimental rather than political, so that the rhetoric of the image is entirely dissipated in an affective fog. Fourth, in the course of the play each monumentalizes the other by an obsessive relationship to memory – as when Antony recalls first seeing Cleopatra, a passage incidentally from Plutarch, not Shakespeare (III, 168–87) – which we should not confuse with a genuine relationship to history or the past. Fifth, the tendency to objectify and hypostatize representation migrates into the characters' behavior towards individual words, which, at the moment they appear in speech, are suddenly held up, as if the word-as-object has transformed into a slightly impenetrable emblem for microscopic and almost physical scrutiny, the word frozen as an anaesthetized patient on the table. That words lose their inner life relative to syntax and context itself describes how fully the atmosphere that Antony and Cleopatra breathe is divorced from historical time and political space. Finally, with the rival queens' entry from opposite doors in the rear of the stage, Act III spatializes a fundamental feature of Ventidius's and Dolabella's roles. Characters try to maneuver other characters into assuming postures *within* the syntax of some orchestrated or discrete tableau, just as when Ventidius tries spatially to maneuver Antony into a proper spousal relation to Octavia and their children, or when he commits suicide as a predictably ineffective example to Antony. The instant and catastrophic effects of Alexas' lies on what Ventidius tries to effect through such tableaux reveals how completely brittle – almost literally superficial – they are. The implication is that representation is now worn so thin that when it fractures, the only option is death or suicide.

Dryden in effect contrasts the marmoreal bankruptcy of this world with Danby's success in husbanding England's acknowledged transformation into a commercial power to be reckoned with, with the accompanying view that commerce – an English virtue – rather than glory – a French vice – will strengthen the nation's sinews. As in *The Rover*, that other "Mediterranean" play from the same season of 1677, the opposition between markets – a fluid system of negotiation and exchange already made imaginatively likely in William Harvey's discovery of the circulation of the blood – and more antique and static systems of honor is suggested by the play itself.[12] As many commentators on the history of economics make clear, the discourse of trade (developed especially in England after about 1620) was centrally a means of adjudicating the relative wealth of European nations, especially with the collapse of Portuguese and Spanish colonial hegemony and with the emergence of Holland as the continental *entrepôt*; and it was, to put it only slightly differently, a means of adjudicating the relative integrity of political bodies that were now distinctively nation-states. As we have seen, both the imaginative transformation of physiology that occurred after *De Motu Cordis*, in which the entire body participates in a single circulatory mechanism, and the net result of the three Dutch Wars, whose consequences in favor of English seaborne trade became increasingly clear after the mid 1670s, move in similar directions which are visible in the dramas of that decade. Thus in the Preface to *All for Love*, Dryden expresses resentment against Rochester and the court wits, as well as the French love of ceremony, and contrasts it with a different literary order, one based on merit, and one permitting social mobility based on the market. The world of privilege he associates with Nero, by contrast with which "the true poets were they who made the best markets, for they had wit enough to yield the prize with good grace, and not contend with him who had thirty legions" (20). As a piece of political advice, Dryden intends, in *All for Love*, for Charles II to see himself as two figures at once: positively as Octavius, involving an ideal view of the polity that favors a blue-water policy of the kind Danby, in effect, represents; and negatively as Antony, whose obsession with an Eastern queen prevents him from thinking or acting politically from the start. Throughout the play, Octavius is at sea in the Mediterranean, whose commercial possibilities were already obvious to Englishmen in the 1670s, and for that reason Antony dismisses him as a mere usurer and tradesman: "nature meant him for an usurer: / He's fit indeed to buy, not conquer kingdoms" (III, 214–15). By contrast, like the Spanish in *The Rover*, Antony and Cleopatra are marooned on the gold standard, a world of intrinsic and transparent value. It is Antony in Act V who most clearly invokes the opposition of his world to a commercial, seaborne economy, for, suddenly convinced of Cleopatra's death by Alexas, he contemplates the alternative:

> She is [fled]; my eyes
> Are open to her falsehood. My whole life
> Has been a golden dream of love and friendship:
> But now I wake, I'm like a merchant roused
> From soft repose to see his vessel sinking,
> And all his wealth cast o'er . . .
>
> (V, 203–8)

A little later, he exhausts that metaphor, resigning the world to Octavius:

> What should I fight for now? My queen is dead.
> I was but great for her; my power, my empire
> Were but my merchandise to buy her love,
> And conquered kings, my factors. Now she's dead,
> Let Caesar take the world –
> An empty circle since the jewel's gone
> Which made it worth my strife; my being's nauseous,
> For all the bribes of life are gone away.
>
> (V, 269–76)

CHAPTER 10

The double logic of Don Sebastian: the Oedipal conscience at the Glorious Revolution

By 1688, Dryden's residual Toryism, as well as his alignment with the moderate and indigenous Catholic tradition after his conversion to Rome, both served, though in different ways, to create a profound disappointment in James II. James had, by all accounts, begun his reign as the single strongest Stuart monarch in the seventeenth century, applauded by the nation and voted a generous income by his first parliament.[1] Even late in 1687, to many contemporary observers James's position, backed by a large, well-trained army of about 20,000 men and a powerful navy, seemed impregnable.[2] Therefore both *Don Sebastian* (performed at the end of 1689) and *Amphitryon* (performed in the fall of 1690) comprise meditations on what were in Dryden's view a series of catastrophes for which James was responsible and from which – in the openly political sense – there could be no recovery. ("One of the strangest catastophes that is in any history," wrote Gilbert Burnet.) Dryden's sympathetic identification with a politically shipwrecked Milton seems to have intensified at this time because Dryden was more able than ever to see his own fate anticipated in the older poet. Both men lived to see history destroy the political causes to which they were yoked, so that at one point in *Don Sebastian* Dorax cries out, "Some Kings are resolute to their own ruin."[3]

I thus disagree with David Bywaters's contention that *Don Sebastian*, performed before the Battle of the Boyne, still entertained hopes of a Jacobite *revanche*. Such a view – I believe – emerges from too minute a focus on thematic correspondences between dramatic and political events, so that what is in fact a political parallel, whose application to local particulars comes and goes, and whose capacities for moral equivocation Dryden exploits, serves instead as a fairly direct allegory on events.[4] One purpose of both *Don Sebastian* and *Amphitryon* is, precisely, to frustrate such equivalences and so to comment on the best ways of reading them; so they show, almost mercilessly, how a reflection model of the literary text turns out to be insistently self-negating or paradoxical. Indeed – in a scene with multiple resonances – Dryden partly warns against such readings in *Don Sebastian* itself, since the Emperor demands that the Mufti force the Koran to mirror his lust for Almeyda:

Mufti.   Why verily the Law is monstrous plain:
              There's not one doubtful Text in all the Alcoran,
              Which can be wrench'd in favor to your Project.
Emp.   Forge one, and foist it into some by-place
              Of some old rotten Roll . . .

                                                            (III, i, 69–73)

It is *Amphitryon*, the simpler play, that can briefly show us here how Dryden resists systematic applications of this sort.

Obviously, the play is about usurpation, since Jupiter – that most lustful and metamorphic deity – conspires to possess Amphitryon's wife, Alcmena, by assuming her husband's form. It is tempting to allegorize the play by treating Jupiter as the usurper William III, the despoiler of his father-in-law's rightful inheritance, and Amphitryon himself as the dispossessed James. But such an application ignores too much of what we are required to admit: the lustful Amphitryon is also a composite Stuart, a figure certainly of the licentious Charles II as well as, by association, of the adulterous James II (who blamed his demise on his sexual exploits).[5] (William III was by contrast reputed to be a closet homosexual, which has some important consequences for *Don Sebastian*.)[6]

Moreover, we should not overlook the staginess of the play, for that rhetoric also serves to point the relative weight of the characters. The effect is to suggest that no character becomes an unequivocal moral pole either for good or ill. Thus, though he may also reflect Milton's Satan, Jupiter as lover and seducer is a far more attractive stage figure than the true Amphitryon, whose dutiful murmurings pale by comparison with Jupiter's ardor, an ardor the poet not only created for Betterton but could only, at one level, relish. (Betterton had assumed the equivocal role of Dorax, not Don Sebastian, in the earlier play.) Evidently, Dryden feels that some magic goes out of the world when it becomes morally sanitized.

Significantly, hope is offered at the end of *Amphitryon* in the person of Hercules – neither divine nor mortal, or alternatively, both god and man. This hero's identity is neither single nor stable, embodied in no preordained taxonomy of value. The ending of the play thus flows almost seamlessly from one of its strangest and funniest threads, namely Sosia's musings on what it is to be both himself ("*S.O.S.I.A.*" that is) and yet not himself (since Mercury "is" also Sosia). Sosia is quicker to see the problem than Amphitryon, to whom he explains it thus:

I tell you once again in plain sincerity, and simplicity of Heart, that before last
Night I never took my self but for one single individual *Sosia*; but, coming to
our Door, I found my self, I know not how, divided, and as it were split into two
Sosia's. (III, i, 82–6)

The most vivid image Sosia uses to convey his parlous identity is numis-
matic. The split coin he describes presents us with not one but two monarchs' heads:

Have you not seen a Six-pence split into two halves, by some ingenious
School-Boy; which bore on either side the Impression of the Monarchs Face?
now . . . those moieties were two Three-pences, and yet in effect but one
Six-pence – . (III, i, 96–9)

This moment epitomizes the royalist conundrum in 1689 or 1690, since
royalist precept opposes usurpation yet argues that the present monarch
must be deemed to rule providentially: the execution of Charles I had
opened up a conceptual divide between two incommensurables, namely a
king de jure and a king de facto.[7] And now the King de jure was in France,
in the arms of an acknowledged enemy, and the King de facto was a for-
eigner, an apparently ungrateful son-in-law, and perhaps unwillingly thrust
onto the nation's confidence. Keith Feiling puts the problem pithily: "The
Revolution had shattered the old Tory basis . . . [The Tories] were drawn
by their political reason to support the Crown, but by their sentiment to
hate usurpation and Dutch wars."[8] I don't know for certain where Dryden
himself stood or how he experienced the world of internally divided values rendered by Sosia in comic terms. This is chiefly because – as James
Winn points out – Dryden's opinions must be inferred either by reference
to the general political, intellectual, and literary climate within which he
moved or from his own literary creations.[9] The latter case is particularly
intransigent: where Dryden's views only derive from a given reading of a
literary text, they cannot be said to explain its origin. All the same, I do not
believe that close readings of *Don Sebastian* or *Amphitryon* justify either the
notion that Dryden adopted a polemical view of the Revolution or that
he adopted a kind of irenist or defeatist posture towards the outcome. His
anger and disappointment were altogether more productively channelled.
Rather, events encouraged Dryden, already an old man, to develop into a
profound political philosopher and anthropologist, such that the baroque
texture of his late plays permits him to treat the events of a dramatic plot
as a myth of Stuart history, a history viewed from the elegiac perspective of
a marooned loyalist.

In the wake of the Glorious Revolution, the Tory or loyalist position was almost impossible. Any scrupulous royalist in the seventeenth century generally subscribed to some form of Divine Right theory, until recently more an imaginative complex of attitudes, ideas, and images than a coherent political philosophy. The tensions inhabiting the debate after 1688 have a good deal to do with the fact that British constitutional theory was largely customary and that the King's powers were rarely thought of in contractual terms, though the arguments had achieved increasingly greater focus during the Long Parliament, after 1649, and in the Exclusion Crisis.[10] Events were demanding that a state of mind that was closer to myth or folklore respond in systematic terms to the new polemical atmosphere. The contractual view was associated with radical and Whiggish thought to which few parliamentarians were sympathetic, and it is a marked feature of the period between 1688 and 1690 that the contractarian arguments presented by Locke in the *Two Treatises* in 1690 failed to appeal.[11] Inasmuch as arguments from agreement or compact were made, they rested on individual and local precedents in English history, and avoided the fiction of original contract altogether.[12] The systematization of the Revolution Settlement as a Lockean efflorescence was a recursive action from the less marshy ground of the eighteenth century.[13] The final decision of the Convention Parliament, in intense negotiations with William, was to declare that James II had abdicated from, not deserted, the throne, which was "thereby become vacant."[14] But that was only the least uncomfortable and untenable of several fictions debated early in 1689.[15] All parties were agreed that by fleeing to France, the King had forfeited his right to rule; and legal opinion influencing the deliberations of the Convention Parliament was that the King's legal authority had lapsed the moment he left England.[16] We must also recall a psycho-historical state of mind that remembered how the Civil Wars and Interregnum had rent the national fabric; and it seems that parties of all political persuasions tacitly agreed that 1660 represented a precipice in the past beyond which none should venture. In *A Sermon Preached June the 17th 1688. Upon the Birth of the Prince*, John Turner said, "There is no Form of Government so bad, so ill contrived, but it is still infinitely better than no Government at all."[17] By the end of March 1688, even a Tory like Danby was drawn to parallels between the unwise policies of James II and Cromwell as if to underscore the taboo against reawakening the chaos of the Civil Wars.[18]

Historians are quick to point out that in the long run the compromise at the Revolution fitted the Whigs as ill as the Tories.[19] But the Tories or loyalists suffered most immediately and violently from the way that history had forced them to strain or abjure their principles. They were the natural inheritors of the doctrine of Divine Right, which had a complex genealogy, one ancient and one comparatively modern. Despite J. P. Sommerville's confidence that Divine Right theory "was not an odd devotion to analogies or historical precedent, but a set of simple rational arguments,"[20] on the one hand one could argue that the English doctrine has a pedigree in folklore, pagan myth, Biblical precedent, and ad hoc theories of kingship especially from the Norman Conquest on. The Henrician reformation marked a critical juncture because Henry VIII argued that he was King by direct divine decree free of Papal sanction, so that in England the doctrine tended to have a nativist and Protestant bias.[21]

There is general agreement that it was the Stuarts who elaborated and capitalized on Divine Right theory most fully, though James II's demise projected the theory increasingly into the realm of Jacobite nostalgia. Paradoxically, the Long Parliament, the execution of Charles I, and the Restoration combined to catalyze Divine Right theory into its fullest expression, as if it arrived historically too late to help those who needed it most. I believe that Dryden was conscious from 1660 of the belatedness of the doctrine, such that his Jacobitism, though tragic, is marked by none of the nostalgia that we see, for example, in Aphra Behn's *Oroonoko*, which also responds to the events of 1688. By the middle of the century, Divine Right theory could be summarized in the following propositions: monarchy is a divinely ordained institution; hereditary right is indefeasible; kings are accountable to God alone; and nonresistance and passive obedience are enjoined by God.[22]

In the event, James's political maneuverings, which were rapid, inscrutable, and contradictory, rendered loyalists' experience of these principles between 1686 and 1689 internally divisive. Already from November 1686 to April 1687, James, realizing that Tories like Rochester on whom he had relied would resist the abolition of the Test Acts, turned to the Whigs, as well as to William Penn.[23] The Tories had hitherto represented the core of loyalist feeling, which James now rebuffed; and this internal tension is also clear in three other incidents: James's sudden back-pedaling in 1688; the loyalist *volte-face* in 1688 and 1689; and the single most precipitous event in the Revolution, namely the trial and acquittal of the Seven Bishops, five of whom were to become nonjurors after William was declared King. Observing the Emperor similarly driven between conflicting impulses, Sebastian exclaims, "Was ever Man so ruin'd by himself!" (II,i,411).

I believe that the period between May 1688 and the end of 1689, when *Don Sebastian* was performed, set the terms for Dryden's play, but not only, and not centrally, for thematic reasons. This period in English history massively amplified a presiding interest in the relationship between the individual conscience and public duties to the monarch and the nation. Though the debate about conscience long predated James's accession, it was revived in the early 1680s and intensified after 1685.[24] The first local occasion was the Seven Bishops' refusal to direct Anglican clergymen to read the second Declaration of Indulgence, originally issued in April 1688. The second occasion, which followed closely, was the refusal by most of those bishops, and a substantial minority of Anglican clergy besides, to take the oath of allegiance to William and Mary. Both of these actions severely jeopardized the individuals involved – the nonjurors lost their benefices in the event – and it is important to see that Sancroft and his allies could not readily be charged with simply trying to secure Anglican hegemony. Their true motives for crossing both the Stuart and Orange regimes remained in doubt and seemed to demand the kinds of explanation that were then offered: the Bishops were following their consciences. But if this was the case, the nature and claims of private conscience, when confronted by public events and public obligations, themselves remained obscure.

In the context of public policy, of reasons of state, such uncertainties were deeply vexing, both on political and epistemological grounds. So Antonio remarks sardonically, "I see the Doctrine of Non-Resistance is never practic'd thoroughly but when a Man can't help himself" (I,i,521–2). That the claims of conscience were profound, and supplied a true motive for action, few seem to have doubted. The difficulty came with the attempt to describe its positive content and prerogatives, especially since some writers – including, it seems, Dryden in *Don Sebastian* – argued that the King might also issue repugnant commands out of his own conscience.[25] Moreover, the Anglicans had denied liberty of conscience to dissenters, but their leaders were now appealing to a very similar principle. Indeed, the Declaration of Indulgence was rightly advertised as the systematic extension of liberty of conscience to nonconformists and Catholics – by comparison, the Act of Toleration was an anemic document – even if many suspected James's covert motives. The problem, of course, is that, relative to what we can know and judge with any confidence – facts lying unequivocally in the realm of the "public" – conscience is a negative and critical posture towards the givens of common political and social life. What makes it so troubling for politicians is that it seems to have such an immediate claim on the individual's attention, which becomes distracted from the business of state. Thus the conflict between James and those who cited conscientious reasons for resisting him intensified a tendentious parallel with the problem that Julian the Apostate posed for the early Christians, as if, for Protestants, James's Catholicism was a form of pagan oppression.[26] Significantly for my title, the writer of *A Discourse of Conscience* (1688) (following Taylor's *Ductor Dubitantium*) defines this attitude as "double doubt," and as "*The Suspence of a mans Judgment in a Question about the Duty or the Sin of a Action, occasioned by the Equal (or near Equal) Probabilities on both sides.*"[27] Arguing that the mere presence of doubt is not in itself enough to resist a lawful command, since "that *Command* is (generally speaking) a sufficient Warrant for a Man to do that Action, though he *Doubts* whether in it self it be lawful or no," the writer hesitates to enforce such obedience in the face of conscientious scruples. "Far are we . . . from asserting," he concedes,

That whatever our Governours do command, the Subject is bound to perform, so long as he only *Doubts*, but is not *perswaded* of the unlawfulness of the thing commanded: And if there be any sin in the Action, he that *commands* it is to answer for it, and not he that *obeys*. For we do believe, that in matters where a mans *Conscience* is concerned, every one is to be a *Judge* for himself, and must *answer* for himself. And therefore if our Superiours do command us to do an Action which *their Superiour* God Almighty hath forbid; we are offenders if we do that Action, as well as they in commanding it, and that whether we do it *Doubtingly*, or with a *Perswasion* of its Lawfulness.[28]

Whatever Dryden thought of the Bishops' role in bringing down James, by the end of 1689 his own position echoed theirs. Like them, he was a conscientious objector to the new regime. Accordingly, throughout *Don Sebastian* Dryden imagines the political order as necessarily composed of such unstable relations between unlikes, where neither for the individual nor for the state can any element exist autonomously. For this reason, Dryden returns both to the heroic mode, a casuistical forum (Alan Roper has argued) for debating the conflicting claims of love and honor;[29] and to the tragicomic double plot, which ever since Beaumont and Fletcher had permitted playwrights to view Stuart rule from a profoundly ironic perspective.

Dryden's personal case is further complicated because the loyalists lost faith in James largely over his Catholicizing policies which Dryden could be deemed to represent. There are plenty of indications in *Don Sebastian* of Dryden's anger at churchmen's meddling – as he saw it – in the affairs of state. (In Act III, Dorax says, "Churchmen hold the Reins; / And, when ere Kings wou'd lower Clergy greatness, / They learn too late what pow'r the Preachers have" [III,i, 414–16].) Nevertheless, I would argue that the logic of *Don Sebastian* shows that Dryden could sympathize with the loyalists' frustration, because what forced their hand, Feiling argues, was less the content than the manner of James's policies. All commentators see James's attitudes and methods as rash, arrogant, self-deluded, and out of touch with local opinion. Of course the case of the Seven Bishops captures the issues most vividly. The Anglican church had carefully expanded the doctrine of nonresistance under Charles I, and yet James II, as nominal head of the church, seemed intent on driving the country onto the rock of Catholicism, the harbinger of the profoundest irrational fears in the seventeenth century. Anxieties were intensified by the revocation of the Edict of Nantes in 1685 (not to mention Louis's viciously expansionist policies which were the prime cause of William's decision to invade), resulting in the Huguenots' suffering.

Thus the officers of the church rejected a key article of Anglican doctrine in order to buttress the fabric of a national institution: they violated the principle of nonresistance when they refused to read the Second Declaration of Indulgence after it was issued on 27 April 1688.[30] Yet although their acquittal after their trial was the most intensely charged popular stimulus to reject James, five of those Bishops resolutely refused in 1689 to swear allegiance to William. They continued to reject nonresistance to the de facto magistrate on the theory that James, not William, was legally still the head of church and state. Maitland makes the simple point that strictly according to law they were right.[31] The dating of *Don Sebastian* is particularly relevant here, for if it was performed in December 1689, as Miner conjectures, this follows by some months Archbishop Sancroft's suspension on 1 August 1689 (he was not formally deprived of office until 1 February 1690).[32] In *A Prophylactick from Disloyalty in these Perilous Times* (1688), Thomas Pierce vividly imagines the conundrum at the heart of the Bishops' experience. The doctrine of nonresistance amounts to the principle that "When God and his Deputies do stand in Competition for our Obedience, God must have our whole *Active*, and his deputies our *Passive* Obedience only." But the consequence for Pierce as a sympathetic witness was that "when I observed the different Judgments, of *Seven* Bishops on one side, and *Six* of another, I stood pendulous for a time between *Six* and *Seven*; like an hovering Piece of Iron between two Loadstones."[33]

Whatever Dryden thought of Protestant loyalism, Pierce's image perfectly describes the position of the native and moderate Catholic opinion with which Dryden was allied. That James was embarked on a Catholicizing policy, and that he went about it rashly, is clear. There is some debate about whether in offering full toleration to all creeds, James's motives were in fact as generous as they could be made to appear. Those who have examined the issue most closely seem to think not. And for that very reason, most agree, it is unlikely that native Catholics favored James's actions, for they were keen to be seen as loyal Englishmen; they did not want to attract unfavorable attention from the nation at large; and they were uncomfortably aware – until an heir was, against all odds, born in 1688 – that James's successors would be Protestant. Moreover, James's political behavior in general can be described as hermetic, for the Catholics at court represented a society and attitudes as much out of tune with Catholics in the country as with its Protestant majority. In his deafness to moderate counsel, James was rehearsing the key weaknesses associated with the historical Sebastian I, King of Portugal. As de Oliveira Marques puts it, Sebastian "despised the old and the prudent, surrounding himself with a bunch of young aristocrats, almost as insane and immature as himself. . . Only through flattery could one gain access to him."[34] That life at court was segregated from general feeling is epitomized in James's selecting the widely hated Jesuit, Father Petre, as an advisor. Thus there were good grounds for post-Revolutionary propaganda to blame James's demise (like that of his father) on bad counselors. John Miller argues that James entertained the pathetic conviction that if only Englishmen could give Catholics a fair hearing, there would be mass conversions.[35] The King seems to have learnt little from his own daughter Anne's resistance to pressures applied towards her conversion. In the single most elegant assessment of Dryden's moderate Catholic loyalties, Louis Bredvold concludes that "The Catholics themselves were divided into two factions: those who wanted James to confine himself to moderate courses and keep up a good understanding with William; and those who thought that the king must act swiftly to liberate English Catholics from all their legal penalties and make the Catholic Church in England absolutely secure from legal oppression forever." James bungled things so badly that, in the long run, "Ironically enough, the very people whom James endeavored to liberate preserved his memory with detestation."[36]

It is therefore my contention that Dryden's loyalist inclinations, inflected by his commitments to a nativist Catholicism, caused him to view both William and James – that is, kings as such – with a profound and yet an imaginatively constitutive ambivalence. After 1688, loyalists were forced to admit that the usurper had succeeded, such that the King de facto was William, while the King de jure, James, had brought ruin upon himself and his supporters. In sustaining their allegiance to James, nonjuring churchmen and native Catholics, whom James had effectively abandoned, shared the problem of articulating their grounds of resistance to constituted powers. In *The Doctrine of Passive Obedience and Jure Divino Disproved* (1689),

George Hickes bluntly dismisses the legitimacy of the nonjurors' position, for, as he puts it,

Allegiance is due to a King in Possession, (who is called a King *De Facto*,) and Treason may be committed against him, as well as against a King by regular descent . . . whereas, on the contrary, all . . . acts done by a King *de Jure*, who is not in possession of the Crown, are totally void . . .[37]

Or, as the *Agreement Betwixt the Present and the Former Government* (1689) has it, "the *Law* allows a King *de facto* the Name, and Dignity, and Authority, and Defence of a King."[38] Such politically and epistemologically confident positions allowed those who supported the Williamite succession seamlessly to translate their obligations from the House of Stuart to the House of Orange. It was often averred that William had simply restored Englishmen to their native possession, the constitution. But this was to beg the very question that Dryden asks in *Don Sebastian*, since such comfort, not to say smugness, was denied a large number of Englishmen at this juncture, who were left wrestling with their consciences.

The play puts the problem very clearly. It is set in Morocco in 1578, immediately after the battle of Alcazar-quivir, and occurs at that town, though Dryden confusingly refers to the North African locale only as "Alcazar." Sebastian's grandiose narcissism was the sole cause of this disastrous Moorish victory; and the particulars of its aftermath also demand applications to the Glorious Revolution, because the battle provided the occasion for the forced union of Portugal and Spain under Philip II, who was half Portuguese and (like William) used his connections in the Portuguese camp to orchestrate his entry into Portugal in December 1580.[39] It was only in 1640 that the Braganza family could reestablish Portuguese independence; but the Portuguese were never to recover the prestige associated with Henry the Navigator, and one story to which Dryden alludes maintained that, because no one had actually witnessed his battlefield death, the Spanish had murdered Don Sebastian. In fact, popular myths of his survival resulted in the emergence, over time, of no fewer than four Pretenders who claimed to be Sebastian redux; all were executed.[40] On these myths two slightly different disenfranchised communities pinned their hopes: the *sebastianitas*, who saw in Sebastian the seed of Portuguese national revival; and the Jews who converted to Christianity after the expulsion in 1507, the "new Christians," who spoke of Sebastian as *O Encoberto* ("the Hidden One") "who would establish a millennial reign of peace and prosperity."[41] The applications for Jacobites and disenfranchised Catholics after 1688 are obvious; and it is also important to note that any narrative of the reign of Sebastian I and its aftermath must account for the historical force of popular beliefs that imaginatively conflated historical fact with myth.

The play itself is organized around a double plot. The high plot involves the current Moorish emperor, Muley-Moluch, who has gained power by usurping the father of Almeyda, an "African" princess (it seems) whom he desires, but with whom Don Sebastian will fall in love. The Moors have just defeated the Portuguese and have full possession of Alcazar, which provides the setting of the action. In the Muslim camp we also find the emperor's brother, Muley-Zeydan, a scheming favorite called Benducar (who plans to use Mustapha and the mob for his own political ends), and the Mufti (the chief Muslim clergyman).

The Mufti is also the occasion for the low plot because (as a materialist of the first order) he is one beneficiary of the auction of Christian prisoners that occurs in Act I. Purchasing Antonio as a slave, he gets more than he bargained for: Antonio's charms catalyze a sexual rivalry between Morayma and Johayma, the Mufti's daughter and his wife, though things are nicely settled at the end with Antonio's betrothal to Morayma, a comic version of Don Sebastian's marriage to Almeyda.

The high plot moves along parallel lines, one involving Don Sebastian and Almeyda. In defiance of the rumors about Don Sebastian's disappearance, Dryden introduces Don Sebastian as one of the several Christian prisoners, who also include (besides Antonio), Almeyda and Alvarez, whom Don Sebastian reveres as "my second Father" (II,i,593), and who has earlier warned Almeyda against marrying Sebastian. By displaying his nobility in defeat, Don Sebastian prompts Muley-Moluch to commute his sentence and treat him, Almeyda, and Alvarez with the dignity they deserve. But in Act III, Muley-Moluch is enraged to discover that Sebastian and Almeyda have indeed married. He orders their arrest, which causes visible distress in Dorax, a Portuguese former Christian who has converted to Islam.

Dorax's principled ambivalence becomes a political threat to Benducar and the Mufti, both of whom poison his drink at the end of Act III. Benducar's and the Mufti's machinations comprise the second thread of the high plot, since they each contemplate treason against Muley-Moluch. The one succeeds in orchestrating mob violence to unseat the emperor and desires additionally to gain possession of Almeyda – the main action of Act IV; the other seeks to ensure the continual control of state affairs by the clergy, who are represented here as venal and power-hungry.

The events of Act IV, in which the mob kills and beheads the emperor, leave Don Sebastian's claims to the throne and to Almeyda unchallenged because Antonio (arriving in the castle grounds from the Mufti's garden) protects Almeyda against Benducar's lust, just as his love for Morayma will free her from Muslim oppression. Because the two poisons have cancelled each other out, Dorax returns to reveal himself to Don Sebastian (and to berate him) as his former friend whom Sebastian betrayed, Alonzo.

In Act V, Don Sebastian, with Muley-Zeydan in custody, seems on the brink of securing his inheritance when he discovers from Alvarez that Almeyda is his sister. Prevented from suicide, he concludes the play by deciding to become an anchorite, so allowing for a new political compromise in which a malleable Muley-Zeydan will rule with Dorax's counsel.

That there are no foundational or purely indigenous claims to power or culture is argued by the fact that there are three lawful rulers in the play, all of whose claims to legitimacy are deeply fissured: Don Sebastian, an elusive figure from romance, the "true" but incestuous King of Portugal; Muley-Moluch, a usurper but nevertheless a de facto ruler who is unjustly murdered; and Muley-Zeydan, the beneficiary of the final political *détente*.

Attention to Dorax's and Muley-Zeydan's roles in the plot should reveal that Dryden's central point in his play, as well as its governing structural and rhetorical principle, is that any truly conscious agent experiences history as a series of invariably painful discrepancies between an immediate response to public events and their meaning in some larger or more transcendental scheme. Allegiance to either interpretive framework alone may yield a certain comfort perhaps, but it is an illusory relief from interpretive anxiety. A trust in the immediate and most evident features of historical experience comprises a materialist fallacy, in which, for example, the Williamite succession amounts to the triumph of populist self-interest, the rule of what the Mufti refers to as "these three P's, Self-Preservation, our Property, and our Prophet" (IV,iii,110–11), in which (as the rabble puts it), "Religion and Trade always go together" (IV,iii,85–6). A recourse to a ready-made transcendental account of things imports a different set of dangers, since, isolated from the contingencies of historical accident, it abstracts us altogether from those distinctively human properties, the passions, the body, and moral equivocation. In the dedication to *Don Sebastian*, Dryden writes,

True Philosophy is certainly of a more pliant Nature, and more accommodated to human use; *Homo sum, humani ame nihil alienum puto.* A wise man will never attempt an impossibility; and such it is to strain himself beyond the nature of his Being; either to become a Deity, by being above suffering, or to debase himself into a Stock or Stone, by pretending not to feel it. (62)

Don Sebastian is accordingly full of doublings of many different kinds – almost obsessively so – doublings whose purpose is to celebrate our experience of history, as well as those literary texts like Dryden's (and Plutarch's) which rehearse and recommend the moralizing force of historical example.

The dynamic and movement of history depends on two profound disequilibria. First we have an experiential disequilibrium that catapults one historical moment into the next, so weaving the web by which we recognize "history" at all. In *Totem and Taboo*, Freud asks, "How much can we attribute to psychical continuity in the sequence of generations? and what are the ways and means employed by one generation in order to hand on its mental states to the next one?"[42] These are very much questions on Dryden's mind, since the fate of James II seemed inextricably bound at an imaginative level with that of his father, so that like Freud he sees the continuities of seventeenth-century history largely through the family romance, the past shadowing the present. Similarly, the fictional Almeyda is haunted by the memory of "My murther'd Father, and my Brother's Ghost" (I,i,446).

And second, we have a more conceptual disequilibrium that reminds us that raw events always happen in some charged, ironic, potentially disruptive relation to our sense of moral order. This disequilibrium, we must recall, describes Dryden's very assumption about literature-in-history, since the parallel embedded in the literary fable purposely frustrates a total interpretation of the history to which it responds. Part of the moral condition of our applications is that they are individual and contingent, always on the brink of revision, since our developing encounters with the literary (or historical) narrative will invariably unsettle interpretation. Literature and history demand each other, but never become mutually exhausted. This is exactly one thread of argument in the preface to *Don Sebastian* ("*where the event of a great action is left doubtful,*" Dryden writes, "*there the Poet is left Master*" [68]). This disequilibrium is also what Jeremy Taylor has in mind in *Ductor Dubitantium* when he speaks of history as governed both by motives of prudence and by motives of conscience which operate eccentrically relative to each other.[43] It is worth remembering too that Dryden was soon to embark on his great translation of the *Aeneid*, a text which is precisely about this dynamic of disequilibrium. Virgil secures the very possibility of his poem by revealing how the struggle between Venus and Juno creates potentially endless delays and disasters for Aeneas and the Trojans, so that it becomes difficult to tell what happens "inside" and what "outside" public history. The hiatus so created – between leaving Troy and arriving in Latium – becomes the narrative we have.

Typically, Dryden establishes the symbolic economy of his play in his dedication to Leicester. The choice of dedicatee is itself highly significant.

Here is a member of the Sidney clan – another Philip Sidney no less –
whose public political affiliations had been at the opposite pole to Dryden's.
The elder brother of Algernon, whom Charles II had executed for his
alleged complicity in the Rye House plot, Leicester had been appointed
one of the judges of Charles I at his trial, but had declined to act. He
had enjoyed Cromwell's favor and signed the declaration naming Richard
the new Protector in 1658. However, his relative lack of political standing
meant a ready pardon after the Restoration. Significantly for *Don Sebastian*,
Leicester had dropped out of public affairs thereafter, choosing instead to
patronize literature, a patronage which had earned Dryden's gratitude. It
is as though the realm of literature allows a point of contact, a kind of
no-fire zone, for two men (Leicester and Dryden) with opposed political
pasts. In offering a shared critical perspective on public affairs, literature
itself becomes a medium of conscience within public life. The point is all
the more charged, since Leicester's eldest son had, on 11 July 1689, been
summoned by William III to the Lords as Baron Sidney of Penshurst, so
that Dryden's experience of the Sidneys is a strange amalgam of affection
and distance.[44]

That Dryden is thinking in these curiously dialectical ways is confirmed
by some of the chief analogies with which he lards the dedication. The
explicitly political one creates a double parallel: the relationship between
Cicero and Atticus is rehearsed in the relationship between Dryden and
Leicester; and since Dryden mentions "changes of Government" (59), which
seem to affect Leicester very little, Dryden also aligns himself with an
endangered Cicero whose assassination was one precondition of Augustus'
preeminence. Though this parallel is unstated, I think it sufficiently implied
in Dryden's lifelong use of the Augustan myth of power, not least of course
in his greatest heroic play, *All for Love*. Thus as Augustus rises, Cicero falls.
Dryden wonders too about the need even to point the parallel, since history
itself may already have, in the figure of Atticus, prefigured Leicester's virtue.
Just as conscience shadows public history, so the past shadows the present.
The poet wonders "Whether I need to name a second *Atticus*; or whether
the World has not already prevented me, and fix'd it there without my
naming?" (61). And just as conscience stands as a fixed principle before the
fluctuations of fortune – "the variety of Revolutions" – so Leicester will
serve as the chief planet in a Copernican moral cosmos "who centring on
himself, remains immovable and smiles at the madness of the dance about
him" (60). Finally, Leicester will act as a stable principle of value in a more
literal sense: where the moral coin of the realm experiences fluctuations of
value, "The leading men still bring their bullion to your mint, to receive the

stamp of their intrinsick value, that they may afterwards hope to pass with human kind" (59–60). Thus Dryden can later, in the preface, imply that persecution forces a man "*to set a value on himself*" (72), for a knowledge of ourselves depends paradoxically on the instabilities of fortune.

The preface to the reader expands the dialectical principle into the play, the play conceived of here, like kingship itself, as a cultural artifact. Thus Dryden meditates richly on the distinctions between the text as originally written, as acted, and as printed, which returns it to a state close to the original conception. (Dryden also discusses two other doublings in the play: the "*double poyson*" issued to Dorax [70] and, more elliptically, "*another Moral*" in addition to "*the general Moral*" [71].) Dryden writes that "*there is a vast difference betwixt a publick entertainment on the Theatre, and a private reading in the Closet*" (66). Of course we are speaking of a single play, whose nature is also provocatively a series of doublings. The play is most embodied at the moment of inception, revealing in its "lustre" the "masculine vigour in which it was first written" (66). But the limits of the theater reveal that "*the body was swoln into too large a bulk for the representation of the Stage*" (66), requiring the playwright to trim the "*Descriptions, Images, Similitudes, and Moral Sentences*" (66), which only the reader, permitted time to pause and reflect, can enjoy. The experience of the stage rushes us along in the "*tumult and hurry*" of the action (66); reading alone supplies leisure for criticism and reflection.

Simply by describing the phenomenology of theater, Dryden has quite brilliantly supplied a key to what follows in the text proper. The play, he insists, is one object; yet it is strangely amphibious, because the more we contemplate the values associated with a series of heuristic dyads (writing and orality; stage and page; masculine and feminine), the more they become in practice mutually inextricable. The original script, Dryden says, is embodied, rugged, graphic, masculine; the acted script is implicitly more abstracted, streamlined, oral, perhaps feminized. Yet at the same time (Dryden knows) we often think of stage action as more embodied, and thus masculine; while the luxury of privacy and critical reflection can seem altogether more refined, more feminine.

Thus the mere fact of drama itself raises a problem which informs the low plot of *Don Sebastian*, which meditates on the relations between body and soul; as well as the relationship between its low and high plots. The high plot concerns the business of state; the low plot, the erotic competition between Morayma (daughter) and Johayma (mother, and wife to the Mufti) for Antonio's favors. This might suggest that the abstractions of public political debate (a masculine world) and the rough and tumble of private sexual farce (a more feminine world) remain – as they do in *Marriage a la Mode* – largely segregated. But they do not. Like Davenant, Dryden is energetically working out the post-Cartesian mind–body problem through an entirely political matrix.[45] As we will see, for him, politics and erotics are different ways of attacking a single problem in culture. It is possible that the erotic chase might remain merely carnal, since Muslim theology has failed (we learn) to supply women with souls ("Our Law says plainly women have no Souls" [I,i,263]). Yet the eventual union of Antonio the Christian with Morayma the Muslim establishes, symbolically, the union of body and soul, and the confirmation that "we women are allow'd the priviledge of having Souls" (V,i,109).

For exactly equivalent reasons, in Act IV, the low plot spills into the high plot. The Mufti's garden directly borders the castle grounds, so that Benducar, planning (with the Mufti) to use mob violence against the emperor Muley-Moluch, and replace him with his brother Muley-Zeydan, commands his servant to "set wide the *Mufti*'s Garden Gate, / Which is his private passage to the Palace" (IV,i,194–5). The erotic and irrational violently destabilize politics; and the resulting mix of "high" and "low," of "public" and "private," supplies the conditions for the assassination of Muley-Moluch, and the legitimation of Don Sebastian as rightful heir.

Yet it is a conjunction that Dryden can only have viewed ambivalently. He makes clear – strictly observing this feature of royalist principle – that though Muley-Moluch has gained his title by usurpation, the populace is still subject to his authority. Dorax emphasizes his gratitude to the emperor to underscore this obligation (II,i,288–98). Thus the monarch's demise serves two incommensurable purposes at once. It symbolically reenacts the fate of Oliver Cromwell (both the fictional and actual usurpers' heads being impaled for public display). And it also serves to attack the populist rejection of James as lawfully constituted monarch.

Because it expresses a love-hate relationship to the monarch or primal father, this ambivalence is most powerfully extended to the eponymous hero. This is hardly surprising. Don Sebastian himself recognizes that Muley-Moluch and he express two dimensions of the same symbolic order: "Sure our two Souls have somewhere been acquainted / In former beings; or, struck out together, / One spark to *Affrick* flew, and one to *Portugal*" (II,i,370–2). The attitude is mutual. Muley-Moluch, using language that could apply only to Charles I, sees Don Sebastian as an example of "Suff'ring Majesty" (I,i,343). For like the martyred King, and like James his son, Don Sebastian is a symptom of the recrudescence of a royalist romance that had been gathering force throughout the seventeenth century, and which I believe Dryden both harnesses and exorcizes in his play. That fantasies of kingship are immersed in popular mythology is also one of Dryden's central points in his preface. The very existence of Don Sebastian in the plot is a fabulous denial of death, for history has it that

the body of Don Sebastian *was never found in the Field of Battel; which gave occasion for many to believe, that he was not slain: that some years after, when the* Spaniards *with a pretended title, by force of Arms had Usurp'd the Crown of* Portugal, *from the House of* Braganza, *a certain Person who call'd himself* Don Sebastian, *and had all the marks of his body and features of his face, appear'd at* Venice, *where he was own'd by some of his Country-men; but being seiz'd by the* Spaniards *was first Imprison'd, then sent to the Gallies, and at last put to Death in private.* (67)

If, in imitation of popular myth, Dryden returns Don Sebastian into imaginative history for four acts of his play, he finally evacuates him definitively by enmeshing him in an Oedipal plot. This is no mere convenience of closure, since Dryden exploits the tremendous force of the taboos expressed in the Oedipus myth for his entire political argument. As Freud puts it, "the beginnings of religion, morals, society and art converge in the Oedipus complex."[46] Dryden (with Lee) had published his own version of *Oedipus* in 1679, on the brink of the Exclusion Crisis, and *Don Sebastian* is liberally sprinkled with references to that archetypal plot.[47] The immediate cause of Don Sebastian's self-banishment in Act V is that he discovers that he has married his sister Almeyda. The breaking of the taboo is owing in part to their father whose licentiousness – in imitation of Charles II and James II – means that accidents can happen. But Don Sebastian's disregard of the incest taboo (like Stuart self-regard) is systemic: he represents a resistance to the principle of disequilibrium recommended at every other level of the plot and governing all exogamous sexual practices.

Dorax – played by Betterton – serves as a pointed contrast to Don Sebastian. That he is alienated from the seductions of monarchy is expressed in his comment that "my Soul's a Regicide" (IV,ii,611). Most spectacularly, as we have seen, Dorax survives two simultaneous attempts to poison him in Act III. Benducar and then the Mufti doctor his drink; but he survives because the two poisons cancel each other out, producing what Dorax calls the "double poysons cure" (IV,iii,330). This complex doubling characterizes Dorax's entire story, for he was formerly Alonzo, Don Sebastian's friend from an earlier life. But Alonzo converted to Islam, repelled by Don Sebastian's homosexual favoritism towards Enriquez, "thy Man Mistress" (IV,ii,459). In his homosexual liaisons as well as in incest, Don Sebastian evidently represents that cultural impossibility, a principle of total equivalence resisted both by the play as such and by Dorax, who insists that he is not what he once was: "*Dorax* cannot answer to *Alonzo*" (IV,iii,616). Don Sebastian's sexual history represents a primitive or a-social condition contradicting the differential psychodynamics of history as such, so that he must banish himself from history by becoming an anchorite. And since history is a sum of disequilibria of the many kinds we have considered, Almeyda and Don Sebastian are convicted of their incest because the two rings they wear make a perfect fit: "a Curious Artist wrought 'em, / With joynts so close, as not to be perceiv'd; / Yet are they both each others Counterpart" (V,i,413–15).

In evacuating Don Sebastian from history Dryden reveals the depth of his anthropological understanding of monarchy, an understanding not coincidentally explored by Freud in *Totem and Taboo*, for which one of the prime historical cases is the fate of the Stuart kings. Dryden's play does not end in Act IV with the elimination of external threats to Don Sebastian. Rather, Act V reveals that the greatest threat to the King is the King himself. The confluence of circumstances surrounding James's demise almost uncannily reproduces Freud's description of the tribe's ambivalence to the primal father. First, the burst of intensely royalist propaganda that accompanied James's accession both insists on Divine Right in all its nakedness and commits the same fallacy – if it can be described as such – as that in *Totem and Taboo*. Just as Freud's analysis of the individual family romance becomes an analysis of tribal neuroses about the King, so discussions of royal prerogative – even at the very end of the seventeenth century – consistently depend on the analogy with powerful fathers of families. Preaching immediately after the death of Charles II, Augustine Frezer proclaimed that "Kings . . . are our civil Parents," but this was a fatherhood whose powers were often represented as unlimited and even magical.[48] Thus royal prerogative was only partly grounded in legal or constitutional arguments. It was just as often asserted that it came directly from God. Descanting on the doctrine of passive obedience, James Ellesby writes,

No Force or Violence, no Opposition or Resistance can lawfully be made against a Sovereign Prince, who receives his Power immediately from God, and therefore to him alone can be accountable for it.[49]

Even more suggestively, the pamphlet *Edovardus Confessor Redivivus. The Piety and Vertues of Holy Edward the Confessor, Reviv'd in the Sacred Majesty of King James the II* resurrects an ancient, almost mythical King. This occurs exactly by the contagious process described by Freud. And so Don Sebastian speaks of himself as a kind of contagion: "If burnt and scatter'd in the air,

the Winds / That strow my dust diffuse my royalty, / And spread me
o'er your Clime: for where one Atome / Of mine shall light; know there
Sebastian Reigns" (I,i,364–7). Thus James inherits Edward's magical and
thaumaturgic powers by contact rather than legal descent. James could
heal scrofula because he wore at his coronation a crucifix unearthed from
Edward's tomb, disturbed in the preparations for the service, which also
transfused James IV's powers into his descendant: "the Virtual and Warlike
Genius of the Famous *JAMES*, is, by Generative Descent, (I will not say,
Pythagorean Transmigration) streamed down into himself."[50]

Second, the plot of *Don Sebastian* seems to show that by the end of
1689 Dryden saw the Stuarts as trapped in a repetitively morbid history.
Don Sebastian only enters the play in defiance of popular beliefs that he is
dead, and the discovery of his homosexual past and his incestuous marriage
render his institutional viability chimerical. For the play, for Oedipus, for
the Revolution, the past weighs fatally on the present. It is almost as if the
royalist pamphlets' insistence on the parallel between Charles I and James
II unconsciously wished on the son the father's fate: the original sacrifice of
the father that Freud describes, expressing intense fear of and devotion to
his powers, must be "represented twice over – as the god and as the totemic
animal victim."[51] The insidious force of Pythagorean transmigration represents a kingly power towards which Dryden always expressed ambivalence,
so that he expects us to reserve judgment on the emperor's declaration that
"Kings, like Gods, / Are every where; walk in th'abyss of minds, / And view
the dark recesses of the Soul" (III,i,158–60). Dryden must have been aware
of the profound historical irony in the widespread republication of early
Stuart pamphlets to address the new crisis. Anthony Ascham (who died in
1650) seems exactly to have anticipated the fate of James II in that of Charles
I, because he epitomizes (in *A Seasonable Discourse, wherein is Examined
what is Lawful during the Confusions and Revolutions of Government; Especially in the Case of a King Deserting his Kingdoms* [1649; reprinted in 1689]),
the *dénouement* of Dryden's play: "the Action was more than Kingly; For
to lay down a Crown is more majestical than to wear it."[52]

That James had in effect rehearsed his father's demise is one of the arguments made increasingly after 1688. *Some Considerations Touching Succession
and Allegiance* (1689) says that in deserting the kingdom, James had suffered a "*Demise du Roy*," which, "does not in itself signify death," but rather
"a Separation of the Regal Authority from the Person of the King."[53] But
numerous other tracts invite the analogy between abandoning the kingdom
and a symbolic death. The *Agreement Betwixt the Present and the Former
Government* (1689) states that "though the King in his personal or natural

Capacity cannot . . . forfeit his Life, yet he may *die* or *kill* himself";[54] Richard Booker writes that "the King may divest himself of all Authority and Power, and when this is done the obligation ceaseth, as if he were really Dead";[55] and Ascham had already styled the subordination of a King to a new power "a Civil Death."[56]

The view that James had in a sense died does not seem restricted to those who urged the oath of allegiance on William and Mary. For, quite apart from its Oedipal core, the plot of *Don Sebastian* shows Don Sebastian literally dicing with death. The Christians, taken prisoner just before the opening of the play, are forced in Act I to draw lots (black or white balls) which will determine whether they are to die. Sebastian is the only prisoner to draw a black ball (pronouncing his doom), which he does twice. This emboldens him to declare himself King of Portugal, but the greatness of his mind prompts Muley-Moluch not only to see in him the emblem of suffering majesty, but to reprieve him.

That his reprieve has little concrete effect on the outcome captures, I think, the logic of Dryden's peculiar loyalism after 1688. Both *Don Sebastian* and *Amphitryon* seem finally to be propounding a double thesis about monarchy at the end of the seventeenth century which has little to do with Jacobite nostalgia. First, actual kings – even those to whom we feel allegiance – are highly problematic, not to say self-defeating, entities. As Freud puts it, "The ruler cannot be trusted to make use of his immense powers in the right way, that is, for the benefit of his subjects and for his own protection."[57] And second (a logical entailment), in some ways the "best" king is not so much no king at all, but an absent king or a king virtually dead. With his powers at a distance, we can more safely and selectively call on them to legitimate the patriarchy: in this scheme the absent king acts as the transcendental signifier for the system, securing but not disrupting it, and securing it merely opportunistically. This is, I believe, centrally the force of Walter Benjamin's observation that "In the *Trauerspiel* of the seventeenth century, the corpse becomes quite simply the pre-eminent emblematic property."[58] And Freud writes in recognition of the powers of the dead, and almost as if he had James II in mind, "The living did not feel safe from the attacks of the dead till there was a sheet of water between them."[59] If (as even royalists might argue) William was to have legitimacy, it was, like James II's very different prerogative, uncomfortably predicated on the ritual sacrifice of a Stuart King.

CHAPTER 11

Epilogue: Congreve as Whig: the politics of equivalence in The Way of the World

Famously, the aging Dryden handed the laurels to Congreve, his successor, in his dedicatory poem to *The Double Dealer*, printed in 1694, the year in which the Bank of England was founded largely to finance William III's wars on the continent. There is no reason to question the depth of Dryden's appreciation for the much younger poet, whose *The Way of the World*, performed six years later, is, along with Etherege's *The Man of Mode*, the most beautifully finished Restoration comedy. But there are reasons to pay close attention to the highly ambiguous terms through which Dryden's passing the torch is expressed, for, as an inventor of English literary history, Dryden makes Congreve's claims emerge as a condition of the history of seventeenth-century drama, a drama which in Dryden's mind is always and at the same time literary and political. It is important to notice the sense in which Dryden sees both himself and Congreve as belated figures maturing – though at different times – after "the giant race before the Flood" has been swept away. For Dryden, all culture after the early Stuart period has something of the postlapsarian and radically historical and temporal character imagined in *Paradise Lost*, though Dryden is here trying to distinguish the literary economy of his generation from that represented by a much younger generation of playwrights like Congreve and Vanbrugh. Shakespeare as always represents such a capacious and primal store of literary wealth that he leaves no stable inheritance, which leaves the field open to Fletcher and Jonson, each in his way bequeathing strengths and weaknesses to their immediate successors, chief among them Davenant and Dryden, Jonson's two heirs as Poets Laureate. These are memories secured by Congreve in Dryden's dedication to *The Double Dealer* and by a series of allusions, in *The Way of the World*, to Davenant's *The Siege of Rhodes*. There are two things to notice about Dryden's stance: his entirely constitutional or principled ambivalence – or the sense that the dramatic culture he represents and over which he presided is perhaps more restrained, less fecund than early Stuart drama, and at the same time less finished than Congreve's art – so that it supplies a strange and prodigious interval in the history of seventeenth-century poesy; and by the same token, his remarkable capacity to objectify his own place in time, a time which, because he sees it as past, he can ironize by a kind of ethnographic imagination which he subtly turns both against himself and his master, Charles II. (This is a marked feature of Dryden's imaginative and critical genius throughout his career, but this habit was to intensify after the disasters of 1688):

> Like *Janus* he the stubborn Soil manur'd,
> With Rules of Husbandry the rankness cur'd:
> Tam'd us to manners, when the Stage was rude;
> And boistrous *English* wit, with Art indu'd.
> Our Age was cultivated thus at length;
> But what we gain'd in skill we lost in strength.[1]

After Charles's exploits with women and the Exclusion Crisis partly engendered by his bastard son, Monmouth, any reference to Charles's sowing and tilling, his husbandry, is intrinsically unstable, producing once again a dialectical effect within the structure of analogy which Dryden had been cultivating as early as *Astrea Redux* in 1660: whether we think of Charles as the May King in that poem, or Charles as David in *Absalom and Achitophel*, the analogy always harnesses as much critical as celebratory force, so that the poet, throughout his career, seeks to summon the Stuarts away from the status quo. Just as Dryden's royalism always preserves within it the memory or trace of the ideal monarch to which their poet invariably holds Charles and James accountable, so Dryden's first royal master appears as the archetypal split figure of Janus, whose double head was, according to the Oxford Classical Dictionary, often crudely attached to a body: Dryden's image brilliantly distills the problem that occupied the dramatic tradition to which he belonged and over which he can be said to have presided. That is, what Dryden represents as a loss of strength after the early Stuart period purchases in its stead greater analytic precision or "skill," because tragicomedy in particular permitted the poet to ironize and debate the conditions of power. Thus, influenced by the tragicomic tradition epitomized in Beaumont and Fletcher, the theatrical culture to which Congreve is so obviously a latecomer, and represented in Dryden's poem by Etherege's "courtship," Southerne's "purity," and Wycherley's manliness, had, especially in the 1670s, consistently made drama the condition for sustained and methodical deliberation on the problems of state which focused on the internal contradictions of power and the proper relation of its head to the body politic.

In the 1690s, Dryden makes clear, we are in a different intellectual and dramatic climate from that which went before. In fact, John Dennis, looking back on the entire Restoration period from the first quarter of the eighteenth century, conveys a story of rapid decline. He writes,

In the Reign of King Charles the second there flourishd a number of Contemporary poets, who were most of them excellent in their Different Manners, as Milton, Denham, Waller, Cowley, Butler, Dryden, Rochester, Dorsett, Otway, Wycherley, Etherege, Shadwell &c. In the Reign of King William things began apace to Degenerate, and yet even then we had Two Comick poets, of whom one is still living, of each of whom we may boldly pronounce, that He is magnorum Haud quaquam Indignus Avorum.[2]

It is true that now much of the contingent, open, and experimental quality of the relations among political theory, commerce, and physiology has evaporated, so that although histories of economic theory treat Nicholas Barbon and Charles Davenant as progressive thinkers favoring free trade, *A Discourse of Trade* (1690) and *An Essay upon the Probable Methods of Making a People Gainers in the Balance of Trade* (1700) exude a much greater confidence in the kind of disciplinary enterprise on which they are engaged as well as their relations to related disciplines.[3] This produces a paradox of sorts, since the explicit confidence in free trade rests on an implicit epistemic and ideological conviction that few trade theorists after Malynes had enjoyed, so that the official liberalism of free trade theory does not rest on the experimental methods we could associate with Dryden, Mun, and Misselden. Both Barbon and Davenant write in the confidence that commerce and political theory can harmonize – that there is such a genre as political economy – and that Harvey's discovery of the circulation of the blood endows the entire enterprise with a conceptual and systematic coherence, often expressed in the language of "proportion." Thus Barbon, glancing back to Mun:

TRADE is now become as necessary to Preserve Governments, as it is useful to make them Rich. . .

The Reasons why many Men have not a true *IDEA* of *TRADE*, is, Because they Apply their Thoughts to particular Parts of *TRADE*, wherein they are chiefly concerned in Interest; and having found out the best Rules and Laws for forming that particular Part, they govern their Thoughts by the same *NOTIONS* in forming the Great *BODY* of *TRADE*, and not reflecting on the different Rules of Proportions betwixt the Body and Parts, have a very disagreeable Conception.[4]

Similarly, though more comprehensively, Charles Davenant writes:

> It shall not be here argued, whether the skill of physic be now brought to perfection, or whether it is yet capable of further improvements; but this may be safely pronounced, that the knowledge of the sinews, muscles, arteries and veins, with the late discovery of the circulation of the blood and all the parts of anatomy, conduce very much to render this dark science more plain and certain.
>
> In the same manner, such as would understand the body politic, its true constitution, its state of health, its growth or decay, its strength or weakness, and how to apply remedies to the various distempers to which it is incident, must study and look narrowly into all the distinct parts of the commonwealth, its Trade, the current money, (which is its flowing blood) the arts, labour, and manufactures, and the number of its people; with many other things which altogether are the members of which the great body is composed.[5]

By analogy, writing as a literary anthropologist, Dryden in the 1690s also seems aware of a shift of the cultural climate away from the rich dialectical tensions of an age riven by dynastic uncertainty to a more self-confident, not to say smug, age in which manners – and the sequestered world of the private – increasingly substitute for constitutional – and more insistently noisy and public – debates about the fate of the nation. Indeed, he seems to be addressing it directly, and addressing it in ways that, as we have seen in *Of Dramatic Poesy*, treats the formal and epistemological conundra of drama as expressions of its political commitments. Dryden's extraordinary maturity as a cultural commentator is epitomized, I believe, in the degree to which his political alienation after the Glorious Revolution finds expression in the most rigorous commitment to the split dramatic plot we find in the Drydenian canon, as if, in hewing to the critical power he associates with tragicomedy, he can express his distaste for the new political order. As we have seen, it is precisely by such a formal device that in two of his greatest plays, namely the heroic tragicomedy *Don Sebastian* and the comedy bordering on farce, *Amphytrion*, Dryden subjects the entire tragic history of Stuart rule to his own form of ironic analysis.

Thus it is that Dryden's panegyric to Congreve is shot through with an apprehension of the ideological and formal differences between the contingent, unfinished, and open quality of the products of his specific literary generation, and the greater aesthetic and political securities available to the beneficiaries of the Glorious Revolution, which had occurred when Congreve was eighteen and Addison only sixteen. Congreve's achievement in *The Double Dealer* obviously appears to Dryden as an architectural device, but one less open-ended than before, though still gently aware of the distinctions among the orders. Like the marmorial designs in Isaac Ware's edition of *The Four Books of Architecture*, Congreve's slightly obsessive relation to the unities in this play representing a kind of permanence and stability Dryden implicitly contrasts especially to the Fletcherian canon that had dominated the first decade of the Restoration theatre, not least because Congreve harmonizes implicitly competitive modes, uniting the strengths of Fletcher and Jonson, just as now, rather than creating variety and dialectic, Doric and Corinthian combine in a single statement. The suggestion is that what was a political rhetoric has now become a social style. Hence:

> Our Builders were, with want of Genius, curs'd;
> The second Temple was not like the first:
> Till You, the best *Vitruvius*, come at length;
> Our Beauties equal; but excel our strength.
> Firm *Dorique* Pillars found Your solid Base:
> The Fair *Corinthian* crowns the higher space;
> Thus all below is strength, and all above is grace.
>
> (ll. 13–19)

Perhaps it is Congreve's very youthfulness that allows him, in his Dedication to Montague, to echo Dryden's compliment to him and apply it to his play. He admits that *The Double Dealer* may have its faults, but

Yet I must take the boldness to say, I have not miscarried the whole; for the mechanical part of it is perfect. That I may say with as little vanity, as a Builder may say he has built a House according to the Model laid down before him; or a Gardiner that he has set his Flowers in a knot of such or such a Figure. I design'd the Moral first, and to that Moral I invented the Fable, and do not know that I have borrow'd one hint of it any where. I made the Plot as strong as I could, because it was single, and I made it single, because I would avoid confusion and was resolved to preserve the three Unities of the Drama, which I have visibly done to the utmost severity.[6]

Quite apart from the splendid creation of Millamant, one of the many things that makes *The Way of the World* so impressive is precisely its adherence to the unities, an encouragement Congreve almost certainly received from the influential translation of the Abbé d'Aubignac's *La Prâtique du Théatre* which had appeared in 1684 as *The Whole Art of the Stage*.[7] In confining his masterpiece to London and making "The Time equal to that of the Presentation," Congreve was following d'Aubignac's view that "'Tis certain, that the Stage is but a Picture or Image of Humane Life; and as a Picture cannot show us at the same time two Originals, and be an accomplished Picture: It is likewise impossible that two Actions, I mean principal ones, should be represented reasonably by one Play" (81). Indeed the play is – outside of Racine and of Dryden's *All for Love* – a textbook exposition of *liaison de scènes*: thus at the end of Act IV, Marwood tries, seemingly in vain, to blow Waitwell's cover as "Sir Rowland" courting the superannuated Lady Wishfort; while Act V begins with the plot unmasked, and the outraged dowager about to execute revenge on Foible, Waitwell's wife and accomplice in the scheme.

At the same time, Congreve already seems aware in the Dedication to *The Double Dealer* that neoclassical precept might prevail at the cost of some constriction or what he calls "severity." One expression of this narrowness of effect in *The Way of the World* occurs as what I will call, by reference to the language of political economy that seems to link Congreve's play with the trade theorists we have examined, a general stabilization of value. In the critical reception of Congreve's play, this problem of value manifests itself most consistently in the lurking suspicion that the plot, and Mirabell's schemes within it, are causally slightly illusory. This is because one of the premises of Mirabell's already having reformed as a rake is that Mrs. Fainall, with whom he has earlier had a liaison, is protected from the worst consequences of her marriage of convenience to Fainall by the contents of the black box, which lurks, as it were, behind the scenes, is first mentioned by Waitwell in Act IV, and proves to be the prime legal and fiscal *deus ex machina* for the comic outcome in Act V: Mrs. Fainall is secured as an independent lady by having signed her wealth over to Mirabell before her marriage to Fainall, and well before the play began; and because Lady Wishfort is now grateful to Mirabell, she will allow him to marry Millamant with all of her huge fortune of £12,000. It is understandable that a certain tradition of criticism feels slightly cheated by the sudden introduction and surprising effects of this device, as if all of Mirabell's other schemes, all of Fainall's and Marwood's plots, all of Sir Wilfull Witwoud's bumblings, and all of Lady Wishfort's anger and disappointment prove only elliptical or equivocal agents of an outcome more solidly secured by means outside or beyond the plot proper.

It might be useful to compare the singularity or equilibrium of the play's design especially with *The Man of Mode*, since Dorimant and Mirabell are so obviously cousins, as are, in their way, Harriet and Millamant. Both Dorimant and Mirabell represent a threat to Harriet and Millamant, because for both women, as for every Austen heroine, the unavoidable teleology of marriage also involves an inevitable loss of power over oneself, one's body, and one's fortune. As in *Pride and Prejudice*, the function of the plot is to allow the heroine to adjudicate the degree of danger involved in selecting this potential husband over any other suitor (the Collinses and the

Wickhams of this world, for example), and in that sense the project is essentially epistemological. But Etherege's play is more rigorously skeptical and experimental than either Congreve's play or Austen's novel, though one might remark that the older Austen became, the closer she came to the Etheregean ethos. Apart from the endangered heroine contemplating the rake from an ironic distance, superficially Congreve's play shares many features with Etherege's: the opposition between the wits and witwouds, between the town and the country, between the older and younger generations, the lure of the pastoral as a figure of escape from the moral compromises of the urbane world, and the blocking figure of the enraged ex-lover – Mrs. Barry, the tragic actress, played both Etherege's Loveit and Congreve's Marwood, as if to make the point.

But the tonal and moral differences are marked and significant: the first act of *The Man of Mode* reveals Dorimant as alpha male abusing the servants not only as suppliers of commodities, but also as commodities or animals themselves; and though Harriet does not arrive until Act II, we know by the end of Act I that Dorimant has already trashed two women – the illiterate Molly, and Loveit, whom he will later sadistically humiliate – and is on the verge of trashing Bellinda, who quickly learns from witnessing Dorimant's display of power over Loveit, but not before she has served as a convenient stop-gap for Dorimant's sexual *ennui*. The country is only the object of horror and detestation, and the competition between the older and younger folk has an explicitly constitutional resonance, because it pits the pre- against the post-Civil War generations. At one level, the dialectical tensions among its various terms is the subject of the play, since it ends with the famously suspended conclusion: Harriet presents Dorimant with the bleak prospect of a huge drafty country house, the ladies perched on chairs in the hall, and the dismal cawing of the crows outside.

We could see *The Man of Mode* as a Hobbesian device, a self-affirming artifact, whose refusal of resolutions throws us back on the artifice of the play itself, while taxonomizing the contesting elements of power that underwrite its world. But everything that remains suspended and competitive in Etherege's world is reconciled and naturalized, rendered into a series of equivalences, by Congreve's plot: the country – in the benign if occasionally drunken shape of Sir Wilfull Witwoud – serves as the stabilizer of value and as the probable object of refinement; the servants, as we have seen, are essential to Mirabell's schemes as well as the means for blowing Marwood and Fainall's cover; the older generation has lost its constitutional aura, so that although Lady Wishfort acts as an archetypal blocking figure, she represents centrally Millamant's private fate as a woman, that she will grow old and lose her purchase on the sexual marketplace; and whereas the tendency of the older plays is to migrate out from the rake's closet into public spaces like the Mall or St. James's Park, the New Exchange, the theater, or to taverns like Long's or Locket's, the movement of this play is from the Chocolate House (Act I) to the Park (Act II) and finally in the last three acts to the private space of Lady Wishfort's house. And whereas the resolutions, such as they are, in *Marriage a la Mode*, or *The Man of Mode*, or *The Country Wife*, or *The Rover* occur only as a form of *détente* entirely conditioned by the phenomenal conditions of what is public and negotiable, so that the stage space also becomes a figure of the classical forum as well as the experimental laboratory, the resolutions of *The Way of the World* depend on unsupervised forms of trust. In fact, ideologically, trust of this sort plays exactly the obfuscatory role as "abstraction" in Adorno and Horkheimer's *Dialectic of Enlightenment*, where they write, "Bourgeois society is ruled by equivalence. It makes the dissimilar comparable by reducing it to abstract qualities."[8] The kind of trust Congreve imagines is never subjected to the forensic skepticism of the drama of the 1670s and secures seemingly untroubled relations – or, as Adorno and Horkheimer put it, "equivalence" – among different generations, among masters and servants, and between men and women. Mrs. Fainall trusts that Mirabell will not abscond with her money; Mirabell trusts that Waitwell and Foible will execute his schemes; and most importantly, the principals trust each other in the famous proviso scene, which – unlike equivalent scenes in earlier plays – remains unsupervised by a third party. And whereas in *The Country Wife* there is some palpable distribution of power and desire between Horner and Lady Fidget, the proviso scene segregates the prerogative of man and wife into, respectively, the public and private realms: in this arrangement Millamant may be an empress, but only empress of the tea-table, so obeying the strictures on female conduct that Addison rendered programmatic in *The Spectator*.

It is of course not original to argue that Congreve represents the political and cultural climate after 1688, but that is normally associated with Congreve's softening of effect in response to Jeremy Collier's *Short View of the Immorality and Profaneness of the English Stage*, which Congreve slyly insinuates into Lady Wishfort's closet, and with the wider project to reform manners that seems to have followed the Revolution. I have argued elsewhere that the black box and the terms of the proviso scene represent one of the legal fictions that – at least recursively – were employed to legitimate William and Mary's claim to the throne, namely the Lockean notion of compact, an agreement that has something like a pre-contractual or informal power to bind.[9] But I will here return to the language of value and the methodological as well as substantive challenge it poses, because, to rephrase my position, it is also my belief that Restoration drama as a whole provided the discursive conditions not only for political or constitutional debate, but for the emergence of political economy as an authoritative means for analyzing society. This should not surprise us, not only because Dryden makes the case in *Of Dramatic Poesy*, but because Stuart constitutional crises had almost invariably to do with the king's and the nation's finances. Time and again, Restoration plays invoke the economic model as a means to discuss the larger cultural and political concerns which are almost always their central focus, whether we think of Dryden's Dedication to Danby in *All for Love*, in which Dryden praises Danby for placing the nation's finances on a better footing, so compensating for the damage resulting from Charles's Stop on the Exchequer in 1672, which was one cause for the disasters of the third Dutch War; or whether we think of the opposition between the competing English mercantile and the Spanish bullionist accounts of value in Behn's *The Rover*. Congreve implicitly invokes this alliance of politics and economics in his dedications to *The Double Dealer* and *The Way of the World*, the first to Charles Montagu and the second to Ralph Montagu (apparently no close relation). Both Montagus were at critical junctures ardent Williamites, and they each in a different way represent for Congreve a stabilizing effect, so whereas Ralph is praised for his country retirement, Charles's significance is centrally that he engineered the first million-dollar loan to William's government in March 1692 and sponsored the bill establishing the Bank of England. After he had served as Congreve's dedicatee, however, he became involved in the recoinage scheme which also occupied the energies of Somers, Locke, Newton, and Halley.

Given the enormous national energies devoted to the recoinage scheme in the 1690s, when *The Way of the World* must have been in gestation, I will close by reference to Locke's contribution to the recoinage debate, namely *Some Considerations of the Consequences of the Lowering of Interest and Raising the Value of Money* (1696). Locke is certainly aware of the range of options open to him from the first important debate stimulated by the coinage crisis of 1620, and refers to Mun's *A Discourse of Trade*. What was at stake by the end of the seventeenth century were a number of issues of both practical and conceptual significance, and trade theorists were sophisticated enough to know it. The central fact was that clipping of coins – minted of gold and silver – had resulted in a massive discrepancy between the bullion weight of coins in circulation and their nominal face value. Having invented the technology to make milled coins, which were both regular relative to each other and unclippable, the government realized that it had to call in the old coins and remint them. This determination immediately crystallized a series of debates not only about the practicalities but about the implications for the economy at large. First, the century had increasingly developed a conceptual distinction between coins as bullion and coins as nominal counters of trade, between what contemporaries called the "intrinsick" and "extrinsick" value of money.[10] Second, there was anxiety that international fluctuations in the value of gold and silver meant that coins would be exported out of the country when their bullion value exceeded their nominal value. Third, most theorists had difficulty accounting for the fact that the values of gold and silver were bound to fluctuate relative to each other. Fourth, the loss of coin in circulation by the end of the century raised concerns about the money supply, and forced theorists to ask how money supply might be related to rates of interest, and how rates of interest might reflect or stimulate national wealth. And finally, many theorists recognized that the fascination with specie may have been outdated by the creation of credit in the form of the Bank of England, which resulted in the national debt. In his *Review of the Universal Remedy for all Diseases Incident to Coin* (1696), William Freke sums up the general problem:

[Clipping] made an Inequality in the Intrinsick Value of different pieces of our Coin, which passed still under the same Denomination: An Absurdity easily remarkable; A Force upon Nature which could not hold. And what were the Consequences of it? Nature wrought still in her own Methods. At Home, whilst no Remedy was applied, the Corruption spread, the Disease increased. . . And as the Body of the Nation labour'd more and more under this Uneasiness, it began to seek for Ease (If I may use the Metaphor) by shifting of Postures. Is there no Remedy (said the Tradesman) to be had from any publick Physician?[11]

The response of the most sophisticated polemics in the recoinage crisis was to argue that money only had a symbolic role in determining the value of goods and that it was also a commodity in its own right, so that the purpose of international trade was never to acquire large quantities of bullion. The value of gold and silver was arbitrary and had to do with their scarcity relative to other commodities. Thus Rice Vaughan writes, "The first Invention of *Money* was for a Pledg and instead of a Surety, for when men did live by Exchange of their *Wants* and *Superfluities*, both parties could not always fit one another at the present";[12] or alternatively, Sir Humphrey Mackworth: "Money is but a *medium* of Commerce, a Security which we part with, to enjoy the like in Value, and is the Standard of all Commodities, and esteemed so by the world."[13]

Competition for mutual esteem seems much closer to the ethos of *The Country Wife* than *The Way of the World*, which seems altogether closer to the principles governing Locke's (and Freke's) responses to the recoinage, responses which, as a matter of historical fact, prevailed. Like John Evelyn and, later, Addison, Dryden seems to have cultivated some interest in numismatics, and in widely separated poems, namely *Absalom and Achitophel* and *Alexander's Feast* – his most virulently anti-Williamite piece, published only a year after Locke's *Considerations* – he treats the impulse to yoke the extrinsic and intrinsic value of coins as an expression of self-indulgence and of Satanic force. But both Locke and Freke are too driven by a fear of the corruption of the coinage to demand anything else, such that Joyce Appleby is right to argue that, by an historical irony, Locke's success at the mint meant the temporary triumph of an archaic form of bullionism.[14] Defending "its intrinsick Value," Locke argues that it is not "the denomination but the *quantity* of Silver, that gives the value to any coin."[15] It is Freke who reveals quite clearly how these economic issues migrate into the kinds of moral concern that are central to *The Way of the World*, since Congreve, like Freke, is responding to the wider demand to reform manners. Freke writes that "our National Disease is not simple, but complicated; That we labour under a consumptive Trade, under an expensive War, and (worse than all) under a general Corruption of Manners." Both Congreve's and Freke's answers seem – in their different ways – to cultivate a regime of equivalence in the body politic at large. Whereas in celebrating the Revolution settlement, Congreve's play adheres rigorously to the unities, for Freke, all bills of exchange must find an immediate correspondence in coins, and coins in bullion, so that "it will occasion a certain fixt Difference of Estimation to be settled, between . . . Bills and running Cash; Not fluctuating as it is now, up and down, in incomputable Uncertainties."[16]

Notes

1 "THIS WAR OF OPINIONS" IN THE "EMPIRE OF WIT":
TRAGICOMEDY, POLITICS, AND TRADE

1 John Dryden, *Of Dramatic Poesy and Other Critical Essays*, ed. George Watson, 2 vols. (London: Everyman, 1962), I: 12. All subsequent references are to this edition and will appear in my text.

2 The standard account of Restoration tragicomedy is Nancy Klein Maguire, *Regicide and Restoration: English Tragicomedy, 1660–1671* (Cambridge: Cambridge University Press, 1992), and also Maguire, "Tragicomedy," in Deborah Payne Fisk, ed. *The Cambridge Companion to English Restoration Theatre* (Cambridge: Cambridge University Press, 2000), 86–106. See also A. P. Dani, *Coherence in Hip-Hop Art: Dryden's Tragicomedies* (New Delhi: Creative Books, 2005).

3 See E. N. Hooker, H. T. Swedenberg, Jr., *et al.* eds. *The Works of John Dryden*, 20 vols. (Los Angeles: University of California Press, 1956–89), XI: 625. Henceforth cited as *California Dryden*.

4 For example, John Harold Wilson, *The Influence of Beaumont and Fletcher on Restoration Drama* (Columbus: Ohio State University Press, 1928), records that in the season of 1661–2, "there were at least nine performances of eight plays by Shakespeare, forty one of twenty one by Beaumont and Fletcher, and ten of three by Jonson" (12). That the Fletcherian mode had permeated deep into ordinary people's lives by the 1640s is suggested by the experience of the century's two greatest diarists. Pepys played a role in a domestic production of *Philaster* when still a boy, possibly in 1642; and Evelyn records on 5 February 1648 that he "Saw a tragi-comedy acted in the Cock-pit, after there had been none of these diversions for many years during the war." See Claire Tomalin, *Samuel Pepys: The Unequalled Self* (New York: Knopf, 2002), 10; and William Bray, ed. *The Diary and Correspondence of John Evelyn, F. R. S.*, 4 vols. (London: George Bell, 1898), I: 254. The fluctuating fortunes of Beaumont and Fletcher are the subject of Arthur Colby Sprague, *Beaumont and Fletcher on the Restoration Stage* (1926; rpt. New York: Blom, 1965), and Lawrence B. Wallis, *Fletcher, Beaumont and Company: Entertainers to the Jacobean Gentry* (Morningside Heights, NY: King's Crown, 1947), 243–9. Sprague details a vigorous interest in Beaumont and Fletcher after the closing of the theaters, and the plays were also performed as "drolls" (3–6).

5 Thomas Rymer, *The Tragedies of the Last Age Consider'd* (1678), in J. E. Spingarn, ed. *Critical Essays of the Seventeenth Century*, 3 vols. (1957; rpt. Bloomington: Indiana University Press, 1963), II: 190.

6 Francis Beaumont and John Fletcher, *The Maid's Tragedy*, ed. T. W. Craik (Manchester: Manchester University Press, 1988), 13. All subsequent references to the play are to this edition and will appear in my text.

7 See Alan Roper's superb commentary on *The Conquest of Granada* in *California Dryden*, XI: 411–35.

8 For a further definition of casuistry, see John M. Wallace, *Destiny His Choice: The Loyalism of Andrew Marvell* (Cambridge: Cambridge University Press, 1968), 10. See Antony Ascham, *A Discourse Wherein is Examined What is Particularly Lawfull During the Confusions and Revolutions of Government* (London, 1648), 83; 85; 6–7.

9 Gerald Eades Bentley, *The Professions of Player and Dramatist in Shakespeare's Time, 1590–1642* (Princeton: Princeton University Press, 1986), 199. See also Andrew Gurr, *The Shakespearean Stage, 1574–1642*, 2nd edn. (Cambridge: Cambridge University Press, 1980), 20.

10 Oliver Lawson Dick, ed. *Aubrey's Brief Lives* (1949; rpt. Boston: Godine, 1999), 21. See also Langbaine's account: "I am now arrived at a brace of Authors, who like the *Dioscuri, Castor* and *Pollux*, succeeded in Conjunction more happily than any Poets of their own, or this Age, to the reserve of the Venerable *Shakespear*, and the Learned and Judicious *Johnson*." See Gerard Langbaine, *An Account of the English Dramatick Poets* (1691), ed. John Loftis, 2 vols. (Los Angeles: William Andrews Clark Memorial Library, 1971), I: 203.

11 *The Subjects Libertie. Set Forth in the Royall and Politique Power of England* (London, 1643), 25.

12 Quentin Skinner, *The Foundations of Modern Political Thought*, 2 vols. (Cambridge: Cambridge University Press, 1978), II: 148–62. Hunton, for example, is fully conscious of Roman Catholic theories of resistance. See Philip Hunton, *A Treatise of Monarchy* (1643; rpt. London, 1680), 77–9.

13 See Robert Eccleshall, *Order and Reason in Politics: Theories of Absolute and Limited Monarchy in Early Modern England* (Oxford: Oxford University Press for University of Hull, 1978); Margaret Atwood Judson, *The Crisis of the Constitution: An Essay in Constitutional and Political Thought in England, 1603–1645* (1949; rpt. New York: Octagon, 1980), 4; Wallace Notestein, *The Winning of the Initiative by the House of Commons* (London: Oxford University Press for the British Academy, 1924).

14 David Wootton, ed. *Divine Right and Democracy* (Harmondsworth: Penguin, 1986), 24.

15 Sir David Lindsay Keir, *The Constitutional History of Modern Britain since 1485*, 8th edn. (New York: Norton, 1966), 154–229; F. W. Maitland, *The Constitutional History of England* (1908; rpt. Cambridge: Cambridge University Press, 1965), 238–75; Notestein, *Winning of the Initiative*, 4 and *passim*; J. R. Tanner, *English Constitutional Conflicts of the Seventeenth Century, 1603–1689* (1928; rpt. Cambridge: Cambridge University Press, 1957), 5–7.

16 Notestein, *Winning of the Initiative*, 13.

17 Judson, *Crisis*, 154.

18 J. G. A. Pocock, *The Machiavellian Moment: Florentine Political Thought and the Atlantic Republican Tradition* (Princeton: Princeton University Press, 1975), 374.

19 See Tanner, *English Constitutional Conflicts*; and J. P. Kenyon, *The Stuart Constitution, 1603–1688: Documents and Commentary*, 2nd edn. (Cambridge: Cambridge University Press, 1986), 1–3.

20 Notestein, *Winning of the Initiative*, 32–3.

21 Cited in Judson, *Crisis*, 113.

22 See ibid., 433.

23 *Subjects Libertie*, 30.

24 Harvey opens up the tension between private and public processes in *De Motu Cordis*: "the heart . . . alone of all the parts (though it has for its private use the coronal vein and arterie) does contain in its concavities, as in cisterns or celler . . . blood for the public use of the body." *De Motu Cordis*, in Geoffrey Keynes, ed. *The Anatomical Exercises of Dr. William Harvey* (London: Nonesuch, 1928), 95. Hereafter cited as "Keynes."

25 Of the confused relations between conceptions of the private and public, Judson writes, "in the seventeenth century most forms and procedures protecting private rights were inextricably mixed with those assuring public rights" (*Crisis*, 272).

26 John Neville Figgis, *The Divine Right of Kings* (1896; rpt. New York: Harper, 1965); and Corinne Comstock Weston and Janelle Renfrew Greenberg, *Subjects and Sovereigns: The Grand Controversy over Legal Sovereignty in Stuart England* (Cambridge: Cambridge University Press, 1981), 119.

27 Figgis, *Divine Right*, 246.

28 Ibid., 235.

29 Weston and Greenberg, *Subjects and Sovereigns*, 18.

30 Skinner, *Foundations*, II: 356.

31 Figgis, *Divine Right*, 212; 252.

32 James Shirley, "To the Reader," in *Comedies and Tragedies Written by Francis Beaumont and John Fletcher* (London, 1647), Sigs. A3r–A3v.

33 Pocock, *Machiavellian Moment*, 361; Wallace, *Destiny His Choice*, 15; Weston and Greenberg, *Subjects and Sovereigns*, 38.

34 Kenyon, *Stuart Constitution*, 18.

35 Charles Herle, *A Fuller Answer to a Treatise Written by Doctor Ferne* (London, 1642), 3.

36 Hunton, *A Treatise of Monarchy*, 7.

37 Ibid.

38 Ibid., 42; 62; 99; 86. The relationship between the architectonic and the physiological is a basic analogy in Harvey and is suggested by the fact that Wren was responsible for the diagrams of the nervous system incorporated into Thomas Willis, *Practice of Physick* (London, 1681). Willis was one of the most prolific medical writers during the Restoration, and the *Practice* was merely a translated

compendium of many of his already huge works. Harvey clearly thinks about the body in architectural terms (see *De Motu Cordis*, in Keynes, 37).

39 Howard Nenner, *The Right to be King: The Succession to the Crown of England, 1603–1714* (Chapel Hill: University of North Carolina Press, 1995), 1–12; Weston and Greenberg, *Subjects and Sovereigns*, 110.

40 I depart here from Christopher Hill's reading of the implicit politics of Harvey which directly influences John Rogers. Hill argues that between 1628 and 1651 Harvey abandons the view that the heart is the monarch of the system in *De Motu Cordis*, favoring instead the autonomous action of the blood in *De Generatione*, which Hill sees as an abandonment of simple royalism in favor of what Rogers anachronistically calls a "liberal" alternative. This reading involves some highly selective approaches to both texts, as well as ignoring *De Circulationis* (1649), and neglecting the fact that each of these texts plays a different rhetorical role for Harvey, and that they are therefore generically discontinuous. Moreover, the fact that all were reissued in translation in 1653 lends priority to none. Apart from the dedication to the King, Harvey only at one point speaks in *De Motu* of the heart as the "Prince in the Commonwealth" (Keynes, 115), but he makes it clear at the end of *De Circulationis* that the blood's action depends on the heart (Keynes, 188). The dedicatory poem to the 1653 *De Generatione* first praises Harvey for telling us about the heart and then about circulation (*Anatomical Exercitations concerning the Generation of Living Creatures* [London, 1653], Sigs. a2v–a3r). And the purpose of *De Generatione* is to determine how life is formed, using a chicken egg as an example, so the question of whether blood or the heart comes first is almost literally a chicken-and-egg problem. Part-way through, moreover, Harvey notices that the sperm precedes blood in the embryo, and that it itself contains no blood (*Anatomical Exercitations*, 80). There is no evidence in Harvey's language of what Rogers calls "radical egalitarianism" (John Rogers, *The Matter of Revolution: Science, Poetry and Politics in the Age of Milton* [Ithaca: Cornell University Press, 1996], 27); the model seems to be one of co-ordination in the state, as when Harvey writes, "the heart . . . is the beginning of all things in the body, the spring, fountain, and first causer of life, [and] is . . . to be taken, as being joyn'd together with the veins, and all the arteries, and the blood which is contained in them" (*De Circulatione*, Keynes, 186). I would argue that circulation in all texts represents, as Dryden argues, a new approach to systematacity, and that they manifest what most historians of science have recognized, namely that Harvey vacillates between qualitative and quantitative views of the body. If anything, the greater stress on the qualitative in the later texts represents a regression, as I will show that the Restoration opposes a qualitative epistemology – denoting a dogmatic view of the world – to a systemic or methodical view – which is more skeptical about different postulates in the system, and therefore more "liberal" in the precise sense of the word. See Christopher Hill, "William Harvey and the Idea of Monarchy"; Gweneth Whitteridge, "William Harvey: A Royalist and No Parliamentarian"; and Hill, "William Harvey (No Parliamentarian, No Heretic) and the Idea of Monarchy," in Charles Webster, ed. *The Intellectual Revolution of the Seventeenth*

Century (London: Routledge and Kegan Paul, 1974), 160–96. See also Rogers, *The Matter of Revolution*, 16–27.

41 Harvey, *De Motu Cordis*, Keynes, 38.

42 Hunton, *A Treatise of Monarchy*, 61.

43 Ascham, *Discourse*, 67.

44 Harvey, *De Motu Cordis*, Keynes, 9.

45 Hunton, *A Treatise of Monarchy*, 71.

46 Harvey, *De Motu Cordis*, Keynes, 3.

47 *Subjects Libertie*, 36–7.

48 Harvey, *Anatomical Exercitations*, Sig. a3r.

49 John Ogilby, *The Entertainment of His Most Excellent Majestie Charles II*, intro. Ronald Knowles (Binghamton, NY: Medieval and Renaissance Texts and Studies, 1988); and Blair Hoxby, "The Government of Trade: Commerce, Politics, and the Courtly Art of the Restoration," *ELH* 66 (1999): 591–627. Knowles presents a facsimile of Ogilby's expanded second edition of 1662, whereas I use the first edition of 1661. References in the text are to this first edition (London, 1661).

50 Sir Jonas Moore, *A New System of the Mathematicks* (London, 1681), Sigs. a1v; a2r–a2v. At least two more treatises for the Royal Mathematical School were published in the Restoration, including P. Perkins, *The Seaman's Tutor* (London, 1682), and Samuel Newton, *An Idea of Geography and Navigation* (London, 1695).

51 Similarly, *A Description of the Office of Credit* (London, 1665) hopes that "*England* . . . may . . . become the *Emporium* of *Europe*, if not of the World" (9).

52 Dryden speaks of the organic form of the poem as having an "Oeconomy," which allows him to think of it both through physiological metaphors and metaphors of trade. See Dedication of the *Aeneis*, in *California Dryden*, V: 268; 270. At 234, he directly refers to the recoinage debate which also occupied Locke, and at 337 he writes, "If sounding Words are not of our growth and Manufacture, who shall hinder me to Import them, from a Foreign Country? I carry not out the Treasure of the Nation, which is never to return: but what I bring from *Italy*, I spend in *England*: Here it remains, and here it circulates; for if the Coyn be good, it will pass from one hand to another. I Trade both with the Living and the Dead, for the enrichment of our Native Language."

53 For reexports, see Ralph Davis, *English Overseas Trade, 1500–1700* (London: Macmillan, 1973), 36–7.

54 Ralph Davis, "English Foreign Trade, 1660–1700," *Economic History Review* n.s. 6 (1954): 150–66. In *English Overseas Trade*, Davis revises these estimates, suggesting instead an expansion from 50,000 lbs. to 30,000,000 lbs. (35). See also W. E. Minchington, ed. and intro., *The Growth of English Overseas Trade in the Seventeenth and Eighteenth Centuries* (London: Methuen, 1969).

55 Ralph Davis, *English Merchant Shipping and Anglo-Dutch Rivalry in the Seventeenth Century* (London: National Maritime Museum, 1975), 1. See also Davis, *The Rise of the English Shipping Industry in the Seventeenth and Eighteenth Centuries* (Newton Abbot: David and Charles, 1962), 388–9.

56 Steven Pincus, "Neither Machiavellian Moment nor Possessive Individualism: Commercial Society and the Defenders of the English Commonwealth," *The American Historical Review* 103 (1998): 705–36. See also J. R. Jones, *The Anglo-Dutch Wars of the Seventeenth Century* (London: Longman, 1996).

57 For an excellent account of Milton's fluctuating attitude to trade in his career, see Blair Hoxby, *Mammon's Music: Literature and Economics in the Age of Milton* (New Haven: Yale University Press, 2002).

58 Notestein, *Winning of the Initiative*, 31.

59 Jan de Vries, *The Economy of Europe in an Age of Crisis, 1600–1750* (Cambridge: Cambridge University Press, 1976), 20.

60 E. A. J. Johnson, *Predecessors of Adam Smith: The Growth of British Economic Thought* (1937; rpt. New York: Augustus Kelley, 1960), 3–16; William Letwin, *The Origins of Scientific Economics* (New York: Doubleday, 1964), v–vii; Joseph A. Schumpeter, *History of Economic Analysis* (1954; rpt. New York: Oxford University Press, 1961), 3–11.

61 See B. E. Supple, *Commercial Crisis and Change in England, 1600–1642* (Cambridge: Cambridge University Press, 1959).

62 See for example Davis, *Rise of the English Shipping Industry*, 9.

63 Thus, in *Essays on Trade and Navigation* (London, 1695), Francis Brewster writes, "we need go no further than the *Dutch* and *Spaniards* for Demonstration" (1). On the decline of Antwerp and the rise of the Dutch carrying trade, see Jonathan I. Israel, *Dutch Primacy in World Trade, 1585–1740* (Oxford: Clarendon Press, 1989), 28–37; and Jan de Vries and Ad van der Woude, *The First Modern Economy: Success, Failure, and Perseverance of the Dutch Economy, 1500–1815* (Cambridge: Cambridge University Press, 1997), 362–76.

64 See also *The Hollanders Declaration of the Affairs of the East Indies* (Amsterdam, 1622).

65 Joyce Oldham Appleby, *Economic Thought and Ideology in Seventeenth-Century England* (Princeton: Princeton University Press, 1978), 45.

66 Gerard de Malynes, *England's View in the Unmasking of Two Paradoxes* (London, 1603), 6; *Saint George for England, Allegorically Described* (London, 1601), 42.

67 *England's View*, 5.

68 *Saint George for England*, 13–14.

69 Ibid., Sig. A6r.

70 *England's View*, 3–4. In his dedication to the King in *Consuetudo, Vel Lex Mercatoria, or the Ancient Law Merchant* (London, 1622), Malynes almost directly cites James I's *Trew Law of Free Monarchies* (Sig. A3r).

71 Malynes, *The Maintainance of Free Trade, According to the Three Essentiall Parts of Traffique* (London, 1622), 5; *England's View*, 1.

72 Malynes, *A Treatise of the Canker of Englands Commonwealth* (London, 1601), 14.

73 Andrea Finkelstein, *Harmony and the Balance: An Intellectual History of Seventeenth-Century English Economic Thought* (Ann Arbor: University of Michigan Press, 2000), 11. Finkelstein complains in particular about the failure to account for Harvey.

74 Thus in the Restoration, Dudley North could write in his *Observations and Advices Oeconomical* (London, 1669), that "*Oeconomy* is an Art, and every Artist ought to be curious in the choyce of his Instruments, and not onely so, but to trust chiefly to his own eye, cast either upon the whole work it self, or upon those who act in it" (43).

75 Malynes, *Maintainance of Free Trade*, Sig.¶4v; Mun, *A Discourse of Trade* (London, 1621), 53.

76 Mun, *Discourse of Trade*, 25.

77 Mun, *England's Treasure by Forraign Trade. Or, the Ballance of our Foreign Trade is the Rule of our Treasure* (London, 1664), 103.

78 Ibid., 37.

79 Malynes, *The Center of the Circle of Commerce* (London, 1623), Sig. A3v.

80 Ibid., 2.

81 Edward Misselden, *The Circle of Commerce. Or, The Balance of Trade, in Defence of Free Trade* (London, 1623), 6; 2–3.

82 Mun, *England's Treasure*, 47.

83 Malynes complains of the disparate motives of merchants in *Lex Mercatoria*, 59, whereas Mun treats the merchant as "*The Steward of the Kingdoms Stock*" (*England's Treasure*, 3). For a balance between royal initiative and the merchant community, see Misselden, *Free Trade or, The meanes to make trade florish (London, 1622)*, 53–4.

84 Misselden, *Circle of Commerce*, 98; Mun, *England's Treasure*, 84.

85 Malynes, *Saint George for England*, 78.

86 Ibid., Sig. A8r.

87 Misselden, *Circle of Commerce*, 91.

88 Mun, *England's Treasure*, 116.

89 Appleby, *Economic Thought*, 5; 48.

90 Misselden, *Circle of Commerce*, 142.

91 Mun writes of "the whole body of the trade" (*England's Treasure*, 84).

92 See the full title of Malynes's *A Treatise of the Canker of Englands Commonwealth . . . Wherein the Author Imitating the Rule of Good Phisitions, First, Declareth the Disease. Secondarily, Sheweth the Efficient Cause thereof. Lastly, a Remedy for the Same.*

93 Malynes, *Lex Mercatoria*, 86.

94 [James Howell], *Cottoni Posthuma* (London, 1651), 294.

95 Mun, *England's Treasure*, 42.

96 Malynes, *Lex Mercatoria*, 59.

97 Ibid., 64–5.

98 Mun, *England's Treasure*, 173.

99 Misselden, *Free Trade*, 19; see also 10.

100 Mun, *Discourse of Trade*, 40.

101 Malynes, *Lex Mercatoria*, 64; in *The Canker of England's Commonwealth*, Malynes refers to the flow of trade as an "Ocean" (10).

102 Malynes, *Lex Mercatoria*, 95.

103 Ibid.

104 Perry Gauci, *The Politics of Trade: The Overseas Merchant in State and Society, 1660–1720* (Oxford: Oxford University Press, 2001), 12 and *passim*; and see *England's Great Happiness* (London, 1677), in J. R. McCulloch, ed. *Early English Tracts on Trade* (Cambridge: Cambridge University Press, 1954), 269. Hereafter cited as "McCulloch."

105 Charles Wilson, *England's Apprenticeship, 1603–1763*, 2nd edn. (London: Longman, 1984), 63.

106 Ibid., 168.

107 Thomas Willis, *The Practice of Physick*, 2nd edn. (London, 1684), 48; 133.

108 R. H. Tawney, *Religion and the Rise of Capitalism* (1926; rpt. New Brunswick, NJ: Transaction, 1998), 10; Letwin, *Origins of Scientific Economics*, vii.

109 William Petty, *Verbum Sapienti*, in *A Collection of Tracts and Treatises [on] Ireland*, 2 vols. (Dublin, 1861), II: 136–7.

110 Petty, *The Political Anatomy of Ireland*, in *A Collection of Tracts and Treatises*, II: 7.

111 *A Description of the Office of Credit* (London, 1665), 13.

112 Nicholas Barbon, *An Apology for the Builder* (London, 1685), 30.

113 [Daniel Defoe], *Taxes No Charge* (London, 1690), 11.

114 Sir Humphrey Mackworth, *England's Glory* (London, 1694), 11–12.

115 William Freke, *A Review of the Universal Remedy for all Diseases Incident to Coin* (London, 1696), 11.

116 Charles Davenant, *An Essay on the Probable Methods of Making a People Gainers in the Balance of Trade*, in *The Political and Commercial Works*, 5 vols. (London, 1771), II: 169–70.

117 Appleby, *Economic Thought*, 242–57.

118 Pincus, "Neither Machiavellian Moment nor Possessive Individualism," 724–7.

119 Samuel Fortrey, *Englands Interest and Improvement*, in McCulloch, 218.

120 Rice Vaughan, *A Discourse of Coin and Coinage* (London, 1675), 248.

121 Carew Reynel, *The True English Interest* (London, 1674), Sig. A4v.

122 John Evelyn, *Navigation and Commerce* (London, 1674), 10.

123 *Britannia Languens* (1680), in McCulloch, 289.

124 Sir Francis Brewster, *Essays on Trade and Navigation* (London, 1695), esp. Ch. 1.

125 For a different reading of the Lord Mayor's Shows, see Susan J. Owen, *Restoration Theatre and Crisis* (Oxford: Clarendon Press, 1996), 275–99. I don't agree with Owen's argument that Jordan's promotion of trade and moderation makes him Whiggish, especially since his position seems to have been consistent from 1671, when that kind of identification is less decisive than during the Exclusion Crisis which provides Owen's focus.

126 See for example, *Pictures of Passions, Fancies, and Affections* (London, 1641), Sig. B1v.

127 *Fancy's Festivals* (London, 1657), Sigs. B3r; B1r; A4r.

128 *London's Triumphs* (London, 1674), 9.

129 *London's Resurrection* (London, 1671), 4; 8.

130 *The Triumphs of London* (London, 1675), Sig. A2v.
131 *London's Splendor* (London, 1673), 8.
132 *The Triumphs of London*, 9.
133 *London's Triumphs*, 6.
134 Weston and Greenberg, *Subjects and Sovereigns*, 152.
135 Ibid., 10.
136 *London's Resurrection*, 12.
137 *The Triumphs of London*, 13.
138 *London's Resurrection*, 9.
139 Ibid., 19.
140 *London's Joy* (London, 1681), 12; 13.
141 *London's Triumphs*, 14.
142 *London's Joy*, 5.
143 *London's Resurrection*, 3.
144 Ibid., 5.
145 Ibid., 4.
146 *London's Triumphs*, 6–7.
147 Ibid., 10.
148 Ibid., 12–13.
149 Ibid., 15–19.
150 Evelyn, *Diary*, I: 395. Calling the play "a Tragi-Comedy," Langbaine writes that *The Adventures* is "One of the best Plays now extant, for Oeconomy and Contrivance" (*An Account*, II: 505).
151 William Van Lennep *et al.*, eds. *The London Stage, 1660–1800*, 5 vols. (Carbondale, IL: Southern Illinois University Press, 1965), I: 174.
152 Sir Samuel Tuke, *The Adventures of Five Hours*, in David Womersley, ed. *Restoration Drama: An Anthology* (Oxford: Blackwell, 2000), Epilogue, 55. All subsequent references to the play will be to this edition and will appear in the text.
153 *The London Stage*, I: xxxv.

2 "THIS MIMIC STATE": CICERO, QUINTILIAN, AND THE
THEATRICAL SCENE OF CULTURE

1 Joseph Wood Krutch, *Comedy and Conscience after the Restoration* (New York: Columbia University Press, 1924), 259–64. For the relation to the French, see A. F. B. Clark, *Boileau and the French Neoclassical Critics in England, 1660–1830* (1925; rpt. New York: Burt Franklin, 1970).
2 Writing in the *Orator*, Cicero discusses the role of tragicomedy, imagined as a chiastic relationship between Roscius, the comedian capable of tragedy, and Aesopius, the tragedian capable of comedy: "We have seen actors whose superiors in their own class cannot be found, who not only gained approval in utterly different parts while confining themselves to their own proper spheres of tragedy and comedy, but we have also seen a comedian highly successful in tragedy and a tragedian in comedy." See Cicero, *Brutus, Orator*, trans. G. L.

Hendrickson and H. M. Hubbell (Cambridge, MA: Harvard University Press, 1938), *Orator* xxxi,109. All references will appear by section number in the text.

3 Writing of mixed plots in *Of Dramatic Poesy*, Dryden uses the Ciceronian terms, saying that the English want *variety* and *copiousness*. John Dryden, *Of Dramatic Poesy and Other Critical Essays*, ed. George Watson, 2 vols. (London: Everyman, 1962), I: 65.

4 Aphra Behn, Dedication to *The Lucky Chance*, in Montague Summers, ed. *The Works of Aphra Behn*, 6 vols. (1915; rpt. New York: Phaeton, 1967), III: 183.

5 Abbé D'Aubignac, *The Whole Art of the Stage*, 2 parts (London, 1684), I: 70.

6 Ibid., I: 14.

7 Ibid., I: 22–3.

8 D'Aubignac recommends "those great Figures which express the things themselves" (ibid., II: 49).

9 Ibid., II: 14; 25; I: 99; 111; 64.

10 Ibid., I: 115.

11 Ibid., I: 38; 40; 55.

12 Ibid., I: 38.

13 Ibid., I: 81.

14 For comparisons with the original, see Abbé D'Aubignac, *La Prâtique du Théatre*, ed. Helène Baby (Paris: Honoré Champion, 2001).

15 Ibid., I: 84.

16 Ibid., I: 86. A little later he writes, "the second Story must not be equal in its Subject, nor in its Necessity, to that which is the foundation of the Play, but must be subordinate to it, and so depend upon it" (I: 96). Dryden is clearly alive to the political resonances in such statements.

17 Ibid., I: 103.

18 Ibid., II: 139; 145. D'Aubignac remarks that Plautus uses the term in the preface to *Amphitryon*, but not in the current sense (II: 146).

19 Ibid., I: 49.

20 This charge against Dryden Dubos repeats from Langbaine.

21 Gerard Langbaine, *An Account of the English Dramatick Poets* (1691), Intro. John Loftis, 2 vols. (Los Angeles: William Andrews Clark Memorial Library, 1971), I: 223.

22 See John W. Cunliffe, ed. *The Complete Works of George Gascoigne*, 2 vols. (Cambridge: Cambridge University Press, 1910), II: 1.

23 Langbaine, *An Account*, I: 228–9.

24 Ibid., I: 229.

25 [René Rapin], *A Comparison between the Eloquence of Demosthenes and Cicero* (Oxford, 1672), 117–19.

26 In the *Institutes*, Quintilian writes that "this much is certain and incontrovertible, that Euripides will be found of far greater service [than the other Greek tragedians] to those who are training themselves for pleading in court" (X, i, 67). Quintilian, *Institutio Oratoria*, trans. H. E. Butler, 4 vols. (Cambridge, MA: Harvard University Press, 1922). All references will appear by section number in the text.

27 Gascoigne, *Works*, II: 30–1.

28 For a thorough description, see Sister Rose Anthony, S.C., *The Jeremy Collier Stage Controversy, 1698–1726* (Milwaukee, WI: Marquette University Press, 1937).

29 Edward Niles Hooker, ed. *The Critical Works of John Dennis*, 2 vols. (Baltimore: The Johns Hopkins University Press, 1939–43), I: 159.

30 [Charles Gildon], *The Life of Mr. Thomas Betterton* (London, 1710), 1.

31 Ibid., 2.

32 Ibid., ix.

33 See Harry Mortimer Hubbell, *The Influence of Isocrates on Cicero, Dionysius, and Aristides* (New Haven: Yale University Press, 1903).

34 René Rapin, *Reflections upon the Eloquence of these Times* (London, 1672), 2.

35 Ibid., 10–11.

36 Ibid., 12–15.

37 John Bulwer, *Chironomia* (London, 1644), Sigs. A7v; A8r.

38 Ibid., 10.

39 Rapin, *Reflections upon the Eloquence of these Times*, 16.

40 Rapin, *A Comparison between Demosthenes and Cicero*, 36.

41 Ibid., 90.

42 Ibid., 166.

43 Gildon, *Life of Betterton*, 6.

44 Ibid., 11–12.

45 Ibid., 13.

46 Ibid., 14.

47 See for example, ibid., x; 25; 51; 65; 79; 97; 137.

48 Ibid., 3.

49 Ibid., 19.

50 Ibid., 26; 28.

51 Abbé Dubos, *Critical Reflections on Poetry, Painting, and Music*, 3 vols. (London, 1748), I: 372–3.

52 Ibid., III: 237.

53 Ibid., II: 102–3.

54 Ibid., II: 103.

55 Ibid., I: 29.

56 Ibid., II: 351; see also 365.

57 Ibid., II: 102.

58 Ibid., II: 166–9.

59 The standard account of Cicero's role in humanism is still Jerrold Siegel, *Rhetoric and Philosophy in Renaissance Humanism: The Union of Eloquence and Wisdom, Petrarch to Valla* (Princeton: Princeton University Press, 1968). Charles Sears Baldwin writes that "Cicero remains after 2000 years the typical orator writing on oratory. The most eminent orator of Roman civilization, he wrote more than any other author has written on rhetoric; and historically he has been more than any other an ideal and model" (*Ancient Rhetoric and Poetic* [New York: Macmillan, 1924], 37). See also R. R. Bolgar, *The Classical Heritage*

and its Beneficiaries from the Carolingian Age to the End of the Renaissance (1954; New York: Harper and Row, 1964), esp. Ch. 7; Kenneth Charlton, *Education in Renaissance England* (London: Routledge and Kegan Paul, 1965). And in *William Shakespeare's Small Latine and Lesse Greeke*, 2 vols. (Urbana: University of Illinois Press, 1944), T. W. Baldwin writes, "it is clear that England's fundamental rhetorical standards were those of Europe, and the standards of Europe were predominantly Ciceronic" (II: 68).

60 See for example, William Harrison Woodward, *Vittorino da Feltre and Other Humanist Educators* (1897; rpt. New York: Teachers College, Columbia University, 1963), 25–7.

61 Erasmus, *Ciceronianus*, in A. H. T. Levi, ed. *The Collected Works of Erasmus: Literary and Educational Writings 6* (Toronto: University of Toronto Press, 1986), 346.

62 Ibid., 368. Very similar sentiments about Cicero as a guide to style and to method occur in Johann Sturm, *A Ritch Storehouse or Treasurie for Nobilitie and Gentlemen* (London, 1570), esp. Sigs. 35v–36r.

63 Erasmus, *On Copia of Words and Ideas*, trans. Donald B. King and H. David Rix (Milwaukee: Marquette University Press, 1963), 9; 12. Though the cultural history is more mythical altogether, we see a remarkably similar sentiment in Heinrich Cornelius Agrippa von Nettesheim, *The Vanity of Arts and Sciences* (London, 1676): "There was also a Rhetorical Gesticulation, not much differing from Stage-Action, but more careless, which *Socrates, Plato, Cicero, Quintilian*, and most of the Stoicks have deem'd most necessary and commendable in a Rhetorician, and an Orator" (65).

64 Henry Peacham, *The Compleat Gentleman* (London, 1634), 2; 44–5.

65 M. L. Clarke, *Classical Education in Britain, 1500–1700* (Cambridge: Cambridge University Press, 1959), 36.

66 E. N. Hooker and H. T. Swedenberg, eds. *The Works of John Dryden*, 20 vols. (Los Angeles: University of California Press, 1956–89), XVII: 356. For a general assessment of Dryden's debts to Cicero and Quintilian, see Lillian Feder, "John Dryden's Use of Classical Rhetoric," *PMLA* 69 (1954): 1258–78.

67 Cicero, *De Oratore*, trans. E. W. Sutton and H. Rackham, 2 vols. (Cambridge, MA: Harvard University Press, 1929), I,ii,28. All references will appear by section number in the text.

68 See R. L. Howland, "The Attack on Isocrates in the *Phaedrus*," *The Classical Quarterly* 31 (1937): 152. Maureen Daly Goggin and Elenore Long, in "A Tincture of Philosophy, A Tincture of Hope: The Portrayal of Isocrates in Plato's *Phaedrus*," *Rhetoric Review* 11 (1993): 302; 319, deny that Plato is attacking Isocrates. For Isocrates' success as a teacher, see H. I. Marrou, *A History of Education in Antiquity* (1948; rpt. and trans. Madison: University of Wisconsin Press, 1956), 79.

69 Cicero himself refers to Carneades and the New Academy at *De Oratore* (henceforth *DO*) III,xviii,68; *Orator* (henceforth *Or*) iii,12; xvi,51.

70 On the New Academy, see Richard McKeon, Introduction, Cicero, *Brutus, On the Nature of the Gods, On Divination, On Duties*, trans. Hubert

M. Poteat (Chicago: University of Chicago Press, 1950), 35–8; and McKeon refers to "the negative dialectic of the New Academy" (44). See also Harald Thorsrud, "Cicero on his Academic Predecessors: The Fallibilism of Arcesilaus and Carneades," *Journal of the History of Philosophy* 40 (2002): 1–2; 4. Cicero discusses the principle of *in utramque partem* at *DO* I,xxxiv,158; lvi,240; lvii,244; II,liii,215; III,xxi,79; xxvii,107; xxxvi,145; *Or* xiv,47–xv,48.

71 See also *DO* III,xviii,68.

72 For Cicero, contingency is marked existentially by death, not only deaths recorded in *De Oratore*, but the death of Quintus Hortensius which opens the *Brutus* (i,1). In language it is best expressed by jokes and laughter, for which, as he remarks, there can be no theories, since to explain the rules of a joke is to kill it. It depends entirely on mastery of idiom, inflection, and occasion. (*DO* II,livi,217–19; III,lviii,235–6ff.) The methodical connection between death and jokes provides Quintilian's *Institutio Oratoria* with its architecture, Book VI half-way through beginning with an elegy on the loss of his family and comprising a meditation on jokes, issues reintroduced in Book XI, which addresses those aspects of rhetoric that have to do with context and circumstance, namely memory and delivery.

73 G. L. Hendrickson writes that for Aristotle, rhetoric is a form of dialectic but adapted for an audience ("The Origin and Meaning of the Ancient Characters of Style," *The American Journal of Philology* 26 [1905]: 254).

74 S. E. Smethurst, "Cicero and Isocrates," *Transactions and Proceedings of the American Philological Association* 84 (1953): 276.

75 In this context, Hall remarks that Cicero's use of aristocratic conversation is one way of assuaging the Roman suspicion of "theory" (Jon Hall, "Social Evasion and Aristocratic Manners in Cicero's *De Oratore*," *American Journal of Philology* 117 [1996]: 95). Much the same could be said of Neander's aristocratic company: these are men of affairs closely associated with high politics.

76 Dryden, *Of Dramatic Poesy*, I: 20.

77 See for example, Isocrates' comment in the *Antidosis*: Gymnastics and philosophy "are complementary, interconnected, and consistent with each other, and through them those who have mastered them make the soul more intelligent and the body more useful." *Isocrates I*, trans. David C. Mirhady and Yun Lee Too (Austin: University of Texas Press, 2000), 239. Anticipating a later argument in this chapter, but closely related, Cicero writes in the *Orator*, "[philosophy] helps the orator as physical training helps the actor" (iv,14).

78 Friederich Solmsen, "The Aristotelian Tradition in Ancient Rhetoric," *The American Journal of Philology* 62 (1941): 42. Aristotle can also be credited with distinguishing clearly among the deliberative, the forensic, and the epideictic modes (ibid.).

79 Cicero mentions Roscius at *DO* I,xxvii,124–xxviii,130; I,xxix,132; I,lix,251–I,lxi,259; II,lvii,233–4; II,lix,242; III,xxv,102; III,lix,221; *Br* lxxxiv,290. He mentions acting more generally, always being careful to distinguish between decorous action and farce or pantomime, at *DO* II,xlvi,198; II,lix,242; II,lx,247;

II,lxii,251; II,lxiv,259; III, xxii,83; III,xxvi,102; III,lvi,214; III,lvii,217; *Br* xxx,116; *Or* xxv,86; xxxix,134.

80 Erasmus, *On Copia*, 15. Sandys similarly refers to "Rhodian eclecticism" (John Edwin Sandys, ed. Cicero, *Ad Marcum Brutum Orator* [1885; rpt. Hildesheim: Georg Olms, 1973], xl).

81 The dialectical principle in the Sophists is marvellously analyzed in Mario Untersteiner, *The Sophists* (Oxford: Blackwell, 1954). See esp. p. 53 on Protagoras.

82 On these doublings, which prefigure the threefold characters of style, see Hendrickson, "Origin and Meaning," 265.

83 Hendrickson writes that this ideal is first announced in the *Orator*, not *De Oratore* ("Cicero De Optimo Genere Oratorum," *The American Journal of Philology* 47 [1926]: 112).

84 Hendrickson, "Origin and Meaning," 250.

85 Ibid., 255.

86 Hendrickson, "The Peripatetic Mean of Style and the Three Stylistic Characters," *The American Journal of Philology* 25 (1904): 125.

87 Solmsen, "Aristotelian Tradition," 183: "Since this is the theory which the Romans beginning with Cicero revive, we note an important divergence between them and their Greek colleagues, who think of style primarily as an 'ornament' and tend to ignore the instructive and informative function of language . . . as well as the requirement of a proper relation between style and subject matter, etc. (*to prepon*)."

88 Smethurst, "Cicero and Isocrates," 298.

89 Ibid., 274.

90 Ibid., 284–5. For Cicero's ideals in *De Republica*, see W. W. How, "Cicero's Ideal in his *De Republica*," *The Journal of Roman Studies* 20 (1930): 26–9; and Marcus Wheeler, "Cicero's Political Ideal," *Greece and Rome* 21 (1952): 49–56.

91 See *DO* II,lxxxii,337: "But the chief essential for giving counsel on affairs of state is a knowledge of the constitution of the state, whereas the thing that is essential for persuasive speaking is a knowledge of the national character; and as this frequently alters, it is often necessary also to alter the style of speaking employed." Also Philip George Neserius, "Isocrates' Political and Social Ideas," *International Journal of Ethics* 43 (1933): 315. A. D. Leeman analyzes the relationship between the three characters of style and the mixed republic in *Orationis Ratio: The Stylistic Theories and Practice of the Roman Orators, Historians, and Philosophers* (1963; rpt. Amsterdam: Hakkert, 1986), 148–9.

92 Solmsen, "Aristotelian Tradition," 45.

93 Mary A. Grant and George Converse Fiske, "Cicero's *Orator* and Horace's *Ars Poetica*," *Harvard Studies in Classical Philology* 35 (1924): 9; 39. See also Fiske and Grant, *Cicero's "De Oratore" and Horace's "Ars Poetica"* (Madison: University of Wisconsin Studies in Language and Literature, No. 27, 1929).

94 Ibid., 24.

95 Hendrickson, "Origin and Meaning," 288.

96 For *membrum*, usually in the plural, see *DO* II,lxxxvii,359; III,xiii,50; III,xxv,96; III,xlviii,186; *Br* xvi,64; xvii,69; xliv,162; lvii,209.

97 Per Fjelstad, "Restraint and Emotion in Cicero's *De Oratore*," *Philosophy and Rhetoric* 36 (2003): 40.

3 "THE CIVILITY OF THE STAGE": DAVENANT'S CRITICAL ROYALISM

1 See John Freehafer, "The Formation of the London Patent Companies in 1660," *Theatre News* 20 (1965): 6–30.

2 Gerard Langbaine, *An Account of the English Dramatick Poets*, ed. John Loftis, 2 vols. (Los Angeles: William Andrews Clark Memorial Library, 1971), I: 115.

3 Stephen Orgel, *The Jonsonian Masque* (Cambridge, MA: Harvard University Press, 1965).

4 Stephen Orgel and Roy Strong, *Inigo Jones: The Theatre of the Stuart Court*, 2 vols. (London/Berkeley: Sotheby Parke Bernet/University of California Press, 1973), I: 58; 50–2.

5 Ibid., I: 72. Elsewhere, though briefly, Roy Strong admits the dependence of the Webb/Davenant reform of the stage on Inigo Jones, so linking the Caroline and Carolean periods. (See John Harris *et al.* eds. *The King's Arcadia: Inigo Jones and the Stuart Court* [London: Arts Council of Great Britain, 1973], 208).

6 Ibid., I: 17. Though often cited by theater historians, the British Library Lansdowne MS 1171 provides for the most part equivocal evidence. Of the ten designs, only four are identified, and some of the designs – such as the first – are not to scale. The most unequivocal evidence occurs in the form of the groundplans for *Salmacida Spolia* (plan 2) and *Florimène* (plan 10), which seem clearly to show that in both cases the depth from the front of the stage to the backshutters is 16 feet. The problem with Orgel's account is that he first seems to argue that the stage for *Florimène* is deeper than that of most masques (which may be true), then comments that the groundplan for *Salmacida Spolia* is more cramped (which is more difficult to prove) without remarking on the important fact that the stage itself is equally deep.

7 This is the topic of Inga-Stina Ewbank, "'These Pretty Devices': A Study of Masques in Plays," in *A Book of Masques, in Honour of Allardyce Nicoll* (Cambridge: Cambridge University Press, 1967), 407–48.

8 Keith Sturgess, *Jacobean Private Theatre* (London: Routledge and Kegan Paul, 1987), 54. Also Andrew Gurr, *The Shakespearean Stage, 1574–1642*, 2nd edn. (Cambridge: Cambridge University Press, 1980), 24–6; Ch. 4. Gurr points out that there is little evidence of stage design for the public theaters and even less for the private theaters. Sturgess and Gurr concur in thinking that the design of the stage remained the same in both venues but that the indoor theaters were much smaller and often relied exclusively on artificial lighting, allowing for a very different experience of a play. Sturgess asks us to think of the difference between a large sporting event and indoor entertainment. Both critics agree that the scenic and proscenium stage are exclusively Restoration

forms introduced by Davenant, though Orrell lays great store by Jones's designs
for the Cockpit, Drury Lane, which could accommodate scenes in ways that
anticipated Davenant's reforms.

9 Sturgess, *Jacobean Private Theatre*, 160.

10 Ibid., 18. Orrell hazards a guess that the setting may have been Somerset House
   (John Orrell, *The Theatres of Inigo Jones and John Webb* [Cambridge: Cambridge
   University Press, 1985], 88).

11 Sturgess, *Jacobean Private Theatre*, 148.

12 See Orrell, *The Theatres of Inigo Jones and John Webb*; and *The Human Stage:
   English Theatre Design, 1567–1640* (Cambridge: Cambridge University Press,
   1988).

13 William Grant Keith, "The Designs for the First Movable Scenery on the
   English Court Stage," *Burlington Magazine* 25 (1914): 29–33; 85–98; and see
   also Keith, "A Theatre Project by Inigo Jones," *Burlington Magazine* 31 (1917):
   61–70; 105–11, an argument about Jones as architect that anticipates mine
   below.

14 Richard Southern, "Observations on Lansdowne MS. 1171," *Theatre Notebook*
   2 (1947): 6.

15 I thus take issue with Orgel's tendency to treat "rhetoric" as purely discursive
   and as a mode to be distinguished from the theatrical or dramatic. Orgel shows
   no interest in the Roman grounds of humanism, exclusively citing Plato and
   Aristotle as the chief influences on seventeenth-century dramatic theory and
   rhetoric. See Orgel and Strong, *Inigo Jones*, 9–10; and Orgel, "The Poetics
   of Spectacle," *New Literary History* 2 (1971): 381; though Orgel qualifies his
   position somewhat in *The Illusion of Power: Political Theater in the English
   Renaissance* (Berkeley: University of California Press, 1975), 18–19.

16 D. J. Gordon, "Poet and Architect: The Intellectual Setting of the Quarrel
   between Ben Jonson and Inigo Jones," *Journal of the Warburg and Courtauld
   Institutes* 12 (1949): 152–78.

17 For more commentary on the quarrel between Jonson and Jones, see Richard
   Southern, *Changeable Scenery: Its Origin and Development in the British Theatre*
   (London: Faber and Faber, 1952), Ch. 6.

18 The relationship between the stage conditions of Blackfriars and tragicomedy
   is the topic of a superb essay by R. A. Foakes, "Tragicomedy and Comic
   Form," in A. R. Braunmuller and J. C. Bulman, eds. *Comedy from Shakespeare
   to Sheridan: Change and Continuity in the English and European Dramatic
   Tradition* (Newark: University of Delaware Press, 1986), 74–88.

19 Andrew Gurr, *Playgoing in Shakespeare's London*, 2nd edn. (Cambridge: Cambridge University Press, 1996), 27.

20 See for example Rudolf Wittkower, *Palladio and English Palladianism* (New
   York: Thames and Hudson, 1985), 51.

21 Orrell, *The Human Stage*, 165; this motif also distinguishes Wren, according to
   John Summerson, who emphasizes "the Latinity of the Sheldonian," Wren's
   first essay in architecture (John Summerson, *Architecture in Britain, 1530–1830*,
   4th edn. [Harmondsworth: Penguin, 1963], 114).

22 Serlio was one theorist unwilling to distinguish the classical orders absolutely from the Gothic.

23 Though there is some question as to whether Serlio also thought in these somatic terms, Orrell argues that he did (*The Human Stage*, 137–8; 146–7).

24 William Bray, ed. *The Diary and Correspondence of John Evelyn, F.R.S.*, 4 vols. (London: George Bell, 1898), I: 211.

25 Orrell, *The Human Stage*, 126; also Ch. 9.

26 Orrell, *The Theatres of Inigo Jones and John Webb*, 70–3.

27 Alfred Harbage, *Sir William Davenant, Poet, Venturer, 1606–1668* (1935; rpt. New York: Octagon, 1971), 148.

28 I am grateful to Max Novak and Alan Roper for help on this point.

29 John Downes, *Roscius Anglicanus*, ed. Montague Summers (1929; rpt. New York: Benjamin Blom, 1968), 20–2.

30 William Van Lennep *et al.*, eds. *The London Stage, 1660–1800*, 5 vols. (Carbondale, IL: Southern Illinois University Press, 1965), I: 185.

31 John Summerson, *Sir Christopher Wren* (London: Collins, 1953), 44–8.

32 Ibid.

33 Orrell, *The Human Stage*, 202.

34 Thomas Carew, "To My Worthy Friend, M. Davenant, upon his Excellent Play, *The Just Italian*," in *The Works of Sir William Davenant* 2 vols. (1673; rpt. New York/London:, Benjamin Blom, 1968), II: 442. Quotations from *The Cruel Brother, The Just Italian, Love and Honour*, and *The Platonick Lovers* all come from this volume of the *Works* and refer to act, scene, page, and column numbers.

35 I agree with Kevin Sharpe that Caroline literature represents a sympathetic critique of the monarchy, but whereas Sharpe looks thematically to the extent to which "court" writers respect "country" values, I am more concerned with the extent to which the action of the theatre represents a methodical critique of power more generally. See Kevin Sharpe, *Criticism and Compliment: The Politics of Literature in the England of Charles I* (Cambridge: Cambridge University Press, 1987), esp. Ch. 2 on Davenant. Apart from Harbage's book cited above (note 27), major studies of Davenant include Philip Bordinat and Sophia B. Blaydes, *Sir William Davenant* (Boston: Twayne, 1981); Mary Edmond, *Rare Sir William Davenant* (Manchester: Manchester University Press, 1987); and "Sir William Davenant," in Montague Summers, *The Playhouse of Pepys* (1935; rpt. New York: Humanities Press, 1964), Ch. 1.

36 A useful list of plays performed at Blackfriars appears in Irwin Smith, *Shakespeare's Blackfriars Playhouse: Its History and Its Design* (New York: New York University Press, 1964), 214–19.

37 For monopolies, see I,i,466a.

38 Lee Bliss, "Pastiche, Burlesque, Tragicomedy," in A. R. Braunmuller and Michael Hattaway, eds. *The Cambridge Companion to English Renaissance Drama*, 2nd edn. (Cambridge: Cambridge University Press, 2003), 237; and R. A. Foakes, "Tragicomedy and Comic Form," cited above.

39 Sturgess, *Jacobean Private Theatre*, 41.

40 See Gurr, *The Shakespearean Stage*, 14; Gurr, *Playgoing in Shakespeare's London*, 184.

41 Jonathan Barnes, ed. *The Complete Works of Aristotle*, 2 vols. (Princeton: Princeton University Press, 1984), I: 716.

42 Ibid.

4 "THE VITRUVIUS OF HIS AGE": INIGO JONES, THE RHETORIC OF
STAGE DESIGN, AND ARCHITECTURAL THEORY

1 See John Bold, *John Webb: Architectural Theory and Practice in the Seventeenth Century* (Oxford: Clarendon Press, 1989); and also some typically stimulating comments in John Summerson, *Architecture in Britain: 1530–1830*, 4th edn. (Harmondsworth: Penguin, 1963), 83–4. On Wren, see John Summerson, *Sir Christopher Wren* (London: Collins, 1953); and Adrian Tinniswood, *His Invention so Fertile: A Life of Sir Christopher Wren* (London: Pimlico, 2002).

2 See especially Stephen Orgel and Roy Strong, *Inigo Jones: The Theatre of the Stuart Court*, 2 vols. (London/Berkeley: Sotheby Parke Burnet/University of California Press, 1973), esp. I: 1–28; 49–75; Strong, *Splendour at Court: Renaissance Spectacle and Illusion* (London: Weidenfeld and Nicolson, 1973), 216; Orgel, *The Illusion of Power: Political Theater in the English Renaissance* (Berkeley: University of California Press, 1975); Orgel, "Plato, the Magi, and Caroline Politics: A Reading of *The Temple of Love*," *Word and Image* 4 (1988): 663–77; Gordon Toplis, "The Sources of Jones's Mind and Imagination," in John Harris *et. al.*, eds. *The King's Arcadia: Inigo Jones and the Stuart Court* (London: Arts Council of Great Britain, 1973), 61–3, where Toplis argues, improbably, that it was not until Newton that a "Platonic cosmology" was displaced, which omits the scientific revolution brought about by atomism, whose Lucretian resonances are important for my story here; Orgel, "The Royal Masques, 1631–40," in *The King's Arcadia*, 165, where Orgel speaks of the masques as "Magic mirrors"; Graham Parry, *The Golden Age Restor'd: The Culture of the Stuart Court* (Manchester: Manchester University Press, 1981); David Lindley, "Introduction," in *The Court Masque*, ed. Lindley (Manchester: Manchester University Press, 1984), 6. One of the most inflected essays speaking of Jones as neoplatonic is to be found in A. W. Johnson, ed. and intro., *Three Volumes Annotated by Inigo Jones* (Åbo: Åbo Akademi University Press, 1997), xiii–lxxvii.

3 George Kennedy, *The Art of Persuasion in Greece* (Princeton: Princeton University Press, 1963), 8.

4 In *The Most Notable Antiquity of Great Britain, Vulgarly Called Stoneheng* [or, *Stoneheng Restored*] (London, 1655), Jones makes it clear that his Italian travels were stimulated by his youthful interest in the "*The Arts of Design*," and that as a result architectural theory became an abiding interest (*Stoneheng Restored*, 1). I am most influenced by John Summerson's hard-headed, balanced, and intelligent appraisal of Jones, which has never been superseded. See Summerson, *Architecture in Britain*, 61–84, and his superb little book, *Inigo Jones* (Harmondsworth: Penguin, 1966), to which I owe many important insights in

this chapter. See also Michael Leapman, *Inigo: The Life of Inigo Jones, Architect of the English Renaissance* (London: Review, 2003). In the notes that follow I distinguish between the original texts of architectural theorists and Jones's annotated copies. There are no standard editions of the annotations, but two sets of annotations appear in modern editions. A. E. Johnson has published transcriptions of Jones's annotations to Vasari's *Lives* (1568), Plutarch's *Moralia* (1614), and Plato's *Republic* (1554) – all in Italian – in *Three Volumes Annotated by Inigo Jones* (see note 2 above); Jones's notes to Palladio, *I Quattro Libri dell'Architettura* (Venice, 1601) appear in Bruce Allsop and R. A. Sayce, eds. *Inigo Jones on Palladio*, 2 vols. (Newcastle-upon-Tyne: Oriel Press, 1970). Jones's other books at Worcester College, Oxford include: Alberti, *L'Architettura*, trans. Cosimo Bartoli (Monte Regale, 1565); Philibert de L'Orme, *Le Premier Tome de l'Architecture* (Paris, 1567); Vincenzo Scamozzi, *L'Idea della Architettura Universale* (Venice, 1615); and Giacomo Barozzi da Vignola, *Regola delli Cinque Ordini d'Architettura* (Rome, 1607). Jones's copy of Vitruvius, *I Dieci Libri dell'Architettura*, trans. Daniel Barbaro (Venice, 1567) is at Chatsworth, and I use the transcriptions made by Dr. John Newman, now available in typescript at Worcester College; Jones's 1600 copy of Sebastiano Serlio, *Tutte l'Opere d'Architettura* (Venice) is at the Centre Canadienne d'Architecture, Montreal; and his 1619 copy of Serlio is at the Royal Institute of British Architects, Portland Place, London. By examining Jones's handwriting, John Newman argues that Jones began his engagement with architectural theory as early as 1608. See John Newman, "Inigo Jones's Architectural Education before 1614," *Architectural History* 35 (1992): 18–50; and also Gordon Higgott, "Inigo Jones in Provence," *Architectural History* 26 (1983): 24–34;123–31.

5 Robert Tavernor, *Palladio and Palladianism* (London: Thames and Hudson, 1991), 21.

6 Vitruvius argues, for example, that number and proportion were derived empirically from observing the proportions of the human body. See Vitruvius, *Ten Books on Architecture*, Ingrid Rowland *et al.*, trans. and ed. (Cambridge: Cambridge University Press, 1999), 48. The Ciceronian correspondence between members and the body is central to Serlio too. See Sebastiano Serlio, *On Architecture*, trans. Vaughan Hart and Peter Hicks, 2 vols. (New Haven: Yale University Press, 1996), I: 99. Obviously Plato's organicism still has some influence on the conception, as Alberti's notion of *concinnitas* admits. But it seems to me that having a notion of numerical proportion based on the observable proportions of the human body does not automatically commit you to what Tavernor calls "the Pythagorean-Platonic number sequences," though writers in this vein also point to the notion that a proportionate building reflects the divine order in echoing, for example, Solomon's Temple (*Palladio and Palladianism*, 37). This issue is handled with considerable tact by James S. Ackerman, who shows that Palladio was influenced by sixteenth-century developments in mathematics which emphasized ratios and proportion, and that for the same reasons he was interested in music, both traditions which originate in Pythagoras if not before, without suggesting that Palladio was either Pythagorean or neoplatonic in tem-

perament (*Palladio* [Harmondsworth: Penguin, 1966], 162–7). The criterion
of decorum argues, in contradistinction to any transcendental postulate, that
truth is purely circumstantial. Echoing Cicero, Alberti compares the architect's
knowledge of painting and mathematics to the poet's knowledge of tone and
meter. Though Roman ideas about meter have their origins in Greek theories
of musical modes, as they operate in Cicero they serve an entirely skeptical
approach to representation. See Leon Battista Alberti, *On the Art of Building
in Ten Books*, trans. Joseph Rykwert *et. al.* (Cambridge, MA: MIT Press, 1988),
317.

7 Aristotle, *On Rhetoric: A Theory of Civil Discourse*, trans. George Kennedy
(New York: Oxford University Press, 1991), 235. This purely somatic and contingent notion of proportion informs, I believe, many of Jones's annotations,
as in "Of the proportion of children" (Roman notebook), and "the Thiknes of
walls *proportioned* to collumbs" (Jones/Alberti, VII,x). In fact, in his *Elements of
Architecture*, the second major English architectural treatise to be issued, Henry
Wotton, discussing the Tuscan order, cites Protagoras' man-measure argument,
as if specifically to undercut the Platonic implications of human proportion;
though in 1662, Balthazar Gerbier D'Onvilly links the mysterious appeal of proportion to the fact that God is a divine architect, and dictated the proportions
of Noah's Ark and the Temple. See Henry Wotton, *The Elements of Architecture*
(London, 1624), 34; Sir Balthazar Gerbier D'Onvilly, *A Brief Discourse concerning the Three Chief Principles of Magnificent Building* (London, 1662), 2–3. Jones
alludes to Pythagorean and Platonic number theory in Jones/De L'Orme, II:
35; 38.

8 Andrea Palladio, *The Four Books of Architecture*, trans. Isaac Ware (1738; rpt. New
York: Dover, 1965), 1. Wotton writes, "*Symmetria* is the *conveniencie* that runneth
between the *Parts* and the *Whole*, whereof I have formerly spoken. *Décor* is the
keeping of a due *Respect* between the *Inhabitant*, and the *Habitation*" (*Elements
of Architecture*, 119).

9 Vaughan Hart, *Art and Magic in the Court of the Stuarts* (London: Routledge,
1994), 8.

10 Vitruvius also sought to imitate Ciceronian style. See Vitruvius, *Ten Books*, xiii;
7; 16–17. Vitruvius himself connects Lucretius and Cicero (ibid., 109). Alina A.
Payne expounds the Ciceronian and humanistic grounds of this tradition in *The
Architectural Treatise in the Italian Renaissance: Architectural Invention, Ornament, and Literary Culture* (Cambridge: Cambridge University Press, 1999). See
also Christine Smith, *Architecture in the Culture of Early Humanism: Ethics,
Aesthetics, and Eloquence* (New York: Oxford University Press, 1992). The sole
exception seems to be Scamozzi, but there is disagreement as to whether he can
be described as neoplatonic or Aristotelian. (See Marco Frascari, "The Mirror
Theatre of Vincenzo Scamozzi," in Vaughan Hart and Peter Hicks, ed. *Paper
Palaces: The Rise of the Renaissance Architectural Treatise* [New Haven: Yale University Press, 1998], 258; Payne, *The Architectural Treatise*, 215.) On Alberti as
humanist, see also Anthony Grafton, *Leon Battista Alberti* (New York: Hill and
Wang, 2000).

11 Payne, *The Architectural Treatise*, 53.
12 Thus Alberti cites Cicero in particular, not Plato or Pythagoras, to support the view that "Beauty is the reasoned harmony of all the parts within a body, so that nothing may be added, taken away, or altered, but for the worse. It is a great and holy matter; all our resources of skill and ingenuity will be taxed in achieving it; and rarely is it granted, even to Nature herself, to produce anything that is entirely complete and perfect in every respect." Alberti attended the same humanist academy as Vittorino da Feltre (*On the Art of Building*, xi; 156). See also Christy Anderson, "Learning to Read Architecture in the English Renaissance," in Lucy Gent, ed. *Albion's Classicism: The Visual Arts in Britain, 1550–1660* (New Haven: Yale University Press, 1995), 248. Alberti is known to have owned Cicero's *Brutus* (Caroline van Eck, "Architecture, Language, and Rhetoric in Alberti's *De Re Aedificatoria*," in Georgia Clarke and Paul Crossley, eds. *Architecture and Language: Constructing Identity in European Architecture, c. 1000–c. 1650* [Cambridge: Cambridge University Press, 2000], 75).
13 Alberti, *On the Art of Building*, x; xv.
14 See Frédérique Lemerle, "On Guillaume Philandrier: Forms and Norm," in *Paper Palaces*, 186–97; also Payne, *The Architectural Treatise*, 27.
15 Michael Baxandall, *Giotto and the Orators: Humanist Observers of Painting in Italy and the Discovery of Pictorial Composition, 1350–1450* (Oxford: Clarendon Press, 1971).
16 Thus Alberti states unequivocally that we have little access to the truths of nature: "Nature is not at all easy to understand and very perplexing." Alberti, *On the Art of Building*, 327.
17 Jones/De L'Orme, III: 65.
18 Vitruvius, *Ten Books*, 26; 65–70; Alberti, *On the Art of Building*, 268–82; Serlio, *On Architecture*, I: 83–93; 136–41; Palladio seems more interested in temples as expressions of the same principles, a connection suggested by Jones's design for St. Paul's, Covent Garden. For theatre design in the Italian Renaissance and the Teatro Olimpico's place in it, see Ackerman, *Palladio*, 177–82.
19 See for example, Yves Pauwels, "The Rhetorical Model in the Formation of French Architectural Language in the Sixteenth Century: The Triumphal Arch as Commonplace," in *Architecture and Language*, 134–47.
20 Jones/Vitruvius, 25; 162; 279.
21 Jones/Plutarch, in Johnson, *Three Volumes*, 35; 43.
22 Vitruvius, *Ten Books*, 13.
23 Wotton, *Elements of Architecture*, 122.
24 Alberti, *On the Art of Building*, 5; 95.
25 Robert Tavernor, "Palladio's 'Corpus': *I Quattro Libri dell'Architettura*," in *Paper Palaces*, 234.
26 Jones/Palladio, I: 27.
27 Precisely along these lines, Vitruvius describes the cosmos as "the all-encompassing system of everything in nature" (*Ten Books*, 109).
28 Ibid., 47.
29 Jones/Scamozzi, I,i,xiv,46; I,iii,xx,312; Jones/Vitruvius, 109; 164.

30 Jones/Alberti, IX,v,256.

31 Alberti, *On the Art of Building*, 5; 7; 73; 79; 85; 86.

32 Cicero directly compares architecture to medicine. See John Onians, *Bearers of Meaning: The Classical Orders in Antiquity, the Middle Ages, and the Renaisssance* (Princeton: Princeton University Press, 1988), 33.

33 Payne, *The Architectural Treatise*, 6; the textual model is clear, for example, in Henry Wotton's *Elements of Architecture*, 118–19.

34 See for example Vaughan Hart, "'Paper Palaces': From Alberti to Scamozzi," in *Paper Palaces*, 3.

35 Alberti, *On the Art of Building*, 155.

36 Harris, *The King's Arcadia*, 153.

37 Frascari, "The Mirror Theatre of Vincento Scamozzi," in *Paper Palaces*, 253.

38 Tavernor, "Palladio's 'Corpus,'" in *Paper Palaces*, 240.

39 Frascari, "The Mirror Theatre of Vincento Scamozzi," in *Paper Palaces*, 259.

40 William Davenant, "The Author's Preface," *Gondibert*, ed. David Gladish (Oxford: Clarendon Press, 1971), 8.

41 Payne, *The Architectural Treatise*, 63.

42 See Anthony Geraghty, "Wren's Preliminary Design for the Sheldonian Theatre," *Architectural History* 45 (2002): 282. Vitruvius specifically connects the siting of theaters to matters of health (*Ten Books*, 65).

43 Vitruvius writes, for example, referring to the elements or atoms of nature in the Democritean scheme, "all things seem to come together and be born from the conjunction of these bodies, and are distributed into infinite types of natural objects, [so] I thought I should expound on their varieties and the criteria for their use, as well as what qualities they have in building" (ibid., 35). Commenting on Vitruvius, Jones implies that the key criteria are "order" and "disposition," and he writes too that force in architecture consists of six principles that in Barbaro's translation appear as "ordini," "dispositione," "bel numero" (for Jones, "Eurithmia"), "compartimento" (what Jones calls "Simitria"), "decoro," and "distributione" (Jones/Vitruvius, 27; 26). Jones offers the analogy between Lucretian and Pythagorean elements (Jones/Vitruvius, 72).

44 Jones/Vitruvius, 22.

45 Hart, "From Alberti to Scamozzi," in *Paper Palaces*, 19. Thus Jones expands on the principle in his copy of De L'Orme: "it faut que ledit Architect soit diligent à cognoistre l'assiette du lieu, & sçavoir ou doit ester posée une chacune chose, selon quelle le requiert. Pareillement entendre quel regard doiuent auoir les chambers & autres lieux, le tout aueques bonnes inuentions & la positions, après avoir entendu le plaisir, pour mieux tout accommoder. Mais s'il n'estoit capable de sçavoir discerner qui luy sera bon, il faut que l'Architecte le conseille & le serve fidelement selon son estat & qualité" (Jones/De L'Orme, III: 65).

46 Alberti, *On the Art of Building*, 8; see also 23; 163.

47 Payne, *The Architectural Treatise*, 73.

48 Samuel Daniel, *Tethys' Festival*, in David Lindley, ed. *Court Masques* (Oxford: Oxford University Press, 1995), 55.

49 See for example Alina A. Payne, "Architects and Academies: Architectural Theories of *Imitatio* and the Literary Debates on Language and Style," in *Architecture and Language*, 118–33.

50 For Cicero, rhetoric is a species of philosophy in being able to marshall elements of speech and knowledge for a given circumstance (Cicero, *De Oratore*, trans. E. W. Sutton and H. Rackham, 2 vols. [Cambridge, MA: Harvard University Press, 1929; 1932], I,xli,187–8).

51 G. W. Pigman, "Versions of Imitation in the Renaissance," *Renaissance Quarterly* 33 (1980): 1–32; and Thomas M. Greene, *The Light in Troy: Imitation and Discovery in Renaissance Poetry* (New Haven: Yale University Press, 1982). Onians writes, "Just as Cicero and his contemporaries developed their own rhetorical style by studying that of the period and people whose speeches they most admired, so Serlio felt that the same could be done for architecture" (*Bearers of Meaning*, 269). See also Quintilian, *Institutio Oratoria*, trans. H. E. Butler, 4 vols. (Cambridge, MA: Harvard University Press, 1922), X,ii.

52 See H. D. F. Kitto, *The Greeks* (Harmondsworth: Penguin, 1957), and George A. Kennedy, *The Art of Rhetoric in the Roman World* (Princeton: Princeton University Press, 1972), esp. 383ff.

53 Vitruvius, *Ten Books*, 25; Serlio, *On Architecture*, I: 263; Alberti, *On the Art of Building*, 23; see also 163. The range and flexibility of approaches to invention and imitation are variously described by Vitruvius' editors (Vitruvius, *Ten Books*, 16); Hart, "From Alberti to Scamozzi," in *Paper Palaces*, 18; Hart and Hicks, "On Sebastiano Serlio," in *Paper Palaces*, 156–7; Onians, *Bearers of Meaning*, 153; 269; and Payne, *The Architectural Treatise*, 6; 34; 57–8; and 82, where expression allowed by different columnar styles permits varieties of "innuendo."

54 Hart and Hicks, "On Sebastiano Serlio," in *Paper Palaces*, 147. Important steps to clarifying the distinctions among the orders were taken by Brunelleschi and Raphael. See Onians, *Bearers of Meaning*, 136; 272; 273; and Ingrid D. Rowland's superb "Raphael, Angelo Colocci, and the Genesis of the Architectural Orders," *The Art Bulletin* 76 (1994): 81–104.

55 See for example Orgel and Strong, *Inigo Jones*, I: 16, though this impression is offset by comparing designs for masques with illustrations from Serlio in general; and John Orrell, *The Theatres of Inigo Jones and John Webb* (Cambridge: Cambridge University Press, 1985), *passim*; Orrell, *The Human Stage: English Theatre Design, 1567–1640* (Cambridge: Cambridge University Press, 1988).

56 For a list of Jones's books, see John Harris *et. al.*, eds. *The King's Arcadia*, 217–18.

57 Alberti, *On the Art of Building*, 317.

58 Jones/Serlio (1619), III, 100. See also Jones/Serlio (1600), Sig. B2v.

59 Jones/Vitruvius, 36; 115.

60 According to Onians, this principle of differentiation is first clearly visible in the Hellenistic period and influenced the Romans (*Bearers of Meaning*, 26; 29–30).

61 Vitruvius, *Ten Books*, 55.

62 See Payne, *The Architectural Treatise*, 44; Onians remarks that Serlio systematized the anthropomorphic conception more thoroughly than Vitruvius (*Bearers of Meaning*, 148). Quintilian compares the developing styles of sculpture to

the orders, so that for him the primitive style of Callon and Hegesias is "Tuscanic" (*Institutio Oratoria*, XII,x,7).

63 Onians, *Bearers of Meaning*, 38.
64 Alberti, *On the Art of Building*, 155.
65 Tacitus, *A Dialogue on Oratory*, in *The Complete Works of Tacitus*, trans. and ed. Alfred John Church *et al.* (New York: Modern Library, 1942), 751.
66 Ibid., 752.
67 Onians remarks that by contrast the origin of the Corinthian order is obscure (*Bearers of Meaning*, 19).
68 Alberti, *On the Art of Building*, 19; 23; 24; 34.
69 Onians, *Bearers of Meaning*, 3; 155.
70 Richard J. Tuttle, "On Vignola's *Rule of the Five Orders of Architecture*," in *Paper Palaces*, 206; Payne, *The Architectural Treatise*, 75; 64; 139. See also Vitruvius, *Ten Books*, 23; 24; 150.
71 Alberti, *On the Art of Building*, 100; 117; 61.
72 Onians, *Bearers of Meaning*, 35; 39.
73 Alberti makes this argument in relation to the Doric, from which the Tuscan was derived (*On the Art of Building*, 201).
74 Onians, *Bearers of Meaning*, 277; 282. Serlio, *On Architecture*, 254.
75 Onians, *Bearers of Meaning*, 131.
76 Ibid., 150; 153. Alberti, *On the Art of Building*, 201; Serlio, *On Architecture*, 364. See also Payne, *The Architectural Treatise*, 61.
77 Onians, *Bearers of Meaning*, 286.
78 Joseph Rykwert, *The Dancing Column: On Order in Architecture* (Cambridge, MA: MIT Press, 1996), 357.
79 John Shute, *The First and Chief Groundes of Architecture* (London, 1563), Sigs. A2v–A3r.
80 Ibid., Sig. B2r.
81 Vaughan Hart, "Early English Vitruvian Books," in *Paper Palaces*, 304; 309.
82 Alberti, *On the Art of Building*, 157. Onians writes, of the greater expressive freedom of Roman architecture, that "the greater richness of the Roman structural vocabulary which exploited piers and arches as readily as columns and entablatures enabled the contrast between elegance and strength to be made more forcibly" (*Bearers of Meaning*, 30–1).
83 Alberti, *On the Art of Building*, 158; Vitruvius, *Ten Books*, 1; Onians, *Bearers of Meaning*, 28; 274; 310; Payne, *The Architectural Treatise*, 6; 15; 19; 72; 118.
84 Vitruvius, *Ten Books*, 77; Alberti, *On the Art of Building*, 92–3. Alberti remarks that two different styles are needed to distinguish the secular and sacred aspects of civic life (ibid., 125; 130).
85 This is a point Jones makes clearly in his annotations to Alberti (Jones/Alberti,VIII,iii,253).
86 Vitruvius, *Ten Books*, 63.
87 Ibid., 70.
88 Ibid., 66; Payne, *The Architectural Treatise*, 20; Joseph Rykwert, "Theory as Rhetoric: Leon Battista Alberti," in *Paper Palaces*, 43.

89 Ackerman, *Palladio*, 75–87.
90 Hart, "Early English Vitruvian Books," in *Paper Palaces*, 310.
91 Orgel and Strong, *Inigo Jones*, I: 34–6; John Harris and Gordon Higgott, *Inigo Jones: Complete Architectural Drawings* (New York: The Drawing Center, 1989), 29; also Summerson, *Architecture in Britain*, 63–4.
92 Harris and Higgott, *Inigo Jones*, 64.
93 Jones/Alberti, IX,vii,263.
94 Jones's writing is typically difficult to interpret, but the only likely Tuesday would be the 24th, not the 21st, as may at first appear to be the case.
95 Jones/Scamozzi, II,vi,v,14.
96 Jones/Alberti, IX,v,256–7.
97 Jones/Vitruvius, 28.
98 Jones/Scamozzi, II,vi,xvi,57.
99 Jones/Vitruvius, 98; 164.
100 Jones/Vasari, in Johnson, *Three Volumes*, 18.
101 Jones/Scamozzi, II,vi,i,3; I,i,xiv,46.
102 Serlio, *On Architecture*, II: 254.
103 Harris, *The King's Arcadia*, 200.
104 Ibid., 68.
105 Ibid., 120.
106 Jones/Scamozzi, II,vi,iii,8.
107 Harris, *The King's Arcadia*, 143.
108 Jones/Vitruvius, 192.
109 Jones, *Stoneheng Restored*, 8; 13; 40. Page numbers appear hereafter in the text.
110 Martin Butler, "Early Stuart Culture: Compliment or Criticism?" *The Historical Journal* 32 (1989): 425–35.
111 [Thomas Carew], *Coelum Britannicum*, in *The Works of Sir William Davenant*, 2 vols. (1673; rpt. New York/London: Benjamin Blom, 1968), I: 362–7. Citations henceforth appear parenthetically in my text.
112 William Davenant, *The Triumphs of the Prince D'Amour*, in *The Works of Sir William Davenant* I: 396. Citations henceforth appear parenthetically in my text.
113 William Davenant/Inigo Jones, *The Temple of Love* (1635), in Orgel and Strong, *Inigo Jones*, II: 601. Citations henceforth appear parenthetically in my text.
114 William Davenant/Inigo Jones, *Britannia Triumphans* (London, 1637), 2. Citations henceforth appear parenthetically in my text.
115 David Howarth, "The Politics of Inigo Jones," in David Howarth, ed. *Art and Patronage in the Caroline Courts* (Cambridge: Cambridge University Press, 1993), 79.
116 C. V. Wedgwood, "The Last Masque," in *Truth and Opinion* (New York: Macmillan, 1960), 139–56.
117 William Davenant/Inigo Jones, *Salmacida Spolia*, in Lindley, *Court Masques*, 211.

5 "THIS NEW BUILDING": DAVENANT'S LAST PHASE

1 Sir Willliam Davenant, *Gondibert*, ed. David F. Gladish (Oxford: Clarendon Press, 1971), 3. All references to *Gondibert* will appear henceforth parenthetically in the text, either as page numbers, or as Book, Canto, and Stanza numbers. For major studies of Davenant, see Chapter Three, note 35.

2 Clear references to Harveian physiology occur at II,iii,37; II,iv,25; III,iv,11.

3 Jacob Burckhardt, *The Civilization of the Renaissance in Italy* (New York: Random House, 2002), 72; 59.

4 *The Works of Sir William Davenant*, 2 vols. (1673; rpt. New York/London: Benjamin Blom, 1968), I: 341. All further references to the play appear in my text.

5 William Davenant, *The Cruelty of the Spaniards in Peru* (London, 1658), 14. All references are to this edition and will appear in my text.

6 William Davenant, *The Siege of Rhodes, Made a Representation by the Art of Prospective in Scenes. And the Story sung in Recitative Musick* (London, 1656), Sig. A2v. All references to this edition will appear parenthetically in my text.

7 William Davenant, *The Siege of Rhodes. The First and Second Part* (London, 1672), 35. All references to the 1661 versions of both parts will be to this edition, which was incorporated into the *Works* of 1673.

8 See Katherine Eisaman Maus, "Arcadia Lost: Politics and Revision in *The Tempest*," *Renaissance Drama* 13 (1982): 189–209.

9 See E. N. Hooker, H. T. Swedenberg, Jr., *et al.* eds. *The Works of John Dryden*, 20 vols. (Los Angeles: University of California Press, 1956–89), X: 8. References to *The Tempest, or The Enchanted Island* will be cited in the text.

10 See Richard Kroll, "Emblem and Expression in Davenant's *Macbeth*," *ELH* 57 (1990): 835–64.

6 INSTITUTING EMPIRICISM: HOBBES AND DRYDEN'S
MARRIAGE A LA MODE

1 See Laura S. Brown, "The Divided Plot: Tragicomic Form in the Restoration," *ELH* 47 (1980): 67–79; J. Douglas Canfield, "The Ideology of Restoration Tragicomedy," *ELH* 51 (1984): 447–64; David Rodes's commentary on *Marriage a la Mode* in E. N. Hooker, H. T. Swedenberg, Jr., *et al.* eds. *The Works of John Dryden*, 20 vols. (Los Angeles: University of California Press, 1956–89), XI. All subsequent references to the play are to this edition and will appear in my text. See also Eric Rothstein and Frances Kavenick, *The "Designs" of Carolean Comedy* (Carbondale: Southern Illinois University Press, 1988).

2 Michael McKeon, "Marxist Criticism and *Marriage a la Mode*," *The Eighteenth Century: Theory and Interpretation* 24 (1983): 141–62.

3 John Dryden, *Of Dramatic Poesy and Other Critical Essays*, ed. George Watson, 2 vols. (London: Everyman, 1962), II: 274. All subsequent references are to this edition and will appear in my text.

4 Gregory S. Kavka, *Hobbesian Moral and Political Theory* (Princeton: Princeton University Press, 1986).

5 See Quentin Skinner, "Conquest and Consent: Thomas Hobbes and the Engagement Controversy," in G. E. Aylmer, ed. *The Interregnum: The Quest for Settlement* (London: Macmillan, 1972), 78–98; and J. G. A. Pocock, "Time, History, and Eschatology in the Thought of Thomas Hobbes," in *Politics, Language, and Time: Essays in Political Thought and History* (New York: Atheneum, 1973), 148–201.

6 Steven Shapin and Simon Schaffer, *Leviathan and the Air Pump: Hobbes, Boyle, and the Experimental Life* (Princeton: Princeton University Press, 1985).

7 See C. B. MacPherson, *The Political Theory of Possessive Individualism* (Oxford: Oxford University Press, 1962), 29; also "Hobbes's Bourgeois Man," in Keith C. Brown, ed. *Hobbes Studies* (Oxford: Blackwell, 1965), 169–83.

8 MacPherson, *The Political Theory*, 179.

9 Keith Thomas, "The Social Origins of Hobbes's Political Thought," in *Hobbes Studies*, 193.

10 Ibid., 207.

11 Michael Oakeshott, *Hobbes on Civil Association* (Oxford: Blackwell, 1975), 117.

12 Thomas Creech, trans. *T. Lucretius Carus the Epicurean Philosopher, his Six Books De Rerum Natura* (Oxford, 1682), 174–5.

13 Thomas Hobbes, *Leviathan*, ed. C. B. MacPherson (Harmondsworth: Penguin, 1968), 82. All references are to this edition and will appear in the text.

14 Victoria Silver, "The Fiction of Self-Evidence in Hobbes's *Leviathan*," *ELH* 55 (1988): 351–79.

15 Derek Hughes, "The Unity of Dryden's *Marriage a la Mode*," *Philological Quarterly* 61 (1982): 125–42.

7 EQUITY AND EXCHANGE – OR TRADE AND CONTINGENCY – IN *THE PLAIN DEALER*

1 See Helen Burke, "'Law -Suits' and 'Love-Suits,' and the Family Property in Wycherley's *The Plain Dealer*," in J. Douglas Canfield and Deborah C. Payne, eds. *Cultural Readings of Restoration and Eighteenth-Century English Theater* (Athens: University of Georgia Press, 1995), 89. For the reasons educed below, I do not, however, agree with Burke that the over-focus on character is owing to "the humanist tradition of critical thinking" (89). Peter Holland, "Text and Performance (2): Wycherley's *The Plain Dealer*," in *The Ornament of Action: Text and Performance in Restoration Comedy* (Cambridge: Cambridge University Press, 1979), 192.

2 Derek Cohen, "The Alternating Styles of *The Plain Dealer*," *Restoration and 18th-Century Theatre Research* 2nd ser. 2 (1987): 19; 28.

3 Laura Morrow, "Phenomenological Psychology and Comic Form in *The Plain Dealer*," *Restoration and 18th-Century Theatre Research* 2nd ser. 3 (1988): 1.

4 Robert F. Bode, "'Try Me, At Least': The Dispensing of Justice in *The Plain Dealer*," *Restoration and 18th-Century Theatre Research* 2nd ser. 4 (1989): 1.

5 Anthony Kaufman, "Idealization, Disillusion, and Narcissistic Rage in Wycherley's *The Plain Dealer*," *Criticism* 21 (1979): 119–33; W. Gerald Marshall, "Wycherley's Drama of Madness: *The Plain Dealer*," *Philological Quarterly* 59 (1980): 26–35.

6 Bode, "'Try Me, At Least'," 2–3.

7 One major exploration of Wycherley and satire is Rose A. Zimbardo, *Wycherley's Drama: A Link in the Development of English Satire* (New Haven: Yale University Press, 1965). Along with books by Thomas Fujimura, Norman Holland, and Dale Underwood, Zimbardo's book helped establish the terms by which modern critics could take Restoration drama seriously.

8 See Derek Hughes, "*The Plain Dealer*: A Reappraisal," *Modern Language Quarterly* 43 (1982): 315–36; Ronald Berman, "Wycherley's Unheroic Society," *ELH* 51 (1984): 465–78; and Holland, "Text and Performance," cited above.

9 Berman, "Wycherley's Unheroic Society," 466.

10 Hughes, "*The Plain Dealer*," 322.

11 Ibid., 329.

12 Holland, "Text and Performance," 172; 180; Bode, "'Try Me, At Least'," 2; Burke, "'Law-Suits,'" 92.

13 William Wycherley, *The Plain Dealer*, ed. Leo Hughes (Lincoln: University of Nebraska Press, 1967), V,ii,222. All references are to this edition and will be cited in the text.

14 Holland, "Text and Performance," 200.

15 Berman, "Wycherley's Unheroic Society," 468; Holland, "Text and Performance," 182.

8 MERCHANTS AND BULLIONISTS IN BEHN'S *THE ROVER*

1 Maureen Duffy, *The Passionate Shepherdess: The Life of Aphra Behn, 1640–1689* (1977; rpt. London: Phoenix, 1989), 156.

2 Robert Markley, "'Be Impudent, Be Saucy, Forward, Bold, Touzing, and Leud': The Politics of Masculine Sexuality and Feminine Desire in Behn's Tory Comedies," in J. Douglas Canfield and Deborah C. Payne, eds. *Cultural Readings of Restoration and Eighteenth-Century Theater* (Athens: University of Georgia Press, 1995), 137.

3 Ibid., 117; 116. On "royalist ideology," see also Stephen Szilagyi, "The Sexual Politics of Behn's *Rover*: After Patriarchy," *Studies in Philology* 95 (1998): 450.

4 Heidi Hutner, "Revisioning the Female Body: Aphra Behn's *The Rover*, Parts I and II," in Hutner, ed. *Rereading Aphra Behn: History, Theory, and Criticism* (Charlottesville: University Press of Virginia, 1993), 103.

5 See for example Nancy Copeland, *Staging Gender in Behn and Centlivre: Women's Comedy and the Theatre* (Aldershot: Ashgate, 2004), 33.

6 Derek Hughes, *The Theatre of Aphra Behn* (Basingstoke: Palgrave Macmillan, 2001), 84–5. Also Taylor Corse, "Seventeenth-Century Naples and Aphra

Behn's *The Rover*," *Restoration* 29 (2005): 41–51. In a different essay, Hughes on scholarly grounds demolishes one of the most often cited articles on Behn's status as author. See Hughes, "The Masked Woman Revealed; or, The Prostitute and Playwright in Aphra Behn Criticism," *Women's Writing* 7 (2000): 149–64. Hughes is responding to Catherine Gallagher, "Who was that Masked Woman? The Prostitute and the Playwright in the Comedies of Aphra Behn," *Women's Studies* 15 (1988): 25–42. See also Laura J. Rosenthal, *Playwrights and Plagiarists in Early Modern England* (Ithaca: Cornell University Press, 1996), 110–31.

7 On carnival, see Linda R. Payne, "The Carnivalesque Regeneration of Corrupt Economies in *The Rover*," *Restoration* 22 (1998): 40–9.

8 For full accounts, see Eric Cochrane, *Italy, 1530–1630* (London: Longman, 1988), 19–54; and Domenico Sella, *Italy in the Seventeenth Century* (London: Longman, 1997), 1–18.

9 Sella, *Italy in the Seventeenth Century*, 30.

10 Ibid., 33.

11 Ibid., 36.

12 Gregory Hanlon, *Early Modern Italy, 1550–1800* (Basingstoke: Macmillan, 2000), 201.

13 See Aphra Behn, *The Rover*, ed. Frederick M. Link (Lincoln: University of Nebraska Press, 1967), I,i,87; I,i,141; I,ii,284. All referencs are from this edition and will be cited in the text.

14 See also Joseph F. Musser, Jr., "'Imposing Nought but Constancy in Love': Aphra Behn Snares *The Rover*," *Restoration* 3 (1979): 17–25. I disagree with Musser's view that Angellica – like Harriet – is the key to the play.

15 Elin Diamond, "Gestus and Signature in Aphra Behn's *The Rover*," in Janet Todd, ed. *Aphra Behn Studies* (Cambridge: Cambridge University Press, 1996), 32–56.

9 THE POLITICAL ECONOMY OF *ALL FOR LOVE*

1 See David Ogg, *England in the Reign of Charles II*, 2nd edn. (Oxford: Oxford University Press, 1963).

2 John Neville Figgis, *The Divine Right of Kings*, 2nd edn. (Cambridge: Cambridge University Press, 1922).

3 For example, the Stop on the Exchequer had personal consequences for Dryden. See James Anderson Winn, *John Dryden and His World* (New Haven: Yale University Press, 1987), 232.

4 Andrew Browning, *Thomas Osborne, Earl of Danby and Duke of Leeds, 1632–1712*, 3 vols. (Glasgow: Jackson and Son, 1951), I: 117.

5 See for example Blair Hoxby, "The Government of Trade: Commerce, Politics, and the Courtly Art of the Restoration," *ELH* 66 (1999): 591–627.

6 John Dryden, *All for Love*, ed. David M. Vieth (Lincoln: University of Nebraska Press, 1972), 4. All references are to this edition, and will appear in the text.

7 Browning, *Danby*, I: 232.

8 Ibid., 227; 227 note.

9 E. N. Hooker, H. T. Swedenberg, Jr., *et al.* eds. *The Works of John Dryden*, 20 vols. (Los Angeles: University of California Press, 1956–89), XIII: 363–89.

10 Given the extent to which I am arguing for a kind of negative dialectics in *All for Love*, it is worth recalling that Dryden co-translated Plutarch. Plutarch's "parallels" are presented as pairs of ancients, whose values are often juxtaposed in some mutually critical relation. Plutarch does not, it is true, compare Cicero and Antony directly, but he makes clear that Cicero was often governed by expedient rather than principle, yet that Antony was sordidly implicated in his assassination, so that the implied contrast produces no simple moral allegory of virtue.

11 Roland Barthes, *On Racine* (Berkeley: University of California Press, 1992).

12 For an exploration of the effects of the Harveian revolution on the discourse of trade, see Richard Kroll, "Pope and Drugs: The Pharmacology of *The Rape of the Lock*," *ELH* 67 (2000): 99–141.

10 THE DOUBLE LOGIC OF *DON SEBASTIAN*: THE OEDIPAL CONSCIENCE AT THE GLORIOUS REVOLUTION

1 Keith Feiling, *A History of the Tory Party, 1640–1714* (1924; rpt. Oxford: Clarendon, 1959), 205; Geoffrey Holmes, *The Making of a Great Power: Late Stuart and Early Georgian Britain, 1660–1722* (London: Longman, 1993), 166–7; David Ogg, *England in the Reigns of James II and William III* (Oxford: Clarendon, 1966), 139–43.

2 Holmes, *The Making of a Great Power*, 177.

3 John Dryden, *Don Sebastian*, III,i,421, in E. N. Hooker, H. T. Swedenberg, Jr., *et al.* eds. *The Works of John Dryden*, 20 vols. (Los Angeles: University of California Press, 1956–89), XV. Henceforth *California Dryden*. Quotations from *Don Sebastian* and *Amphitryon* are from this edition and will be cited in the text. Major readings of *Don Sebastian* include David A. Bywaters, *Dryden in Revolutionary England* (Berkeley: University of California Press, 1991), Ch. 2; and Steven Zwicker, *Lines of Authority: Politics and English Literary Culture, 1649–1689* (Ithaca: Cornell University Press, 1993), Ch. 6. I particularly disagree with Zwicker's contention that "Rather than a revolutionary text, Dryden's *Don Sebastian* is a reactionary creed" (175). Dryden's dialectical politics cannot aptly be described in either of these ways.

4 Bywaters, *Dryden in Revolutionary England*, 55.

5 J. P. Kenyon, *Stuart England*, 2nd edn. (Harmondsworth: Pelican, 1985), 246.

6 The accusations emerged from William's intense personal relationship with William Bentinck and seem already to have been current in 1689. See "Satire on Bent[in]g" (March 1689), in John Harold Wilson, ed. *Court Satires of the Restoration* (Columbus, OH: Ohio State University Press, 1976), 217–21. Wilson notes that the "private reasons" alluded to in line 16 "were presumed to be homosexual" (222 note 15). *A Satyr upon King William; Being the Secret*

History of his Life and Reign (London, 1703) is a defense of William, but addresses the rumor: "As for that Unnatural Vice which some said he was addicted to, (to my certain knowledge) he was as free from it, as *Lot* when he left *Sodom*" (Sig. B1v). In his commentary on *Don Sebastian* for the California Dryden, Earl Miner writes, "The historical king of Portugal disdained any interest in women and is thought to have been homosexual" (*California Dryden*, XV: 388).

7 John Neville Figgis, *The Divine Right of Kings*, 2nd edn. (Cambridge: Cambridge University Press, 1922), 143–4; Ogg, *England in the Reigns of James II and William III*, 166–7.

8 Feiling, *History of the Tory Party*, 275.

9 James Anderson Winn, *John Dryden and His World* (New Haven: Yale University Press, 1987), xiii.

10 Figgis, *Divine Right*, 141–7; Ogg, *England in the Reigns of James II and William III*, 177. Dryden legitimates custom as a ground of political appeal in *Don Sebastian*, III,i,75–80, where the custom of marriage resists Muley-Moluch's attempts to revise it for his own interests.

11 J. P. Kenyon, *Revolution Principles: The Politics of Party, 1689–1720* (Cambridge: Cambridge University Press, 1977), 2; 200; Ogg, *England in the Reigns of James II and William III*, 243. The two most comprehensive treatments of the Glorious Revolution are J. R. Jones, *The Revolution of 1688 in England* (New York: Norton, 1972); and W. A. Speck, *Reluctant Revolutionaries: Englishmen and the Revolution of 1688* (New York: Oxford University Press, 1988).

12 Kenyon, *Revolution Principles*, 2; 16.

13 Holmes, *The Making of a Great Power*, Ch. 13.

14 Kenyon, *Revolution Principles*, 10.

15 Kenyon, *Stuart England*, 275; Ogg, *England in the Reigns of James II and William III*, 226–27; and for the debate, see E. Neville Williams, *The Eighteenth-Century Constitution, 1688–1815: Documents and Commentary* (Cambridge: Cambridge University Press, 1960), 20–6.

16 Kenyon, *Stuart England*, 270; 273.

17 John Turner, *A Sermon Preached June the 17th 1688. Upon the Birth of the Prince* (London, 1688), 3.

18 Feiling, *History of the Tory Party*, 226.

19 Ibid., 275.

20 J. P. Sommerville, *Politics and Ideology in England, 1603–1640* (London: Longman, 1986), 50.

21 Figgis, *Divine Right*, Ch. 1.

22 Ibid., 5–6. See, for example, James Ussher, *The Power Communicated by God to the Prince, and the Obedience Required of the Subject*, 2nd edn. (London, 1683). The first edition was published in 1660, though it was reportedly written under Charles I. Also, John Wilson, *A Discourse of Monarchy* (London, 1684). A contemporary account of different views of monarchy and the recent systematization of Divine Right theory, see John Somers, *A Brief History of the Succession of the Crown of England* (London, 1688/89), esp. 10; 14, which puts

the lie to J. P. Sommerville's claim that historiographical arguments did not in themselves constitute political theory at this period.

23 Jones, *The Revolution of 1688*, 99.

24 The most impressive indigenous primer in casuistry, Taylor's *Ductor Dubitantium*, was published throughout the Restoration period: 1660, 1671, 1676, 1696.

25 For example, *A Letter from a Clergy-Man in the Country, to the Clergy-Man in the City . . . Shewing the Insufficiency of his Reasons . . . for not Reading the Declaration* (London, 1688), 26. Dryden's remark comes at II,i,199, where the Mufti says, "He prates as if Kings had not Consciences." Other references to the debate about conscience occur at I,i,482; II,i,171–213; III,ii,94–100.

26 The parallel with Julian the Apostate – which enters into much of the literature of the Revolution – was largely owing to a series of tracts written by Samuel Johnson, the first of which he published in 1682, in which, in the wake of the Exclusion Crisis, Johnson intended the offensive parallel between the Duke of York and Julian. In *Julian the Apostate: Being a Short Account of his Life* (London, 1682), xxv, Johnson writes: "the Christian Souldiers served under this Infidel Emperor, and where their Religion was not concern'd, made Conscience of obeying him; but where indeed it came to the Cause of Christ, there they made as much Conscience of disobeying him." Johnson's tracts supply a direct polemical connection between the Exclusion Crisis and the Revolution. *Julian the Apostate* was published thrice in 1682–3, with a "third" edition in 1688 and a "fourth" in 1689. Similarly, the reader is told, in Johnson's *Julian's Arts to Undermine and Extirpate Christianity* (London, 1689), that "The present Impression of this Book was made in the Year 1683" (Sig. A2v).

27 *A Discourse of Conscience. The Second Part. Concerning a Doubting Conscience* (London, 1688), 6.

28 Ibid., 33; 35.

29 See Alan Roper, Commentary on *The Conquest of Granada*, in *California Dryden*, XI: 411–35.

30 See Narcissus Luttrell, *A Brief Historical Relation of State Affairs*, 6 vols. (Oxford: Oxford University Press, 1857), I: 440.

31 F. W. Maitland, *The Constitutional History of England* (Cambridge: Cambridge University Press, 1919), 283–5.

32 *Dictionary of National Biography*. Also Earl Miner, Commentary on *Don Sebastian*, in *California Dryden*, XV: 382.

33 Thomas Pierce, *A Prophylactick from Disloyalty in these Perilous Times* (London, 1688), 3; 5.

34 A. H. de Oliveira Marques, *History of Portugal*, 2 vols. (New York: Columbia University Press, 1972), I: 311.

35 John Miller, *Popery and Politics in England, 1660–1688* (Cambridge: Cambridge University Press, 1973), 201–2.

36 Louis I. Bredvold, *The Intellectual Milieu of John Dryden* (Ann Arbor: University of Michigan Press, 1956), 161; 163.

37 George Hickes, *The Doctrine of Passive Obedience and Jure Divino Disproved* (London, 1689), 2.

38 *Agreement Betwixt the Present and the Former Government* (London, 1689), 53.

39 See H. V. Livermore, *A New History of Portugal* (Cambridge: Cambridge University Press, 1972), 162–3.

40 Mary Elizabeth Brooks, *A King for Portugal: The Madrigal Conspiracy, 1594–95* (Madison: University of Wisconsin Press, 1964), 4.

41 Ibid., 6; 9.

42 Sigmund Freud, *Totem and Taboo* (New York: Norton, 1989), 196.

43 Jeremy Taylor, *Ductor Dubitantium, Or, The Rule of Conscience in all her Generall Measures; Serving as a Great Instrument for the Determination of Cases of Conscience*, 2 vols. (London, 1660), I: 11: "There are many actions in which prudence is not at all concerned as being wholly indifferent to this or that for matter of advantage; but there is no action but must pass under the file and censure of Conscience."

44 *Dictionary of National Biography*.

45 Thus John Wilson, in *Jus Regium Coronae* (London, 1688): "Sovereignty is a Commission granted by God to the Prince, who is the Soul that informs, and actuates, that incorporated Body, the People" (34).

46 Freud, *Totem and Taboo*, 194.

47 See, for example, I,i,500; II,i,3 ("The thoughts of Kings are like Religious Groves," which I take to be an allusion to *Oedipus at Colonus*); II,i,275; II,i,583; IV,ii,72–4.

48 Augustine Frezer, *The Divine Original and the Supreme Dignity of Kings, No Defensative against Death* (Rotterdam, 1685), 5.

49 James Ellesby, *The Doctrine of Passive Obedience* (London, 1685), 2.

50 *Edovardus Confessor Redivivus* (London, 1688), 33.

51 Freud, *Totem and Taboo*, 185.

52 Anthony Ascham, *A Seasonable Discourse* (1649; rpt. London, 1689), 47. Sebastian anticipates his own end in very similar terms: "I'll shew thee / How a Man shou'd, and how a King dare dye! / So even, that my Soul shall walk with ease / Out of its flesh, and shut out Life as calmly / As it does Words; without a Sigh, to note / One struggle in the smooth dissolving frame" (III,i, 214–19).

53 *Some Considerations Touching Succession and Allegiance* (London, 1689), 5–6.

54 *Agreement Betwixt the Present and the Former Government; Or, A Discourse of this Monarchy, Whether Elective or Hereditary?* (London, 1689), 33.

55 Richard Booker, *Satisfaction Tendred to all that Pretend Conscience for Non-Submission to our Present Governours* (London, 1689), 2.

56 Ascham, *Seasonable Discourse*, 46.

57 Freud, *Totem and Taboo*, 61.

58 Walter Benjamin, *The Origin of German Tragic Drama* (London: Verso, 1998), 218.

59 Freud, *Totem and Taboo*, 77.

11 EPILOGUE: CONGREVE AS WHIG: THE POLITICS OF EQUIVALENCE
IN *THE WAY OF THE WORLD*

1 John Dryden, "To my Dear Friend Mr. Congreve, On His Comedy, call'd, *The Double Dealer*," in E. N. Hooker, H. T. Swedenberg, Jr., *et al.* eds. *The Works of John Dryden*, 20 vols. (Los Angeles: University of California Press, 1956–89), IV, ll. 7–12. All subsequent references are to this edition and will appear in the text.

2 John Dennis, *The Causes of the Decay and Defects Of Dramatick Poetry, and of the Degeneracy Of the Publick Tast* (1725[?]), a manuscript reproduced in Edward Niles Hooker, ed. *The Critical Works of John Dennis*, 2 vols. (Baltimore: The Johns Hopkins University Press, 1939–43), II: 275.

3 It is interesting to see that this sense of disciplinary coherence is already visible in a tract like North's *Observations*, in which he writes, "*Oeconomy* is an Art, and every Artist ought to be curious in the choyce of his Instruments, and not onely so, but to trust chiefly to his own eye, cast either upon the whole work it self, or upon those who act in it" (Dudley North, *Observations and Advices Oeconomical* [London, 1669], 43).

4 Nicholas Barbon, *A Discourse of Trade*, ed. Jacob B. Hollander (1903; rpt. Baltimore: The Johns Hopkins University Press, 1934), 5; 7.

5 Charles Davenant, *An Essay on the Probable Methods of Making a People Gainers in the Balance of Trade*, in *The Political and Commercial Works*, 5 vols. (London, 1771), II: 169–70.

6 Herbert Davis, ed. *The Complete Plays of William Congreve* (Chicago: University of Chicago Press, 1967), 118–19.

7 I owe this observation to a comment made many years ago by Alan Roper.

8 Max Horkheimer and Theodor W. Adorno, *Dialectic of Enlightenment* (1972; rpt. New York: Continuum, 2000), 7.

9 Richard Kroll, "Discourse and Power in *The Way of the World*," *ELH* 53 (1986): 727–58.

10 See for example Prat: "*Extrinsick Value* of Money is the Denomination and Power that is given it by Authority. *Intrinsick Value* is the Necessary and Natural Value, always and everywhere inherent in the Species" (Samuel Prat, *The Regulating Silver Coin, Made Practicable and Easie* [London, 1696], 6).

11 William Freke, *A Review of the Universal Remedy for all Diseases Incident to Coin* (London, 1696), 12–13.

12 Rice Vaughan, *A Discourse of Coin and Coinage* (London, 1675), 1.

13 Sir Humphrey Mackworth, *England's Glory; or The Great Improvement of Trade in General, by a Royal Bank, or Office of Credit* (London, 1694), 5.

14 Joyce Oldham Appleby, *Economic Thought and Ideology in Seventeenth-Century England* (Princeton: Princeton University Press, 1978), 219–41.

15 Patrick Hyde Kelley, ed. *Locke on Money*, 2 vols. (Oxford: Clarendon Press, 1991), I: 308; 310.

16 Freke, *A Review*, 25; 29.

Index